Roman Egypt

Egypt played a crucial role in the Roman Empire for seven centuries. It was wealthy and occupied a strategic position between the Mediterranean and Indian Ocean worlds, while its uniquely fertile lands helped to feed the imperial capitals at Rome and then Constantinople. The cultural and religious landscape of Egypt today owes much to developments during the Roman period, including in particular the forms taken by Egyptian Christianity. Moreover, we have an abundance of sources for its history during this time, especially because of the recovery of vast numbers of written texts giving an almost uniquely detailed picture of its society, economy, government, and culture. This book, the work of six historians and archaeologists from Egypt, the US, and the UK, provides students and a general audience with a readable new introduction to the period and includes many illustrations of art, archaeological sites, and documents, and quotations from primary sources.

ROGER S. BAGNALL is Professor Emeritus of Ancient History and founding Leon Levy Director Emeritus at the Institute for the Study of the Ancient World at New York University. His publications include numerous books on the documents and social and economic history of Roman and Late Antique Egypt.

Roman Egypt

A History

———

Edited by

ROGER S. BAGNALL

New York University

with contributions from Mona Haggag, T. M. Hickey,

Mohamed G. Elmaghrabi, Arietta Papaconstantinou, and

Dorothy J. Thompson

CAMBRIDGE
UNIVERSITY PRESS

CAMBRIDGE
UNIVERSITY PRESS

University Printing House, Cambridge CB2 8BS, United Kingdom

One Liberty Plaza, 20th Floor, New York, NY 10006, USA

477 Williamstown Road, Port Melbourne, VIC 3207, Australia

314–321, 3rd Floor, Plot 3, Splendor Forum, Jasola District Centre,
New Delhi – 110025, India

103 Penang Road, #05–06/07, Visioncrest Commercial, Singapore 238467

Cambridge University Press is part of the University of Cambridge.

It furthers the University's mission by disseminating knowledge in the pursuit of
education, learning, and research at the highest international levels of excellence.

www.cambridge.org
Information on this title: www.cambridge.org/9781108844901
DOI: 10.1017/9781108953948

© Cambridge University Press 2021

First published 2021

Printed in the United Kingdom by TJ Books Limited, Padstow Cornwall

A catalogue record for this publication is available from the British Library.

Library of Congress Cataloging-in-Publication Data
Names: Bagnall, Roger S, editor.
Title: Roman Egypt : a history edited by Roger S Bagnall.
Description: Cambridge, United Kingdom ; New York, NY : Cambridge University Press,
2021. | Includes bibliographical references and index.
Identifiers: LCCN 2021007638 (print) | LCCN 2021007639 (ebook) | ISBN 9781108844901
(hardback) | ISBN 9781108953948 (ebook)
Subjects: LCSH: Egypt – History – 30 B.C.-640 A.D. | Romans – Egypt. | BISAC: HISTORY /
Ancient / General | HISTORY / Ancient / General
Classification: LCC DT93 .R66 2021 (print) | LCC DT93 (ebook) | DDC 932/.022–dc23
LC record available at https://lccn.loc.gov/2021007638
LC ebook record available at https://lccn.loc.gov/2021007639

ISBN 978-1-108-84490-1 Hardback
ISBN 978-1-108-94900-2 Paperback

Contents

List of illustrations   [*page* viii]
List of maps   [xvii]
List of boxes   [xviii]
List of contributors   [xxi]
Preface   [xxiii]
Chronology   [xxviii]

1   Laying the foundations for Roman Egypt
    (Dorothy J. Thompson)   [1]
    1.1   The pharaonic background and the Third Intermediate Period
           (1069–664 BC)   [1]
    1.2   Rebuilding a centralized state: Saite rule   [3]
    1.3   Two Persian occupations and sixty years of independence   [5]
    1.4   Greeks in Egypt before Alexander   [9]
    1.5   Alexander and the Ptolemies   [11]
    1.6   Resistance to foreign rule   [17]
    1.7   Alexandria and other urban centers   [20]
    1.8   The world of the temples   [25]
    1.9   The population of Egypt   [29]
    1.10   A multilingual environment   [33]
    1.11   Greek and Egyptian education in Ptolemaic Egypt   [35]
    1.12   The Hellenization of the Egyptian administration   [37]
    1.13   A mixed economy   [39]
    1.14   Romans in Egypt before the Roman conquest   [42]

2   The coming of Roman rule   [46]
    2.1   Government and administration: continuity and change
           from the Ptolemies to the Romans (Mohamed G.
           Elmaghrabi)   [46]
    2.2   The Roman army in Egypt (Mohamed G. Elmaghrabi)   [60]
    2.3   Languages in Roman Egypt (T. M. Hickey)   [67]
    2.4   The central role of Alexandria (Mohamed G. Elmaghrabi)   [71]
    2.5   Egypt's integration into the Roman economy
           (T. M. Hickey)   [87]
    2.6   The development of urban elites (Roger S. Bagnall)   [92]

2.7   The treatment of the temples and its implications
       (T. M. Hickey)   [95]
2.8   The Jewish communities of Egypt, especially Alexandria
       (Roger S. Bagnall)   [102]
2.9   Religious change under Roman rule (Dorothy J.
       Thompson)   [106]
2.10   The people of Roman Egypt (Roger S. Bagnall)   [112]
2.11   The origins of Christianity in Egypt (Roger S. Bagnall)   [117]

3 Development and crisis in a Roman province   [121]
3.1   The continued rise of urbanism and the elite (Roger S.
       Bagnall)   [121]
3.2   Violence from inside, above, and outside (Roger S.
       Bagnall)   [130]
3.3   Intensification of high-value agriculture (T. M. Hickey)   [137]
3.4   The Antonine plague and its debated consequences (Mohamed
       G. Elmaghrabi)   [142]
3.5   Twilight of the temples (Roger S. Bagnall)   [145]
3.6   The emergence of the Alexandrian church, then city bishops;
       the persecutions of Christians (Roger S. Bagnall)   [152]
3.7   The invention of the Coptic writing system (Roger S.
       Bagnall)   [162]

4 The making of Late Antique Egypt   [169]
4.1   Diocletian's reforms of administration, coinage, and taxation
       (Mona Haggag)   [169]
4.2   An Egyptian nation in a Roman nation (Roger S.
       Bagnall)   [178]
4.3   Turbulence and renewal in Alexandria (Mona
       Haggag)   [180]
4.4   Elite struggles for wealth and power and the rise of a new
       aristocracy (T. M. Hickey)   [186]
4.5   Paganism, Christianity, and religious pluralism (Mona
       Haggag)   [190]
4.6   The emergence of Christian institutions in public; the church
       and imperial politics (Roger S. Bagnall)   [200]
4.7   The reappearance of a Jewish community in Egypt
       (Roger S. Bagnall)   [203]
4.8   The invention of charitable institutions (Roger S.
       Bagnall)   [206]
4.9   Monasticism (Mona Haggag)   [210]
4.10   The development of a Christian literary culture in Coptic
       (Roger S. Bagnall)   [217]
4.11   The development of a Christian educational culture
       (Roger S. Bagnall)   [220]

5 Divergence and division   [225]
  5.1 Patriarchs and church politics from Chalcedon to Justinian
       (Arietta Papaconstantinou)   [225]
  5.2 Conflicts over doctrine and power from Justinian to Heraclius
       (Arietta Papaconstantinou)   [233]
  5.3 Alexandria as a university city; the auditoria of Kom el-Dikka
       (Mona Haggag)   [243]
  5.4 Egyptian villages in Late Antiquity (Roger S. Bagnall)   [250]
  5.5 The dominance of the wealthy elite (T. M. Hickey)   [258]
  5.6 City and country: dependence and divergence (Roger S.
       Bagnall)   [263]
  5.7 Coptic develops a literature and bids for official status (Arietta
       Papaconstantinou)   [268]

6 The Persians, the Arab conquest, and another
  transformation of Egypt (Arietta
  Papaconstantinou)   [276]
  6.1 The Sasanians in Egypt (T. M. Hickey)   [276]
  6.2 The conquest and lingering uncertainties   [280]
  6.3 Administrative continuity and evolution   [290]
  6.4 Old and new elites   [296]
  6.5 Impact on the rural population   [303]
  6.6 The evolution of the church and the dominance of the
       Miaphysites   [314]
  6.7 The formation of a Coptic identity   [319]
  6.8 The evolution of language use and gradual extinction of Coptic
       as spoken and business/legal language   [327]
  6.9 Linguistic change and religious conversion   [335]

  Epilogue   [344]

  Glossary   [347]
  Bibliography   [350]
  Index   [373]

Illustrations

Chapter 1

1.1.1   The Union of Upper and Lower Egypt, on the great temple of Rameses II (Dynasty 19) at Abu Simbel. Photo by Prisma/ UIG/Getty Images   *[page 2]*

1.2.1   Block statue of Pedon, found in Priene. Photo from Ç. Şahin, "Zwei Inschriften aus dem südwestlichen Kleinasien," *Epigraphica Anatolica* 10:1–2 (1987) plates 1 and 2; W. Blümel and R. Merkelbach, *Die Inschriften von Priene* (Bonn 2014): 408, used courtesy of W. Blümel on behalf of the editors of *Epigraphica Anatolica.*   [5]

1.3.1   Statue of Udjahorresnet from Sais. Vatican museums cat. no. 22690.   [7]

1.4.1   Dedication of a statuette to Apis by a Greek. BM 1898,0225.1. © The Trustees of the British Museum.   [11]

1.5.1   Oracle temple at Siwa. Photo by Roger Bagnall.   [13]

1.5.2   Orders of Alexander's general Peukestas. Photo by E. G. Turner. After Turner, E. G. (1974) *JEA* 60: pl. LV. Courtesy of the Egypt Exploration Society.   [15]

1.6.1   Canopus decree. Egyptian Museum, Cairo, CG 22186; JE 37548. Photo: P. M. Fraser archive, Centre for the Study of Ancient Documents, Oxford.   [19]

1.8.1   Edfu temple. Photo A. K. Bowman.   [26]

1.8.2   Vase of Arsinoe II. British Museum no. 1873,0820.389. © The Trustees of the British Museum.   [27]

1.10.1   Dedication to Isis-Astarte with Phoenician dedication. Cairo, Egyptian Museum, Catalogue (1962) no. 4751.   [35]

1.13.1   Tetradrachm of Ptolemy I Soter. American Numismatic Society 1944.100.75899.   [42]

1.14.1   Cleopatra VII in Egyptian dress on the Dendera temple. Photo Olaf Tausch: commons.wikimedia.org/wiki/File: Dendera_Tempel_Kleopatra_Cäsarion_05.jpg.   [44]

Chapter 2

2.1.1   Chart of papyrus finds distribution. Courtesy Mark Depauw, derived from the data of *Trismegistos*.   [48]

2.1.2   Edict of Tiberius Julius Alexander. Photo "NeferTiyi": www.flickr.com/photos/nefertiyi/8853838884/.   [50]

2.1.3   Decision about a foundling child by the *strategos*. *P.Oxy.* 1.37. Photo courtesy British Library.   [55]

2.2.1   Letter about enlistment in the fleet. Berlin, Staatliche Museen P. 7950. Photo Aegyptisches Museum und Papyrussammlung, Staatliche Museen, Berlin/Art Resource, New York.   [61]

2.2.2   A stele from Nikopolis. Greco-Roman Museum, Alexandria, inv. 252.   [62]

2.2.3   The fort of Dios in the Eastern Desert. From M. Reddé, "The Fortlets of the Eastern Desert of Egypt," in J.-P. Brun, T. Faucher, B. Redon, *et al.*, *The Eastern Desert of Egypt during the Greco-Roman Period: Archaeological Reports* (books.openedition.org/cdf/5248), Figs. 11, 23, and 29. Courtesy of Michel Reddé.   [64]

2.2.4   Ostracon with a letter of the prefect concerning deserters. *P.Bagnall* 8. Photo courtesy Adam Bülow-Jacobsen.   [66]

2.3.1   Demotic abstract of a contract. *P.Tebt.* 1.227. Photo courtesy the Center for the Tebtunis Papyri, The Bancroft Library, University of California, Berkeley.   [68]

2.4.1   Plan of Alexandria. From Bagnall and Rathbone 2017: Fig. 2.1.1.   [73]

2.4.2   Bronze drachma coin of Antoninus Pius. American Numismatic Society 1944.100.60756.   [74]

2.4.3   Bronze crab from obelisk in Alexandria. Metropolitan Museum of Art, accession 81.2.2.   [75]

2.4.4   Mosaic from the Villa of Birds, Alexandria. Ancient World Image Bank, Institute for the Study of the Ancient World, NYU.   [76]

2.4.5   Roman tomb from Alexandria. Photo Rüdiger Stehn: www.flickr.com/photos/rstehn/32883277522/.   [77]

2.5.1   Bronze drachma coin of Hadrian with Isis Pharia and the Pharos. American Numismatic Society 1944.100.57679.   [89]

2.5.2   The "Torlonia relief" showing Roman merchant vessels.
         (Rome, Museo Torlonia, inv. 430). Photo used courtesy of
         the Fondazione Torlonia, Rome.   [90]
2.5.3   Berenike, plan of site. Map by Martin Hense.   [91]
2.6.1   Agricultural development around a well in the Dakhla oasis.
         Photo by Roger S. Bagnall.   [95]
2.7.1   Plan of the Edfu temple. From Bagnall and Rathbone 2017:
         229.   [96]
2.7.2   Petition to the prefect of Egypt: *P.Tebt.* 2.302. Photo
         courtesy the Center for the Tebtunis Papyri, The Bancroft
         Library, University of California, Berkeley.   [99]
2.7.3   Colored drawing on a demotic account showing Tutu and
         Bes. P.Tebt. frag. 13,385. Photo courtesy the Center for the
         Tebtunis Papyri, The Bancroft Library, University of
         California, Berkeley.   [101]
2.8.1   Letter of Claudius to the Alexandrians. *P.Lond.* 6.1912v,
         British Library Papyrus 2248. Photo courtesy British
         Library.   [104]
2.9.1   Isis with Harpokrates in wall painting from Karanis.
         Facsimile painting by Hamzeh Carr over existing
         photograph (2003.02.0002). Photo courtesy of the Kelsey
         Museum of Archaeology, University of Michigan.   [107]
2.9.2   Anubis from Kom el-Shoqafa. Photo André Pelle, ©
         Archaeological Society of Alexandria and Centre d'études
         Alexandrines.   [108]
2.9.3   Head of Augustus from Meroe. British Museum cat. no.
         1911,0901.1. © The Trustees of the British Museum.   [110]
2.10.1   Mummy portrait of Eutyches. Metropolitan Museum of Art,
         18.9.2.   [114]
2.11.1   Christian manuscript, Gospel of John, assigned to the
         second century. *P.Ryl.* 457. Photo courtesy of the John
         Rylands University Library, Manchester.   [119]

Chapter 3
3.1.1   Antinoopolis, gateway to the theater. *Description de l'Égypte*
         IV 55.   [122]
3.1.2   Funerary shroud of a woman, dated *c.* 170–200. Metropolitan
         Museum of Art, 9.181.8.   [123]

3.1.3   Fragment of Thucydides' *Histories* from Oxyrhynchos.
        P.Oxy. 34.2703. Photo courtesy of the Egypt Exploration Society
        and the University of Oxford Imaging Papyri Project.   [128]

3.1.4   Hermopolis, monumental center as reconstructed. From
        D. M. Bailey, *British Museum Expedition to Middle Egypt.*
        Excavations at El-Ashmunein, IV. Hermopolis Magna:
        Buildings of the Roman Period (London 1991), pl. 23. © The
        Trustees of the British Museum.   [130]

3.2.1   The Serapeum in Alexandria as rebuilt in the third century
        AD. Axonometric reconstruction by Judith McKenzie. From
        Bagnall and Rathbone 2017: 63.   [134]

3.3.1   Drawings of *saqiya*-type water-lifting devices. After M. Venit,
        (2002) *The Monumental Tombs of Ancient Alexandria:*
        The Theater of the Dead (Cambridge) fig. 98, 97.   [139]

3.3.2   Ancient winery south of Marea. Photo Nicola Aravecchia,
        2007: flic.kr/p/8VGps2.   [140]

3.5.1   Mud-brick temple at Umm el-Dabadib, Kharga oasis. Photo
        Roger S. Bagnall, 2002.   [146]

3.5.2   A gravestone from Terenouthis. University of Missouri
        Museum of Art and Archaeology 2011.25. Photo courtesy of
        Museum of Art and Archaeology, University of
        Missouri.   [148]

3.5.3   Roman military camp at Luxor, reconstruction. From
        Bagnall and Rathbone 2017: 201, based on a drawing in
        M. El-Saghir et al., *Le camp romain de Louqsor* (Cairo
        1986), pl. XX.   [149]

3.6.1   Early Christian papyrus letter from the Fayyum. *P.Bas.* 2.43v.
        Photo: University of Basel, Peter Fornaro.   [155]

3.6.2   Certificate of sacrifice to the gods. *SB* 1.4439. Photo Staats-
        und Universitätsbibliothek Hamburg.   [156]

3.6.3   Bilingual papyrus with Coptic and Greek handwritings.
        P.Brux.Bawit 22. Berlin Papyrussammlung, P.22159.   [158]

3.6.4   The Reader who does not know how to read. *P.Oxy.* 33.2673.
        Photo courtesy Egypt Exploration Society and the University
        of Oxford Imaging Papyri Project.   [160]

3.7.1   Egyptian in Greek, with extra signs. *O.Narm.Dem.* 2.37.
        Facsimile courtesy of Paolo Gallo.   [164]

3.7.2   Letter of John, probably John of Lykopolis. *P.Amh.* 2.145.
        Photo from plate in the original publication.   [167]

Chapter 4

4.1.1–2   Pre-reform tetradrachm of Diocletian, Alexandria, AD 293/
294. American Numismatic Society 1935.117.1029. [172]

4.1.3–4   Post-reform bronze follis of Diocletian, Alexandria, AD
302/303. American Numismatic Society
1944.100.1359. [173]

4.1.5–6   Pre-reform billon tetradrachm of Domitius Domitianus,
Alexandria, AD 296/297. American Numismatic Society
1944.100.62002. [174]

4.1.7–8   Post-reform bronze follis of Domitius Domitianus,
Alexandria, AD 297/298. American Numismatic Society
1944.100.1225. [175]

4.1.9   Diocletian's pillar, AD 298–299 ("Pompey's pillar"), in the
Serapeum at Alexandria. Photo: Judith McKenzie, Manar
al-Athar. [176]

4.3.1   Tetradrachm from the Palmyrene occupation, Alexandria.
British Museum IOLC.4744. © The Trustees of the British
Museum. [181]

4.3.2   Plan of Kom el-Dikka. Courtesy of the Polish Centre of
Mediterranean Archaeology of the University of Warsaw
(drawing Wojciech Kołątaj, Aureliusz Pisarzewski and
Sara Arbter). [183]

4.4.1   Gold *solidus* of Constantine I, Constantinople, AD 330.
American Numismatic Society 1967.153.48. [189]

4.5.1   Eucharist scene in the Tomb of Wescher, Kom El-Shoqafa.
After McKenzie 2007: Figure 404, reproduced there from
C. Wescher, "Un ipogeo cristiano antichissimo di
Alessandria in Egitto," *Bulletino di archeologia cristiana* 3
no. 8 (1865) 57–61. [195]

4.5.2   Tomb VII in Tabiet Saleh, with Christian symbols on the
eastern wall of a tomb at Gabbari. Photo G. Grimm, used
by courtesy of Mrs. G. Grimm. [195]

4.5.3   Theophilus standing over the ruins of the Serapeum. After
McKenzie 2007: Figure 411, reproduced there from A.
Bauer and J. Strzygowski, *Eine alexandrinische
Weltchronik* (Vienna 1905). [197]

4.8.1   The Monastery of St. Shenoute or "White Monastery."
Photo: Judith McKenzie, Manar al-Athar. [208]

4.9.1   Monastic cell at Deir el-Naqlun. Photo Darlene L. Brooks
Hedstrom. [216]

4.11.1   Didymos the Blind, *Commentary on the Psalms.* Photo courtesy L. Tom Perry Special Collections, Brigham Young University Library.   [223]

Chapter 5

5.1.1   Ivory relief depicting a preaching apostle. Louvre, OA 3317. Photo Marie-Lan Nguyen: commons.wikimedia.org/wiki/ File:Fragment_relief_Louvre_OA3317.jpg.   [227]

5.1.2   Vatican stamp commemorating the 1500th anniversary of the Council of Chalcedon. Smithsonian, National Postal Museum, no. 2008.2009.147. Photo courtesy of the National Postal Museum, Smithsonian Institution.   [229]

5.1.3   Emperor Zeno represented on a gold solidus, Constantinople, 476–491. Dumbarton Oaks, accession no. BZC.1948.17.1240. © Dumbarton Oaks, Byzantine Collection, Washington, D.C.   [232]

5.2.1   Bronze coins (*nummi*) of Justinian, Alexandria, sixth century. (a) BZC.1948.17.1529, DOC 1:158, no. 273; (b) BZC.1967.17.3; DOC 1:158, no. 276; (c) BZC.1948.17.1534, DOC 1:158, no. 275; (d) BZC.1948.17.1530, DOC 1:158, no. 274. © Dumbarton Oaks, Byzantine Collection, Washington, D.C.   [234]

5.2.2   Portrait of the empress Theodora from Ravenna. Photo Petar Milošević: commons.wikimedia.org/wiki/File:Mosaic_of_ Theodora_-_Basilica_San_Vitale_(Ravenna,_Italy).jpg.   [236]

5.2.3   Portrait of Bishop Abraham of Hermonthis. Bode Museum, Berlin, Museum of Byzantine Art, inv. 6114. Photo by Anagoria: commons.wikimedia.org/wiki/File:0595_ Tafelbildnis_Bischof_Abraham_von_Hermonthis_ Bodemuseum_anagoria.JPG.   [241]

5.2.4   Ivory diptych with list of bishops, Theban region. British Museum, BEP 1920,1214.1. © The Trustees of the British Museum.   [242]

5.3.1   Kom el-Dikka, view of auditoria with street and theater. Photo Judith McKenzie, Manar al-Athar.   [247]

5.3.2   Kom el-Dikka, theater. Photo Judith McKenzie, Manar al-Athar.   [248]

5.3.3   Kom el-Dikka, individual auditorium with apse. Photo Judith McKenzie, Manar al-Athar.   [249]

5.4.1   House of Serenos at Trimithis (Amheida), Dakhla oasis, view from above. Photo Bruno Bazzani, Excavations at Amheida.   [252]

5.4.2   View of Jeme with Late Antique houses. Photo courtesy of T.G. Wilfong.   [253]

5.4.3   Church at Ain el-Gedida, Dakhla oasis. Photo Nicola Aravecchia.   [254]

5.5.1   Consular diptych of Apion II. Photo courtesy of the Catedral de Oviedo.   [259]

5.5.2   Aerial image of Oxyrhynchos possibly showing house of Apion family. Photo courtesy of Thomas Sagory.   [262]

5.6.1   Deir el-Bahri, Monastery of St. Phoibammon. Photo H. Carter negative DB-HAT.NEG.C.15a, courtesy of the Egypt Exploration Society.   [265]

5.6.2   Basilica of Hermopolis. Photo Roger S. Bagnall.   [267]

5.7.1   Coptic funerary stela from Esna/Latopolis, sixth–seventh century. British Museum, EA714. © The Trustees of the British Museum.   [272]

5.7.2   Ostracon with a letter from Bishop Abraham of Hermonthis. British Museum, EA32782. © The Trustees of the British Museum.   [274]

Chapter 6

6.1.1   Dodecanummium minted under Sasanian rule, Alexandria. American Numismatic Society 1954.126.144.   [277]

6.1.2   Fragment of a Pahlavi letter. Metropolitan Museum of Art 90.5.960.   [279]

6.2.1   Gold solidus of Heraclius, Constantinople, 610–613. American Numismatic Society 1944.100.13561.   [281]

6.2.2   Roman fortress of Babylon. From Sheehan 2010, fig. 27, courtesy of Peter Sheehan.   [282]

6.2.3   The new capital at Fusṭāṭ. From Whitcomb 2015: 96, fig. 11.4. Photo courtesy Donald Whitcomb.   [288]

6.3.1   Receipt for requisitioned sheep: *SB* 6.9676. P.Vindob. G 39726. Photo © Österreichische Nationalbibliothek.   [291]

6.3.2   Old Cairo – Fusṭāṭ, aerial photograph. From Treptow 2015: 99, fig. 12.1. Photograph by Rajan Patel, reproduced by permission of the American Research Center in Egypt, Inc. (ARCE).   [294]

6.3.3   Mosque of 'Amr. Photo by "Sherief1969": commons
        .wikimedia.org/wiki/File:Amr_Ibn_Al_As_Mosque_3.jpg.
        [295]

6.4.1   Gold necklace and armbands, Asyut, *c.* 600. British Museum,
        BEP 1916, 0704, 2-4. © The Trustees of the British
        Museum.   [299]

6.4.2   Fragment of a woolen hanging, seventh–ninth century.
        Dumbarton Oaks, BZ.1937.14. © Dumbarton Oaks,
        Byzantine Collection, Washington, D.C.   [302]

6.5.1   Spindles from textile production, Thebes. Metropolitan
        Museum of Art; (a) 14.1.475; (b) 08.202.29.   [305]

6.5.2   Monastery of Apa Jeremias at Saqqara, ground plan. Plan by
        Peter Grossmann.   [309]

6.5.3   Objects of everyday life. Metropolitan Museum of Art:
        (a) terracotta oil lamp, inv. 14.1.378; (b) spoon, inv. 14.1.263;
        (a) fishnet, inv. 14.1.560; (d) lock and key, inv. 14.1.242 and
        14.1.243.   [310]

6.5.4   Hanging decorated with crosses and floral motifs, from
        Bawit. Harvard Art Museums/Arthur M. Sackler Museum,
        1975.41.31. Gift of the Hagop Kevorkian Foundation in
        memory of Hagop Kevorkian. © President and Fellows of
        Harvard College.   [313]

6.6.1   Fresco from the Monastery of Apa Jeremias, Saqqara,
        showing a group of monks. Now in the Coptic Museum,
        Cairo. Photo Alamy.   [318]

6.7.1   Icon with Patriarchs of Alexandria, from the church of St.
        Merkourios in Old Cairo. From Gabra, G. (2014) *Coptic
        Civilization: Two Thousand Years of Christianity in Egypt.*
        Cairo: Figure 4.2. Photo courtesy Gawdat Gabra.   [322]

6.7.2   Painting showing monks, from the Monastery of St. Antony.
        From Bolman, E. (2002) *Monastic Visions: Wall Paintings in
        the Monastery of St. Antony at the Red Sea.* New Haven: 52,
        fig. 4.22. Photograph by Patrick Godeau, reproduced by
        permission of the American Research Center in Egypt, Inc.
        (ARCE). This project was funded by the United States
        Agency for International Development (USAID).   [324]

6.7.3   Monastery of Samuel of Qalamun. Photo Roland Unger:
        commons.wikimedia.org/wiki/File:DeirSamuelEntrance
        .jpg.   [325]

6.8.1   Bilingual tax demand, Aphrodito, 709. P.Heid. inv. Arab 13r.
        © Institut für Papyrologie, Universität Heidelberg.   [328]
6.8.2   Indian textile found in Egypt. Dumbarton Oaks, BZ.1993.49.
        © Dumbarton Oaks, Byzantine Collection, Washington,
        D.C.   [332]
6.9.1   Bilingual manuscript with sections of the New Testament.
        From the Church of St. Merkourios (Abu Sayfayn), Old
        Cairo. Coptic Museum, inv. 146: www.coptic-cairo.com/
        museum/selection/manuscript/manuscript/files/page50-
        1002-full.html. Courtesy of the Coptic Museum.   [337]
6.9.2   Shawl with bilingual inscription. Musée du Louvre, E25405.
        Photo Musée du Louvre/ Art Resource, New York.   [338]
6.9.3   Gold dinar of Fatimid caliph al-Mu'izz. Courtesy The David
        Collection, Copenhagen, inv. C 478. Photo by Pernille
        Klemp.   [341]

Maps

1 Egypt   [*page* xxxv]
2 Delta   [xxxvi]
3 Lower Egypt   [xxxvii]
4 Fayyum   [xxxviii]
5 Upper Egypt   [xxxix]
6 Great Oasis/Western Desert   [xl]
7 Eastern Desert   [xli]

Boxes

1.5.1   Plutarch, *Life of Alexander* 27.3–5   [*page* 14]

1.5.2   Alexander's Egyptian titles, in an inscription from the
        Bahariya oasis   [14]

1.5.3   Royal decree concerning choice of courts: *P.Tebt.* 1.5.207–
        220 (118 BC)   [17]

1.7.1   Imported goods: *P.Cair.Zen.* 5.59823 (253 BC)   [23]

1.9.1   Complaint by a non-Greek: *P.Col.Zen.* 2.66   [32]

1.11.1 Exemption from salt-tax: *P.Hal.* 1.260–265   [36]

2.1.1   Edict of Subatianus Aquila: *P.Yale* 1.61   [51]

2.1.2   Edict of Tiberius Julius Alexander (Hibis Temple, Kharga
        oasis): *OGIS* 669   [51]

2.1.3   The governor's judgment: *P.Oxy.* 1.37   [56]

2.2.1   Letter of Antonius Maximus: *BGU* 2.423   [61]

2.2.2   Trilingual inscription of Cornelius Gallus: *CIL*
        3.14147   [65]

2.2.3   Letter about barbarian attacks: *P.Bagnall* 8   [66]

2.3.1   Knowledge of Egyptian as a basis for entry into the
        priesthood: *P.Tebt.* 2.291   [69]

2.4.1   Plutarch, *Alex.* 26 on the foundation of Alexandria   [72]

2.4.2   Edict of Caracalla: *P.Giss.* 40   [78]

2.4.3   The Muziris papyrus: *SB* 18.13167 recto   [82]

2.4.4   Letter about desired books: *P.Mil.Vogl.* 1.11   [87]

2.5.1   A letter home from a sailor in the grain fleet: *W.Chr.* 445.
        (2nd or 3rd cent. AD)   [89]

2.7.1   Regulations concerning the priesthood: Selections from
        BGU 5.1210 (after AD 149), the *Gnomon of the* idios
        logos   [100]

2.8.1   Claudius' letter to the Alexandrians, lines 73–104: *P.Lond.*
        6.1912   [105]

2.9.1   Karanis prayer papyrus: *P.Mich.* 21.827, column 1   [111]

2.10.1 The barbarians attack: *O.Krok.* 1.87.26–44   [115]

2.11.1 The Ethiopic *History of the Episcopate of Alexandria*   [118]

3.1.1   Receipt for entrance fee to the council of Oxyrhynchos, AD
        233: *P.Oxy.* 44.3175   [125]

3.1.2   List of persons: *P.Amst.* 1.72.1–20 (cf. van Minnen
        1986)   [127]

3.2.1   Excerpts from the reports on trouble in the Delta, from
        P.Thmouis 1   [132]

3.3.1   A landholder in trouble in the early Roman Fayyum. *BGU*
        2.530 (1st C. AD)   [138]

3.3.2   Restoring vineyards on the Appianus estate: *P.Flor.* 2.148
        (AD 265/266)   [141]

3.4.1   Deaths at Soknopaiou Nesos, *SB* 16.12816, col. 4 (AD
        179)   [143]

3.6.1   Certificate of sacrifice: *SB* 1.4435   [159]

3.6.2   From the Letter of Phileas of Thmouis: Eusebius, *Eccl. Hist.*
        8.10   [162]

4.4.1   Landholdings of a son of Hyperechios: *P.Herm.Landl.*
        2.241–253   [187]

4.4.2   A wealthy landowner, Apion II (**5.5**), accepts responsibility
        for functions of the city council: *SB* 12.11079 (571)   [190]

4.5.1   A magical amulet: *P.Oxy.* 7.1060   [193]

4.5.2   Athanasius on prohibited books: *Festal Letter*
        39.21–23   [199]

4.7.1   Manumission of a slave from the Jewish community of
        Oxyrhynchos: *P.Oxy.* 9.1205.1–9, AD 291   [204]

4.9.1   Philo on the *therapeutai*: *On the Contemplative Life*,
        22–39   [211]

4.9.2   Childhood of Antony: Athanasius, *Life of Antony*, 1   [211]

4.10.1 Letter of Shenoute: *My heart is crushed, Canon 8*, XO 84:
        i.3–ii.18   [219]

4.11.1 Didymos the Blind in the classroom on Psalm 34:9   [223]

5.1.1   *Acts of the Council of Chalcedon*, Third Session   [230]

5.2.1   Letter to Bishop Pisenthios: *SBKopt.* I 295   [240]

5.5.1   The emperor's right-hand man: From the medieval Greek
        Narrative on the Construction of Hagia Sophia   [260]

5.7.1   Arbitration by Bishop Abraham: *BKU* 2.318 (Hermonthis,
        early seventh century)   [275]

6.1.1   Feasting the Persian governor: *BGU* 2.377 (619–629)   [278]

6.2.1   On the second conquest of Alexandria: *History of the
        Patriarchs* Benjamin I, *Patrologia Orientalis* 1 (1904)
        494–495   [284]

6.2.2 Census declaration: *P.Lond.Copt.* 1079 [286]

6.3.1 Receipt for requisitioned goods: *SB* 6.9676 (643, Herakleopolis) [292]

6.4.1 Letter from the governor to a local official showing concern about equality of treatment: *P.Lond. 4.1345* [301]

6.5.1 List of fugitives: *P.Lond.* 4.1460, 38–48 (Aphrodito, 709) [307]

6.5.2 Child donation of Tachel: *P.KRU* 86 (29 August 766) [311]

6.6.1 The meeting of Benjamin and ʿAmr: *HPA* Benjamin I, *PO* 1 (1904) 495–497 [316]

6.7.1 Samuel tears up a letter from Cyrus: Passage from the *Life of Samuel of Qalamun* pp. 80–81 Alcock [326]

6.8.1 Arabic replaces Coptic: Apollo of Qalamun, *Discourse* [*"Apocalypse"] of Samuel, head of the Monastery of Qalamun*, Ziadeh 379–381 [334]

6.9.1 Graffito from Bawit with a short prayer: text from Fournet 2009b [339]

6.9.2 On languages of trade: al-Muqaddasi, *The Best Divisions for Knowledge of the Regions* (Collins 2001) [340]

Contributors

Roger S. Bagnall is Professor of Ancient History and Leon Levy Director, emeritus, Institute for the Study of the Ancient World, New York University, as well as Jay Professor of Greek and Latin and Professor of History, emeritus, at Columbia University. He is the director of the excavations at Amheida and the co-author of the recent volume on those excavations, *An Oasis City*. His interests lie mainly in the social, economic, and administrative history of Egypt from the Hellenistic to the Late Antique period and in the papyrological documentation of that period.

Mona Haggag is Professor Emerita of Classical Archaeology in the Department of Archaeology and Classical Studies, Faculty of Arts, Alexandria University, Egypt; President of the Archaeological Society of Alexandria (founded 1893); and President of the Scientific Permanent Committee for the Academic Promotion of Egyptian Universities' Staff. Her main domain of interest is the monuments and heritage of Egypt during Ptolemaic and Roman times, with special focus on Alexandrian tangible heritage. Her awards include the Alexandria University Award for Scientific Distinction; the 2016 Award of Honor of the Union of Arab Archaeologists; the Hypatia Prize from the Hellenic Association for Women Scientists, Athens; and the Egyptian State Award of Excellency in Social Sciences, Egypt.

Todd M. Hickey is Professor of Classics at the University of California, Berkeley, and the current President of the American Society of Papyrologists. He also directs Berkeley's Center for the Tebtunis Papyri and serves as Faculty Curator for Graeco-Roman Egypt at the Phoebe Apperson Hearst Museum of Anthropology. His research interests include social relations in Roman and Late Antique Egypt and the history of papyrology, including the provenance of collections.

Mohamed G. Elmaghrabi is Professor of Graeco-Roman History and Civilization at Alexandria University, and Acting Vice Dean of the Faculty of Archaeology and Languages at Matrouh University. His publications are mainly editions of Greek documentary papyri of early Roman Egypt.

Arietta Papaconstantinou is Associate Professor of Ancient History at the University of Reading and Associate Member of the Faculty of Oriental Studies at the University of Oxford. She is the author of *Le culte des saints en Égypte des Byzantins aux Abbassides* (2001), and has published widely on the religious, linguistic, social, and economic aspects of the transition from Rome to the Caliphate in the Eastern Mediterranean, focusing more specifically on the history of Late Antique and early medieval Egypt.

Dorothy J. Thompson, a Fellow of Girton College, Cambridge, is an ancient historian with a particular interest in Hellenistic Egypt. She is a Fellow of the British Academy and an Honorary President of the International Society of Papyrologists. The second edition of her prize-winning *Memphis under the Ptolemies* was published by Princeton University Press in 2012 and her most recent book, together with Thorolf Christensen and Katelijn Vandorpe, is *Land and Taxes in Ptolemaic Egypt: An Edition, Translation and Commentary for the Edfu Land Survey*, published by Cambridge University Press in 2017.

Preface

Egypt has a long history. Even leaving aside the predynastic period, this history stretches for more than five thousand years, from the earliest pharaonic dynasties to the present. To both students and a wider public around the world, the period from the Old Kingdom to the end of the New Kingdom (about 2686 to 1080 BC) is certainly the best known. In Egypt itself, this pharaonic period as well as the history of Egypt from the arrival of Arab armies in the seventh century to the present are important parts of the school curriculum. Less often taught are the three-quarters of a millennium between the end of the New Kingdom and the arrival of Alexander the Great in 332 BC. Even less well known to a general public or an educational focus is the millennium from the conquest of Alexander to the arrival of Arab armies in 639–640. Tourists in Egypt are likely to have acquired at least some acquaintance with the superb monuments dating from the periods of Islamic rule. But apart from a perhaps brief exposure to Alexandria, there is little that a casual visitor will learn about the period when Greek was widely spoken and written in Egypt, and particularly the period when it was under Roman rule. And yet these centuries not only witnessed many of the most dramatic events of Egyptian history, they also created the essential foundations of the society that 'Amr ibn el-As found in the seventh century and that still shape significant aspects of the Egyptian religious and cultural landscape. This book is intended to bring the history of these critical centuries of Egyptian history to a broad audience.

During these centuries Egypt played a central role in the Mediterranean world, serving for much of the period as a critical link between the Mediterranean and the sphere of the Indian Ocean. Control of Egypt's wealth was a chief objective for successive empires over a long span of history: Kush, Assyria, Persia, Macedon, Rome, and Byzantium. Egypt was by most reckonings the wealthiest state of its time, with an enormous amount of productive land, watered by the Nile and refertilized each year with the silt brought by the Nile's flood. With no more than one-twelfth of its present population at most – even at its peak – Egypt already had under cultivation most of the land that is farmed today and produced far more abundant crops than other regions. In the Roman period Egypt fed Rome and then Constantinople, the largest cities of their time, and even then did not exhaust its surplus. Controlling Egypt was thus vital to the survival of successive Roman governments.

Egypt's importance was therefore closely tied to the particular geographical and ecological features of the country. Proverbially the "gift of the Nile," for most of the period covered in this book the country stretched the length of the Nile from just south of Aswan for some 840 km (520 miles) to the Mediterranean coast. The valley was generally narrow, bordered by desert on either side, until it reached Heliopolis (Cairo) at the head of the Nile delta *c.* 685 km (425 miles) downstream. Here the Nile branched out into a network of channels and canals (Map 1), making it difficult to cross the Delta; those who entered Egypt would come south along one of the branches of the Nile. Both these Delta channels and the mainstream of the Nile were subject to movement over time with the effect that ancient settlements that once stood on the banks of the river now lie some distance away. In the western desert a line of oases was linked both eastward to the valley and to Nubia in the south; across the Eastern Desert ran routes to ports on the Red Sea coast. The Fayyum basin, 100 km (around 60 miles) south of Cairo, provided a further area of agricultural land, especially after its reclamation under the early Ptolemies. Overall, there were some 60,000 square km (23,000 square miles) of fertile land in the country and the wealth of Egypt's agriculture, dependent on the annual flood of the Nile, will be a recurring theme in the following chapters.

This period is rich in evidence concerning many aspects of life. True, the monuments are perhaps less impressive than for earlier periods, and inscriptions far less numerous and informative than those of the pharaonic period, although the great temples of Edfu and Dendera do belong to the Ptolemaic period. Narrative sources are scanty, and statistics lacking. But in compensation we have far greater quantities of everyday textual evidence, mostly in Egyptian, Greek, Aramaic, Latin, and Arabic, from ancient authors preserved in medieval manuscripts but mostly in the hundreds of thousands of papyrus texts found in Egypt over the last two hundred years. Although only part of this immense treasure has so far been published, it is enough to enable us to examine everything from the workings of government to the private lives of ordinary people, often in great detail. Sometimes a group of texts – an archive – centers on one person or family. Although these sources are often fragmentary and difficult to understand, they enable us to see something of the economic, social, administrative, and cultural lives of the population to a degree impossible in most other places of the ancient world, with the partial exception of Mesopotamia (roughly, modern Iraq). This evidence thus offers an exceptional opportunity to understand how a society with a deep-rooted and vigorous indigenous culture evolved over a long period of interaction with neighboring societies while retaining a distinctive identity.

This book seeks to bring these richly documented millennia between the New Kingdom and the Arab conquest to a broad readership. Its focus is on the period of the Roman Empire, including the centuries in which Egypt was ruled from Constantinople after the center of power in the empire moved east in the fourth century AD. During this time Egyptian Christianity took form in ways that remain profoundly embedded in society today. But because Roman Egypt was shaped in part by the changes of the preceding intervals of both Egyptian and foreign rule, our introduction takes us back to the Third Intermediate Period and the Saite, Persian, and Ptolemaic kings.

Egypt's history before the coming of the Ptolemies is conventionally studied in "dynasties," series of rulers usually with a relationship to one another. Our idea of these dynasties goes back to ancient Egyptian temple records as reflected in the work of the Egyptian priest Manetho, who produced his history of the country for Ptolemy II in the third century BC (**1.5**). We use this dynastic framework to introduce Egypt's history before Alexander the Great. Modern scholars of the nineteenth and earlier twentieth centuries sometimes jumped too quickly to the view that the Greeks brought immediate and radical change to Egypt, supposed to have been a closed and backward society until then. But more recent Egyptological work has shown that Egypt before Alexander was already deeply integrated into the Near Eastern world and exchanged ideas and technologies with its neighbors in all directions. Many immigrants from all over the Eastern Mediterranean lived in Egypt and became Egyptian to some degree. That is not to say that the three hundred years of Ptolemaic rule did not bring change – they did. But the story is much more complicated and the change more gradual than has been assumed.

The Romans from the start tried to make Egypt more like other parts of their large empire. But once again, there was much that did not change, and the changes that did take place have been made out to be greater than they were. Ultimately, some of the innovations of Roman rule transformed Egyptian society more profoundly than any Ptolemaic developments had done. It is not always easy, however, to discern why changes took place. Of particular relevance to this book, it is hard to tell just why the slow decline of the Egyptian temples accelerated in the third century and created the conditions that allowed Christianity to spread and become more established in the country, leading to Egypt becoming almost entirely a Christian country in the centuries down to and beyond the arrival of the Arabs. We have tried to follow this development without going too deeply into the details of the theological controversies that split the Christian community in Late Antiquity. Our account continues after the Arab conquest in order to show how the changes that it brought, both directly and indirectly, helped to shape medieval, and even modern, Egypt, a world in which the consonant stem of the word "Egyptian" (in various ancient languages) came to be used to mean specifically "Copt," i.e. Egyptian Orthodox Christian rather than Arab or Muslim Egyptian.

Because we lack ancient narrative sources for much of the period we cover, this book does not try to tell a continuous story. But where we can reconstruct the course of events we provide pieces of what such a narrative would be. By contrast, the wealth of documentary sources and archaeological evidence would allow many aspects of life in Roman Egypt to be covered in more detail than is possible in a book on this scale. Our work thus complements rather than replaces more thematic books about daily life such as Anna Boozer's forthcoming *At Home in Roman Egypt* (Cambridge University Press).

The sources on which our account is based cannot be cited in detail in a book of this nature, but we give references to documents directly cited or quoted, and after each section we provide a selection of works in which the evidence is fully cited. The ancient sources and modern scholarship alike offer a rich vocabulary of technical terms in Greek, Egyptian, Latin, and Arabic, which can be overwhelming to most readers. We translate these terms and give the original word, wherever we think it useful, inside parentheses. A glossary at the end provides definitions of the ancient terms.

This book originated in a plea by Wassif Boutros Ghali, President of the Société d'Archéologie Copte (Society for Coptic Archaeology), to create an account of Roman and Byzantine Egypt, to be published in both English and Arabic, that would be accessible to a broad public, including students. He was particularly concerned that the book should give a sense of the development of Roman Egypt into its Late Antique form and of the organic formation of the Christian community of Egypt. We are grateful for this challenge and for his comments on a draft of the book. Sadek Wahba has also offered useful comments and ensured that funding was available to produce the book. Financial support has come from the Wahba Family Trust, Mohamed Adel El Gazzar, Teymour Boutros-Ghali, and Hamed El Chiaty. We are grateful to all of them for making this book possible.

Editing a volume composed of contributions from six authors is always a challenge. I have tried to unify the presentation as far as possible and to provide enough cross-references for the reader to find the many sections in which a particular subject may be covered. But individual authorial views remain; even among ourselves we differ in analysis and emphasis, just as any group of scholars will. Although a book of this kind is unavoidably written with a high level of generalization and seeming authority, readers should always keep in mind that controversies lurk behind almost any statement. The manuscript was read by Stephen Davis, Dominic Rathbone, and three anonymous readers for the Cambridge University Press, whose detailed remarks were exceptionally helpful in the process of revision. As always, wherever we have not taken their advice, the responsibility is ours alone. We are also indebted to Rona Johnston-Gordon and Mary Woolsey for a careful stylistic revision of the text.

Chronology

BC

Predynastic Period: to 3000
Early Dynastic Period: *c.* 3000–2686
Old Kingdom: *c*. 2686–2181
First Intermediate Period: *c*. 2180–2040
Middle Kingdom: *c*. 2040–1730
Second Intermediate Period: *c.* 1730–1550
New Kingdom: *c.* 1550–1069
Third Intermediate Period: *c.* 1069–664
Late Period: 664–332

Dynasty 26 (Saite)

Psammetichos I: 664–610
Foundation of Naukratis: *c.* 630/570
Necho II: 610–595
Psammetichos II: 595–589
Apries: 589–570
Amasis: 570–526
Psammetichos III: 526–525

Dynasty 27 (1st Persian Occupation)

Cambyses: 525–522
Darius I: 522–486
Xerxes: 486–465

Dynasty 28

Amyrtaios: 404–399

Dynasty 29

Hakoris: 393–380

Dynasty 30

Nektanebo I: 380–362
Nektanebo II: 360–343
Tachos: 361–359

2nd Persian Occupation

Artaxerxes III: 343–338
Darius III: 336–332

Macedonian dynasty

Alexander the Great: 332–323
Foundation of Alexandria: 331
Philip III Arrhidaios: 323–317
Alexander IV (d. 310): 323–306
Ptolemy son of Lagos, satrap of Egypt: 323–306

Ptolemaic dynasty

Ptolemy I Soter (with Berenike I): 306–282
Battle of lpsos: 301
Ptolemy II Philadelphos (with Arsinoe II, d. 270/268): 282–246
Ptolemy III Euergetes I (with Berenike II): 246–221
Canopus decree: 238

Ptolemy IV Philopator (with Arsinoe III): 221–204
Battle of Raphia: 217
Revolt in the Thebaid under Haronnophris and Chaonnophris: 206–186
Ptolemy V Epiphanes (with Cleopatra I): 204–180
Battle of Panion: 200
Memphis decree (Rosetta Stone): 196
Ptolemy VI Philometor and Cleopatra I: 180–177
Ptolemy VI and Cleopatra II: 177–170
Ptolemy VI, Ptolemy VIII and Cleopatra II: 170–164
Antiochus IV invades Egypt: 170–168
Ptolemy VIII Euergetes II ("Physkon"): 164–163
Ptolemy VI and Cleopatra II: 163–145
Ptolemy VIII: 145–116
Cleopatra III and Ptolemy IX Soter II ("Lathyros"): 116–107
Cleopatra III and Ptolemy X Alexander I: 107–101
Ptolemy X and Cleopatra Berenike III: 101–88
Ptolemy IX Soter II: 88–80
Ptolemy XII Neos Dionysos ("Auletes"): 80–58
Berenike IV: 58–55
Ptolemy XII: 55–51
Cleopatra VII Philopator and Ptolemy XIII: 51–47
Julius Caesar in Egypt: 48/47
Cleopatra VII and Ptolemy XIV: 47– 44
Cleopatra VII and Ptolemy XV ("Caesarion"): 44–30
Mark Antony sometimes in Egypt: 41–30
Battle of Actium: 31

AD

Roman emperors

Augustus (previously Octavian): 27 (BC)–14
Tiberius: 14–37
Gaius (Caligula): 37–41
Alexandrian Greeks attack the Jews: 38
Claudius: 41–54
Nero: 54–68
Galba, Otho, Vitellius: 68–69
Vespasian: 69–79

Titus: 79–81

Domitian: 81–96

Nerva: 96–98

Trajan: 98–117

Jewish revolt in Egypt: 115–117

Hadrian: 117–138

Hadrian visits Egypt: 129–130

Antoninus Pius: 138–161

Marcus Aurelius: 161–180

Lucius Verus: 161–169

Antonine plague in Egypt: 167–*c.* 179

Revolt of Boukoloi in the Delta: 172–175

Commodus: 180–192

Septimius Severus: 193–211

Septimius Severus visits Egypt: 200–201

Caracalla: 211–217

Constitutio Antoniniana (grant of Roman citizenship): 212

Macrinus: 217–218

Antoninus (Elagabalus): 218–222

Severus Alexander: 222–235

Maximinus the Thracian: 235–238

Gordian III: 238–244

Philip the Arab: 244–249

Decius: 249–251

Decian "persecution" of Christians: 250

Trebonianus Gallus: 251–253

Valerian and Gallienus: 253–260

Gallienus (alone): 260–268

Claudius II the Goth: 268–270

Palmyrenes control Egypt: 270–272

Aurelian: 270–275

Tacitus: 275–276

Probus: 276–282

Late Antique/Byzantine emperors

Diocletian: 284–305

Diocletian in Egypt: 298

The Great Persecution: 303–313

Constantine I: 306–337
Licinius: 308–324
Athanasius bishop of Alexandria: 328–373
Constantine II: 337–340
Constans: 337–350
Constantius II: 337–361
Julian ("the Apostate"): 361–363
Jovian: 363–364
Valens: 364–378
Theodosius I: 379–395
Roman Empire divided into eastern and western halves: 395
Arcadius: 395–408
Theodosius II: 408–450
Marcian: 450–457
Council of Chalcedon condemns Miaphysites: 451
Leo I: 457–474
Zeno: 474–491
Anastasius: 491–518
Justin I: 518–527
Justinian: 527–565
Justin II: 565–578
Tiberius II: 578–582
Maurice: 582–602
Phocas: 602–610
Heraclius: 610–641
Sasanian Persians occupy Egypt: 619–629
Arab conquest: 639–642
Umayyad khalifate: 642–750
Abbasid khalifate: 750–868

Alexandrian patriarchs from Demetrius on

Demetrius I: 189–231
Heraclas: 231–247
Dionysius: 247–264
Maximus: 264–282
Theonas: 282–300
Peter I: 300–311
Achillas: 312

Alexander I: 312–328
Athanasius I: 328–373
Peter II: 373–380
Timothy I: 380–385
Theophilus: 385–412
Cyril I: 412–444
Dioscorus I: 444–454
Timothy II Aelurus ("the Cat"): 457–477
Peter III Mongus ("the hoarse"): 477–490
Athanasius II: 490–496
John I Hemula: 490–505
John II Nicaiotes: 505–516
Dioscorus II: 516–517
Timothy III: 517–535
Theodosius I: 536–566
Peter IV: 576–577
Damianus: 578–607
Anastasius: 607–619
Andronicus: 619–626
Benjamin: 623–662
Agathon: 662–680
John III: 680–689
Isaac: 690–692
Simon: 692–700
Alexander II: 704–729
Kosmas I: 729–730
Theodore: 730–742
Michael I: 743–767
Menas I: 767–776
John IV: 777–799
Mark II: 799–819
Jacob: 819–830
Simon II: 830
Yusab I: 831–849
Michael II: 849–851
Kosmas II: 851–858
Shenoute I: 859–880
Michael III: 880–907
Gabriel I: 909–920
Kosmas III: 920–932

Makarios I: 932–952
Theophanios: 952–956
Menas II: 956–974
Abraham: 975–978
Philotheos: 979–1003
Zacharias: 1004–1032
Shenoute II: 1032–1046
Christodoulos: 1046–1077
Cyril II: 1078–1092

Chalcedonian patriarchs from Justinian on

Paul Tabennesiota: 538–540
Zoilus: 540–551
Apollinaris: 551–570
John: 570–581
Dynasties, kings, and emperors drawn from Bagnall and Rathbone 2017
Patriarchs list drawn from Davis 2004, Appendixes 1 and 3

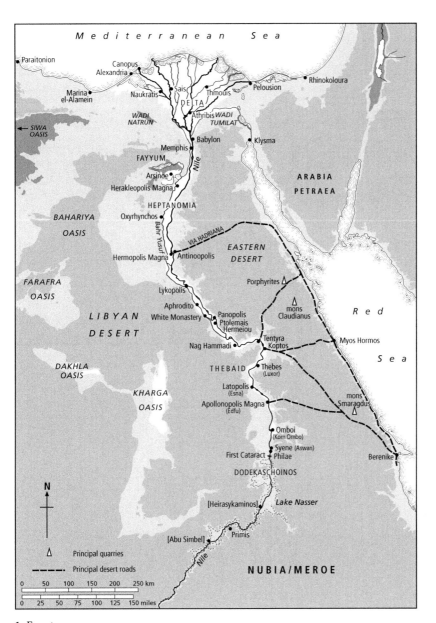

1 Egypt

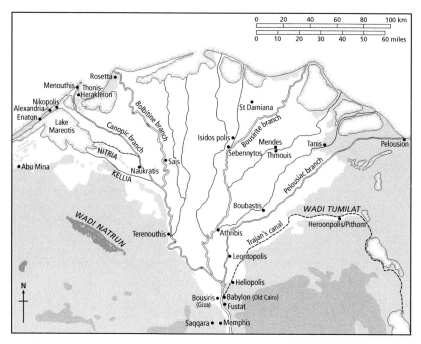

2 Delta

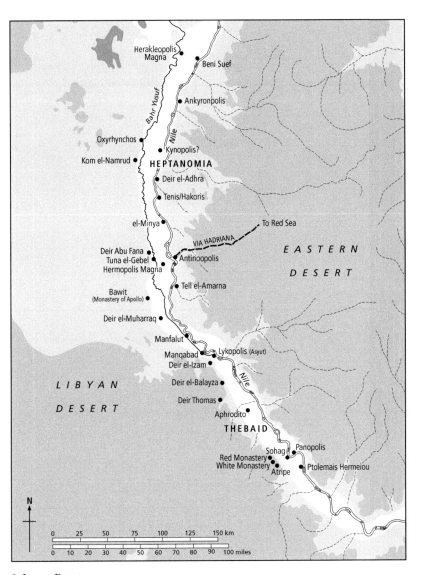

Herakleopolis
Magna
● Beni Suef

● Ankyronpolis

Oxyrhynchos ● Kynopolis?
Kom el-Namrud ●
HEPTANOMIA

● Deir el-Adhra

● Tenis/Hakoris

el-Minya ●
To Red Sea
VIA HADRIANA
EASTERN
Deir Abu Fana ●
Tuna el-Gebel ● ● Antinoopolis
Hermopolis Magna ●
DESERT
● Tell el-Amarna
Bawit
(Monastery of Apollo) ●

Deir el-Muharraq ●

Manfalut ●
Manqabad ● ● Lykopolis (Asyut)
Deir el-Izam ●

LIBYAN Deir el-Balayza ●
Nile
DESERT Deir Thomas ●

Aphrodito ●

THEBAID

● Panopolis
Sohag ●
Red Monastery ●
White Monastery ● ● Ptolemais Hermeiou
Atripe

Bahr Yusuf
Nile

N

0   25   50   75   100   125   150 km
0 10 20 30 40 50 60 70 80 90 100 miles

3 Lower Egypt

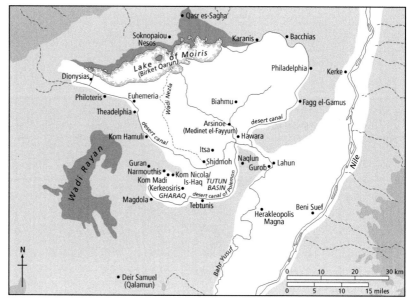

4 Fayyum

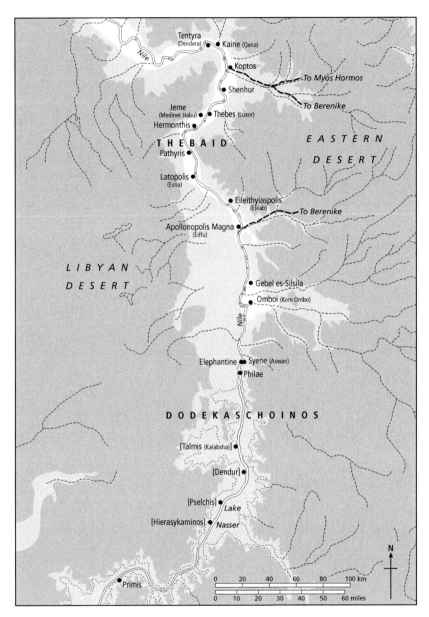

5 Upper Egypt

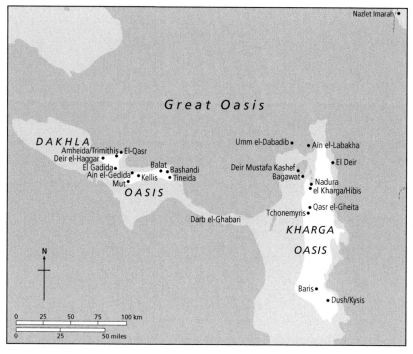

6 Great Oasis/Western Desert

7 Eastern Desert

1 | Laying the foundations for Roman Egypt

1.1 The pharaonic background and the Third Intermediate Period (1069–664 BC)

As Ruler of the Two Lands, Egypt's pharaoh wore the double *pschent* crown: the red crown of Lower Egypt, in the north, surrounding the white crown of Upper Egypt, in the south. Personified in the ruler, this union remained a central ideal throughout Egyptian history. The unity of Upper and Lower Egypt, also symbolized in the knot tied between papyrus and reed, was long seen as key to Egypt's success. (Figure 1.1.1) In practice, however, the country was diverse in many ways, with an ongoing struggle between the central ideologies of unity and uniformity and the realities on the ground. Egypt was a self-consciously distinctive culture that also constantly received and absorbed immigrants from many countries into its society.

After the strong centralized monarchy of the Ramessids in the late second millennium BC (Dynasties 19–20), with its grandiose monuments and stable rule, the four hundred years of the Third Intermediate Period (Dynasties 21–25) saw the unifying knot become loose and at times untied, with different rulers based in different areas for much of the period. Many of these leaders originated from beyond Egypt's heartland of the Delta and the valley. Libyan rulers came into the Delta from the west, while others from the land of Kush (Nubia; what is now southern Egypt and northern Sudan) established themselves in the south. Egypt was also invaded in the seventh century BC by Assyrians from the east in a struggle to control the Levant that would often be replayed in later times.

Egypt's permeable western border with Libya is a desert, as hard to control then as now. The penetration of migrant groups into the Delta had started early, and, in a decentralized and fragmented country, Libyans were a presence to be reckoned with. Some were already settled as captives in the late New Kingdom by Rameses III, and others later served as Egyptian troops. In most respects, these Libyans became strongly

Figure 1.1.1 The Union of Upper and Lower Egypt, on the great temple of Rameses II (Dynasty 19) at Abu Simbel
The Union of Upper and Lower Egypt is signified in the knot held firm by Hapy, god of the Nile, in this image from the great temple of Rameses II (Dynasty 19) at Abu Simbel. On the left Hapy stands for Upper Egypt, land of the papyrus, and on the right for Lower Egypt, land of the reed, as shown in both his headdress and at his feet.

Egyptianized. The pharaoh Shoshenq I from Boubastis (945–924 BC, Dynasty 22), known as Great Chief of the Meshwesh (a Libyan tribe), was successful in extending his power beyond the Delta. He installed his son in Thebes (Luxor) and briefly controlled the whole of Egypt. This unity did not last. In Dynasty 23 (818–715 BC), Libyan kings again ruled from various centers, including Herakleopolis (Ihnasya el-Medina). In the Delta, Sais (Sa el-Hagar) later became the center of influence, and in Upper Egypt the main Theban priesthood of Amun-Ra remained import-ant as a series of different rulers controlled the south.

Around the mid-eighth century BC, Thebes came under the control of a new line of Nubian pharaohs (Dynasty 25). A royal princess named Amenirdis was appointed to the central priesthood as God's Wife of Amun – an appointment that was also political, as is clear from later choices for this post. When, under growing pressure from rival powers, the Nubian ruler Piy moved north to subdue Hermopolis (Ashmunein), Memphis (Mit Rahineh), and finally the Delta, the unity of Upper and Lower Egypt was once again established, now under a dynasty of black pharaohs from the south. Shortly thereafter, Memphis was recognized as the new capital of Egypt. Thebes, however, continued to be important as the main city of Upper Egypt, key to control of the south. Construction in the great Theban temple of Amun-Ra is evidence of the concerns and success of these strongly Egyptianized Nubian pharaohs. But problems now came from the east.

Egypt had lost her external possessions along the Levantine coast at the end of the New Kingdom. In 720 BC Assyrian forces defeated the Egyptians at Raphia, located in what is now the Gaza strip. Some fifty years later, under pharaoh Taharqa (690–664 BC, Dynasty 25), conflict again surfaced between these two powers. The Assyrians twice invaded Egypt, reaching Memphis and even Thebes on the second occasion, which they sacked. The Assyrians imposed a tribute, and set up vassal administrators in Delta towns. One of these was Psammetichos (Psamtek), who after a time asserted his independence from the Assyrians, ejected rival chiefs from the Delta, and established himself as ruler of a united and independent Egypt, founding the Saite dynasty (Dynasty 26). Once again the knot was tied.

Bibliography
Jansen-Winkeln 2012; Kitchen 1986; Morkot 2000; Myśliwiec 2000; Naunton 2010

1.2 Rebuilding a centralized state: Saite rule

With their capital now based at Sais in the Delta, the pharaohs of Dynasty 26 (664–525 BC) presided internally over a fairly successful and economically prosperous period. By the ninth year of his reign, Psammetichos I had taken Thebes and, in a move to reinforce control of the south, like the Nubian pharaohs before him he installed his daughter Nitocris as God's Wife of Amun, the highest priestly position in Thebes in this period, one that was later also held by the daughter of Psammetichos II (595–589 BC).

As always, Egypt's wealth lay in her agriculture, which in turn depended on the annual flood of the Nile (**Preface** and **1.13**). Egypt's rich harvests were the envy of the ancient world. Under the Saites, a strong financial structure was developed to exploit this agricultural wealth, with a financial official known as a *senti* in overall control. At the same time, overseas trade expanded, especially in the Eastern Mediterranean, along the coast of Phoenicia and northward into the Aegean. Even more than in earlier periods, Egypt welcomed traders who sailed there, and many stayed. With this greater interest in the sea, Egypt for the first time developed a significant navy.

The new regime embarked on an ambitious temple-building program. Starting under Psammetichos I, construction significantly increased, especially in Sais and the Delta but also in major cult centers along the Nile and in the western oases. In this way, pharaoh honored the gods of Egypt, in whose name he ruled and on whose support and protection he relied. But not all construction was of temples. At Memphis, the great palace-fort of pharaoh Apries (589–570 BC), with its huge fortified platform and surrounding ditch, still presents a lasting image of strength. The project to build a canal between the Red Sea gulf and the Nile, initiated under Necho II (610–595 BC) and finally completed three centuries later under Ptolemy II, is a measure of the confidence and stability enjoyed in this period, when Upper and Lower Egypt were united and the country turned its interest seaward.

Keeping control also required strong armies. In his initial campaigns to establish himself, Psammetichos I had employed foreign troops from Asia Minor. Some left a record. Pedon son of Amphinneus, from Caria (now southern Turkey), who fought for pharaoh, was rewarded with the gift of a city and a golden bangle, which he recorded on an Egyptian statue that he dedicated back home (Figure 1.2.1). The son of Greek immigrants Alexikles and Zenodote, in contrast, remained in Egypt. His Egyptian name *Wahibre-em-akhet* ("king Apries is in the horizon") was probably acquired when he entered court circles. After an impressive career in the administration, Wahibre-em-akhet was buried at Saqqara (the great cemetery area of Memphis) in an Egyptian-style sarcophagus with a full set of traditional funeral equipment (Vittmann 2003: Taf. 21–22a; Villing 2018). Most foreign troops were settled in the Delta to protect Egypt's eastern border against the Assyrians, and later, after the fall of the Assyrian empire, against the Babylonians and Persians. In the south, a military garrison was established at Elephantine, at the first cataract of the Nile. To the west, conflict continued intermittently. Under pharaoh Apries, Egypt supported the Libyan king against the Greek city of Cyrene. Amasis, the general sent by Apries to quell unrest among his defeated Egyptian troops, instead ousted his own ruler and established himself on the throne. During Amasis' long reign (570–526 BC) the country continued to prosper both at home and abroad. Shortly after Amasis' death, the Persian king Cambyses invaded Egypt, putting an end to the Saite period.

Figure 1.2.1 Block statue of Pedon, found in Priene
This Egyptian "block statue" of Pedon son of Amphinneus, found in Priene, carries a
sixth-century Greek inscription on its front surface. Dedicated by Pedon, who had
brought it from Egypt, it records gifts granted him by the Egyptian king Psammetichos
II as a reward of valor: a golden bracelet and a city. The statue (without its head)
measures 21 x 17 x 17 cm (8¼ x 6¾ x 6¾ in) and is now in the Denizli-Hierapolis
Archaeological Museum, inv. no. 3162.

Bibliography
Agut–Labordère 2013; Lloyd 2000; Villing 2018; Vittmann 2003; Yoyotte
1989

1.3 Two Persian occupations and sixty years of independence

In the course of the next two centuries, Egypt was occupied by the Persians
for two periods, one long (525–404 BC) and one short (343–332 BC). As
was true later under the Romans, Egypt's ruler was now an absentee
pharaoh who, supported by garrisons at the borders, governed through
a provincial governor, based at Memphis. The Persians introduced
Aramaic – the most widely used language of the Near East – as the language
of rule, though Egyptian continued in use in local administration,
economic life, and elsewhere.

Our knowledge of the first Persian invasion and occupation comes from a variety of sources. The Greek historian Herodotus from Halicarnassus, who visited Egypt under Persian rule, wrote at length on Egyptian geography, history, religion, and customs in books 2 and 3 of his *History*. Archaeology is, as always, an important source of information. For example, not only do we find the inscriptions of the Persian kings on temple walls, but Persian efforts to expand cultivated land in the Kharga oasis are revealed by the buildings and irrigation systems excavated there. Aramaic papyri provide details of the lives and practices of the new immigrants, especially the mainly Judaean troops stationed in Elephantine and Syene (Aswan) who, settled with their families, protected the southern border (*Pap.Eleph.Engl.*). Relations with local Egyptians are further illuminated by contracts, letters, and other documents written in demotic, the cursive Egyptian script developed under the Saites. Hieroglyphic texts record the careers of several prominent individuals. For instance, the inscription on the green basalt statue of Udjahorresnet (Figure 1.3.1) records his career (Kuhrt 2007: 117–122). He first served as a naval officer under the last two Saite pharaohs; surviving the end of that dynasty, he was taken to the court of Cambyses in Persia (modern Iran). There he composed an Egyptian titulary (a set of royal titles to be inscribed in hieroglyphs, the traditional sacred script of Egypt) for the Persian king as the new ruler of Upper and Lower Egypt. In recognition of his services, Cambyses appointed him priest of the goddess Neith and chief physician, and Udjahorresnet exploited his influence at court to bring about the reconstruction, with generous endowments, of the great temple of Neith at Sais. Eventually, the inscription records, he was sent back to Egypt by Cambyses' successor Darius I in order to revive the House of Life at Sais (the temple library and medical school). The collaboration of such men was key to how the Persians ruled. After their initial conquest, the new rulers, while ruling from afar, opted to act as pharaohs should, offering respect and support for the temples and gods of Egypt.

The wealth of Egypt was thus now exploited by a foreign power. According to Herodotus (3.91.2–3), a tribute of 700 talents was imposed – more than classical Athens originally collected from its entire confederacy in the fifth century BC. Garrisons were to be supported locally; the profits of the fisheries of Lake Moeris in the Fayyum went to the great king, with salt and Nile water for his table; and the town of Anthylla in the northern Delta provided shoes, girdles, and needles for the Persian queen. As elsewhere in the Persian empire, the building and upkeep of roads supported a well-regulated postal system. Furthermore, large Egyptian estates were granted to

Figure 1.3.1 Statue of Udjahorresnet from Sais
Statue made of green basalt of the chief physician Udjahorresnet from Sais. His life and
career under Egypt's Persian rulers Cambyses and Darius I are recorded in the
hieroglyphic inscription that covers its surface. Udjahorresnet, 58 cm (23 in) high without
his head, is shown holding a small shrine that contains a figure of the god Osiris.

high-ranking Persians, such as the fifth century BC satrap (governor)
Arshama, whose Aramaic correspondence with his local steward
Nakhtihor survives, written on skins – the standard writing material of the
Persian empire (Hdt. 5.58.3). Later rulers also adopted the practice of
rewarding loyalty with significant land grants, as in the case of Ptolemaic
gift-estates (**1.12**). In the western oases, the Persians introduced a new
technology for irrigation. Excavated tunnels (or *qanats*) used the natural
slope of the land to bring water in over long distances from underground
reservoirs. Agriculture flourished and, as before, its produce was taxed. The
Persian "artaba" was introduced to Egypt as the measure for grain, and

Persian artistic forms, such as metalwork bowls, were adopted. Egypt's active Greek and Levantine trade is visible both in an Aramaic record of customs dues (475 BC; Kuhrt 2007: 681–703) and in the archaeological record – for example, in the finds from the recent underwater excavations at Thonis-Herakleion at the Canopic mouth of the Nile (**1.4**). Below the level of satrap, the administration mainly continued as before, with local officials in post.

As ruler of Upper and Lower Egypt, Darius I effectively put down an initial uprising. He boasted of further work on the Red Sea canal and, as part of an empire-wide project, supported the codification of Egyptian laws in the *Demotic Law Code* (Mattha and Hughes 1975). His fifth-century successors faced more severe trouble, both in Egypt and closer to home. Under Artaxerxes I, a Libyan prince named Inaros, supported by Athens, led a rebellion, centered in the Delta and Memphis, that was quelled only after several years, in 454 BC. From Sais, Inaros' associate Amyrtaios continued the struggle in the Delta, and yet a further uprising took place under Darius II. The Persians were losing control. In 404 BC, distracted by dynastic conflict on the death of Darius II and confronted with a new rebellion under Amyrtaios II, Persia finally abandoned Egypt.

The sixty years of Egyptian independence running from 404 BC to 343 BC (Dynasties 28–30) were marked by conflicting claims to rule and disputes between rival factions. Persia loomed as a constant threat. Egyptian rulers further built up naval strength in the Eastern Mediterranean and increasingly used their wealth to employ foreign troops to assist local forces.

Of these latest native pharaohs, Hakoris ruled the longest (393–380 BC). A far-reaching program of temple-building under him left still visible traces on the ground, and cults received their customary royal support. Egypt's military position improved considerably. Starting under Nektanebo I (380–362 BC) in Dynasty 30, impressive fortifications were built along the coast and in the northeast Delta. Strong protective walls of mud brick are a widespread feature of the period, and may still be seen, for instance, at Elkab in the south. A further striking feature of this time is the growing popularity of animal cults. Sacred animals and birds were bred for mummification, dedicated by pilgrims, and buried in vaults along the desert edge. Providing a steady business for their priests, these typically Egyptian cults may have strengthened a sense of Egyptian identity in the context of a widening world. So, probably, did the increasing use of the Egyptian demotic script with its rich literature.

After capturing Phoenicia and Cyprus, King Artaxerxes III took Egypt back into Persian control (343 BC). The resulting shortage of papyrus in the market, noted by the Athenian philosopher Speusippus, is a measure of how deeply Egypt was involved in the Aegean world and how any interruption of Egyptian trade could have far-reaching consequences. Pharaoh Nektanebo II fled to Nubia, from where, according to the far later *Alexander Romance*, he supposedly visited Macedon and fathered Alexander the Great with the Macedonian queen Olympias thanks to a magical disguise.

Any new regime needs to establish legitimacy, but the new Persian rulers who controlled Egypt from 343 to 332 BC had little time for this. Relying on their satraps, and with local magnates to represent them on the ground (men like Somtutefnakht or Petosiris of Hermopolis, whose statues or tombs have survived), these absentee rulers were less concerned than their predecessors to present themselves in Egyptian guise. Greek sources are regularly hostile to the Persians, while demotic papyri suggest that much in Egypt continued undisturbed.

Bibliography
Agut-Labordère 2014; Colburn 2019; Defernez 2012; Kuhrt 2007; Lichtheim 1980; Ray 1988; Tuplin and Ma 2020

1.4 Greeks in Egypt before Alexander

When Alexander invaded Egypt in 332 BC, he found a significant Greek presence there, dating back to at least the seventh century. Greeks had come to Egypt primarily as troops, traders, and tourists. Ionian and Carian troops from Asia Minor were employed by Psammetichos I to establish his rule in the seventh century BC (**1.2**). Settled in camps in the Delta, they continued to protect the borders. Amasis later transferred these foreign fighters to Memphis, where, as Hellenomemphites ("Greek Memphites") and Caromemphites ("Carian Memphites"), they became well integrated in the city. Furthermore, they provided a ready source of information on their adopted homeland for Greek visitors such as Herodotus (cf. **1.3**) and later settlers.

In the fourth century BC, the Greek troops who became involved in disputes between Egyptian kings served under their own experienced generals. The Athenian Chabrias secured the throne for Nektanebo I and later headed his successor Tachos' navy. Tachos also hired a Spartan king, Agesilaos, and his troops. When Agesilaos switched sides in a further family struggle for power, Nektanebo II prevailed with his support. Agesilaos departed the country a wealthy man but, perishing en route home, arrived as a corpse embalmed in honey.

As Egypt turned toward the Mediterranean, immigrant traders played an increasingly significant role in economic development. The Delta city of Naukratis (Kom Giᶜeif, el-Nibeira, el-Niqrash) on the Canopic branch of the Nile was designated for settlement by Amasis sometime in the mid-sixth century BC, with land and cult centers for visiting traders. The main quarter of Naukratis was the Hellenion, founded by prominent cities from Ionian and Dorian Asia Minor, along with Mytilene on Lesbos. These founder cities provided officials to control trading matters in a community where many Egyptians also resided. Other Greek communities – Aegina, Samos, and Miletos – had their own cult centers in Naukratis. Thonis-Herakleion at the mouth of the Canopic branch of the Nile became a major port for Mediterranean commerce, as recent underwater excavations have shown, and with Naukratis upstream the Canopic branch dominated Mediterranean trade long before the foundation of Alexandria (Iskanderiya) in the same region.

The Delta region flourished and grew, as is clear from excavations and inscriptions. Twin hieroglyphic decrees, dated to year 1 of Nektanebo I (380 BC), record his grant of one-tenth of the royal revenue on imports through Thonis-Herakleion – gold, silver, timber, and wooden objects are specified – and on goods produced in Naukratis – such as perfume, faience, scarabs, and other amulets – to support the nearby temple of Neith at Sais (Masson-Berghoff and Villing 2016: 51; Lichtheim 1980: 86–89). Herodotus (2.175) describes the magnificent adornment of this temple by Amasis; he identified the goddess to whom it was dedicated with the Greek Athena. Naukratite production and trade joined agriculture as a source of wealth for the country. Egypt's first indigenous coinage, struck in imitation of Athenian tetradrachms, introduced a new method of facilitating payment for troops and possibly trade.

Not to be neglected are the Greek tourists who had visited Egypt over the centuries – according to Herodotus, this was a land of wisdom and marvels. In his poetry the Athenian statesman Solon recorded his presence in the Canopic region *c.* 600 BC. From the mid-fifth century a fine bronze statuette of an Apis bull from Memphis bears the name of its Greek dedicant Sokydes (Figure 1.4.1). These visitors were only two of many.

Bibliography
Huss 2001; Masson-Berghoff and Villing 2016; Rutherford 2016

Figure 1.4.1 Dedication of a statuette to Apis by a Greek
Dedication to Apis by a Greek. This small bronze statuette, just over 10 cm (about 4 in) in height, records its Greek dedication to Apis on its base: Sokydes set this up to Panepi. The Apis bull bears a sundisk between its horns above the uraeus, the rearing cobra that here symbolizes its divinity; its distinctive markings are clearly visible with an inverted triangle on its forehead and outspread falcon and vulture wings across its back. Dating from the late sixth century BC, this statuette from the Delta is clear evidence for the respect shown to Apis by a visiting or resident Greek. Later, under Ptolemy I, the Memphite god Apis was adapted, with human form, into the Greek god Sarapis.

1.5 Alexander and the Ptolemies

When Alexander of Macedon entered the easternmost Egyptian port of Pelusium (Tell el-Farama) in late 332 BC, early in his long campaign to conquer the Persian empire, the satrap Mazakes surrendered. Alexander made for Heliopolis (Tell el-Hisn), which occupied a crucial position at the Delta apex, and from there joined his army at Memphis, the capital of Egypt. Here he set a precedent for his successors as he combined Greek-style celebratory games with sacrifice to the gods and particularly to the

Apis bull, a deity with strong royal connections already well known to the Greeks, whose cult and burial vaults were centered in Memphis (Arrian, *Anab.* 3.1.4). The Ptolemies later supported this bull-cult, publicly contrasting themselves with the reputation – if not the reality – of their predecessors. According to anti-Persian propaganda, indeed, both Cambyses and Artaxerxes III had slaughtered an Apis bull, although the contemporary record suggests this is untrue. Continuing his concern for native cults, when he founded the new city of Alexandria on the coast (**1.7**), Alexander's initial plan included temples not only to the Greek gods but also to the Egyptian Isis, who was already well known in the Greek world (Arrian, *Anab.* 3.1.5).

From Alexandria Alexander proceeded westward in the direction of Cyrene; at Paraetonium (Mersa Matruh), he marched south through the desert to the Siwa oasis (Figure 1.5.1), where he claimed that the oracle had recognized him as son of Ammon, the name the Libyans (under Cyrenean influence) gave to Egyptian Amun, whom they identified with the Greek god Zeus. Alexander's daring personal project thus had longer-term political consequences as the new ruler of Egypt was integrated into the local pantheon.

Around the same time, Alexander acquired a full pharaonic titulary of five names. For both Greeks and Egyptians, as ruler he was now endowed with divine support. His image as pharaoh can still be seen on the walls of a chapel in the Luxor temple at Thebes.

Although the acceptability of the conqueror as pharaoh was important, above all Alexander was a military man who relied on his army. Egypt was "spear-won" territory, and garrisons with good commanders were crucial for the future. So on his departure in late spring 331 BC, after less than a year, Alexander left garrisons in Memphis and Pelusium, with a continuing military presence in the south. Two Macedonian generals were placed in overall control. A contemporary papyrus preserves an "out-of-bounds" order for troops from one of these commanders (Peukestas son of Makartatos), apparently once posted up on the priestly building that it orders troops not to enter (Figure 1.5.2).

Placed in charge of the country's finances was Kleomenes from Naukratis. In addition to native informants, especially priests, Alexander and his successors made use of Greeks already resident in the country for information and support. Kleomenes' success in building up reserves is evident in the enormous sum of 8,000 talents that the first Ptolemy found when he returned to take control of Egypt after Alexander's death.

Figure 1.5.1 Oracle temple at Siwa
Oracle temple at Siwa. This oracle temple sacred to Ammon in the Siwa oasis was visited by Alexander of Macedon early on in his visit to Egypt; there, the oracle recognized him as son of the god.

Despite Alexander's short stay in Egypt, he left good management in place; his policies continued after his departure. The foundation of Alexandria as a second Greek-style city (*polis*) brought a stronger Mediterranean-facing focus to the country while, elsewhere, existing structures were largely left in place.

Alexander thus set the scene, but his general Ptolemy son of Lagos was the man who, on Alexander's unexpected early death in 323 BC, seized the

---

Box 1.5.1 Plutarch, *Life of Alexander* 27.3–5

And having traversed the desert, Alexander reached the place where the prophet of Ammon addressed him with greetings from the god, as if from his father. [Questions follow about the fate of those who had murdered his father Philip] ... This is the account that most writers give about the oracular responses but Alexander himself, in a letter to his mother, says that he received some prophecies that were to remain secret; he would communicate these to her alone on his return. And some say that the prophet in a desire to show courtesy in speaking to him in Greek addressed him as *O paidion* ("my son") but with his foreign pronunciation put an "s" at the end of the words instead of an "n," so saying "*O paidios.*" Alexander, they report, was not displeased at the mistaken pronunciation and the story went around that the god had addressed him as "*O pai Dios*" ("O son of Zeus").

Box 1.5.2 Alexander's Egyptian titles, in an inscription from the Bahariya oasis

(Horus name) the young one, strong in power; (Two Ladies name) loved by the gods, to whom is given the office of his father; (Horus-on-the-Gold name) ruler on the whole earth; (Praenomen or *nsw.t-bity* name) who rejoices the heart of Ra, loved by Amun; (Son-of-Ra name) Alexandros.

Source: Bosch-Puche 2008

---

chance to establish a new family dynasty in Egypt. Acquiring Egypt in the division of Alexander's kingdom, he ruled for forty years, first nominally as governor for Alexander's young children, and then from 304 BC onward with the title of king. This long period allowed him to put Egypt on a strong footing in military, economic, religious, and cultural matters, in the development of a working administration, and in the management of relations between the local population and immigrant settlers. Most importantly, unlike foreign predecessors, notably the Persian kings, Ptolemy was a resident pharaoh; Egypt was now his home.

Militarily, Ptolemy I sought not only to preserve control within the borders of Egypt but also, in the competitive world of the Hellenistic kingdoms, to ensure a long-term supply of troops for his army. Already under the Persians native soldiers were given plots of tax-free land in return for service (Herodotus 2.168). This system of land grants (commonly termed

Figure 1.5.2 Orders of Alexander's general Peukestas
The orders of Alexander's general Peukestas were once posted up on papyrus in a sacred area of the Memphite necropolis at Saqqara; note the barely visible nail holes. The text reads: *Orders of Peukestas. No entry. Priestly property.* The concern of a key Macedonian commander for Egyptian temple property foreshadows the later attitude of the Ptolemaic regime. Egypt, Saqqara, excavations of the Egypt Exploration Society 1972-G.P. 3.

"cleruchy" or allotment) was adopted by the Ptolemies for both immigrant and local troops, thus providing a reward for service and keeping an army-in-waiting without paying salaries continuously. Over time, the cleruchic system was extended, first to the different police forces (regular police, desert guards, river police, etc.) and, from the second century BC, more widely to Egyptian infantrymen with land grants that were much smaller than those of Macedonian cavalrymen, who regularly received 100 arouras (27.5 hectares/ 68 acres). These grants would have long-term effects on the agriculture and land-holding system of Roman Egypt.

Outside his Egyptian homeland, Ptolemy sought to retain a strong presence in the Aegean and Eastern Mediterranean while repelling the threat of other powers, which were keen to take control of Egypt and its wealth. These rivals were above all the Antigonids (Antigonos the One-eyed and his heirs) and the Seleucids, descended from yet another of Alexander's generals – Seleukos – and based in Syria on Egypt's northeastern border. Cyprus and Cyrene formed important centers of Ptolemaic influence for most of the Ptolemaic period, passing to Rome only in the course of the first century BC. However, the more extended Ptolemaic overseas empire, based on the League of Islanders and including areas along the coast of Asia Minor and the north Aegean, was mostly lost to the Ptolemies by the end of the third century BC.

To manage the new regime, the early Ptolemies crucially depended on local knowledge. So, although the top echelons of the administration at first consisted of Greeks, with a finance minister at its head (the *dioiketes,* equivalent to the Egyptian *senti*, cf. **1.2**), at a local level Egyptian input and participation were essential. The old division of the country into forty-two regions (nomes) was retained, with a nomarch in charge of each. The nomarchs were displaced as administrative heads of the nomes by the late third century BC by governors (*strategoi*, "generals," in Greek, though the office was by this point mainly civil). At first these posts were filled by Greeks – or at least by men with Greek names (**1.12**) – but Egyptians provided the local functionaries required to manage the key operations, such as the census and land survey, essential for taxation in both cash and produce.

At least according to their own surviving records, local priests played an important role in communication with the new rulers. The Memphite high priests of Ptah were perhaps the most significant, but the burial complex of the Hermopolite priest Petosiris from the early Ptolemaic period shows a family that managed such a role for five generations under the changing dynasties. No successful pharaoh could ignore these influential men, and Manetho, the third-century priest who recorded the Egyptian pharaonic dynasties in Greek, illustrates the concern of one of the local intelligentsia to make Egyptian history available to their new rulers. To some degree this was a two-way process.

The Ptolemies' respect for local religion may be measured most visibly in the temple-building they undertook. As already noted (**Preface**), the main Egyptian temples still standing were constructed in this period, replacing earlier and more modest structures. As resident pharaohs, the Ptolemies built widely throughout the land. The temple to Horus at Edfu is a striking example, as is that of Hathor at Dendera, where Horus came annually from Edfu to visit his consort. Many other Ptolemaic temples survive only in ruins or not at all. At the time these temples were significant in providing a visible connection between the king and his country's gods.

Along with revenues, any viable state needs a good legal structure. Many matters we would consider legal were handled by crown administrators, but a dual court system was put in place early on, with Greek *chrematistai* acting as circuit judges in Greek legal matters, while people's justices (*laokritai*) were responsible for the Egyptian legal system. The two systems continued throughout the Ptolemaic period, but there was increasing economic and social pressure to move cases into the Greek court system. In the late second century BC, royal legislation provided that the language of a contract normally decided which law, and hence which judiciary, would be applied (*P. Tebt.* 5.207–220 (118 BC)).

> **Box 1.5.3 Royal decree concerning choice of courts:**
> ***P.Tebt.* 1.5.207–220 (118 BC)**
>
> And they [the sovereigns] have decreed, in cases in which Egyptians
> and Greeks are opposed, namely in cases of Greeks who bring actions
> against Egyptians, or of Egyptians against Greeks, with regard to all
> classes except the cultivators of Crown land and the taxpayers and all
> others connected with the revenues, that where Egyptians make an
> agreement with Greeks by contracts written in Greek, they shall give
> and receive satisfaction before the *chrematistai*; but where Greeks make
> agreements by contracts written in Egyptian they shall give satisfaction
> before the native judges [*laokritai*] in accordance with the national
> laws; and that suits of Egyptians against Egyptians shall not be dragged
> by the *chrematistai* into their own courts, but they shall allow them to
> be decided before the native judges in accordance with the national
> laws. (Translation from Bagnall and Derow 2004: 99.)

Finally, Ptolemy I successfully managed the crucial matter of succession. In this family dynasty, all kings were named Ptolemaios, and by joining his younger son with him on the throne for the final three years of his life and sending away potential competitors, Ptolemy ensured that on his death the succession of Ptolemy II was a smooth one. This pattern of succession, developed under Ptolemies I and II, was effectively followed for the next two hundred fifty years – sometimes at the cost of dynastic murders.

Bibliography
Fischer-Bovet 2014; Hölbl 2001; Lloyd 2011; Manning 2010; Thompson 2018

1.6   Resistance to foreign rule

The Ptolemies succeeded in building a rich and powerful state in Egypt and also gained a fine reputation in the Greek world for wealth and culture, with Alexandria serving as a magnet for people from all over the Mediterranean. The following sections of this chapter will explore aspects of this generally successful Ptolemaic state. But we start with major challenges to this success that the new rulers faced – challenges both to their larger Aegean empire and to their rule in Egypt itself. From the mid-third century onward, the Ptolemies confronted various forms of disturbance and unrest in their kingdom. From our vantage point it is not easy to evaluate the complex background to this turmoil. Poor harvests caused by inadequate or excessive Nile floods as well as other economic factors may have exacerbated more general dissatisfaction; hostility to foreign rule was sometimes evident. The first sign of major trouble came shortly after the start of Ptolemy III's reign, when the young king was called home from Syria to deal with unrest. In response, in autumn 243 BC he cut in half the rates for the salt tax, the main tax paid by the whole population. This reduction brought a priestly decree of thanks to the king for benefactions (the so-called Alexandria decree [el-Masri et al. 2012] of 243 BC), and Ptolemy III acquired the cult-title of Euergetes, "Benefactor." A later priestly decree from Canopus (Bagnall and Derow 2004: 268–269), set up in 238 BC in trilingual form (in hieroglyphs, demotic, and Greek), records the king's recent initiative in importing grain when the Nile flood had failed (**1.8**; **1.10**; **1.13**; Figure 1.6.1).

The most serious rebellion came a few decades later in the south; from 206 BC much of Upper Egypt was in revolt. No tax income came in, and Nile traffic was disrupted as rebel kings ruled from Thebes. With the loss of the south, Ptolemy IV came under extreme pressure; his murder in Alexandria (204 BC), followed by trouble at court, only aggravated the situation. When the priests convened at Memphis for the coronation of his son, the young Ptolemy V, known as Epiphanes ("Made Manifest"), their trilingual decree (196 BC, the "Rosetta stone": Bagnall and Derow 2004: 269–273) recorded the successful suppression of a simultaneous rebellion at Lykopolis in the Delta. Upper and Lower Egypt were not reunited until 186 BC. Thebes rebelled again in 88 BC during struggles between the two sons of Ptolemy VIII Euergetes II; its destruction by Ptolemy IX was devastating.

Pressure from abroad also put the Ptolemies under strain in the course of the second century. The country was twice invaded by Antiochus IV of Syria (in 170–168 BC), one of the more aggressive Seleucid kings (**1.5**). Within the royal family, the two sons of Ptolemy V fell out and, in the face of the Syrian threat, their subsequent joint rule (170–164 BC) was far from trouble-free. Later, following the death of Ptolemy VI Philometor ("Mother-loving") in 145 BC, civil war (132–130 BC) broke out involving the two wives (Cleopatra II and III) of his brother Ptolemy VIII Euergetes II. Cleopatra II had earlier been the wife of Ptolemy VI; she was also his sister, according to the marriage pattern of the Ptolemies, who were keen to keep rule within

Figure 1.6.1 Canopus decree
Passed by all the priests of Egypt assembled at the temple of Osiris at Canopus on 7 March 238 BC in favor of the king and his queen Berenike II, the decree was made in recognition of royal benefactions both in the traditional duties of the monarch in regard to the temples, such as care for the sacred animals, the provision of peace, and good government, and more particularly in the import of grain in a period of recent shortages. They decided to add the benefactor gods to the existing ruler cult, to enhance the priesthood in numbers, and to initiate special celebrations. A calendar reform with the provision of a leap year was decreed (though not actually put into effect) and a new Egyptian-style cult was devised for the young princess Berenike, who had recently died. The decree was to be set up inscribed trilingually – in hieroglyphs, demotic, and Greek – in all the temples of Egypt. On this example from Kom el-Hisn near Naukratis a royal scene heads all three texts in the order just indicated. *CPI* 129. White limestone. H: 2.22 m x W: 0.79 m (7ft 3 in x 2 ft 7 in).

the family. Cleopatra III, Ptolemy VIII's second wife, was her daughter by that earlier marriage, so also her second husband's niece. These were difficult times indeed for the Ptolemaic ruling house.

Throughout the period of dynastic conflict, tensions simmered between the court and the Alexandrian population and, on a broader scale, between the capital and countryside. These tensions were exploited by Dionysios Petosarapis, a courtier who started an uprising in Alexandria that speedily spread throughout the countryside. Papyri record sporadic violence – documents were burned, property seized illegally, and local temples attacked – as support for Dionysios spread. Control of the south was only reestablished in 165 BC.

No predominant grievance may be detected in these various out-breaks of discontent. The Greek historian Polybius (5.107.2–3) drew attention to the confidence acquired by Egyptian troops who were armed by Ptolemy IV for his successful campaign against Antiochus III in the Fourth Syrian War (battle of Raphia, 217 BC). The names of the Theban rebel rulers Haronnophris ("Horus is Osiris") and Chaonnophris ("Osiris still lives"), like the surname Petosarapis ("gift of Osorapis") that was attached to Dionysios, imply an element of nationalism. So does the later apocalyptic text called the "Potter's Oracle," which foretold the desertion of Alexandria ("the city by the sea") in favor of Memphis and an end to the rule of the "Girdlewearers" (i.e. the Greeks). However, as so often in civil unrest, more immediate causes are also known: Nile flood failure (in some cases perhaps the result of climatic disruptions caused by volcanic eruptions elsewhere), damage from conflicts, hardship, and local ven-dettas all played their part, as did ongoing weakness in central control. A series of royal and administrative rulings concerning debts, taxes, and other problems reflects the constant pressure on Ptolemaic rule.

Bibliography
Ludlow and Manning 2016; McGing 1997; Pestman 1995; Veïsse 2004

1.7   Alexandria and other urban centers

According to a tradition preserved in the *Alexander Romance* (Ps.-Callisthenes 1.32.10: Stoneman 1991: 65), Alexandria was founded on April 7, 331 BC. Thanks to its natural advantages, mild weather, location at the intersection of the trade routes of the ancient world, and, above all, access to Egypt's abundant resources, Alexandria became the largest and most important political and economic center of the Hellenistic world. With constant activity at its Mediterranean harborfront and inland port on Lake Mareotis (Mariut), Alexandria soon flourished.

When the city was founded, a causeway known as the Heptastadion connected the mainland to the island of Pharos. This causeway formed a division between two harbors. To the east lay the Great Harbor, to the west the port of Eunostos, that of "Good Return." On the island stood the famous lighthouse (the *Pharos*). Several sites have been proposed as its location: the medieval fort Qait Bey, the submerged reef called "Diamond Rock" located east-northeast of Qait Bey, or even the submerged islets close to the modern main entrance to the harbor.

The layout of Alexandria was attributed to the architect Deinokrates of Rhodes. Bordered by the Mediterranean to the north and Lake Mareotis to the south, the city was roughly rectangular in shape, taking the form of the cloak or mantle worn by Macedonian soldiers. It was a fully planned city, laid out on a grid system, with two main intersecting roads, the Canopic Way, which ran from east to west, from the Gate of the Sun to the Gate of the Moon, and a second running from north to south. The streets, laid out so as to exploit the prevailing winds, were lined with fine stone houses; there were tetrastyle porticoes, triumphal arches, monumental gates, and fountain houses. Minor streets connected the city's public and private sectors. The new city was divided into five main quarters named after the first five letters of the Greek alphabet. The courts were located in Alpha; the Egyptians lived in an area called Rakotis, which later included the great Serapeum founded by Ptolemy III. Jews inhabited the fourth or Delta quarter. Under the Ptolemies the Jewish community was active in the political life of both the city and the country at large. On the pattern of Memphis and elsewhere, we can assume that the many ethnic communities of Alexandria, a city thronged with immigrants, would have had their own residential quarters.

Much of the area to the south of the Great Harbor was occupied by the Royal Quarter, the Broucheion, which constituted a quarter or even one-third of the total size of the city. As the site of the royal residence, this was Alexandria's grandest area. Here lay the Ptolemaic palace with its gate-tower, gardens, and collection of exotic animals and birds; nearby were the Mouseion (see below) and Alexander's tomb complex. Greek temples stood in the Royal Quarter and elsewhere in the city, which boasted, in addition, a gymnasium, stadium, theater, and other buildings familiar to Greeks. However, the streets were also adorned with large, Egyptian-style statues of the rulers and monuments from earlier times, brought down the Nile to introduce a sense of Egypt to a mainly Greek city.

Like Naukratis earlier or Ptolemais (El-Mansha) in the south, founded by Ptolemy I as a counterbalance to Thebes, Alexandria was set up as a self-governing Greek-style city with its citizen body artificially divided into groups called (on the model of Athens and other Greek cities) tribes and demes and with – at least at the start – a functioning council (*boule*), assembly (*demos*), and board of officials (*prytaneis*). However, the reality that Alexandria was also the residence of Ptolemy and headquarters of his royal administration limited the degree to which civic decision-making could be truly independent.

As home to its rulers and hub for the Ptolemaic administration, Alexandria also served as center for the Greek-style dynastic cult of the Ptolemies. When Ptolemy son of Lagos seized Alexander the Great's embalmed body and brought this talisman to Egypt in a successful bid to bolster his rule, he first buried him in Memphis, Egypt's long-time capital. Alexander's body was later moved to Alexandria, the new capital he had founded. A royal cult attached to that of Alexander was started under Ptolemy II, and the names of later rulers were added one by one. Under Ptolemy IV a dynastic cult center was established around Alexander's tomb. The priesthoods were held by members of prominent Alexandrian families and, especially in the second century, the changing fortunes of the royal family are visible in the modifications made to the overall cult – the addition, removal, or change of cult-titles and priesthoods for kings and particularly queens. In 215/214 BC, a separate dynastic cult was introduced to Ptolemais in the south, in what may be seen as an (ultimately unsuccessful) attempt by Ptolemy IV to keep Upper and Lower Egypt united under his rule.

Festivals played an important part in the life of the capital – for instance, the birthdays of the kings; the Arsinoeia set up for Ptolemy II's sister-wife Arsinoe II; or the great dynastic Ptolemaieia established by Ptolemy II as an international celebration held every four years with processions and games. These regular festivals served to emphasize the wealth and power of the ruling family.

Much of Alexandria's vibrant economic life revolved around the port, with its double harbor and canal leading through to the Nile. Since the damper climate of the coast means that papyri do not survive from the city itself, we rely on documents from elsewhere and on archaeology to gain a picture of Alexandrian trade. Amphora stamps show the diverse origins of Greek wine imported through the city; papyrus documents

> **Box 1.7.1 Imported goods:** *P.Cair.Zen.* 5.59823 (253 BC)
>
> Promethion to Zenon, greeting. You wrote to me about the wax to say that the cost per talent, including the toll at Memphis, comes to 44 drachmas, whereas you are told that with us it costs 40 drachmas. Now do not listen to the babblers; for it is selling here at 48 drachmas. Please therefore send me as much as you can. Following your instructions I have given your agent Aigyptos 500 drachmas of silver toward the price of the wax, and the remainder, whatever it may be, I will pay immediately to whomever you tell me to. And of honey also let 5 *metretai* be procured for me. I appreciate the kindness and willingness which you always show to me, and if you yourself have need of anything here, do not hesitate to write. Farewell. Year 33, Pharmouth 19. (Address) To Zenon. (Translation from Bagnall and Derow 2004: 161.)

from the Fayyum record Greek cheeses, dried figs, Carian honey, and garlic coming through Alexandria; wood, pitch, and cedar oil from Phoenicia remained in constant demand for both civic and naval construction as well as burials. At the same time, the city produced its own goods for consumption at home and for export: the well-known perfumes of Egypt, papyrus, textiles, jewelry, metalware, glassware, and more. The main export through Alexandria's busy harbor, however, was the tax grain, predominantly wheat, which formed the basis of Ptolemaic royal wealth – and later provided much of the food supply for Rome and contributed to its treasury.

As an international center attracting talent from many lands, Alexandria became a trendsetter of the Hellenistic world. The city's cultural life formed a key part of the Ptolemaic project. By their patronage of culture and science, the first Ptolemies aimed to enhance both their own reputation and the prestige of the new kingdom, aspiring to rival the cultural and scientific achievements of Athens herself. Ptolemaic initiatives emphasized the Greekness of their new state and, whatever the explicit aims, their patronage made the city the center of Hellenistic culture. Philosophers, mathematicians, astronomers, artists, poets, and physicians were all encouraged to come and work there. Callimachus from Cyrene and Theocritus from Syracuse wrote their poetry in the city; the mathematicians Euclid, Archimedes, and Apollonios practiced there; the medical scientist Herophilus worked on human anatomy and the circulation of blood; and the inventor Ktesibios developed pneumatics for technological purposes.

Although the construction of a center to the Muses probably began under Ptolemy I, this institution, known as the Mouseion, became more famous and prestigious under Ptolemy II with the addition of the Library – either a separate building or attached to the Mouseion – and an impressively large collection of texts. Ancient estimates of the size of the library collection vary from 400,000 to 700,000 volumes (book-rolls). These numbers are likely exaggerated – it remains unclear how comprehensive the library's holdings actually were – but even a fraction of what is claimed would have constituted the greatest library of its time. In addition to works of the best-known Greek authors, the library contained Greek translations of works in every branch of learning and literature from many other languages. The translation into Greek of the Hebrew Bible (the Septuagint) was associated with the Mouseion. Appointment as librarian brought distinguished scholars to the city, men such as the poet Apollonius of Rhodes or Eratosthenes from Cyrene, who successfully measured the circumference of the earth. Librarians also on occasion served as tutors to the royal family. With Ptolemaic patronage and scholars based in the Mouseion, literature, learning, mathematics, and science flourished.

Elsewhere in Egypt the Greek word for city-state, *polis*, was attached to the names of the nome capitals – Apollonos polis ("city of Apollo"), for instance, for Edfu – and over time these centers developed, becoming more urbanized with an increase in population and the addition of new buildings. In Krokodeilon polis ("city of crocodiles," named after the Fayyum crocodile cults), for instance, Greek-style baths were erected; in third-century BC Hermopolis a shrine was built for Ptolemy III Euergetes and his queen Berenike II; and in the Fayyum village of Philoteris a gymnasium was constructed as a center for the local Greek community. The term *polis*, as given to nome capitals in Egypt, did not, however, carry the same connotations of autonomy and self-governance as in old Greece. Similarly, when, under Ptolemy VI, settlements termed "citizen bodies" (*politeumata*) were introduced for communities of ethnic troops together with their families, this terminology did not carry earlier Greek-style political implications.

In the same period as these military settlements first occur, a new spate of *poleis* in middle and Upper Egypt resulted from a policy introduced under the two sons of Ptolemy V. During the rule of Ptolemy VI Philometor and his brother Ptolemy VIII Euergetes II, a prominent bodyguard-in-chief and governor of the Thebaid named Boethos was responsible for founding new *poleis*: Philometoris and Kleopatra (named for the queen) in the region south of Aswan, and, later, Euergetis in middle Egypt (*OGIS* I 111.10–11; *SB* 24.15973.2). Such cities were well-appointed –

Euergetis, for instance, featured a civic marketplace (*agora*) – with plots available for settlers, including shops. Significantly, these new urban settlements were located in troublesome areas and may, like the military settlements, be seen as a response to the civil unrest of the period.

Bibliography
Bagnall 2002a; el-Abbadi 1990; Empereur 1998; Fraser 1972; Kramer 1997; McKenzie 2007

1.8   The world of the temples

In pre-Ptolemaic Egypt, temples were in many respects major organs of the state, and the rule of pharaoh was sanctioned by the gods. As intermediary between the gods and his people, pharaoh functioned as chief priest throughout the land. In everyday practice, of course, priestly functions were normally carried out by local priests. Temples were not just centers of cult, essential to the well-being of the state, but also Egypt's wealthiest institutions in terms of land, livestock, and stores. It was essential that the new Ptolemaic pharaohs retain the support of their country's gods and, just as Alexander had recognized the importance of Egyptian deities, so the Ptolemies showed their support for the temples and cults of Egypt (cf. **1.3**, **1.5**).

As good pharaohs, most Ptolemies followed the example of their predecessors in pursuing an active policy of temple-building. They supported local cults with donations and visited temples for key local festivals – in the mid-second century, for instance, rulers regularly came to Memphis for the New Year – and stately royal journeys up and down the Nile involved visits to the main temples as well as local gymnasia. When Ptolemy I made fifty silver talents available toward the embalming of the Apis bull that died early in his reign, he was acting as expected of a pharaoh. Similarly in 118 BC, a royal ruling records that the mummification costs of both Apis and Mnevis (the bull of Heliopolis) should be charged to the royal treasury (*P.Tebt.* 1.5). Expenditure for temple-building was on an even greater scale. The great Ptolemaic temple of Horus at Edfu (Figure 1.8.1), for instance, was started under Ptolemy III in 237 and completed only under Ptolemy XII in 57 BC; this was just one of the many grand temples constructed – especially in Upper Egypt, where the Ptolemies needed to make their mark. The main funding for building the great temples would have come from the royal treasury, but there are indications in papyri that native soldiers receiving land might have been required to contribute. So, when in

Figure 1.8.1 Edfu temple
The great temple of Horus at Edfu. This temple was started under Ptolemy III in 237 BC
and completed in 57 BC. Here two statues of the falcon god Horus may be seen flanking
the main entrance.

135/134 BC seventy-five Egyptian infantrymen were granted 10-aroura
plots, one aroura (0.27 hectare/0.67 acre) per person was dedicated to
supporting work on the Edfu temple (*P.Haun.* 4.70.150–159). Both pharaoh
and his people thus participated in supporting the temples.

At the same time, however, big changes decreased the economic strength
and independence of the temples. Earlier temples had collected rents and
other dues on the land and property they controlled, but under the
Ptolemies this task was increasingly taken over by the royal administration.
The job of tax collection was now auctioned out to the highest bidder, and
for their upkeep – payment for priestly services and cult – temples
depended heavily on subventions from the crown. This latter concept
was a new one; in demotic the word for subvention is simply transcribed
from the Greek term (*syntaxis*). A guarantee that rulers would continue
subventions, as recorded for instance in the priestly decree of 196 BC,
suggests that in practice royal obligations were not always met.

In 263 BC a new means of financing cult was introduced by the crown,
when Ptolemy II decreed (*P.Rev.* cols. 36–37) that a tax on vineyards and
orchards (called the *apomoira*), which previously went to the temples, should
be directed to pay specifically for the cult of his sister-wife Arsinoe II (Figure

Figure 1.8.2 Vase of Arsinoe II
This faience wine jar, once colored aquamarine with some gilding, depicts queen
Arsinoe II standing on a base placed between a tall garlanded pillar and a horned altar.
Round the shoulder runs a Greek inscription recording the dedication: "For Good
Fortune, for Arsinoe Philadelphos (she who loves her brother)." This cultic scene
appears to instantiate some ritual act of worship of and for the queen. H. (of vase) 32.4
cm (12¾ in). Mid-third century BC.

1.8.2). Control of temple finances became the responsibility of a new administrative official, who functioned alongside the chief priest. At the same time,
members of the priestly class, especially its senior members, entered the
Ptolemaic administration. Men such as Ptolemaios son of Pasas from Edfu
(**1.12**) held key positions in their local temples, in the army, and in the
administration. In the later Ptolemaic period, the governors of several
Upper Egyptian nomes combined this role with major priesthoods. In
Lower Egypt, Psenptais, high priest of Ptah in Memphis, responsible for the
royal coronation, boasted on his tombstone of an exchange of visits with the
king (BM 886, with Gorre 2009: 330–333). Temples and their priests remained
crucial to the survival of the Ptolemies.

In addition to innovation in temple administration, new gods were
introduced. In Alexandria, a new deity, Sarapis, owed his origin to the
Apis bull of Memphis. For Egyptians the deified (and mummified) bull was
Osiris-Apis, known as Osorapis in Greek. Early under the Ptolemies,

Osorapis was further hellenized as Sarapis, now worshipped in human form. Together with his consort Isis, Sarapis proved a popular deity among Greeks in Alexandria, with its great Serapeum, and in the Ptolemaic empire overseas. Equally significant was the introduction of the cult of the rulers, both the developed dynastic cult of the royal family and cults of individual rulers, especially queens. Ruler cult took two forms, a Greek cult (**1.7**) based in Alexandria (and later Ptolemais in the south) with official priests and priestesses – posts held by Greeks – and the ruler cult found in Egyptian temples, in which the sovereigns were incorporated into existing sanctuaries alongside the Egyptian gods.

Arsinoe II, the second wife and sister of Ptolemy II, was important in the establishment of ruler cult throughout the country. With her title Philadelphos ("Brother-loving"), this goddess was widely promoted. The Fayyum, known earlier to the Greeks as The Marsh (*Limne*), was renamed the Arsinoite nome, and the new Fayyum settlement of Philadelpheia (Gharabat el-Gerza) was also named for her – the "village of (the goddess) Philadelphos." After death she acquired her own priestess (a "basket-bearer") in the official royal cult. It was, however, as a goddess introduced into the Egyptian temples that Arsinoe was particularly popular. A hieroglyphic decree from Mendes records her installation in 270 BC as a deity beside the ram god of that city (Schäfer 2011: 239–276). In other temples, too, she became a temple-sharing goddess (*synnaos theos*) next to the local deity. This queen cult proved enormously popular, as did that of Berenike, the young daughter of Ptolemy III and Queen Berenike, whose tragic death during the priestly convention at Canopus (238 BC) was followed by a traditional seventy-day period of mourning, mummification, and her introduction as a goddess to the great temple of Osiris there (**1.6**). The popularity of these two cults is reflected in the use of the names Arsinoe and Berenike in Egyptian priestly circles.

Otherwise, Ptolemaic kings and queens are portrayed in ranks on temple walls, wearing the traditional crowns of Egypt and making offerings to the local gods. Such visual images of the rulers presented in Egyptian guise were as pervasive as the Greek-style busts of the kings and queens that appeared on vast numbers of coins in circulation. The world of the Egyptian temples was thus incorporated into the Ptolemaic state.

Bibliography
Caneva 2016; Christensen et al. 2017; Clarysse 2000; Clarysse 2010; Dunand and Zivie-Coche 2004; Quaegebeur 1998; Vandorpe 2010; Vandorpe and Clarysse 2019

1.9 The population of Egypt

With its rich agricultural base, Egypt was one of the most populous lands of the ancient Mediterranean world. We have no good means of knowing how many people lived in Egypt in the Ptolemaic period; most modern scholars have not felt much confidence in the estimate of 3 million in the first century BC that Diodorus of Sicily provides (1.31.7). Egypt undoubtedly had the potential to support a larger population, and the Ptolemies welcomed immigrants: military men, captives, traders, and those simply in search of work and a better life. Although immigration was nothing new to Egypt, now it took place on a far larger scale; as we have seen, Alexandria, Egypt's new capital on the Mediterranean, proved a particular draw.

When still in Egypt, Alexander placed rebels from Chios in his southern garrison at Elephantine: a marriage contract (*P.Eleph.* 1) from little more than a decade after Alexander's death indicates a settlement there of soldiers who came with their families from nearby Cyrene, Gela in Sicily, the island of Kos, and Temnos in Aeolia. Indeed, troops in the armies of Alexander and Ptolemy hailed from all around the Mediterranean. Judging from their ethnic designations, military settlers originated in mainland Greece, Libya, Thrace, the Aegean islands, the Greek cities of Propontis, Pontus, Asia Minor, Italy, Sicily, Idumaea, Judaea, and above all Macedon. Ethnic units of cavalrymen, added under Ptolemy III to the original Macedonian cavalry units, comprised Thracians, Mysians, Persians, and Thessalians along with other Greeks. Such were the fighting men for whose loyalty Hellenistic rulers competed. As noted above, in Egypt soldiers might benefit from cleruchic land-grants (**1.5**); in the words of the Greek poet Theocritus (14.59), "Ptolemy is the best paymaster a free man can have."

However, not all immigrants came of their own accord. After the battle of Gaza in 312 BC, where Ptolemy I defeated Demetrios the Besieger, son of Antigonos the One-eyed, Ptolemy settled 8,000 prisoners of war from Syria and Palestine in Egypt, many of them in the Fayyum, where the village name Samaria (named for the northern part of the present Palestinian territories) suggests the origin of its settlers. Papyri also record Ptolemaic interest in Palestinian slaves. More generally, the slave trade brought quantities of unwilling immigrants into Egypt from many places.

The wide range of civilian settlers may be seen by the middle of the third century BC, both in literature, particularly the poetry of Theocritus and Herodas, and in documents, notably the archive of the Carian immigrant

Zenon (www.trismegistos.org/archive/256). These sources, especially literature, illustrate the diversity of the population in Alexandria, where immigrants practiced their trades and exploited the economic, cultural, and artistic opportunities of the period. Trade flourished, with an expanded market for imported goods among the newcomers (**1.7**).

It is easier to trace the origin and role of immigrants than to assess their overall numbers. Figures in ancient literary sources tend to be symbolic rather than actual, and no full population census survives. It is possible to use names, at least in the early Ptolemaic period, as a guide to ethnic origin, but, although this enables us to identify occupations that may be seen as mainly Greek or Egyptian, it provides no breakdown of different sectors within the population at large. In the mid-third century BC, the Fayyum had a total adult population of almost 59,000, of whom some 29 percent (the military plus civilians who were counted as Hellenes for tax purposes) were perhaps of immigrant origin (*P.Count*). However, the Fayyum, as an area mainly reclaimed in this period, was exceptional rather than typical in the scale of its immigrant settlement. The percentage was probably higher in Alexandria but elsewhere far lower; 10 percent may stand as a very approximate figure for the immigrant population of Ptolemaic Egypt, but even this figure has been challenged as excessive.

Despite the presence of these immigrants and of a foreign pharaoh, Egypt remained home primarily to Egyptians, by far the largest group within the population. Settled in towns, villages, and hamlets the length of the Nile valley, in the Delta, and in the western oases, most of the rural and urban population of the country continued their lives little changed. We have already noted the cooperation shown by some key local families and priests toward the newcomers; both sides made concessions as they adapted to new ways. As noted by Herodotus, Greeks could adopt Egyptian deities as their own: Ptah was identified with Hephaistos at Memphis, Neith with Athena at Sais, and Thoeris with Athena at Oxyrhynchos. Egyptian law, with native justices and contracts written in demotic, remained in use (**1.5**). From 146 BC, however, contracts required a summary docket in Greek for registration, and increasingly contracts were drawn up in Greek (cf. **2.3**).

The community of Ptolemaic Memphis illustrates the ethnic mix of the period. Here, in their own separate quarters centered on their main temples, lived the Hellenomemphites and Caromemphites, originally settled by pharaoh Amasis (**1.4**), but now strengthened by new immigrants. The textile production of Apollonios, finance minister of Ptolemy II, was located in this city, as we learn from the papyri of his manager Zenon, who originally came from Kaunos in Caria. Greeks of various origins joined with Phoenicians (known as Phoenico-Egyptians) in the busy life of the port. Judaeans and other Semitic settlers lived in the city, as did, in the second century BC, a garrison settlement or *politeuma* of Idumaeans, also from Palestine. Nevertheless, Egyptians continued as the majority in Memphis, and the death and burial business of the huge Memphite necropolis at Saqqara with its many cults – above all that of the Apis bull – and its mortuary chapels was an almost exclusively Egyptian realm.

As in earlier times, Lower Egypt also saw immigration from the south, where the population included Nubians, who were also sometimes found in other areas of the country. The Meroitic royal name Kandake, borne by a slave recorded in a second-century BC register from the Fayyum (P.Mon. inv. 343.xx.30), implies a southern origin. On the whole fewer Greeks lived in Upper Egypt, and the Greek communities there were generally located in the larger settlements and nome capitals, where Greek temples and public buildings – baths, gymnasia, theaters, and so on – were added to the cityscape. In middle Egypt, Herakleopolis was home to a large Jewish settlement. Like other ethnic communities with *politeumata*, the Jews had their own official representatives; they also practiced their own private law (*P.Polit.Iud.*).

Relations between the different peoples living in Egypt by this time were inevitably complex, not just in terms of language (**1.10**) but also in everyday matters. Mixed marriages were common, and the tendency for those with higher-status jobs to adopt Greek names, regardless of their origin, complicates the picture. For some generations in the mid-third century, those known as "Hellenes" (i.e. Greeks) enjoyed exemption from the obol-tax, which gave them a minimal but symbolic reduction in tax liability. The category included not just new immigrants from Greek-speaking lands but also some in the police force and other similar positions who chose to adopt Greek names and present themselves as Greek (**1.12**).

Greeks might meet with hostility; at least on occasion they claimed that this was the case, hoping that this might count in their favor with high Greek officials. One papyrus, for instance, preserves the complaint of a Greek living in Krokodeilon polis. He describes the humiliating treatment he suffered in a local village at the hands of an Egyptian woman "because I am a Greek and a stranger" (*P.Enteux.* 79.9–10, 218 BC). Other such complaints survive among the papyri and were clearly thought to matter to the official to whom they were addressed. And the ethnic argument could be used the other way. In 256 BC Zenon received the complaint of a camel driver sent to Syria about mistreatment by Zenon's subordinate: he had not been properly paid, and the wine he was given was of poor quality. He was treated poorly, the writer claims, because he was a "barbarian" – meaning that he did not speak Greek – and did not know Greek ways (*P.Col.Zen.* 2.66, 256 BC; Box 1.9.1). The power dynamic is interesting here, but as always with such appeals we have only half of the story. The fact that complaints like these survive illustrates tensions in Ptolemaic society. It is striking, however, how few such examples there actually are. Given the number of variables in each situation – period, place, context, other possible interpretations, and so on – it may be misguided to make too much of these particular cases. Far more documentation survives for reasonably equable relations in everyday life within the population at large.

Box 1.9.1 Complaint by a non-Greek: *P.Col.Zen.* 2.66

… dab … to Zenon, greeting. You do well if you are healthy. I, too, am well. You know that you left me in Syria with Krotos and I did everything that was ordered with respect to the camels and was blameless toward you. When you sent an order to give me pay, he gave nothing of what you ordered. When I asked repeatedly that he give me what you ordered and Krotos gave me nothing, but kept telling me to remove myself, I held out for a long time waiting for you; but when I was in want of necessities and could not get anything anywhere, I was compelled to run away into Syria so that I might not perish of hunger. So I wrote you that you might know that Krotos was the cause of it. When you sent me again to Philadelphia to Jason, although I do everything that is ordered, for nine months now he gives me nothing of what you ordered me to have, neither oil nor grain, except at two-month periods when he also pays the clothing (allowance). And I am toiling away both summer and winter. And he orders me to accept sour wine for my ration. Well, they have treated me with scorn because I am a "barbarian". I beg you therefore, if it seems good to you, to give them orders that I am to obtain what is owing and that in future they pay me in full, in order that I may not perish of hunger because I do not know how to speak Greek. You, therefore, please pay attention to me. I pray to all the gods and to the guardian divinity of the king that you remain well and come to us soon so that you may yourself see that I am blameless. Farewell. (Address) To Zenon. (Translation from Bagnall and Derow 2004: 230–232.)

In numbers and, apart from Alexandria, probably in culture, too, Egypt remained essentially Egyptian, even as foreign communities were incorporated into the life of the country. The inhabited land was surrounded by desert, but the valley of the Nile provided a generally welcoming environment, as did Egypt's gods. Foreigners over time became integrated within the Egyptian population so that, when finally Rome took control, those Greeks who were not citizens of the few Greek cities or numbered among the metropolitans of a nome could easily be categorized by the new conquerors as Egyptians – as, in a real sense, they were.

Bibliography
Bagnall 1984; Clarysse 2019; Cowey and Maresch 2001; Fischer-Bovet 2011; La'da 2003; Mélèze-Modrejewski 1983; Stefanou 2013; Thompson 2001 and 2012

1.10   A multilingual environment

The mixture of languages found in Ptolemaic Egypt matched the diversity of its population. Outside the capital – and maybe even within it – Egyptian remained the main language in everyday use. While traditional Egyptian hieroglyphs were used primarily in a formal temple environment, Egyptian demotic (**1.3**) continued as the form more widely used. Now, however, Greek was increasingly employed for administrative and legal purposes, as well as being the spoken language of Greeks and of those who mixed with them.

Earlier, the Persians had employed Aramaic – along with some Egyptian demotic – within their administration. The language did not disappear after Alexander's conquest: a salt-tax (**1.6**) receipt from 252 BC survives from the area of Thebes, still written in Aramaic (Porten and Yardeni 1999: D8.13). Tax receipts, normally penned on pieces of broken pottery (ostraca), were, especially in the south, often in demotic, sometimes with a Greek subscription, but sometimes in Greek with a demotic subscription. Papyrus was used for tax registers, land surveys, correspondence, and other official bureaucratic matters, of which there were many. Most of the personnel involved in running the new bureaucracy were Egyptian, and surviving documents suggest widespread bilingualism, especially in the first half of the Ptolemaic period. Under the new regime, Egyptian scribes, accustomed to writing demotic using a rush, speedily retooled themselves to write Greek with a sharpened reed. But demotic continued in use within the same offices alongside Greek, especially at the local level. And when scribes switched from demotic to Greek but failed to change their writing implement, Greek script written with a rush betrays the writer's origin, as do misspellings. Within Egyptian temples, however, hieroglyphs continued to be used in inscriptions, as may be seen from the great priestly decrees set up trilingually (with Egyptian hieroglyphs, demotic, and Greek), such as those of Alexandria (243 BC), Canopus (238 BC), and Memphis (196 BC).

Bilingualism was not confined to scribes and officials. Many Greek settlers married locally, and the mix of Greek and Egyptian names given to children suggests that both languages were often spoken at home. For instance, in the family of the cavalry officer Dryton, who served in Upper Egypt in the second century BC, the males bore Greek names, the females mostly Egyptian; as their documents show, the family used both languages (*P.Dryton*).

As was the case in earlier periods, Ptolemaic Egypt was an open society where many different communities flourished and communicated in their different tongues. And when problems arose, novel means of communication were devised. In second-century BC Memphis, for instance, a visiting Phoenician from the garrison at Thebes left a dedication in his native language to the goddess Isis-Astarte. On top of the dedication stood a black schist stele showing Horus standing on crocodiles; its surface was covered in hieroglyphic spells against snakes and scorpions. The top of the base on which this stele stood was scooped out to let liquid flow into a basin in front. It was not necessary to know hieroglyphs to benefit from these spells. The dedicant and others acquired their protection simply by pouring water over the stele and drinking it from the basin (Figure 1.10.1). In this instance it made little difference whether you could speak or read a particular language.

Other languages may well have included Edomite (from what is today Jordan), as implied by the record of a "foreign language" still in use in the second century AD in Hermopolis, which had been home to a large Idumaean garrison under the Ptolemies (*P.Giss.* 99.9–13; cf. CPI 319, *CPI* 320). An inscription in Nabataean from Daphnai in the Delta dated 39/38 BC suggests the presence of Nabataeans there (Jones et al. 1988: 48). A wider range of languages was probably found in Alexandria and the Red Sea ports.

Figure 1.10.1 Dedication to Isis-Astarte with Phoenician dedication
Inscribed in Phoenician on the lower stone is a dedication to his goddess Astarte, identified here with Egyptian Isis, made by a Phoenician soldier from the garrison at Thebes. He asks the goddess for blessings for himself, his wife, and his family. Above, carved in black schist, the protector god Horus stands on top of two crocodiles. The hieroglyphs around record spells against snakes and scorpions. To benefit from these, any interested party would pour water over the image and ingest its magic by drinking from the basin below. No literacy was required. Second century BC, from Memphis (Mit Rahineh).

Bibliography

Clarysse 1993; Mairs 2018; Papaconstantinou 2010a; Prada 2018; Thompson 2009; Torallas Tovar and Vierros 2019; Vandorpe 2002

1.11 Greek and Egyptian education in Ptolemaic Egypt

In Ptolemaic Egypt education took many forms. As the Sicilian historian Diodorus (1.81) recognized, Egyptian formal education took place mainly in a temple context, much as it had in previous centuries. Within the temples, the House of Life was the central place where both sacred writing (hieroglyphs and their more cursive form, hieratic) and the more everyday (demotic) script were taught to priests and their offspring. Writing had long been valued in Egypt – Greeks considered it an Egyptian invention – and its uses were well embedded in many aspects of life. One text that mentions an actual Ptolemaic school survives from Memphis: The young girls employed to play the twin parts of the goddesses Isis and Nephthys in the ritual mourning of an Apis bull attended the school of Tothes within the Serapeum. Although this text is the record of a dream, it may represent reality (*UPZ* 1.78.9, 159 BC). Generally, in addition to writing, students were taught geometry (important in Egypt for land-measurement) and the arithmetic needed for calculations, especially those concerning the stars, used in the religious realm. For the majority, however, in a society where trades traditionally ran within families, home and occupation formed more important learning contexts. Marking the contrast with Greek practices, Diodorus recounts how neither physical exercise nor music formed part of Egyptian education.

The training of scribes mostly took place on the job, within the registry offices in which contracts were drawn up and stored. The duplication of contracts in witness-copies – six identical copies, for instance, survive of one text, made in different hands – provided plenty of opportunity for practice. With Alexander's conquest, the need for scribes literate in Greek was imperative, and the Ptolemies embarked on an active drive to teach Greek.

Under Ptolemy II, a ruling of the finance minister Apollonios exempted from the salt-tax all teachers, sports trainers, actors, and victors in various games (Box 1.11.1). This line-up of those involved in the dissemination of Greek culture clearly indicates Ptolemaic values. Education was crucial to the regime. Tax-registers show the widespread presence of Greek teachers and sports trainers in the villages and towns of Egypt, especially in areas of military settlement such as the Fayyum

---

Box 1.11.1 Exemption from salt-tax: *P.Hal.* 1.260–265

Apollonios to Zoilos, greeting. We have released the [teachers] of letters and masters of gymnastic and [performers of] the rites of Dionysos and victors in the [Alexandrian contest] and in the Basileia and Ptolemaia from the tax on salt, them and their [household members (?), as the king] has ordered. Farewell.

(*P.Count*). School texts and exercises preserved on ostraca and papyrus show that children were not only taught the basics of reading and arithmetic but also given an introduction to literature, above all the works of Homer; more texts of Homer survive from Egypt than of any other author. Other classical authors (usually verse rather than prose) formed part of the curriculum, as did more recent Alexandrian poets. In the mid-second century BC, a Macedonian soldier's son who had taken refuge within the Memphite Serapeum wrote out and thus preserved for us Poseidippos' poem on the Alexandrian lighthouse, the Pharos (115, ed. Austin/Bastianini). For those of sufficient economic standing and in a suitable location, a broad literate education in Greek was readily available as part of the Ptolemaic enterprise.

Bibliography
Bagnall and Cribiore 2006; Cribiore 2001; Cribiore 2009; Morgan 1998; Vierros 2012; Vleeming 1994

1.12 The Hellenization of the Egyptian administration

The Ptolemies inherited a functioning administration, based on centuries of Egyptian experience and further enhanced by the road and postal systems introduced under Persian rule. For the most part, the country could continue to be run as it had been. Now centered on the new capital of Alexandria, where high officials were close to the court, the bureaucratic structure depended on a multiplicity of scribes – this was a bureaucracy that functioned in writing. We know this because of the survival of many administrative documents, thanks to a new practice in this period: the use of discarded papyri in the manufacture of mummy casing. Written in both Greek and Egyptian demotic, these texts illustrate the bureaucracy at work.

The finance minister (*dioiketes*), who was responsible for the country's income and expenditure, headed a far-reaching apparatus. At its base lay regular land-surveys and censuses of humans and animals, which were used to assess and collect taxes in cash and in kind. Apollonios (under Ptolemy II) is the best-known *dioiketes* (cf. **1.9**); his activities are documented in the papyri of Zenon, who managed the 10,000 aroura gift-estate he was granted by the king. In the third century BC such senior posts were held by Greeks; and throughout the period senior officials routinely have Greek names. Names, however, can be deceptive. Recent attention to the decipherment of Egyptian statues and sarcophagi has added several prominent Egyptian priests to the list of finance ministers. From the second century BC, for example, we find the *dioiketes* Dioskourides who, endowed with the honorific court-rank of bodyguard-in-chief, was buried Egyptian-style in a great basalt sarcophagus; also known from their Egyptian statues inscribed with hieroglyphs are Horpakhepesh son of Teos, also named Dioskourides, and from Mendes Harchebis son of Pamnevis and Senobastis, otherwise known as Archibios, a *dioiketes* as well as priest (Collombert 2000; Klotz and LeBlanc 2012; Klotz 2009). Such men moved with ease between the worlds of court and temple.

From the same period, members of the important Edfu family of another bodyguard-in-chief, Ptolemaios also known as Pamenches son of Pasas (cf. **1.8**), were buried with double tombstones recording different names according to their epitaphs, one in Greek and one in Egyptian hieroglyphs (Yoyotte 1969). Such a dual self-presentation is more regularly documented at the village level. For example, the village scribe of Kerkeosiris (in the south Fayyum), Menches son of Petesouchos, had the status of a Greek born in Egypt and was also known as Asklepiades son of Ammonios. Nevertheless, among his fellow villagers he normally used his Egyptian name in his official dealings. Whether and when those involved in this Hellenized administration saw themselves as Greek, Egyptian, or both is at times obscure.

Taxation remained a central Ptolemaic concern. Taxes were levied in both cash and kind (agricultural products). For collecting money taxes, however, a new system derived from the Greek world was introduced to run in tandem with traditional practice. Taxes were now "farmed"; that is, the contracts for their collection were awarded at auction to those whose bid seemed best (cf. **1.8, 1.13**), and guarantors were identified to provide the requisite guarantees that the bidders could afford to deliver the sums they had promised. In the actual process of collection, however, the tax-farmers worked together with traditional royal agents to get the money in. Such a mix of state and private was a Ptolemaic innovation, which appears on the whole to have worked. Along with money taxes, banks were introduced to Egypt. Most were royal banks, located in urban centers; just a few private banks are documented. Payments in and out were standard banking functions, as were book transfers without any actual movement of coins.

Bibliography
Bogaert 1994; Clarysse 1985; Clarysse and Thompson 2006; Muhs 2018;
Vandorpe 2011

1.13   A mixed economy

The economy of Ptolemaic Egypt is regularly, and rightly, described in modern books as "royal" in the sense that the king headed the administration and governed through royal rulings that directly affected the economy in a variety of ways. The system that the Ptolemies inherited for the management of economic affairs depended on a far-reaching bureaucracy, one in constant need of control. Faced, however, with the challenge of successfully exploiting the potential of their new home, they adapted the existing system to new ends. The result, as indicated above, was a new mixed economy with revenues raised in both cash and kind, with elements from old Greece now incorporated into the system they inherited (cf. **1.12**). As in other aspects of Ptolemaic rule, innovation went hand in hand with traditional practices.

One crucial factor in prosperity demanded immediate attention – the need for successful management of the annual flood of the Nile, on which the agricultural output of Egypt depended. As has been widely recognized since antiquity, premodern Egypt was the "gift of the Nile" (the phrase comes from Herodotus, 2.5.1), and upkeep of the system of dikes and channels for distribution and drainage of water was essential if taxes were to be collected and the population fed. Since, however, even seemingly remote events such as volcanic eruptions elsewhere in the globe could indirectly affect the Nile flood through their impact on rainfall in East Africa, local control was sometimes inadequate. Before the construction of the first Aswan dam, every year from June to September the river rose, spilled over its banks, and left the fields covered with silt rich in minerals. Throughout the valley a system of higher- and lower-level canals brought the water into a network of basins, enabling farmers to take full advantage of the flood. Ptolemaic initiatives led to improvements. In the Fayyum, a program of land reclamation, combining Macedonian expertise in drainage with Egyptian experience in irrigation, brought new areas under cultivation. The main system of locks at the Fayyum entrance was renewed, and canals were extended throughout the area to bring the water in, while a system of drains channeled the runoff of excess water. Innovations were also made in water-lifting machines. Simple lifting devices (called *shaduf*) had long been used in Egypt, but the Archimedes screw and possibly the bucket wheel (*saqiya*) were introduced in the Ptolemaic period. New crops were tried; emmer gradually gave way to the more transportable hard wheat as the main cereal crop. As agricultural produce increased overall, the subsequent tax revenue – charged in wheat, but also payable in other grains – rose, bolstering Egypt's ever-growing reputation for wealth.

Unlike the later Roman system of taxes levied by surface area, Ptolemaic taxes were charged on agricultural production, which was checked at both sowing and harvest. Described as rents on royal land in the north and as harvest tax on so-called private land in the south, these taxes averaged out at under 50 percent of a typical cereal yield. Difficulties arose when the flood was too high or too low, leaving land waterlogged or dry. Sometimes the king took action; we have already seen (**1.6**) that Ptolemy III imported grain from abroad when the harvest had failed (238 BC), and in 118 BC Ptolemy VIII remitted all debts to the treasury. More often, the peasants suffered when the administration pressed hard in collecting their dues. The papyri are full of complaints, with shortages often recorded, especially as the system came under pressure in the second half of the period. In 39 BC, when the priests of Thebes passed a decree in honor of Kallimachos, a key figure in the administration of their area, they recorded their fulsome thanks for all he had done at a time when an unparalleled failure of crops caused famine, devastating the city and its inhabitants; he was truly their savior, they claimed, a bright star and a godlike presence (a *daimon*) (*OGIS* I 194.19; *CPI* 387).

Rents and taxes paid in kind were collected in official royal depots, from where they were transported down the Nile to Alexandria in a fleet of barges that sailed throughout the year. Many such ships belonged to prominent Alexandrians, some to queens. They were managed by contractors, often Greeks, who employed local captains and crew to sail them. Throughout the process, the tax-grain was carefully measured and checked by royal officials, given the likelihood of fraud or theft. Once the grain reached Alexandria, it became available for local consumption as well as for export.

As the new port of Alexandria flourished, trade taxes and harbor dues increased royal revenues (**1.7**). Along with grain, the major export, other products were shipped out, including papyrus, glass, and metalwork, drugs and perfumes, stone and natron (a form of salt used in mummification). Into Alexandria came the wood that Egypt needed for ships, and much else besides: silver and other metals, fine pottery ware, wine and foodstuffs for the city, murex dye, and other raw materials from the Levant and Aegean islands. Trade flourished, and Egypt benefited from her overseas empire – as long as she held onto it – in the Eastern Mediterranean.

The Ptolemaic tax system involved a plethora of low-level taxes on humans and goods, as well as charges on many transactions, such as sales, with tax collection auctioned out (**1.12**). Taxes levied on individuals were charged in cash, as were dues on orchards and vineyards and on some fodder crops, grown for feeding animals. Some goods, such as raw materials used in mummification, vegetable oils, linen, and salt, were subject to a royal monopoly; their production and supply were closely regulated. Under Ptolemy II (in 263 BC) almost all adults became liable to an annual salt-tax levied in cash (cf. **1.6**, **1.11**), together with a tax of one obol (a sixth of a drachma; only for males).

The introduction of such regular dues encouraged the spread of currency in the countryside. Coinage had circulated before in Egypt, where hoards survive from as early as the late sixth century BC. During the fourth century, Athenian coinage predominated, with imitation Athenian tetradrachms minted at Memphis, possibly for military pay. However, gold coins like those minted by Tachos (Dynasty 30; cf. **1.4**) were made on the standard of the Persian coin called the daric. Despite intermittent coinage, in earlier times grain was the main unit of value. Under the Ptolemies, the introduction of a new coinage with issues in gold, silver, and bronze, together with the ubiquitous levy of many low-level taxes in cash, resulted in a more monetized economy, in which prices were keenly watched and increasingly goods were bought and sold, especially in urban centers. Again the Zenon papyri provide our best witness to the lively Greek interest in the financial aspects of the exploitation of Egypt. Ptolemy I was the first Hellenistic king to put an image of his own head on coins (Figure 1.13.1). Although coins were issued in all three metals, the shortage of silver, which was not mined in Egypt, led to the adoption of a lighter-weight standard for the silver currency than elsewhere in the Hellenistic world. In 258 BC, in a period of economic reform, a ruling of Ptolemy II required the reminting of imported coins in precious metal as Ptolemaic coinage (Bagnall and Derow 2004: 163–165), resulting in a closed currency system within the country. From the late third century BC, bronze took over from silver as the actual coinage in everyday use; it was no longer interchangeable with silver at a standard rate of exchange. The frequent retariffing of bronze and the decreasing quality of what silver was coined reflect the political problems of the later Ptolemaic period.

(a)   (b)

Figure 1.13.1 Tetradrachm of Ptolemy I Soter
Coin of Ptolemy I Soter (Savior), minted under his son. This tetradrachm, a silver coin
worth four drachmas, shows on the obverse the strongly profiled head of Ptolemy I. The
ruler wears a diadem round his head and an aegis round his neck. On the reverse a left-
facing eagle, the bird of Zeus which came to symbolize Ptolemaic power at home and
abroad, stands on Zeus' thunderbolt with wings closed. Around the caption in Greek
reads "of Ptolemy, king."

Bibliography
Bingen 2007; Clarysse and Vandorpe 1998; Malouta and Wilson 2013;
Manning 2003; Manning, Ludlow et al. 2017; Monson 2012; Thompson
1999; von Reden 2019

1.14   Romans in Egypt before the Roman conquest

Egypt was the last Hellenistic kingdom to fall to Rome. Relations between
the two powers, however, date back to the reign of Ptolemy II, when some
form of official friendship was established (273 BC). When Italy was later
devastated by Hannibal, Rome sent an embassy in search of Egyptian grain
(210 BC; Polybius 9.11a).

Romans increasingly visited Egypt both on official business and as
tourists. From 116 BC, names written in Latin on the temple of Philae, at
the first cataract of the Nile, record a tourist group. For official visitors,
entertainment was lavish. In 112 BC, for instance, the Roman senator
Lucius Memmius made a trip to the Fayyum; instructions preserved on
papyrus record details of his accommodation and a visit to feed the sacred

crocodiles (*P.Tebt.* 1.33). An earlier Roman embassy, which included Scipio Aemilianus (140/139), reported back with admiration for Egypt's natural resources while deploring the excessive hospitality offered them; all the kingdom lacked, in their view, was rulers worthy of it (Diod. Sic. 33.28b.3).

Rome's most dramatic involvement with Egypt resulted from a Ptolemaic request for help against the second invasion of Antiochus IV (168 BC; cf. **1.6**). A circle in the sand around the Syrian invader, drawn by the envoy C. Popillius Laenas, accompanied Rome's ultimatum that, before leaving this circle, Antiochus agree to withdraw from Egypt by a specified date. Recognizing the unmatched power of Rome, Antiochus complied (Polybius 29.27; Livy 14.12).

Appeals to Rome continued. In 164 BC, Ptolemy VI, ousted by his younger brother Ptolemy VIII, was the first Ptolemy to travel to Rome in person to ask for help in regaining the throne. Others followed suit. In fact, his brother Ptolemy VIII was there two years later, hoping to add control of Cyprus to Cyrene, which he already ruled; he returned in 154 BC.

The Ptolemies initiated a further practice that highlights Rome's predominance – that of bequeathing a kingdom to Rome when under pressure at home. In 155 BC the will of Ptolemy VIII, surviving on stone from Cyrene, names Rome as his heir should he die childless (Bagnall and Derow 2004: 92–93). Although this did not come to pass, by recognizing the new superpower Ptolemy VIII started a trend that others followed: Attalos III of Pergamon, who willed his kingdom to the Romans in 133 BC; Ptolemy Apion, who on his death in 96 BC left Cyrene to Rome; and, in 87 BC, Ptolemy X Alexander, who also willed his kingdom to Rome. That bequest was left in abeyance until 58 BC, when Rome annexed the longtime Ptolemaic possession of Cyprus.

In Alexandria, this annexation resulted in an uproar, and Ptolemy XII, known as Auletes (the Fluteplayer), was ejected. Appealing to Rome, Auletes offered 10,000 talents for his restoration, which finally he achieved. The economic consequences of this enormous payment were devastating for Egypt. A Roman manager (*dioiketes*) was installed to collect what was owed, and when Cleopatra VII succeeded her father in 51 BC, Egypt was still suffering hardship, aggravated by a series of poor Nile floods (cf. **1.13**). Roman conflicts played out in Egypt, too. In 48 BC, Caesar pursued his rival Pompey there; in Alexandria he supported Cleopatra (Figure 1.14.1) against her brother

Figure 1.14.1 Cleopatra VII in Egyptian dress on the Dendera temple
On the back wall of the temple of Hathor at Dendera, Cleopatra VII and her son by
Julius Caesar, known as Caesarion (little Caesar), who as male precedes her, are shown
making offerings to Hathor. As prime ruler the queen wears the sun disk of the god Ra
topped by plumes of Isis; her son wears the double crown of Upper and Lower Egypt
resting on spiral ram's horns.

for the throne (**2.4**). The relationship of Caesar and Cleopatra became
a durable literary theme, portrayed with high romantic coloring. After
Caesar's death (44 BC) Mark Antony replaced him as the queen's
Roman consort, but Cleopatra's luck eventually ran out. She and
Antony lost the battle of Actium, and Octavian (later called
Augustus) captured Alexandria (30 BC). With the deaths by suicide
of Antony and Cleopatra, Egypt finally fell to Rome.

The Roman takeover put an end to what had become an Egyptian
dynasty of Greek pharaohs. Over the three hundred years of Ptolemaic
rule, Egypt had continued its long tradition of welcoming immigrants
who came to adopt many of the ways of their new homeland. The
economy on the whole flourished, but despite land reclamation and
improvements in irrigation, Egypt remained subject to the vagaries of
the Nile flood. The period saw growing urbanization as the elite
moved to the central cities in their local areas. The new capital

Alexandria, with an increasing population that now rivaled that of Rome, had changed the geographical focus of the country. Over time, Hellenization gave rise to a vibrant cultural life, mainly in the capital but also more generally through the country. The strength and openness of Egypt, especially in the religious realm, persisted. Egypt was now both Egyptian and Greek. It was soon to become Roman as well.

Bibliography
Gruen 1984; Jones 2011; Lampela 1998; Van 't Dack 1983; Walker and Ashton 2003

2 | The coming of Roman rule

2.1 Government and administration: continuity and change from the Ptolemies to the Romans

In August 30 BC, less than a year after the defeat of Mark Antony and Cleopatra at the battle of Actium, Octavian (later called Augustus) landed with his troops at Alexandria. Antony and Cleopatra both committed suicide to avoid leaving their fate in his hands. With hardly any resistance, Egypt became subject to Roman rule. Although portrayed in Octavian's propaganda as an alien oriental land, Egypt was central to the maintenance of Roman imperial power and wealth. Its wheat and other agricultural products fed the empire through free distributions in Rome, rations for the army, and sales on the market, and it occupied a strategic location between Rome and the sphere of the Arabian Gulf and Indian Ocean. No emperor could risk losing control of Egypt and its resources.

The transition from Ptolemaic to Roman rule and the resulting social, legal, and fiscal changes, extending from the top of the administrative hierarchy to the operations of daily life, remain a lively area of research and debate. It is generally thought that Egypt, in many important aspects, turned "Roman" in a gradual process starting in the reign of Augustus himself and reaching its final stage at the beginning of fourth century, during the reign of Diocletian, when Egypt was fully integrated into the administrative institutions and taxation practices of the empire (**4.1**). That understanding takes as its starting point the view that Egypt at the outset of Roman rule differed from other provinces in many ways, some of them distinctive. This individual character is in part real, the result of significant continuities from Ptolemaic practices (themselves sometimes inherited from earlier periods) in the administrative system of Roman Egypt in the first and early second century AD. However, the perception of distinctiveness has also been shaped by the survival, thanks to Egypt's unique environmental conditions, of vast amounts of papyrological evidence along with other organic materials. This plethora of papyri offers detailed insights into the daily operations of the Roman provincial administration in Egypt, something not generally available for other provinces. This remarkable knowledge, together with the absence in Egypt of Roman municipalities or Greek autonomous cities – a common feature in the administration of both western and eastern Roman provinces – has been taken as proof of the atypicality of Egypt as a Roman province. How quickly and completely Egypt became Roman in character has been much debated over recent decades, as indicated by two papers delivered at international congresses of papyrology thirty years apart. The first, "The Romanity of Roman Egypt: a growing consensus," by Naphtali Lewis in 1983, was challenged by the more recent paper, by Dominic Rathbone in 2013, titled "The Romanity of Roman Egypt: a faltering consensus?"

As a result of disproportions in the preservation and accessibility of papyrological evidence (Figure 2.1.1), our understanding of "Graeco-Roman Egypt" is skewed in favor of Roman times. The ongoing publication of new material, especially the demotic papyri, keeps altering our understanding of many aspects of the administration of the period, especially the transitional years. Moreover, the extent of Roman innovations and the dates of their introduction are often obscured by the scarcity of documents from the late first century BC and the early first century AD. We have also to keep in mind that Rome annexed Egypt in a time when the nature of the Roman regime itself was changing from republic to principate; the meaning of "Roman" was not fixed. This chapter begins with the administration of the province before moving on to address socioeconomic and religious aspects.

Egypt was no longer a "kingdom." The Ptolemaic court hierarchy was dismantled, and many royal posts and titles simply disappeared. Although now an imperial province, under the direct supervision of the emperor rather than the senate, Egypt was not the emperor's personal possession. In Augustus' record of achievements (the so-called *Res gestae*) and on the base of the obelisk of Psammetichos II that he had ordered transported to Rome (where it was used as the gnomon of a giant sundial), he claimed: "I added Egypt to the power of the Roman people" (*Res Gestae* 27; *ILS* 91; the transportation of two obelisks from Alexandria to Rome is recorded by Pliny *HN* 36.69,72). The revenue of Egypt flowed to the Roman state treasury. The previously royal land in Egypt and the taxes were called "public" (*demosia*: belonging to the people, i.e. the Romans). To be sure, the emperors were portrayed in the temples as pharaohs; their names were written in royal cartouches; and, as was the case with the Ptolemies, documents were dated by the emperors' regnal years, rather than by the names of the two Roman consuls in office that year (for the imperial cult

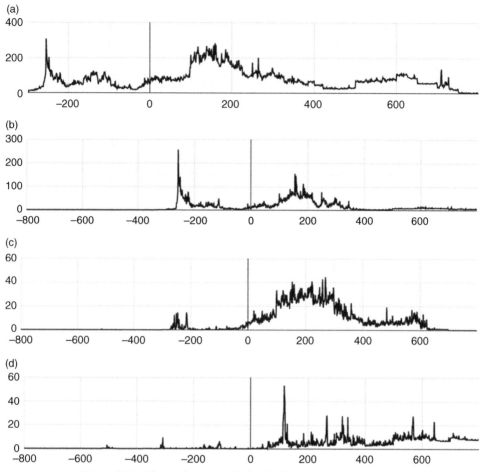

Figure 2.1.1 Chart of papyrus finds distribution
Charts of the distribution of papyrus finds by century: (a) all of Egypt; (b) the Arsinoite nome (Fayyum); (c) Oxyrhynchos; (d) Hermopolis.

see **2.9**). The Roman rulers no longer maintained a residence at Alexandria. After Augustus, and until the Palmyrene occupation of Egypt (270–272) by queen Zenobia (**3.2**), few emperors visited the province for either peaceful or military pursuits (for the visit of the Julio-Claudian prince Germanicus, see **2.9**). After almost a century, Vespasian was proclaimed emperor by the legions in Alexandria in 69; he perhaps relied on the central importance of Egypt's grain supply to bolster his claim. Half a century later, in 130–131, the emperor Hadrian traveled around the country for almost eight months and founded the new city of Antinoopolis (El-Sheikh Abada) to commemorate the memory of his beloved friend Antinoos, who drowned in the waters of the Nile. In 175, the emperor Marcus Aurelius set out to the east to suppress an uprising by the general Avidius Cassius, who had been recognized as emperor in most of the eastern provinces, including Egypt. After reaching Alexandria perhaps in early 176, he treated the city with moderation in spite of its support for Cassius. The visit of the emperor Septimius Severus in 202–203 is perhaps the most important for the changes he made in the administrative realm before and during his stay (**3.1**, **4.2**). The visit of Caracalla, in December 215, was disastrous: When riots broke out in Alexandria, he had Egyptian natives expelled from the city and caused a bloodbath among the elite (**3.2**).

Unlike the Ptolemies, the Roman emperors ruled Egypt in absentia, and could only occasionally and at considerable expense be reached by embassies or addressed through petitions. The emperor would answer certain groups by letter, granting or confirming privileges of the elites in Egyptian society. The most famous of these is the letter of the emperor Claudius to the Alexandrians, which was publicly read and then displayed in Alexandria (**2.8**).

Although the emperor was for the Egyptians a pharaoh, Egypt was actually ruled by a representative called prefect (Latin *praefectus*). His official title, the "governor of Egypt and Alexandria," reflects the distinction between Alexandria and the rest of Egypt, a term that strictly refers only to the Nile valley. This valley territory was often called the *chora*, the countryside. Although many Roman provinces were administered by a governor drawn from the highest class, the senators, Augustus decided that Egypt's governor would be recruited from the next-highest group, the "equestrians," who were much less likely to try to overthrow the emperor and take the office themselves. Moreover, men from the senatorial class and other equestrians were not allowed to visit Egypt without permission from the emperor.

The prefect had, however, basically the same powers and restrictions as governors from the senatorial class. He was forbidden to own property in Egypt, could be replaced at any time, normally served about three years, and took orders and, on important matters such as taxation, needed permission from the emperor, gained probably through long-distance correspondence, which was a crucial key to the functioning of the empire. The historian Cassius Dio (57.10.5) records the emperor Tiberius' much-praised message "I want my sheep shorn, not flayed," sent to the governor of Egypt, when he once sent him more money than was stipulated.

Figure 2.1.2 Edict of Tiberius Julius Alexander
Edict of Tiberius Julius Alexander (AD 69) inscribed on a building at the entrance of the
Temple of Hibis, el-Khargeh Oasis. For the contents see Box 2.1.2.

The prefect held the supreme power in all legal, financial, military, and
administrative matters within the province. He conducted regular round
trips (*conventus*) on the Nile, stopping in a few designated centers for
financial, administrative, and legal inspection. During these circuits the
prefect also held courts and received petitions. During three days of a
conventus of 209 at Arsinoe, one prefect received 1804 petitions (*P. Yale*
1.61: Box 2.1.1). Obviously, a staff was needed to handle such numbers. The
governor was also the source of laws, as he issued edicts that dealt with
various issues, especially the repression of abuses by officials. The prefect's
edicts were written in Latin and then translated into Greek, which
remained the language of the administration throughout Roman rule
(Figure 2.1.2; Box 2.1.2).

Box 2.1.1 Edict of Subatianus Aquila: *P.Yale* 1.61

Announcement of the edict of the prefect Soubatianus Aquila concerning the publication of his answers to the petitions which was handed to him during the *conventus*.

"Sarapion also called Apollon strategos of the Arsinoite for the Themistos and Polemon divisions. The most illustrious prefect Soubatianus Aquila has ordered according to his all-embracing foresight that the petitions handed in to him in Arsinoe on the 26th, 27th and part of the 28th of the month of Phamenoth (22–24.3.210 AD), 1804 in number, having been published in Alexandria also for sufficient days, are also to be published on the spot for three days and to be made clear to those in the nome in order that those wishing to get a copy of what answers pertain to themselves may be able. It is announced, therefore, to those in each village, if any happens to have handed in a petition, that he may come to the metropolis and have a copy made." (Translation in cited edition.)

**Box 2.1.2 Edict of Tiberius Julius Alexander
(Hibis Temple, Kharga oasis): *OGIS* 669**

Julius Demetrius, *strategos* of the oasis of Thebaid:

> I have communicated to you below the copy of the edict which the prefect lord Tiberius Julius Alexander sent to me, so that, having read it, you will enjoy (its) benefits.

Year 2 of Lucius Livius Augustus Sulpicius Galba Imperator, the 1st of Phaophi. (Day) of Iulia Augusta (28 September 68 AD).
Tiberius Julius Alexander says:

> Taking all my care that the city (Alexandria) remains in the proper state, enjoying the benefits it enjoys from the Augusti, and that Egypt contributes zealously, within prosperity, to the grain supply and the great bliss of the present times, without being burdened with new and unjust charges; I have been beseeched, almost from the moment I entered the city, by the petitioners, in small groups and in crowds, both of the most respectable people here as well as cultivators of the "country," who complained of the abuses recently committed, I have not ceased, to the extent of my authority, to rectify urgent matters. But, so that with more confidence, you await everything for your salvation and happiness, from our benefactor Augustus, Emperor, Galba, who shone upon us for the salvation of mankind, and that you realize that I have looked for ways to help you, I have

Box 2.1.2 (cont.)

formally decreed, on each request, what I am allowed to judge and do; as for the more important questions, pertaining to the power and the majesty of the emperor, I will make them known to him in all truth, because the gods have preserved to this most sacred moment the security of the world.

The upper ranks of the central administration of the province were also staffed by Roman citizens from the equestrian rank. Appointed by the emperor, these officials were subordinate to the governor. Some of the former Ptolemaic offices were continued, if only in name, while others were replaced by entirely new officials. The title of the Ptolemaic finance minister (*dioiketes*) was revived in the second century AD for a senior financial official. The *idios logos*, literally the "private account," continued through the Roman period, but shifted from supervising the private account of the Ptolemaic king to managing the financial affairs of the emperor's personal estate in the province, chiefly former possessions of the Ptolemies and irregular revenues, including those from confiscations, auctions, and sales of any property of questionable ownership. A new office, the "estate account" (*ousiakos logos*), was introduced by the Flavian emperors to administer the finances of the former estates of the members of the Julio-Claudian dynasty and their freedmen. In addition to the office of the prefect, the most important Roman innovation in the highest level of administration was the introduction of a minister of justice (*iuridicus*) to help the prefect address issues of civil law.

Within this upper level of central administration, several Roman officials (procurators) were also appointed to supervise certain activities or for state monopolies. In the earliest period, these procurators were appointed from among the emperor's freedmen and slaves, but later only from Romans of equestrian rank. The authority of some civic officials of Alexandria was extended over the country, and these became equestrian offices. The high priest of Alexandria and all Egypt exercised administrative functions in the domain of religion, such as the enrollment of new priests and the receipt and investigation of the temples' reports of personnel, property, and income. The chief judge (*archidikastes*), an office attested at the end of the Ptolemaic period, had judicial and notarial responsibilities in and outside Alexandria. Some Alexandrians (after achieving Roman citizenship and reaching the equestrian rank) were occasionally chosen for the higher central government posts, including the office of the prefect.

In addition, the Romans depended heavily on the Alexandrian indigenous elite to fill lower-level administrative staff posts attached to the office of the prefect. Among the most important were the magistrate responsible for bringing cases into the prefect's court (the *eisagogeus*) and the accountants (*eklogistai* or "auditors") who reviewed the taxes and revenues of the nomes.

Continuity from the pre-Roman era is more visible at the local level than in the central administration. The Romans retained the framework in which the country was divided into more than forty administrative regions called nomes (Greek *nomoi*). The Ptolemies themselves had inherited this system, which dated back to early pharaonic if not predynastic times. The number of nomes fluctuated over time as new nomes were carved out of those that had become more densely populated. The nomes varied in population and size and differed culturally and administratively. Due to the unequal geographical distribution of our papyrological evidence, most of our knowledge comes from two regions: the Arsinoite nome (modern Fayyum) and middle Egypt, particularly from the Oxyrynchite (modern Bahnasa) and Hermopolite (Ashmunayn), both in El-Minya Governorate. The nomes were further divided into smaller administrative districts, called toparchies. These toparchies were designated by their north-south geographical location (lower, middle, upper) or named after a main village. The village was the smallest unit of administration in Graeco-Roman Egypt. Each nome had a capital, called the metropolis ("mother city"), after which the nome was named (e.g. Oxyrhynchos was the capital of the Oxyrhynchite nome). The metropolis was the administrative, social, economic, and cultural center of the nome and was organized into administrative districts on the Roman model.

The Arsinoite, starting in about AD 60, was divided into three administrative units, as if they were three separate nomes. These divisions dated to the Ptolemaic period and were named after Greek personnel who may have been their first administrators: Herakleides, Themistos, and Polemon. In 136/137 the two smaller divisions, the Polemon and Themistos, were merged, and in about 260 the Arsinoite became again a single administrative unit.

Until the reforms of the emperor Diocletian (284–305, see **4.1**), the nomes were grouped in three – later four – wider regional units, called "super-governorships" (*epistrategiai*). Lower Egypt comprised two of these units, the eastern and Western Delta, while middle Egypt, extending south from Memphis to Hermopolis, was the *epistrategia* of the Seven Nomes (Heptanomia) and the Arsinoite. Upper Egypt was the *epistrategia* of the Thebaid including the Small Oasis (modern Bahariya) and the Great Oasis (modern Dakhla and Kharga). Each was under the supervision of a super-governor (*epistrategos*), an office retained from the Ptolemaic period. In the first century the office was held by persons from Egypt, perhaps Alexandrians. However, at some point, probably under the emperor Trajan, the office began to be occupied by Roman equestrian officials, the lowest rank of the imperial officials appointed from Rome. These regional governors linked the central and nome administration; through them the edicts of the prefect were circulated to the lower levels of the government.

External to this organizational scheme, the three Greek cities of the Ptolemaic period (Alexandria, Naukratis, and Ptolemais), and a fourth (Antinoopolis, added in the reign of the emperor Hadrian in 130), enjoyed a certain level of autonomy and independence from the provincial officials in aspects of their internal administration. They possessed their own councils, with the exception of Alexandria, which had lost its council, most probably in the late Ptolemaic period. They also possessed their own civic magistrates, their own laws, and a system of citizenship modeled on the traditional institutions of the Greek *polis* (**1.7**).

In contrast to our sketchy knowledge of the institutions of the cities, we are better informed about the administration of the lower levels in the towns and the villages of the *chora*, the area outside the cities, where Rome tended to preserve the existing administrative structure in the titles of the local officials and the areas of their competence. At the head of each nome was a governor (*strategos*, see **1.5**) and his deputy, the royal scribe. Both offices continued from the Ptolemaic period, and the office of the royal scribe goes back to pharaonic times. By the Roman period the military aspect of the office of the nome governor had long disappeared, although it could resurface in times of crisis, as we see during the Jewish revolt in the second century. The nome governors of the later Ptolemaic period often belonged to influential priestly families who served for long periods and combined court titles with multiple offices in the temples (**1.8**). During the first century of Roman rule, Alexandrian citizens were usually appointed as the *strategoi* and the royal scribes; subsequently, they came largely from the local elites of other nomes. In 139, we find the *strategos* of the Koptite nome complaining to the prefect that private contractors for collecting cash taxes, who are Romans, Alexandrians, or former soldiers, will not submit to his authority, and treat the local tax collectors with contempt (*BGU* 3.747 = *WChr.* 35); by this date many *strategoi* were metropolites, thus of lower status than Romans and Alexandrians, who might challenge their authority.

Strategoi and royal scribes were always appointed to serve outside their own nomes and the nomes in which their properties were located. A series of official diaries recorded on papyri illustrates in detail the daily activities of the *strategos*: for example, his supervision of tax collectors and market officials, and of the public sacrifices (e.g. *P.Par.* 69 = *WChr.* 41). *Strategoi* also appear to have played a significant judicial role. In one famous case, a *strategos* of the Oxyrhynchite in 49 was called to judge the identity of a foundling boy, who had been picked up from the rubbish dump. The man who found the boy had entrusted him to a wet-nurse, who had a son of her own. When one baby died, the survivor was claimed by both the man and the wet-nurse. The governor judged that the survivor was the wet-nurse's son, because he looked like her (*P.Oxy.* 1.37 = *MChr.* 79; Figure 2.1.3, Box 2.1.3). The royal scribe was charged with administrative record-

Figure 2.1.3 Decision about a foundling child by the *strategos*
Decision about a foundling child (*P.Oxy.* 1.37 = *MChr.* 79). London, British Library Papyrus 746. Extract from the court proceedings of Tiberius Claudius Pasion, the *strategos* of the Oxyrhynchite nome (AD 49). The papyrus belongs to the personal archive of Tryphon, a weaver from Oxyrhynchos (for the contents see Box 2.1.3).

Box 2.1.3. The governor's judgment: *P.Oxy.* **1.37**

From the minutes of Tiberius Claudius Pasion, *strategos*. The ninth year of Tiberius Claudius Caesar Augustus Germanicus Imperator, Pharmouthi 3. At the court, Pesouris versus Saraeus.

Aristokles, advocate for Pesouris, (said): "Pesouris, for whom I speak, in the 7th year of our lord Tiberius Claudius Caesar picked up from the garbage dump a male slave child named Heraklas. This he entrusted to the defendant. Thereupon a wet-nurse's contract was made as if for the son of Pesouris. She received her wages for the first year. The payday for the second year came around and again she received them. (To show) that I speak the truth, there are her documents in which she acknowledges that she received payment. As the slave child was being starved, Pesouris took it away. Subsequently, finding an opportunity, she burst into my client's house and carried the slave child off, and she seeks to take for herself the slave child, pretending it is a freeborn person. I have here, firstly, the contract for nursing; I have, secondly, the receipt for the wages. I demand that these be recognized." Saraeus (said): "I weaned my own child, and the slave child of these people was entrusted to me. I received from them the whole eight staters. Subsequently the slave child died, [...] staters were left me being (still) unearned. Now they seek to take away my own child." Theon (said): "We have the documents relating to the slave child."

The strategos (said): "Since from its looks the child appears to be that of Saraeus, if she and her husband will make a sworn declaration in written form that the slave child entrusted to her by Pesouris has died, I give judgment in accordance with the decision of our lord the prefect that on paying back the money which she has received she shall have her own child." (Translation by Palme in Keenan et al. [2014]: 488–489.)

keeping; his duties covered virtually the entire administration of the nome, its population, lands, and animals, much as under the Ptolemies.

In the nome capitals a significant Roman innovation, from at least the mid-first century AD, was the introduction of a semi-civic or municipal government that operated through magisterial offices (**2.6**), taking charge of many functions that the imperial administration did not take on. Despite what may seem like a large number of administrative posts, the Roman government was essentially hostile to the development of a large bureaucracy and in all parts of the empire delegated much to local authorities. In this system, the nome capitals played a limited role in some aspects of internal administration such as public buildings. In the second century, metropolite officials acquired more responsibilities, under the supervision of the central administration and the governor of the nome. (For the introduction of the city council to the nome capitals and its restoration to Alexandria under Septimius Severus, see **3.1**.)

Until the reforms introduced under the emperor Philip the Arab (244–249), the village was headed by a village scribe. His colleague of the Ptolemaic period, the village manager, disappeared by the end of the first century BC, to be reintroduced only in the early third century (cf. **3.6**). The village scribe's competence often comprised several villages, contrary to the Ptolemaic system, in which he administered only one village. His duties were sometimes assumed by boards of village elders. For the sake of impartiality and to avoid conflicts of interest, the village scribes were recruited outside the village (or villages) they were to serve in. Petaus son of Petaus, a well-known village scribe of Ptolemais Hormou (modern El-Lahun at the entrance to the Fayyum) from 184 until 186, was a resident of Karanis (modern Kom Aushim in northern Fayyum). As shown by his papers (*P.Petaus*), he could hardly write his name and depended on numerous subordinates. The village scribe's duties, consisted mostly of the detailed assessment of land taxes and rents and the keeping of population records. In addition to compiling a list of candidates to succeed himself, he was also responsible for finding candidates for unpaid compulsory offices, generally called "liturgies," who, unlike the village scribe, would serve in their home communities.

These liturgists (cf. **3.1**) included the collectors of taxes in cash and in kind as well as a variety of guards. All the offices, below the level of the governor and royal scribe, are usually regarded as liturgies. However, it is possible that these offices were paid in the first and part of the second centuries and had liturgical character only in the method of their appointment, which was determined by the level of income based on property ownership. In this system, which flourished in the second and third centuries AD, only men from the age of fourteen to the age of seventy were appointed to hold liturgical offices. Exempted from liturgies were Roman citizens, citizens of the Greek cities, members of some professions such as philosophers, advocates (known as rhetors), and doctors, as well as fathers of five or more children, and the physically disabled.

The most important responsibility and indeed main purpose of the imperial administration in its various levels, from the prefect to the village scribes, was to extract revenues. Multiple taxes were levied on land, mostly in grain. The people of Rome and a great part of the Roman army in the east depended on grain supplied from the province of Egypt. A plethora of direct and indirect taxes in cash was also levied, most of which had Ptolemaic precedents (**1.6**, **1.10**, **1.12**, **1.13**). Money taxes were paid in an

Alexandrian currency that, just as under the Ptolemies, did not circulate outside the province, and had to be converted to gold before it was sent to Rome. Central to fiscal administration under the Romans was the census, which served as the basis for the principal capitation or poll tax known as *laographia*, either a Roman innovation or a development carried forward from the late Ptolemaic period, especially under Ptolemy XII Auletes and Cleopatra VII. It is probable, however, that Augustus only standardized the existing census and capitation taxes. The Ptolemaic tax would have been collected according to a fixed sum from each village. Under the Romans, however, the tax was estimated per person at a fixed rate and paid only by adult males (including slaves) from age fourteen to sixty-two. The rates differed among regions; the highest rate by far – 40 drachmas – was paid in the Arsinoite nome. The *laographia* was collected together with other minor capitation taxes, such as the dike, pig, bath, and salt taxes. Roman citizens, the citizens of the Greek cities, and a limited number of priests within each temple were exempted. Some parts of the urban population were privileged by paying the poll tax at a lower rate. Members of these groups were subjected to scrutiny in order to maintain their privileged tax status.

Any shortfall in paying the tax, whether owing to individual inability to pay or to depopulation (taxes remained due for individuals who fled the village), was distributed among members of the village community. If a person died, his heirs were obliged to pay on his behalf; if the death took place within the first six months of the year, only half the rate had to be paid. The census, under the Romans, was held every fourteen years to keep the population register updated. Although there was no income tax as such (the administration could not have managed such a tax), most occupations and trades, such as weaving or metalworking, were taxed, and some transactions were subject to sales taxes. License fees were paid by some of the former Ptolemaic monopolies, especially oil production, which the Romans converted to a system of state concessions. Both external and internal custom dues were collected by contractors on imports and exports, the highest being the 25 percent tax on commodities of the foreign trade to the south and east. The administration required detailed information to control the population and raise taxes, and various classes of the population needed to make multiple declarations, for example enumerating flocks of sheep and goats.

Given that record-keeping was essential to administration, a state archive of public records was established in each nome capital. Legal documents were drawn up and recorded through registration offices in various villages, and a special register of land conveyances and property rights to private land was established in each metropolis shortly after 70. Copies of public records and private contracts were kept at two central archives in Alexandria, one at the temple of Isis and another, established later, at the temple of Hadrian.

The coming of the Romans meant the end of the Ptolemaic courts of law, which had used different legal frameworks according to the "ethnic" nationality of the litigants and/or the language of the contracts involved (Box 1.5.3). Now all Egyptians (except Roman citizens and the inhabitants of the three, later four, cities, which had their own civil law) were subject to a unified code of laws that is referred to in documents (mainly from the second century) as "the Law of the Egyptians" (e.g. *P.Oxy.* 4.706 = *MChr.* 81). This code comprised practices of both Egyptian and Greek origins, which had coexisted and evolved, thanks to royal decrees, under the Ptolemies. Roman judges used the Law of the Egyptians in deciding disputes between non-Roman litigants, although the code could be disregarded, modified, or supplemented by a governor, a *iuridicus*, or another juristic official on the local level. The provincial legal experts, the *nomikoi,* interpreted the law in court. Petitions and court proceedings show that litigants, or their representative lawyers, relied in their arguments on prefectural edicts and the accumulated decisions on similar cases as precedents, especially in the second century AD. The Roman government was keen to widely circulate both prefectural edicts and decisions in response to petitions through copies posted prominently in Alexandria and throughout the *chora.*

In the early imperial period, Roman law was minimally applied or adopted in Egypt even by Roman citizens, especially in matters of the law of inheritance. As Egypt gradually became more Roman in other respects, however, Roman legal concepts and practices begin to enter common use, even if modified or misunderstood in some cases. Roman governors resorted to Roman concepts and values in deciding cases in which the local legal system did not make the answer to a problem clear, and Roman ideas and terms for personal business representatives start at an early date to appear in the management of private estates.

Bibliography

Bowman and Rathbone 1992; Capponi 2005; Derda 2019; Haensch 2008; Jördens 2012; Kruse 2019; Lewis 1970; Lewis 1984; Manning 2019; Monson 2012; Monson 2014; Rathbone 1993; Rathbone 2013; Rowlandson 2010; Speidel 2019; Thomas 1983; Yiftach-Firanko 2009; Yiftach-Firanko 2014

2.2   The Roman army in Egypt

The provincial Roman army in Egypt was, at least in principle, no different from its counterparts elsewhere in the empire. The main unit of the army was the legion. Each legion was composed of approximately 5,000 men, and was divided into ten cohorts, the first cohort being twice the size of the others. The cohorts were further divided into centuries. Although the legions were supposedly restricted to Roman citizens, local recruitment of Egyptians, particularly Alexandrians, increased over time. The earliest attested legionary of Egyptian origin is L. Pompeius Niger. He was born as Zoilos son of Syros in Oxyrhynchos in middle Egypt and entered the army about AD 20, not yet a Roman citizen. He acquired this status only on discharge. Evidence also shows that many legionaries serving in Egypt were recruited from Africa. In addition to the legion, there were two main types of non-legionary, or auxiliary, unit: the cohorts, infantry units of about 480 men, and the cavalry units of about 500 (Latin *alae*). The commonest type of auxiliary unit in Roman Egypt was a mixed unit of both infantry and cavalry troops. The troops in the auxiliary units were a mixture of Egyptians, mainly as infantry, and recruits from the neighboring regions such as North Africa, Syria, and Asia Minor. Soldiers serving in the auxiliary units acquired Roman citizenship after discharge from military service. Another, semi-military institution was the *skopelarioi*, lower-class Egyptians who were not soldiers but discharged a kind of compulsory service, defending the roads as tower guards or lookouts.

We do not know much about the organization of the Roman fleet in Egypt. The Alexandrian fleet, composed of the remains of the Ptolemaic fleet, is the principal fleet attested (**2.5**). Its main task was to escort the convoy of grain ships to Rome. The presence of members of the Alexandrian fleet in Akoris (Tehna el-Gabal) and Coptos (Qift) is associated with the fleet's service in the Nile police, the river-guard service. Egyptians were also recruited to serve in the imperial fleet outside Egypt. A letter from the second century AD shows an Egyptian soldier entering the Roman fleet of Misenum in Italy and acquiring the name Antonius Maximus on enlistment (*BGU* 2.423; Box 2.2.1; Figure 2.2.1).

The geographer Strabo, who spent time in Egypt in the first decade of Roman rule, gives a fairly clear picture of the composition of the garrison and the positioning of its various units at the outset of the Roman occupation: "There are three legions of soldiers, one in the city [i.e. Alexandria] and the others in the *chora*. In addition, there are nine Roman cohorts, three in the city, three on the border with Ethiopia at Syene, as a guard for those places, and three elsewhere in the *chora*. There are three horse-units which are likewise positioned in the important places" (Strabo 17.1.2).

© SMB Ägyptisches Museum und Papyrussammlung, Foto: Sandra Steiß

Figure 2.2.1 Letter about enlistment in the fleet
Letter about enlistment in the fleet: *BGU* 2.423 (*WChr.* 480). See Box 2.2.1. Letter sent from Misenum, Italy, by Apion to his father Epimachus in Philadelphia. The letter shows that Egyptians were recruited for military service outside Egypt and demonstrates that soldiers adopted Roman names even before receiving citizenship on discharge.

Box 2.2.1 Letter of Antonius Maximus: *BGU* 2.423

Apion to Epimachus his father and lord, very many greetings. First of all I pray for your good health and that you may always be strong and fortunate, along with my sister, her daughter, and my brother. I give thanks to the lord Serapis because when I was in danger at sea he immediately saved me. When I got to Misenum I received three gold pieces from Caesar as my travelling expenses (*viaticum*). Everything is going well for me. So, I ask you, my lord and father, to write me a letter, first about your welfare, secondly about that of my brother and sister, and thirdly so that I can do reverence to your handwriting, since you educated me well and as a result of that I hope to be advanced quickly, if the gods so wish. Give all my best wishes to Capiton and my brother and sister and Serenilla and my friends. I have sent you through Euctemon a portrait of myself. My name is now Antonius Maximus ... (Translation by Campbell [1994] 13–14.)

The three legions to which Strabo referred (XXII Deiotariana, III
Cyrenaica, and XII Fulminata) were located at three strategic places –
Alexandria, Babylon (Old Cairo), and Thebes – that remained the sites of
military bases until the later Roman period. By AD 23 (if not earlier) the
Legio XII Fulminata was transferred elsewhere (perhaps to Syria), and by
38 at the latest the two permanent Egyptian legions were based at
Nikopolis, at the extended eastern border of Alexandria, reflecting the
more political role of the army in controlling this key point
(Figure 2.2.2). The Legio III Cyrenaica was transferred to Bostra in
Arabia by the emperor Trajan in the first decades of the second century.
The XXII Deiotariana disappeared, perhaps in connection with the Jewish
Rebellion under Bar Kokhba in Palestine in the early 130s. After Trajan's

Figure 2.2.2 A stele from Nikopolis
Funerary stela of Aurelius Sabius, a soldier from Syria, who died at the age of thirty-five
after serving for only one year in the second legion, based at Nikopolis, outside
Alexandria. He is depicted wearing his military cloak and belt and carrying two spears,
with a shield on his left.

Parthian War, the Legio II Traiana Fortis was transferred from Judaea to Egypt and became, until the military reorganization under Diocletian, the sole legion stationed in Egypt, at Nikopolis.

The number and the locations of the auxiliary units are less clear. Evidence shows that, although the number of auxiliaries did not change dramatically in the first and the early second century, by the mid-Antonine period (middle of the second century) the auxiliary forces had increased significantly to seventeen units, with a strength (in theory) of just under 10,000 soldiers.

Almost two-thirds of the auxiliary troops were stationed in Upper Egypt as garrisons for security and order. Three auxiliary cohorts and one cavalry unit were stationed at Syene, Elephantine, and Philae. From these military bases detachments of troops were posted to sites further up the Nile, in lower Nubia. Further units were posted at the heads of major roads at Coptos, Contrapollonopolis Magna (Redesiyah), across from Edfu, and probably Kaine (Qena). We do not have a clear picture of the location of the remaining units throughout the Nile valley, for which our information is based on written papyrological and epigraphical evidence rather than the physical existence of military installations. In the Eastern Desert *praesidia*, however, many well-preserved examples of small forts or outposts have been excavated, some of which have yielded texts concerning the army (Figure 2.2.3).

During most of the Roman period, its army did not face external threats to the frontiers of Egypt. The borders to the south were pacified after the prefect C. Cornelius Gallus defeated the Aethiopians, as Strabo calls them, who had captured most of the Thebaid in Upper Egypt (Box 2.2.2). The next two prefects, Aelius Gallus and Publius Petronius, tried in turn to conquer Nubia. The northeastern frontier did not face any attacks until Palmyra invaded Egypt and took control from 270 to 272 (**3.2**). No evidence survives of any military bases in the Libyan (western) desert during the first two centuries.

On the eastern side of the Nile valley, however, quarrying and mining activities – porphyry from Porphyrites and fine gray granodiorite from Mons Claudianus, not to mention gold and other precious minerals and gems – necessitated a substantial army presence. Troops were deployed to guard these two sites and, starting with Vespasian, detachments were posted in forts (Figure 2.2.3) to protect the caravan routes against the increased "barbarian" attacks of nomadic tribes such as the Blemmyes (Figure 2.2.4; Box 2.2.3), a threat that increased by the late third century.

The concentration of the Roman army – as noted above, one legion as well as auxiliaries – in Alexandria reflects the reality that most of the time

(a)

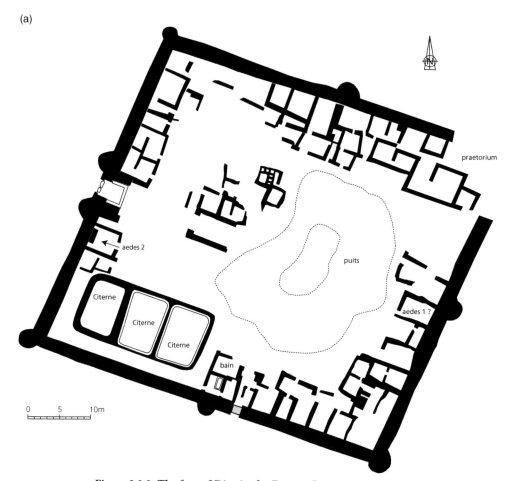

praetorium

aedes 2

Citerne

Citerne

Citerne

puits

aedes 1 ?

bain

0   5   10m

Figure 2.2.3 The fort of Dios in the Eastern Desert
2.2.3 a–c. The *praesidium* (fort) of Dios (Iovis; modern Abu Qurayya), in the Eastern
Desert, founded in AD 114/115. (a) General plan; (b) the headquarters of the fortlet
commander (the *praetorium) with* mosaic floors; (c) the military shrine (*aedes*).

the main role of the army was to keep the restless population of Alexandria
under control. The army intervened in the riots that sprang up in the city
now and then, especially during the conflict between the Alexandrians and
the Jews in Alexandria in the years 38–41 (**2.5**). These troops, however,
could not withstand the two major uprisings in the second century: the
revolt of the Jews in 115–117 and the revolt of the *Boukoloi* in 171–172
(**3.2**). In both cases, the army was almost defeated and intervention of
troops from outside the province was needed. The Boukoloi were defeated
by Avidius Cassius, who attempted to usurp the imperial throne with the
support of the prefect Volusius Maecianus in 175, before he was defeated by

(b)
(c)

Figure 2.2.3 (cont.)

Box 2.2.2 Trilingual inscription of Cornelius Gallus: *CIL* **3.14147**

Gaius Cornelius Gallus, son of Gnaeus, Roman knight, as the first prefect of Alexandria and Egypt after the kings had been defeated by Caesar [i.e. Augustus] son of the divine [i.e. Caesar], defeater of a defection of the Thebaid within fifteen days, in which he defeated the enemy twice in battle, taker of five cities, Boresis, Coptos, Ceramice, Diospolis Magna, Ophieum, with the leaders of those defections cut off, with his army led across beyond the cataract of the Nile, into which place neither by the Roman people nor by the kings of Egypt have arms been carried, with the Thebaid, the common terror of all kings, reduced, with legates of the king of the Ethiopians heard at Philae, with the same king received into guardianship, with a ruler set over the land of the thirty schoenoi on the frontier of Ethiopia, made this dedication to the ancestral gods and to the Nile his assistant.

Marcus Aurelius. Neither revolt, however, caused a permanent increase in the size of the garrison. (Assuming that the units were at their ideal strength, the entire garrison of Roman Egypt can be estimated at around 22,000 at the end of the first century BC, decreasing to about 16,000 at the end of the first century AD, then to 12,000–14,000 in the mid to later second century.) The Roman army in Egypt also seems to have played a considerable role in the control of internal security in the *chora*. This is evident from many petitions concerning local disputes that the villagers

Figure 2.2.4 Ostracon with a letter of the prefect concerning deserters
Ostracon with copy of the letter of Pomponius Faustinus, the prefect of Egypt
(AD 186–187), found at Mons Claudianus, concerning the punishment of two
soldiers who fled from the battlefield. The actual verdict is not stated. The letter
orders copies of the verdict to be posted in the forts. *P.Bagnall* 8, Inv. 7218
(see Box 2.2.3).

Box 2.2.3 Letter about barbarian attacks: *P.Bagnall* 8

Copy of a letter in Latin and a judgment, translated as well as possible.
Pomponius Faustianus to his friend Probus, greetings. I have passed judgment on Iulius Serenus, soldier of the same cohort, and Crepereius Donatus,
soldier of the same cohort, because they have left their fellow soldiers behind
(so that?) they (i.e. the fellow soldiers) were subjected by some weak and
unarmed barbarians. Therefore, along with my verdict, I have ordered that
copies be displayed in the *praesidia* of the quarries, so that it is brought to
the attention of the rest of the soldiers. I order you to do this. (Translation A.
Bülow-Jacobsen in cited edition.)

---

addressed to Roman military officers of the units stationed in their areas,
particularly the centurions.

The presence of the army did not have a major economic impact on
society, in part because it was so small compared to the overall population.
Requisitions, not only for the stationed forces but also for imperial campaigns outside the province, for supplies of grains, animals, boats, and
various kinds of commodities, such as wool clothing for soldiers in
Cappadocia, were usually paid for (perhaps at a lower rate than actual
market price) or receipted for later compensation. The government made
an effort to suppress abuses by soldiers, who excessively and sometimes

forcibly requisitioned boats, animals, and persons, a behavior that generated hostility toward the army (e.g. *PSI* 466).

Families were keen to get their sons enrolled in the imperial garrison. The army offered opportunities for career and social promotion to the elite families who already enjoyed an elevated socioeconomic status in the cities and towns of the *chora*. Perhaps the most important benefit was acquiring, upon discharge, Roman citizenship with all its privileges. Toward the end of the first century and at the beginning of the second century AD, military families of Egyptian origin, such as that of L. Pompeius Niger, become more visible in the papyrological evidence, especially from the Fayyum. The papers, written both in Greek and Latin, of Egyptian families of soldiers and veterans like that of Lucius Bellienus Gemellus (94–110 AD), Gaius Iulius Sabinus and his son Apollinarius (96–118 AD), or Claudius Terentianus (100–125 AD), show the high-ranking position these families held in local society and beyond (Gemellus: *P.Fay.*; Sabinus: *P.Mich.* 8–9; Terentianus: *P.Mich.* 8).

Bibliography
Alston 1995; Brun et al. 2018; Fuhrmann 2012; Haensch 2010; Haensch 2012; Lesquier 1918

2.3   Languages in Roman Egypt

The Roman conquest brought cultural change to Egypt, including changes in the use of language and particularly of scripts. To the languages in use in Ptolemaic Egypt was added Latin, the language of the conquerors and, to a large degree, of their army. We get a taste of the change already in a stela erected at Philae by Cornelius Gallus, the first Roman prefect of Egypt, during the first year of Roman rule (Box 2.2.2). The three languages of the stela are Latin, Greek, and hieroglyphic Egyptian. Missing is the demotic Egyptian familiar from such Hellenistic trilingual inscriptions as the Rosetta stone and the Canopus decree (**1.10**). Though demotic was still relevant at the time of the Gallus stela, Roman rule brought significant shifts in its use, continuing a process that began under the Ptolemies.

The term "demotic" is used both for a distinctive script (Figure 2.3.1), derived ultimately from hieroglyphs, and for a phase in the development of the Egyptian language, which it represents only imperfectly. In the Ptolemaic period, demotic had a considerable range of use despite the

P.Tebt.
0227
Recto

Figure 2.3.1 Demotic abstract of a contract

Demotic abstract of a contract, written using a Greek pen (*kalamos*) instead of the brush typically employed for earlier Egyptian texts. The text, which documents a loan secured by house property, comes from the *grapheion* (registration office) at Tebtunis in the Fayyum. *P.Tebt.* 1.227, 60s BC.

> **Box 2.3.1 Knowledge of Egyptian as a basis for entry into the priesthood: *P.Tebt.* 2.291 (excerpt = *W.Chr.* 137; AD 162)**
>
> Marsisouchos, son of Mar[on?], whose mother is Thenkebkis, having given proof of a knowledge of sacred [i.e. hieratic] and Egyptian [i.e. demotic] writing from a sacred book produced by the priestly scribes in accordance with the memorandum of the 12th of the month Tybi of the present 2nd year, and Pakebkis also called Zosimus, son of Pakebkis, whose mother is Thaisas, on the strength of proofs produced concerning parentage, were respectively shown to be of priestly family. I pray for your health. The 2nd year of Imperator Caesar Marcus Aurelius Antoninus Augustus and Imperator Caesar Lucius Aurelius Verus Augustus, Mecheir 12. (Translation of first edition, modified.)

gradual extension of Greek to more and more spheres. Demotic was used not only in public and private law and administration, along with other private uses, but also as a cultural medium, particularly for religious writings and narrative literature. It must be remembered that the number of published demotic texts is still relatively small, and that the group of texts currently accessible reflects archaeological survival, choice of sites to excavate, and, most critically, the preferences of editors of papyri.

Though the use of demotic writing no doubt diminished under the Romans, there is no reason to consider it any less vigorous as a stage of the Egyptian (spoken) language than its successor Coptic. Even the script remained robust and, indeed, adaptive throughout the Roman period within temple contexts, and it can still be found in graffiti as late as the middle of the fifth century; the number of individuals capable of employing and interpreting the writing system, however, declined. In this respect, the priesthood bears some responsibility, but the priests were by no means isolated from changes occurring in the broader society and culture. Where the use of demotic writing did die out – though hardly immediately – was in legal and administrative settings, more likely because of the costs of using it rather than an active "anti-Egyptian" policy on the part of the Romans. Still, the Romans' lack of interest in local languages (other than Greek) throughout their empire suggests they would have been unwilling to invest in making demotic officially useful.

The erosion of demotic had begun early in the Ptolemaic regime as a by-product of its efforts at centralization and fiscal efficiency.

Specifically, the creation of a registration office with record-keeping responsibilities, which grew over time and added notarial functions (only in Greek), may be cited as a decisive event. The documents produced by this office had extra security because of its record-keeping role; the new scribal responsibility would draw users away from traditional institutions, including the temple notariat. But even earlier, Egyptians would have found the archival services of the office – backed by the state, but offered only in Greek – beneficial for high-value transactions.

An additional important development occurred around 145 BC, at the beginning of the reign of Ptolemy VIII and Cleopatra II, when the registration office was required to abstract all Egyptian contracts in Greek, record them in a registry, and then add a Greek subscription to the original; documents without this treatment were not admissible in court (**1.9**). Further disincentives to the use of demotic instruments would come under the Romans. A requirement for registration of contracts in Alexandria, at the temple of Isis Nanaia, is probably first attested early in the reign of Tiberius. Use of a demotic contract additionally necessitated inclusion of a Greek abstract. Inasmuch as the Greek abstracts of demotic contracts indicated all of a transaction's particulars, the demotic text became superfluous, though instruments with demotic are still found as late as the reign of Marcus Aurelius.

Tax receipts written in demotic, mostly on ostraca (potsherds), are still found in the early Roman period in Upper Egypt, but much less frequently after AD 43, and as a rule the later texts have priestly connections. The near-complete switch to Greek for these receipts is so abrupt that an official origin seems likely, but changes in the private sphere are harder to explain. Oracular inquiries to gods, for example, seem to be limited to Greek during the Roman period. Similarly, private letters in demotic are little known after the beginning of the Roman period, although the preference of editors for more formulaic texts and the difficulty of dating such letters may contribute to their near-invisibility.

Bibliography
Clarysse 1984; Depauw 2003; Hickey 2009; Hoffmann, Minas-Nerpel, and Pfeiffer 2009; Prada 2018; Rahyab 2019; Ripat 2006; Stadler 2008; Yiftach-Firanko 2009

2.4 The central role of Alexandria

As we have seen (**2.1**), when Augustus conquered Egypt, Alexandria lost its role as a royal capital (**1.7**), but it did not lose its importance in other respects, most notably as the hub through which passed much of Rome's grain supply. Although the imperial power lay in Rome, Alexandria, which was described in the first century BC by Diodorus of Sicily (17.53.5) as the "first city of the civilized world," was still after much destruction and suffering (**3.2**) called the "crown of all cities" in the fourth century AD by the historian Ammianus Marcellinus (22.16.7). Many centuries later, it was to dazzle a medieval Arab historian, Ibn Duqmaq, who cited the claim of 'Abd al-Malik Ibn Jurayj that, although he had made the pilgrimage to Mecca sixty times, "if God had suffered me to stay a month at Alexandria and pray on its shores, that month would be dearer to me than the sixty pilgrimages which I have undertaken." Ibn Duqmaq attributed to Ka'b al-Aḥbar the further claim that, according to the Old Testament, "if a man make a pilgrimage around Alexandria in the morning, God will make for him a golden crown set with pearls, perfumed with musk and camphor and shining from the east to the west" (*Al-intesar*, 2.118).

As the founding of the city receded into the past, the stories that accumulated about its origin ignored the Egyptian antecedents of Alexandria, both the settlement there called Rakotis and the more extensive cities in the area of Canopus. The Greek historian Plutarch, writing in the second century AD, reflected the view of an educated Greek of the Roman Empire (*Alex.* 26, Box 2.4.1).

This origin story indicates that Alexander's purpose in founding Alexandria was to leave behind him a "large and populous" Greek city. The choice of the site was advised by Homer, the everlasting symbol of Greek learning, and the founding was accompanied by a good omen that the city would abound in resources and would sustain people from every nation. The story thus encapsulates the three major aspects of the fame of Alexandria at the end of first century and the beginning of the second century AD: its grandeur, its cultural excellence, and its economic prosperity.

The overwhelming beauty of Alexandria, even after the island of Pharos had been laid waste by Julius Caesar, is expressed in a novel of the mid-second century AD by Achilles Tatius, in which Clitophon, the hero, was struck by the city's beauty like a flash of lightning (*Leucippe and Clitophon* 5.1). Most of the ancient city has now disappeared, due in part to natural

Box 2.4.1 Plutarch, *Alex.* 26 on the foundation of Alexandria

If what the Alexandrians say on the authority of Heracleides is true, then it seems that Homer was no idle or useless companion to him on his expedition. They say that after his conquest of Egypt, Alexander resolved to found and leave behind him a large and populous Greek city which would bear his name. On the advice of his architects he was about to measure out and enclose a certain site, when during the night, as he was sleeping, he saw a remarkable vision. He thought he could see a man with very white hair and of venerable appearance [i.e. Homer] standing beside him and speaking these lines:

> Then there is an island in the stormy sea,
> In front of Egypt; they call it Pharos.

He rose at once and went to Pharos, which at that time was still an island a little above the Canopic mouth of the Nile, but which has now been joined to the mainland by a causeway. When he saw that the site was eminently suitable (it is a strip of land similar to a fairly broad isthmus, running between a large lagoon and the sea which terminates in a great harbor), he exclaimed that Homer was admirable in other respects and was also an excellent architect, and ordered the plan of the city to be drawn in conformity with the terrain. Since there was no chalk available, they used barley-meal to describe a rounded area on the dark soil, to whose inner arc straight lines succeeded, starting from what might be called the skirts of the area and narrowing the breadth uniformly, so as to produce the figure of a mantle. The king was delighted with the plan, when suddenly a vast multitude of birds of every kind and size flew from the river and the lagoon on to the site like clouds; nothing was left of the barley-meal and even Alexander was much troubled by the omen. But his seers advised him there was nothing to fear (in their view the city he was founding would abound in resources and would sustain men from every nation); he therefore instructed his overseers to press on with the work.

forces, wartime destruction, and the development of the modern city, and the exact location of its monuments is often not known. Most of what we know about the urban layout of the city (Figure 2.4.1) during the Graeco-Roman period comes from the writings of ancient authors. The earliest topographical description of the city was written by Strabo (17.1), who visited Egypt in the entourage of the prefect Aelius Gallus, and remained in Alexandria between 25 and 20 BC. His description is thus a first-hand observation of the state of the city at the outset of Roman rule.

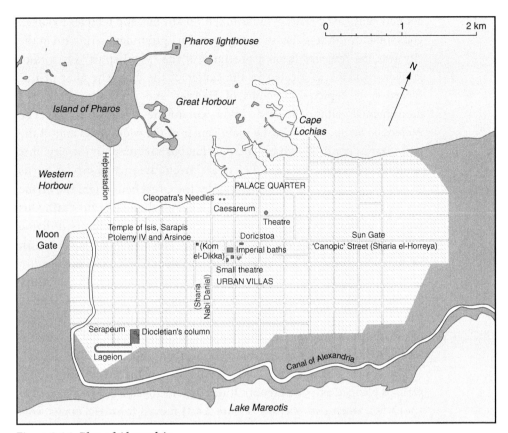

Figure 2.4.1 Plan of Alexandria

The city expanded to the east in the Roman period to include the Ptolemaic cemeteries at Chatby and Hadra. A legionary camp of Nikopolis/Julianopolis was constructed further to the east. But the Roman period also brought damage and destruction. Apart from the harm caused by various military actions (**3.2**, **4.3**), no fewer than twenty-three earthquakes struck the coast between the years AD 320 and 1303, the most severe of which occurred in 365, bringing a tsunami; the harbor floor dropped more than 6 m (20 ft), with much of the Royal Quarter collapsing and sinking beneath the waves. Recent underwater excavations have succeeded in mapping the harbor and the archaeological features of the Royal Quarter, such as the sites of Cleopatra's palace, the Timonium, the Poseideion, and parts of the Emporium.

Alexandria was built following the classical tradition, with buildings and facilities that expressed the Greek way of life: the agora, theater, council halls, law courts, gymnasium, hippodrome, and temples to Greek gods, in addition to a Jewish synagogue. One prominent structure in the city was the *temenos* (sacred precinct) of the "good spirit" or *agathos daimon*, which was located in the center of the city. The altar of this sanctuary is depicted on coins of Hadrian and Antoninus Pius as a monumental altar enclosed by a colonnade (Figure 2.4.2). The Ptolemaic Serapeum (**1.7**), the main center of the widespread cult of the god Sarapis, continued to be the most famous sanctuary of the city. It is the only precinct of which sufficient architectural remains survive for us to form an impression. Just as Alexander the Great had sought the divine oracle of Zeus-Ammon (**1.5**), Vespasian visited the Serapeum during his stay in the city (69–70), where – in a vision – he was promised divine support. The Serapeum burned down in AD 181; rebuilt by AD 217 in an even more monumental form, it flourished until its final destruction (**4.5**). According to Ammianus Marcellinus in the fourth century (22.16.12), the Serapeum was "so adorned with extensive columned halls, with almost breathing statues, and a great number of other works of art, that next to the Capitolium, with which revered Rome elevates herself to eternity, the whole world beholds nothing more magnificent."

The temple dedicated for the imperial cult was the Sebasteion (earlier perhaps planned as a Caesareum). It was built in 26–20 BC then enlarged in 13–12 BC, when two obelisks (Figure 2.4.3) moved from Heliopolis were placed in front of it. (The two obelisks are now in London and New York.) Located right on the harbor, as recorded by Pliny the elder (*HN* 36.69), the

Figure 2.4.2 Bronze drachma coin of Antoninus Pius
Bronze drachma coin of Antoninus Pius, minted in Alexandria, with the altar of Agathos Daimon on the reverse.

Figure 2.4.3 Bronze crab from obelisk in Alexandria
One of the four bronze crabs that were used as supports of corners of the obelisk known as
"Cleopatra's Needle." The obelisk was originally erected by Thutmose III around 1450 BC
in Heliopolis, and was later moved to Alexandria to be placed in front of the Caesareum.
The crab is now at The Metropolitan Museum of Art, while the obelisk itself is standing
in Central Park, New York. The Greek inscription reads in translation "In year 18 of
Caesar (13/12 BC), Barbarus erected [this obelisk]. The architect was Pontius."

Sebasteion remained visible at the time of Napoleon's invasion in 1798. In
the words of the Alexandrian Jewish philosopher Philo (*Leg.* 151): "Nowhere
is there a holy place comparable to the so–called Sebasteion … great and
famous, filled with offerings like nowhere else, surrounded with paintings
and statues of silver and gold, a vast sacred precinct with porticoes (stoas),
libraries, banqueting rooms, sacred groves, monumental gates, large open
spaces, open courts, all decorated in the most extravagant manner." Adjacent
to and south of the Sebasteion was the Forum Iulium. Later renamed the
Forum Augusti, it was a monumental complex of open spaces. The construction of the Temple and the Forum complex may have started under
Cleopatra, possibly in imitation of official buildings of the city of Rome.

Alexandria's main facilities from the Ptolemaic era continued in use
in the Roman period, some with added Roman features, and were
joined by typical Roman public buildings, such as the amphitheater,
imperial baths, and triumphal or commemorative arches. The heart of
city life remained the gymnasium, described by Strabo as a building of
singular magnificence, with colonnades more than a *stadion* (c. 185 m/

600 ft) long, that stretched along the side of the Canopic Street. The complex, situated in the center of the city, included the law courts and the tribunal of the prefect. Papyrological evidence shows that an *atrium magnum,* a Roman-style hall, was added to this complex in the reign of Nero as a part of a *praetorium,* the residence of the prefect and of the emperor during his visits, and a grand new *praetorium* seems to have been built by Hadrian.

Upper-class houses built between the first and mid-third century have been excavated in two areas: the Broucheion near the royal palaces and at Kom el-Dikka. According to earlier city laws, buildings had to stand independently, each within its own set of external walls, although this rule was not followed all the time. The majority of the houses of the wealthy were built on an orthogonal plan, with a porch, a wide reception room, and a distinctive Alexandrian central courtyard paved with large limestone slabs. The main room was always adjacent to the courtyard, connected by a tripartite entrance marked by two columns. In keeping with Hellenistic and Roman building traditions, the rooms were decorated with geometric and figural mosaic floors (Figure 2.4.4) and the walls lavishly adorned with cornices, fluted engaged columns, capitals, and stuccowork.

Figure 2.4.4 Mosaic from the Villa of Birds, Alexandria
Mosaic from the Villa of Birds. Mosaic a-5, panels with birds, bedroom floor. Villa of the Birds, Kom el Dikka, Alexandria (first–second century AD).

Figure 2.4.5 Roman tomb from Alexandria
Roman tomb from Alexandria: the Great Catacomb at Kom el-Shoqafa. The central
niche of the main tomb chamber with a sarcophagus and a relief depicting priests with
masks of the ancient Egyptian gods (from left to right: Horus, Anubis, Thoth) while
performing the lustration of the mummy on an Osiriac lion bier. Only three out of the
normal four canopic jars beneath the bier are depicted.

The city's *necropoleis* are the most distinctive feature of its archaeological remains. Many underground tombs (catacombs) outside the walls
of Alexandria, both to the east and west, are still standing. Although the
precise dates of many of these tombs are disputed, in general they were
constructed from the fourth century BC onward. Alexandrian tombs of the
Roman period are generally similar to the Ptolemaic tombs, with
the Hellenistic-style dining room replaced by a Roman-type dining chamber. The tombs are also characterized by the fusion of Egyptian architectural and iconographic motifs with classical and Roman elements
(Figure 2.4.5).

The people

The population of Alexandria, generally assumed to have been close to half
a million at its peak, was certainly several hundred thousand. The city's
inhabitants came from all over the Greek world and originally included
Macedonians, Syrians, Gauls, Jews, some Persians from the period before
Alexander's conquest, and other peoples from Asia Minor, as well as

Egyptians. By the time of the Roman annexation, the different Greek ethnic categories, such as Macedonian, Thracian, Argive, Cretan, or Athenian, were no longer used, and the "Hellenes" were defined by the Ptolemaic administration as a tax status, a matter not of origin but rather of either their education or a post in the administration. Some Egyptians had been already recognized by the Ptolemies as Hellenes.

The Egyptian population outnumbered the Greeks. The Alexander historian Curtius Rufus (4.8.5) claims that Alexandria was initially largely populated with inhabitants of the neighboring towns (we do not know if he meant Egyptians, or earlier Greek settlers in Egypt). The native Egyptians of Alexandria were favorably characterized as "acute and civilized" by Polybius, quoted by Strabo (17.1.12). A smaller though still significant community of native Egyptian weavers is known to have lived in Rakotis, an area located in the extreme southwest of the city. In the Roman period so many indigenous Egyptians flocked from the *chora* into the city, some fleeing taxes in their home villages, that Caracalla, on his visit to Alexandria in 215, issued an edict ordering their expulsion from the city, with some exceptions. The edict is reported by Cassius Dio (77.23.2) and its Greek version has survived on a papyrus (*P.Giss.* 40, Box 2.4.2).

In addition to Greeks and Egyptians, a diverse third group was made up of mercenaries of the Ptolemaic period who belonged to different ethnicties. Each group constituted an autonomous ethnic organization, a *politeuma*, which had civic rights as permanent residents of a foreign city. The earliest of

---

Box 2.4.2 Edict of Caracalla: *P.Giss.* **40**

All Egyptians in Alexandria, especially the peasants, who have fled hither from other places and can be easily recognized, must be expelled from the City in every possible way. Not, however, dealers in pork, river boatmen, and those who transport reeds for heating the baths. Expel the others who disturb the city by their numbers and uselessness. I understand that Egyptians are accustomed to bring down bulls and other animals for sacrifice at the festival of Serapis, on certain other festival days, and also at other times. For this reason they must not be prevented. Those who must be prevented are the persons who leave their own lands to avoid agricultural work, but not those who travel with a desire to see the most famous city of Alexandria or those for the sake of a more civilized life or for temporary business.

these organizations is attested from the time of Ptolemy VI Philometor. We do not have much information about the persistence of these groups in the Roman period except for the Jewish *politeuma*, which was apparently the strongest and best organized of the capital.

The Romans defined Alexandrian citizenship differently than had the Ptolemies (**2.10**). Not all the Greek population of Alexandria was included in the more restricted citizen-body of "Alexandrians." The Alexandrian citizenship was not, however, closed, and people who did not have citizen parents acquired it through the normal Greek educational institutions of the gymnasium and military training. The number of citizens of Alexandria increased significantly during the Roman period. Claudius, for example, admitted to the body of Alexandrian citizens all those who had registered for military training up to his own reign. Only the actual citizens of Alexandria were now regarded as entitled to privileges that included exemption from the poll tax but also access to the gymnasium and the holding of offices. Everyone else was an "Egyptian," regardless of ancestry, culture, or status under the Ptolemies. Alexandrian citizenship was more-over (according to the emperor Trajan) a prerequisite for the acquisition of the prestigious Roman citizenship and participation in the Roman admin-istration. Hence civic status began to be a lively issue; in particular, tension arose between the Jewish community and Alexandrian citizens over Jewish access to citizenship (**2.8**).

Romans lived in Alexandria before it became a province. The Roman presence in the city is attested from 55 BC, when troops of Aulus Gabinius, the governor of Syria, were settled in Alexandria and mixed with the local population (**1.14**). Later, Caesar quartered three, then four, Roman legions in the city. A large percentage of the armed forces in Egypt during Cleopatra's reign were Roman. In a papyrus claimed to have been signed by Cleopatra herself (*P.Bingen* 45), a Roman general named Publius Canidius, one of Mark Antony's closest allies, was privileged to export wheat from Egypt and to import Cretan wine into the country without paying duty. In addition, he and his tenants were exempt from paying taxes on the land that he owned in Egypt. A Roman senator called Quintus Ovinius was in charge of Cleopatra's woolen and textile factories during the war between Octavian and Antony (Orosius 6.19.20). Under the empire, the number of Roman officials, soldiers, traders, and ordinary travelers increased considerably.

In addition to these groups, trade opportunities brought countless people of other origins to converge on the city. By the late first or early second century, the inhabitants of the city included Syrians, Libyans,

Sicilians, Ethiopians, Arabs, Bactrians, Scythians, Persians, and Indians. Alexandria could rightly be called the world's first cosmopolitan metropolis, yet despite its polyglot nature it remained basically Greek, and these various ethnicities were – at least from an outside perspective – blended into one single "Alexandrian" people. In a first-century visit to the city, the eloquent Dio Chrysostom addressed Alexandrians in Greek, describing the city's central position in the world (*Or.* 32.36):

> Not only have you a monopoly of the shipping of the entire Mediterranean because of the beauty of your harbors, the magnitude of your fleet, and the abundance and marketing of the products of every land, but also the outer waters that lie beyond are in your grasp, both the Red Sea and the Indian Ocean ... The result is that the trade, not merely of islands, ports, a few straits and isthmuses, but of practically the whole world is yours. For Alexandria is situated, as it were, at the crossroads of the whole world, of even its most remote nations, as if it were a market serving a single city, bringing together all men into one place, displaying them to one another and, as far as possible, making them of the same race.

Alexandrian trade

Egyptian foreign trade with the Mediterranean is well attested before the establishment of Alexandria (**1.2**). When Alexandria was established, because it was the seat of the royal residence and also the capital of the Ptolemaic empire, it became the chief trading center of the entire Hellenistic world. In spite of the instabilities during the last decades of the Ptolemaic dynasty, Strabo writing shortly after the Roman occupation states that Alexandria "is the largest trading port (*emporion*) in the world" (17.1.13).

Alexandria and Egypt were, under Roman rule, increasingly tied into the economy of the Mediterranean and places beyond (**2.5**). Alexandria's location facilitated the traffic in both local and international goods. To the north it was connected to the Aegean and Rome through its two harbors. To the south and east, although many roads connected Alexandria to other parts of Egypt such as Pelusium, Memphis, and the Fayyum, most of the traffic went via the Nile through canals to Lake Mareotis, which had a very busy harbor on its northern shore. One of these canals, which started from Schedia, was excavated under Augustus in 11/10 BC and was named Flumen Sebaston ("Augustan river") after him. Alexandria was also linked, through the important Upper Egyptian Nile entrepot of Coptos, to two major eastern trade routes, one that ran along the eastern coast of Africa and another that crossed the water to Arabia and on to the western coast of India. Some of the silk that passed through Petra was carried overland from there through the Sinai to Egypt and Alexandria.

Although the network of trading relations with Africa, Arabia, and India can be traced back to earlier times, trade increased dramatically under the Romans. The Roman economy depended on free markets, but the government took seriously its role of facilitating production and trade. From the very beginning we see Augustus setting his soldiers to work in maintaining and clearing canals that had fallen into decay under the late Ptolemies. The soldiers were also active in building roads in the Eastern Desert, and when the region became less secure in the time of Vespasian, garrisons were put there to protect the caravan routes connecting Coptos and the two major ports on the Red Sea, Myos Hormos and Berenike (**2.2**). The Muziris papyrus (*SB* 18.13167, Box 2.4.3) preserves details of substantial cargoes that were contracted in the second century. The goods were purchased at the port of Muziris in India, shipped probably to Berenike, then transported to Coptos, and thence downriver to Alexandria. The tally for the cargo of this one large ship is impressive; the commodities were worth well over 7 million sesterces.

But Alexandria was not only a way-station for foreign goods: much of the trade activity involved the products of Egypt and Alexandria. The most important product of Egypt was, as we have noted, its grain, both the tax grain collected annually to be sent to feed the population of Rome and the surplus grain sold through commercial channels. Along with the shipment of grain, Alexandrian products were also exported. (It should be noted that Alexandria was itself a major center of consumption, second only to Rome.) The most important products were glass, paper, linen, and works of art, all of which were shipped far and wide. Imported raw materials from the east were worked in Alexandria before being exported. Jewelry was wrought from gold, silver, and a great variety of precious gems, with advances in alchemy at Alexandria leading to work in other metals as well (cf. below). Traders from Alexandria were active in Puteoli, a major Italian harbor town serving Rome and an important port for trade with the East. These traders had connections with traders from Asia Minor and Syria and engaged in transactions with Roman investors and bankers.

Alexandrians were famous for their love of money and work. The *Historia Augusta* (29.8) preserves a letter, supposedly from Hadrian to his brother-in-law Servianus, that alludes to the busy life of the inhabitants of Alexandria:

[It is] a city rich, opulent, productive, in which none lives idle. Some are glass blowers, some makers of papyrus, some linen weavers, all have some art or other. The gouty have something they can do, the blind likewise, not even those with gout in the hand are idle.

Box 2.4.3 The Muziris papyrus: *SB* 18.13167 recto

... your other agents or managers and having weighed I will ... to ... cameleer ... for the shipment of the ... to Coptos and I will bring [sc. the cargo] through the desert with vigilance and precaution up to the public customs warehouses in Coptos and I will put [sc. the cargo] under the power and seal of yourself or your administrators or whoever of them is there up to the loading [sc. of the cargo] on the river and I will load at the required time in a safe river ship and I will convey [sc. the cargo] downstream up to the customs warehouses of the quarter-tax in Alexandria and likewise I will put [sc. the cargo] under your or your people's power and seal for all the expenses from [= met with] the loan from now until the payment of the quarter-tax – the costs of the desert transports, the river freights and the other due outlays – so that, if, on the occurrence of the time established for the repayment in the loan contracts for Muziris, I do not properly pay the aforesaid loan in my name, then you and your agents or managers shall have the choice and complete power, if you choose, to carry out execution without notification or summons and to get possession and own the afore-said security and levy the quarter-tax and transfer the three parts that will remain to whomever you choose and sell and re-hypothecate and cede to another, if you choose, and handle the security whichever way you want and buy for yourself at the then current price and subtract [sc. its value] and reckon the future proceeds from the goods for the payment in full of the loan, with the benefit of assumption regarding the proceeds being on you and your agents or managers, and with us being absolutely free from misrepresentation; the shortfall or surplus with respect to the capital will be on me, the borrower and mortgager ... (Translation De Romanis 2020.)

The Mouseion

The city of Alexandria has played a spectacular role in human cultural history; from 300 BC to AD 200 a vast number of eminent representatives of various branches of knowledge and scientific pursuits were scholars and teachers at Alexandria. Their contribution is manifest in the modern world in the disciplines of medicine, anatomy, physiology, grammar, geography, mechanics, geometry, and literature. Essential to these achievements were two interconnected intellectual centers: the Mouseion and the Royal Library, which together constituted in effect an institution of higher learning (**1.7**). Although these Ptolemaic centers were not as well supported and active in the Roman period, they were still important. Strabo (17.1.8) gives us a brief description of the Mouseion from the earliest period of Roman rule:

> The Museum is also part of the Royal Quarter, having a public walk, seating chamber, and a large building containing the dining-hall of the men of learning who participate in the Museum. This group of men have common property as well as a priest in charge of the Museum, appointed in former times by the Kings, and nowadays by the Emperor.

The Mouseion offered lodgings for its members and rooms for the study of each discipline, along with a garden containing exotic flora and fauna. A semi-religious research institution, the Mouseion was modeled on the Athenian Academy and the Lyceum and devoted to the cult of the Muses. But unlike the Academy and the Lyceum, it was under government control.

Strabo fails to mention the library. In fact, we do not possess any source that mentions both institutions together. It is still unknown whether the library constituted a building of its own and, if it did, whether it was physically separated from the Mouseion; it is more probable that the library was close by the Mouseion. They were, at least administratively, separate institutions, as the library was headed by its own director (*bibliophylax* or *epistates*). In addition to the great library, the "daughter" library, created later, was housed in the temple of Sarapis or the Serapeum in the Rakotis district.

In the Roman period, the Mouseion and the library continued to function under imperial patronage, except for a brief period under Caracalla. Augustus preserved both the funds and the immunities and privileges of the scholars. The Mouseion was even increased by Claudius. According to Suetonius (*Claudius* 42.2), "At last he [Claudius] even wrote historical works in Greek, twenty books of Etruscan History and eight of Carthaginian History. Because of these works there was added to the old Museum at Alexandria a new one called after his name, and it was provided that in the one his Etruscan History should be read each year from beginning to end, and in the other his Carthaginian, by various readers in turn, in the manner of public recitations." Teachers at the imperial court continued to be chosen from among Alexandrian scholars such as Chaeremon, the teacher of Nero, and perhaps Hephaestion, the teacher of the emperor

Lucius Verus. A privileged sector of the community, the members of the Mouseion were granted tax exemptions. A sign of the importance of the Museum membership under the emperors is that it came to be used to reward not only scholars but also important political figures who had no intellectual pursuits, at least none known to us.

The cultural geography of the Mediterranean changed, however, in the imperial period. Even before the advent of the Romans, the prestige of Alexandria as a center of literary culture and scholarship had been harmed when Ptolemy VIII Euergetes II expelled many of its intellectuals around 145 BC. Cultural life seems to have been revived in the following years, especially under Ptolemy XII Auletes and Cleopatra VII and particularly after Athens was sacked by the Romans in the mid-80s BC. Alexandria's reputation was still strong in the time of Caesar, who commissioned one Sosigenes from the city to revise the Roman calendar. But the city was increasingly rivalled by Rome, where the concentration of imperial resources led great numbers of Alexandrian poets, philosophers, and scholars to converge and open schools in the Alexandrian tradition. Among the early scholars was Didymus Chalcenterus ("the bronze-gutted," 80–10 BC), the grammarian reputed for writing more than 3,500 book-rolls and introducing Alexandrian learning to the Romans. Also important was Areius Didymus, a philosopher, who became the personal philosopher of Augustus and was one of the reasons, or so Augustus declared, that he spared Alexandria from destruction. The movement of Alexandrian scholars and intellectuals to Rome and elsewhere continued during the first century AD, leading to the impoverishment of Alexandria's intellectual life. Plutarch, for example, received a fine philosophical education from his Egyptian teacher, Ammonius, at Athens. The study of philosophy later shifted away from Alexandria toward "old Greece" due to the popularity of the Second Sophistic rhetorical movement, centered in Asia Minor, in the late first and second centuries.

This does not mean, however, that intellectual life had vanished from Alexandria. In particular, philological scholarship and literary production continued. Under Nero and the Flavian emperors, the poet Leonidas of Alexandria wrote ingenious panegyric epigrams to the emperors and the imperial family. Alexandria also became the seat of Platonist and Aristotelian philosophy from the first century AD onward. The city remained an important center of rhetorical study in the second and third centuries despite Alexandria's nearly complete absence from the text of Philostratus' *Lives of the Sophists*. Through the whole imperial period Alexandria also retained a certain primacy in scientific work. Some of the greatest intellectuals of their time, including Strabo, Plutarch, Dio Chrysostom, Aelius Aristides, Lucian, and Galen, visited Alexandria, and some of them spent an extended period there. But generally speaking, Alexandrian intellectual life in the imperial period cannot be compared to the achievements of the third and second centuries BC in their pioneering quality and originality.

In addition to lexicography and critical and exegetical commentaries on classical and Hellenistic poetry, original poetry continued to be written. The best-known Alexandrian poet of the Roman period was Dionysios Periegetes, who, in the reign of Hadrian, composed a popular didactic poem in hexameters describing the inhabited world. A new genre of literature – novels – also emerged sometime in the late Hellenistic or early Roman period. Its emergence has been attributed to eastern influence. Egyptian tales were written down long before the Greek novels ever appeared, and some popular Egyptian stories were translated into Greek, including the "Dream of Nektanebo" of the third century BC, and the "Legend of Tefnut," a story assigned to the second century AD. Around the same time, Achilles Tatius of Alexandria composed his erotic romance (*Leucippe and Clitophon*), one of only five surviving ancient Greek novels. Some novel fragments assigned to different authors have turned up on papyrus, such as the "Inundation" novel (*P.Michael.* 4). The papyri also preserved a distinctive literary genre developed in the Alexandrian context, known as the *Acta Alexandrinorum*. These are semi-literary works recording what purport to be the minutes, in a dramatized form, of trials of distinguished Alexandrians before the Roman authorities.

Some significant scientists studied and worked at Alexandria in the early imperial period, including Hero (*c.* AD 100) and Diophantus (*c.* 180) in mathematics. Alexandria continued to be so highly reputed as a center for studies in biology and medicine (especially of the empirical school) that the fourth-century Roman historian Ammianus Marcellinus (22.16.18) mentions that a physician need merely say that he had been trained at Alexandria to commend his knowledge of the art of healing. It is here that Pedanius Dioscorides (*c.* 40–90) probably studied before he moved to Rome and wrote his encyclopedia about herbal medicine – *De materia medica* – which was widely read in Greek, Latin, and Arabic for more than 1,500 years. The Arabs also translated many works of Rufus, who studied medicine and worked in Alexandria in the late first and early second centuries, and falsely attributed three of his works to Galen, the last of the great medical specialists to have studied in Alexandria, around the 150s.

Medicine continued to be taught in Alexandria until the time of Umar Ibn Abd el-Aziz in the early eighth century.

Alchemy originated in Alexandria sometime around AD 100, probably influenced by Egyptian practices. We are in no way certain about the identity or dates of the earliest alchemical authors. Their works partially survive, sometimes only as titles, through quotations in later authors, especially Zosimos of Panopolis (third century AD). The most prominent figures of early Alexandrian alchemy are Mary the Jewess, after whom the *bain-marie* (or double-boiler) is named, and Cleopatra, who is sometimes linked with the famous Ptolemaic queen Cleopatra VII. One of the latter's treatises is titled "Chrysopoeia" (Making of Gold).

In the second half of the second century AD, Claudius Ptolemy synthesized the accumulated knowledge in the sciences of geography and astronomy, going back five centuries to Eratosthenes. His geographical work, the *Geographike Hyphegesis,* and his major astronomical work, the *Almagest,* are the last important works and the only entirely surviving ancient ones in these fields (meaning cartography). These works influenced many scholars for centuries.

Alexandria also played an important role in the cultural life of the ancient world, including Rome, by producing copies of books. The city was famous for exporting papyrus, not only in the form of raw writing material (which was used all over the Roman world) but also as manufactured books. Domitian ordered the texts in Alexandria to be copied for the libraries in Rome. Letters from Oxyrhynchos from the first two centuries show that copies of books made in Alexandria were sent to that town, where more copies could then have been made available. One of these letters (*P.Mil.Vogl.* 1.11, Box 2.4.4) mentions works by Stoic philosophers on self-improvement that were copied in Alexandria.

The Mouseion and the Royal Library both disappear from the historical record in the mid-third century. Apparently they had been destroyed, possibly during the emperor Aurelian's campaign against Zenobia in 272 that devastated the whole Royal Quarter, in which the Mouseion and the library were situated. Sometime in the fourth century the Mouseion appears to have been reestablished on a different site. The fate of the library after the third century is mysterious, but whatever had been in the Royal Quarter had probably been ruined. By the fourth century, the Serapeum and its "daughter" library had become the focus of the intellectual life of the city. The destruction of

Box 2.4.4 Letter about desired books: *P.Mil.Vogl.* **1.11**

Theon to his friend Herakleides, greetings. Just as I devote every effort to obtaining books that are profitable and especially relevant to life, so I think it is incumbent on you, too, not to be casual about reading them, as it is no ordinary benefit that accrues from them to those keen on self-improvement. The list below details what I am sending you via Achillas. Good health to you; I, too, am well. Pass on my greetings as appropriate.

Written in Alexandria.
Boethos *On Ascetic Training* Books 3 and 4
Diogenes *On Marriage*
Diogenes *On Freedom from Pain*
Chrysippos, *On the Treatment of Parents*
Antipatros *On the Treatment of Slaves* Books 1 and 2
Poseidonios *On Moral Exhortation* Book 3.
Reverse: From Theon to Herakleides, the philosopher. (Translation from Trapp [2003]: 139.)

the Serapeum at the end of that century probably spelled the end of a great library in the city, but Alexandria's intellectual life continued, taking new forms in the Late Roman period (**4.3**).

Bibliography
Bagnall 2002a; Benaissa 2012; Delia 1988; Delia 1992; el-Abbadi 1992; Fraser 1972; Haas 1997; Handler 1971; McKenzie 2007; Rowlandson and Harker 2004; Watts 2006

2.5   Egypt's integration into the Roman economy

With the Roman conquest, Egypt became part of a much larger state, one that at its greatest extent would control roughly 5 million square km (1.9 million square miles). Political incorporation also led to economic integration – simply put, the capacity of markets to respond to forces of supply and demand – with the larger state. Although this new connectivity transformed the Hellenistic economic environment, the process of integration was neither immediate nor straightforward. Besides the pace of integration, historians must consider its extent, not only in terms of geography but in terms of economic "sector," as well as its facilitators, both the agents directly seeking it and the indirect factors promoting it. A critical question is the degree to which integration was influenced by imperial policy.

Rather than following a trajectory toward complete connectivity, economic integration waxed and waned in response to a variety of political, fiscal, social, and environmental factors. We cannot track these changes closely. Even in a document-rich province such as Egypt, pertinent written data are hard to come by, while literary texts tend to speak only of decline. Archaeological evidence, our best source for following the movement of goods, for observing changes in diet, and for discerning urban building patterns and techniques as well as other signs of connectivity, is more abundant, but so far its study has mainly served to give impressions or illustrate broad trends. To give just one example: Thanks largely to material evidence we can see that the coming of the Romans had a significant impact on building and mining technologies and techniques.

Integration not only varied over time but also was geographically uneven and variable by sector of the economy, and temporal, geographic, and sectoral conditions were often interrelated. Economic links existed in many dimensions: between Egypt and the imperial center (Italy, in particular Rome); between Egypt and other regions of the empire; between the center, through Egypt, to other parts of the empire; and between Egypt and places beyond the empire's borders, such as India. Generally, connectivity weakened the farther one moved from coastal commercial hubs; land transport was expensive. Certain goods might be traded very far afield, while others had a more limited range or did not even leave their region of production. The reasons for this varied: A product might spoil on a long voyage, or it might be too bulky to transport great distances. High-value items, such as those recorded in the Muziris shipment (**2.4**), tended to travel far, but sometimes we hear about cheap commodities such as vinegar being shipped a distance (Athenaeus 67d, though referring to the pre-Roman period). Our evidence indicates, in any case, that the Mediterranean world under Rome was not a *broad* integrated market.

Certainly the best attested economic tie is the one between province and capital, more specifically the flow of taxes (paid in grain but also gold) from Egypt to Rome (Box 2.5.1). The extensive documentation for this flow, unsurprising given its fiscal character, can, however, obscure aspects of the trade sector and its networks or distort our understanding of them. For one

---

Box 2.5.1 A letter home from a sailor in the grain fleet: *W.Chr.* 445 (2nd or 3rd cent. AD)

Eirenaios to Apolinarios, his dearest brother, many greetings. I pray continually for your health, and I myself am well. I wish you to know that I reached land on the 6th of the month Epeiph and we unloaded our cargo on the 18th of the same month. I went up to Rome on the 25th of the same month and the place welcomed us as the god willed, and we are daily expecting our discharge [= Latin *dimissoria;* issued after the *probatio* or verification of the grain], it so being that up until today nobody in the grain fleet has been released. Many salutations to your wife and to Serenos and to all who love you, each by name. Goodbye. Mesore 9. [Address on the back:] To Apolinarios from his brother Eirenaios. [*Sel. Pap.* 1.113 translation, modified]

Figure 2.5.1 Bronze drachma coin of Hadrian with Isis Pharia and the Pharos
Reverse of a bronze drachma coin of Hadrian, Alexandria mint, AD 133/134. On the left, Isis Pharia, patroness of sailors, advances holding a sail; the Pharos lighthouse is on the right. At the top, the date appears; the "8" in (regnal) "year 18" is damaged.

thing, although it was certainly driven by state demand, the transport itself (at least until after the Antonine plague) was not a compulsory service (**3.1**) but governed by contract, and there was ample opportunity for private enterprise within the fiscal framework. Indeed, the price of wheat in Italy was such that it encouraged private initiative even without state subsidies (Figure 2.5.2). We also know little about the return voyages of the grain ships from Italy to Alexandria: Despite a suggestion to the contrary in Pliny's *Panegyricus* (31), it seems probable that they sailed back to Egypt

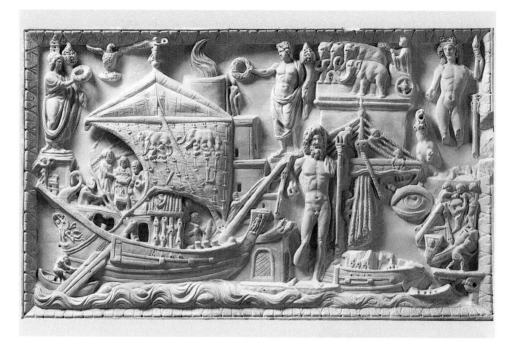

Figure 2.5.2 The "Torlonia relief" showing Roman merchant vessels
The "Torlonia relief," *c.* AD 200, discovered during the mid-nineteenth century in the remains of ancient Portus outside Rome. The rich and intricate iconography of this (once-painted) marble relief, probably a dedication by a shipper of wine or a wine merchant, has been the subject of much scholarly discussion. The ship or ships central to the scene – the one on the left may simply be the moored one at an earlier point in time – are typical Roman merchant vessels, like those that would have sailed from Alexandria. The female figure in the upper left, bearing a lighthouse on her head, faces the Portus lighthouse on her right; she was once regarded as the Tyche (tutelary deity) of Alexandria, and thus these parts of the relief were thought to depict the two endpoints of the *annona* route. She is now generally believed to represent Portus.

with commodities like Italian wine and North African oil, as well as various craft items (fine-ware pottery, for example). In other words, these economic routes were bidirectional or even multicornered. Currency and bullion likewise flowed into Egypt, needed to pay for the spices, perfumes, ivory, and other "luxury" goods that were imported into the empire from India and Arabia through the Red Sea ports (**2.4**); and some of the produce and manufactured goods coming from Italy were intended for the East. Though Egypt served as a transshipment point for this commerce, which even by conservative calculations amounted to a significant portion of the Roman economy, it nonetheless benefited significantly from it. The Red

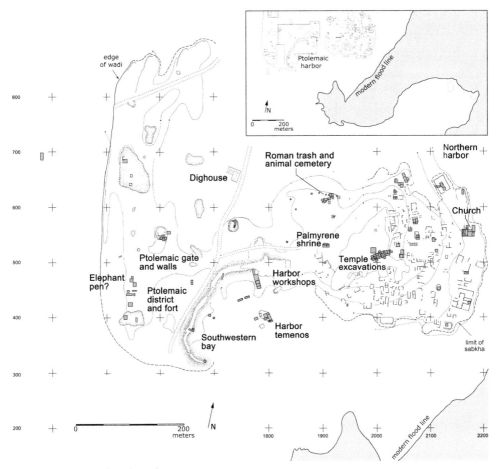

Figure 2.5.3 Berenike, plan of site
Berenike (23° 54.62' N/35° 28.42' E). Founded in the mid-third century BC, this Red
Sea port in the far south of Egypt (c. 675 km [420 miles] south of modern Suez)
primarily served Ptolemaic military needs (the importation of war elephants) early in its
history. By the early Roman period, it had become an important commercial hub in the
trade between the Mediterranean and the East (Arabia, South Asia) and South (coastal
Africa) as well as a cultural "melting pot" in which at least a dozen languages were
employed. By the mid-sixth century the port was no longer in use.

Sea trade served as a stimulus for production and employment all along its
routes: in the ports (Figure 2.5.3), across the Eastern Desert, in Valley
settlements, especially Coptos, and in Alexandria. Indeed, as indicated
above (**2.4**), Alexandria was transformed into the premier commercial
center of the Eastern Mediterranean by virtue of the merchant traffic
associated with the Red Sea trade and the shipment of the tax grain to

Rome. Moreover, a portion of the *tetarte* (25 percent tax) assessed on the high-value Eastern imports – a massive fiscal inflow – remained within the province, as did a portion of the goods themselves.

The state's role in the development of market integration seems less a matter of direct intervention than facilitation. To be sure, there are examples of the former (e.g. laws regarding shippers, the Edict of Maximum Prices), and no one would suggest that the imperial government was uninterested in the successful operation of the *annona*. But just as the *annona* network lowered the transaction costs for private commerce so certain state actions facilitated integration more generally. In this regard, the curbing of piracy and banditry – indeed, the creation of a generally peaceful zone for commerce in and around the Mediterranean – was critical, but other initiatives were also important, such as the maintenance of roads and the setting of low internal customs rates. The practicality of Roman law was also of considerable significance, in particular its relative flexibility regarding non-citizen legal practice and instruments, to say nothing of its protection of private property rights.

Bibliography
Adams 2007; Bowman and Wilson 2009; Lerouxel 2016; Orbis: The Stanford Geospatial Network Model of the Roman World: orbis.stanford .edu.; Rathbone 2007; Sidebotham 2011; Van Minnen 2000

2.6   The development of urban elites

In taking control of Egypt in 30 BC, as we have seen (**2.1**), the Roman government faced the challenge of how to govern and manage its new province. Unlike much of the Eastern Mediterranean, Egypt was not a land full of historically self-governing cities; but neither was it a tribal society or a sparsely populated country. The Romans were not accustomed to governing through elaborate bureaucracies of the kind the Ptolemies deployed and with which we are familiar today. Instead, they preferred to have local elites do the day-to-day work of running the provinces for them, with supervision from Roman governors and a guarantee of security from modest Roman garrisons (**2.2**).

In Egypt, the Romans initially recognized only three Greek cities: the former royal capital of Alexandria, Naukratis in the Delta, and Ptolemais in Upper Egypt. On its foundation in 130, Antinoopolis in Upper Egypt

(Figure 3.1.1) became the fourth Greek city (**2.1**). Only the citizens of these three (later four) cities were treated as Greeks and citizens. Everyone else was legally an "Egyptian" and subject to the poll tax. But the administrative structure of Egypt depended on the nomes and was locally based in their chief towns (*metropoleis*, in Greek). If one did not want to pay a large administrative staff, who was going to run things? Already in the reign of Augustus the need for local elites was obvious, and the first steps were taken toward developing and recognizing them. As part of the regular census, the Roman administration compiled lists of those recognized as Greeks, at least by culture if not by citizenship. In the Fayyum, this group is described as Greek, limited in number, and composed of "settlers" (*katoikoi*), meaning the descendants of Ptolemaic military settlers. In principle, only those whose parents belonged to this group could become members of it; it was thus a closed class. Although legally Egyptians and subject to the poll tax (at a reduced rate, however, like all residents of the *metropoleis*), these people formed a cultural and, eventually, a political elite in the *metropoleis*. Their sons received a training in Greek athletic traditions and other cultural norms in the gymnasium. After the first decades of Roman rule, this institution was found only in the nome capitals and no longer, as in Ptolemaic times, in some villages; membership served as a formal status-marker.

It was apparently in the gymnasia that the long process of turning the nome capitals into fully fledged cities began, as the office of gymnasiarch changed its character from that of the head of a private association to a municipal office (cf. **2.1**). This development probably belongs to the first half of the first century AD. In the following years, two other positions connected with the gymnasium (*exegetes* and *kosmetes*) became municipal offices. Because the holders of these offices are mostly mentioned in documents after their time in office and merely as a form of identification, we know little about the duties associated with these titles. But we can be sure that along with their prestige they brought not only administrative tasks but costs and financial risks. This is a basic characteristic of Roman governance: the power of local elites brought with it expense and responsibilities.

The most central task that the government placed on local elites was that of collecting taxes. Some of this fell on the upper classes of the villages, but at a higher level it was the metropolitans who bore the burden. Particularly the elite among the city population held key positions in the taxation system, especially as the Romans gradually moved away from the practice of con-tracting out tax collection to entrepreneurs. The actual work of collection could be delegated to private staff hired by the responsible officials, but the threat of meeting any shortfall in collection fell on the wealthy elite.

Shouldering such public responsibilities was possible only for the rich. The civic elites of the Roman world depended on income from landed wealth. The landowning elite of late Ptolemaic Egypt were largely the same descendants of military settlers whom the Romans recognized as a socially privileged class, and the Roman government did not disturb their possession of estates that under the Ptolemies were still in theory revocable grants. But even the wealthiest of these descendants did not in general have more than the 100 arouras given to many cavalrymen. The Roman civic elites needed more concentrated wealth (see **3.3**). Roman rule brought changes to make the accumulation of private wealth easier, including full salability of the settlers' allotments and a low, flat tax rate on private land, which encouraged investment and, eventually, greater productivity. And privately owned land that had paid rent to the temples was now treated as private land, with the low tax rate and full freedom to sell. At the village level, the priests formed another elite group, with defined privileges (see **2.7**).

These changes were part of a larger shift in economic and social power. Under the Ptolemies, although private land was not uncommon, access to land depended heavily on one's relationship to institutions, whether those were the temples with their domains or the government with its practice of supporting the military with land grants rather than cash salaries. The Ptolemies had relied on redistributing to the army and officials the agricultural surplus captured through a heavy harvest tax that was effectively a rent. The Romans, in contrast, generated a more robust market economy and incentives to invest in productivity through their low fixed tax rates and the abolition of claims on the country's surplus by privileged groups. With lower taxes and the benefits of investment flowing to the owner, land became much more valuable. The result was economic growth but also increased inequality of wealth; this in turn was central to the Roman political system. This inequality also grew as a result of the larger role of capital investment in agriculture, whether by irrigating more marginal lands in the valley and Delta or by spending to dig wells and irrigation systems in the distant oases of the western desert (Figure 2.6.1).

None of these changes came overnight. The shifts in taxation came early in Roman rule, by the reign of Tiberius, but the movement toward self-government in the nome capitals was a gradual matter; so too was the accumulation of landed wealth on the part of the more successful members of the metropolitan population, which continued in later centuries (see **3.1**, **4.4**). Only occasionally does the evidence enable us to see the formation of the new elite. And the "liturgical" system of administration through

Figure 2.6.1 Agricultural development around a well in the Dakhla oasis
The surroundings are desert, but around the well there is intensive agriculture. The photo shows the view from the second floor of a mud-brick building with storage on the ground floor and a pigeon-house above.

compulsory, temporary service also developed over the first and second centuries (see **3.1**). It is only in the early second century AD that the Roman system seems fully in place.

Bibliography
Bowman and Rathbone 1992; Hagedorn 2007; Monson 2012

2.7 The treatment of the temples and its implications

A modern-day visitor to a well-preserved temple of the Graeco-Roman era, such as that at Edfu (Figure 2.7.1; cf. also Figure 1.8.1), will probably get the impression that these structures were distinct from the settlements in which they were situated. Physically, this is true: Even though most of Edfu's

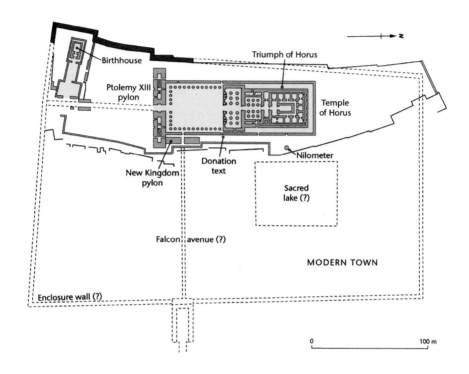

Figure 2.7.1 Plan of the Edfu temple
Plan of the Edfu temple, showing the present remains of the precinct (*temenos*) wall
(upper left) as well as a reconstruction of its ancient course, much of which now lies
under the modern town. The plan also makes clear the size of the imposing pylon of
Ptolemy XII.

temenos wall is missing or lost under the modern town, depriving the visitor
of an immediate grasp of the size of the temple precinct, the massive pylon
and adjoining walls of the extant edifice send a clear enough message: The
temple was a sacred space to which access was controlled.

This distinctive built environment, however, does not mean that temples
and their personnel were poorly integrated into society, still less that they
were a world completely apart. On the contrary, most priests throughout
the Graeco-Roman period fulfilled their religious duties on a part-time
basis, being fully engaged in "secular" activities when they had no hieratic
obligations. And the temples themselves invariably had economic relationships, which in many cases dated back for centuries, with their host

communities and with individuals farther afield. For example, temples required labor and capital to exploit the lands and facilities that they owned. The tenancies that typically furnished these inputs are well documented, but the surviving written record tells only part of the story. Interactions with the local population extended beyond the economic into the social sphere, and in addition to the expected ties connected to cult there were other relationships, such as those governed by patronage.

That a degree of integration of the temples into the community was *present* throughout the period between Alexander's arrival and the closure of the last temple is uncontroversial. The question is rather if, or how, this engagement changed as a result of the transition from Ptolemaic to Roman rule. The traditional view has been that the Roman conquest marked the beginning of the end for the temples. Unlike the Ptolemies, who recognized the power and authority of the indigenous priesthoods and sought to co-opt them to help legitimize their regime (**1.8**), the Romans, according to this narrative, took a confrontational approach: Aware that strong temples had been and might again be focal points for revolt, the new rulers sought to weaken temples by stripping them of their economic power, in particular through the confiscation of their lands; by limiting access to the priesthood through the imposition of new controls, which were eventually overseen by a Roman equestrian-level official, the high priest in Alexandria (cf. **2.1**); and through the creation of onerous new bureaucratic requirements, above all extensive reporting. According to the traditional view, the priests responded to these initiatives with resistance – not typically of the physical variety, but rather cultural: They became more insular, bolting the doors to their precincts and striving to preserve indigenous practice within them, "culture work" that entailed rejecting "Hellenic" or "classical" intrusions.

In part reflective of modern disciplinary boundaries between classicists and ancient historians on the one hand and Egyptologists on the other, this model of confrontation and resistance presents a distorted picture. With the imposition of new power structures – and it cannot be denied that Rome refashioned Egyptian society (cf. **2.6**) – resistance would certainly be expected, but the ways in which it could be manifested were diverse and not necessarily obviously oppositional; subtler responses, involving, for example, language use or the syncretization of gods, were just as, if not more, likely. Moreover, the reactions of the temples (and of individual priests) would not have been uniform but dependent on context.

Is the program Rome adopted for Egypt likely to have differed significantly from those employed in other occupied provinces? Generally speaking, the "Roman" part of provincial administration was a thin veneer; governance relied heavily on the participation of local elites, and the "buy-in" of these individuals was more typically sought through inducements than coercion (see **2.6**). That the Egyptian priesthood was an elite group is unquestionable, though of course there were gradations within the body. Why, then, should we expect the Roman approach toward the priesthood to have been one of confrontation?

The evidence, in fact, suggests that it was not, that the Romans instead recognized the value of engaging the priestly elite in the management of the province. The case for the Romans' most infamous supposed act, the widespread confiscation of temple land (which was then, it is argued, either leased back to the temples or replaced by a state allowance or *syntaxis*), hinges in large part on a single papyrus (*P. Tebt.* 2.302, Figure 2.7.2), whose interpretation is hardly straightforward, and there are plausible alternative explanations of its evidence. Even more suspect are the "access controls" alleged to have been placed upon the priesthood. The priesthood was already a hereditary (and thus "closed") body before the Romans arrived. Roman scrutiny of qualifications, far from being repressive, served to protect or enshrine the pre-existing exclusivity of the group. The examinations (*epikriseis*) employed for the metropolite and gymnasial groups offer a useful comparison (**2.1**). These two bodies – both constructions of the new regime – were privileged entities, expected to participate in government in exchange for the favor that they were shown. The priesthood also received benefits from the state (e.g. exemption from certain compulsory public services and from the poll tax) that were comparable or better than those bestowed upon these "Hellenic" elites, and it is clear that in return it also participated in the administration of the province, most notably through the collection of fiscal dues on temple land and facilities. This arrangement was mutually advantageous: For the Romans – beyond the obvious need for less manpower – it shifted unpopular tasks onto more palatable agents who came from the indigenous population. The priests, meanwhile – besides receiving favors, tangible and otherwise, from the authorities – could portray themselves as a protective barrier between Roman power and the populace while at the same time lessening external interference in their concerns.

If priests did participate in the new Roman power structure, the cultural insularity of the temples is called into question. The fortuitous preservation of a large portion of the temple library at Tebtunis (Umm el-Brigat) allows this question to be addressed, at least for a single institution in an important Fayyum village. A large number of Egyptian ritual and narrative texts

P.Tebt
0302
Frame
1/2
Recto

Figure 2.7.2 Petition to the prefect of Egypt: *P.Tebt.* **2.302**
Top portion of a petition to the prefect of Egypt (probably Lucius Peducaeus Colo[nus])
from priests of the crocodile god Soknebtunis. The document concerns a dispute about
land in which the priests are involved, but the precise nature of this conflict is unclear
owing to the fragmentary state of the text. Supplements proposed by the original editors
have made the petition central to a narrative of Roman antagonism toward Egyptian
temples (part of *P.Tebt.* 2.302, AD 71/72).

Box 2.7.1 Regulations concerning the priesthood

Selections from *BGU* 5.1210 (after AD 149), the *Gnomon* of the idios logos, a compilation of rules concerning various matters of interest to the office of the "special account" (see **2.1**). Items 71–97 regulate cult.

71. Priests may not participate in any *chreia* [= "occupation"? "temple activity"? "public duty"?] other than the service of the gods, nor go forth in woolen garments, nor wear long hair, even if they are barred from the divine procession.
74. A *stolistes* [a high-ranking priest] who deserted his duties was penalized with the loss of his revenue and an additional penalty of 300 drachmas.
77. Where the office of prophet is governed by succession, it is preserved for the family.
78. Where the office of prophet is for sale, it is sold outright and not at public auction.
79. In every temple where there is a shrine, there must be a prophet, and he receives a fifth of the revenues.
[82.] *Pastophoroi* [lower-level temple personnel] may not act as priests.
[84.] Priestly perquisites are safeguarded for a daughter.
[85.] If a temple lacks sufficient staff, priests may be taken from a temple of similar class for religious processions.
[89.] Those who do not send wrappings for the deification of Apis or Mnevis are penalized.
[96.] Private individuals may not occupy a priestly office. (Translation from Johnson [1936]: 648–649, modified.)

---

were copied at Tebtunis, and it has been suggested (with the benefit of hindsight, of course) that this was part of a priestly effort to protect and preserve a threatened tradition. But a subtler view of this copying activity as an imitation or performance of *past* culture is also possible, and furthermore, the copies have yet to be scrutinized for changes or novelties. The Tebtunis priests were in any case hardly resistant to "Hellenic culture." They read Greek works beyond the technical (medical and scientific) treatises in which we might expect them to have an interest, including works of literature such as the *Iliad*, the Hesiodic catalogue, and Xenophon's *Oikonomikos*. Moreover, there is good reason to think that by the second century AD, Greek was their preferred language. Whether

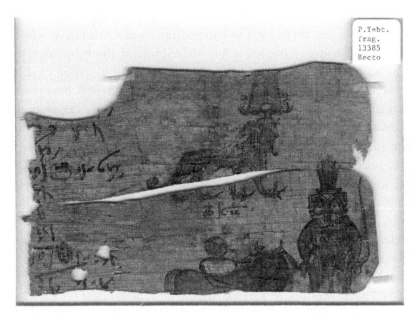

Figure 2.7.3 Colored drawing on a demotic account showing Tutu and Bes
The empty space adjacent to a demotic account (upside down in the image) has been used for a colored drawing; at some later point, the papyrus was employed for funerary cartonnage ("papyrus-mâché"). Depicted are the Egyptian protective deities Tutu (Greek Tithoes, top; "Tutu the Great" is written under his name) and Bes (right). The subject of the third group (bottom) has been the source of debate: It may simply be a priest leading a bull to sacrifice, but it has been argued that it shows Mithras slaying the bull (the tauroctony) and used as evidence for the presence of the Mithras cult already in Ptolemaic Egypt (*P.Tebt.* frag. 13,385).

smaller or more isolated temples reproduced the Tebtunis patterns is another question, but cultural openness is likely to have been even more pronounced in the nome *metropoleis* and cities. The copy work and the reading of Greek were at all events not limited to Tebtunis, as the extensive literary remains found at the much smaller village of Soknopaiou Nesos (modern Dime, on the north side of the Fayyum's lake) show.

This revision of the historical narrative is relevant to understanding the general decline of the temples, which by the third century was rather pronounced. If it is granted that the state was actively invested in their well-being, changes in its own fortunes may well have resulted in diminished economic support, but such reductions are not likely to have been the sole cause of decline. Moreover, the temples were clearly suffering before Rome's prominent periods of crisis, even as early as the later Ptolemaic period. For this reason, it is generally accepted that the decline is not attributable to competition from Christianity, which cannot have had any impact before the middle of the third century. Some economic weakness may have been due to the diversion of elite resources to other needs (see **3.5**). But there could well have been another factor: demography. A series of official temple declarations (*graphai hiereon kai cheirismou*) from Tebtunis vividly depicts the drop in the priesthood's numbers. This decrease becomes particularly pronounced after the Antonine plague (see **3.4**), and it seems likely that the priests, unlike other groups, simply lacked the numbers to recover from the pandemic. In other words, the very exclusivity of the order, its hereditary nature (safeguarded, as we have seen, by the Romans), appears to have been its downfall. The plague may not have been such a decisive factor everywhere – it hit the priests at Soknopaiou Nesos hard, but their numbers were greater – yet it deserves consideration as a cause of temple decline.

Bibliography
Connor 2014; Hickey 2009; Messerer 2012; Messerer 2017; Ryholt 2005; Van Minnen 1998

2.8   The Jewish communities of Egypt, especially Alexandria

There were Judaean military settlers at Elephantine in the service of the Persian monarchy as early as the middle of the fifth century BC, and no doubt there were people of Judaean origin living in Memphis and other Egyptian cities in the fourth century. But large-scale settlement of people from Judaea in Egypt began only under the first Ptolemies, first with war captives and then with voluntary migration. This movement continued over most of the Hellenistic period; for the entire third century, Judaea was part of the Ptolemaic kingdom. The migration resulted in a large Jewish community, spread around the Egyptian countryside as well as in Alexandria, amounting perhaps to a hundred thousand individuals or more in all. Like most other non-Egyptians, Jews were classified legally as Hellenes in the Ptolemaic system.

In Leontopolis, near Heliopolis, there was a temple, built in the second century BC by a high priest displaced from Jerusalem by internal conflict. Prayer houses, probably to be seen as ancestors of the later synagogues, were found in villages where there was Jewish settlement. A Jewish communal body, the *politeuma*, is attested in Herakleopolis, and probably existed elsewhere (**1.9**). It was governed by magistrates who had the competence to settle private legal disputes among Jews, but also apparently some disputes involving non-Jews in the harbor district. Some Jews served in the Ptolemaic army, and a few even rose to high military rank under the kings. The large Alexandrian community was culturally vibrant. It is there that the best-known Greek translation of the Hebrew and Aramaic Jewish scriptures, the Septuagint, was made (cf. **1.7**). Although there may be some signs of conflict between the Jewish community and both the Greek citizens of Alexandria and the wider Egyptian population in the Ptolemaic period, the evidence is limited and perhaps in part fabricated at a later date.

In the Roman organization of Egypt's population, which did not recognize the category of "Greek" (apart from the three Greek cities), the Jews were classified as Egyptians, along with the metropolitan elites of the countryside. They were thus subject to the poll tax, and unlike the metropolitan elites they enjoyed no discount on the rate. The Alexandrian Jews were not treated as Alexandrian citizens and thus were not classified by the Romans among the citizen population, but again as Egyptians. This represented a sharp loss of status for Jews in the Roman era. Nor did Roman law grant the community the limited autonomy that the *politeuma* of the Ptolemaic period had.

These changes no doubt made the Jewish community of Alexandria more vulnerable. But they do not fully explain why the relatively subdued tensions of earlier periods became so much sharper and exploded in a veritable pogrom in AD 38, with much bloodshed and destruction of Jewish property. There had been some jockeying for privileges in the wake of the Augustan settlement, in which each community could feel itself disadvantaged, but it is impossible to say whether this had significant consequences. We have no accounts of the events that are not partisan; indeed, the Jewish philosopher Philo is our main source. It is hard to know which details of his account deserve acceptance, but overall it seems fair to say that the Jews became the losers in a multi-cornered political battle among the Roman government, the Greek population of Alexandria, and the Jews. The prefect, Flaccus, had been in conflict with some parts of the Alexandrian elite, but he found his position precarious at the death of the emperor Tiberius and the accession of Caligula. Rather than fighting each other, the prefect and the Alexandrian notables could agree on the Jews as a common foe. In this way, the hostility of the Alexandrians toward Rome was displaced onto a more acceptable common target, the Jews.

Figure 2.8.1 Letter of Claudius to the Alexandrians
Letter of Claudius to the Alexandrians, in response to their embassy to him about the Jews, AD 41: *P.Lond.* 6.1912v, British Library Papyrus 2248. The letter was copied on the back of a tax register from Philadelpheia in the Fayyum, belonging to the archive of the collector Nemesion.

After the bloodshed, the emperor was brought into the quarrel, but he was also hostile, and the embassy was unsuccessful. It was only at the accession of Claudius to the throne that calm was restored. After hearing embassies from both sides, he sent a sharply worded letter (*P.Lond.* 6.1912; Figure 2.8.1, Box 2.8.1) criticizing the behavior of both the Alexandrian Greeks and the Jews and ordering them to keep to their places and privileges and avoid attacking the other; in it he described the attacks on the Jews as a "war." Perhaps Claudius understood the underlying anti-Roman sentiment only too well.

Despite the damage inflicted by this assault, the Jewish community remained large, active, and rich, still constituting perhaps as much as a third of the city's population and including families holding the contracts for collection of taxes and customs duties on goods coming through the Red Sea ports. It also continued to be a major center of literary and philosophical culture, most notably exemplified by the writer Philo. A later member of Philo's family – his nephew, in fact – was the first Alexandrian to become prefect of Egypt, and indeed the only Jew ever to hold that position; for that matter, his was the only known Alexandrian Jewish family to obtain Roman

> ### Box 2.8.1 Claudius' letter to the Alexandrians, lines 73–104: *P.Lond.* 6.1912
>
> As to the question which of you were responsible for the riot and feud (or rather, if the truth must be told, the war) against the Jews, I was unwilling to commit myself to a decided judgment, though your ambassadors, and particularly Dionysios son of Theon, pleaded your cause with much zeal in confrontation (with their opponents), and I must reserve for myself an unyielding indignation against whoever caused this renewed outbreak; but I tell you plainly that if you do not desist from this baneful and obstinate mutual hostility I shall perforce be compelled to show what a benevolent prince can be when turned to just indignation. Wherefore I conjure you yet again that, on the one side, the Alexandrians show themselves forbearing and kindly toward the Jews who for many years have dwelt in the same city, and offer no outrage to them in the exercise of their traditional worship, but permit them to observe their customs as in the time of the deified Augustus, which customs I also, after hearing both sides, have confirmed; and on the other side, I bid the Jews not to busy themselves about anything beyond what they have held hitherto, and not henceforth, as if you and they lived in two cities, to send two embassies – a thing such as never occurred before now – nor to strive in gymnasiarchic or kosmetic games, but to profit by what they possess, and enjoy in a city not their own an abundance of all good things; and not to introduce or invite Jews who sail down to Alexandria from Syria or Egypt, thus compelling me to conceive the greater suspicion; otherwise I will by all means take vengeance on them as fomenting a general plague for the whole world. If, desisting on both sides from these proceedings, you are willing to live with mutual forbearance and kindliness, I on my side will continue to display the time-honored solicitude for the interests of the city, with which my family has a traditional friendship.

citizenship. The prefect was Tiberius Julius Alexander, who would proclaim Vespasian as emperor in 69.

But Alexander's impact on the Jews of Alexandria was far from what the community might have hoped, for he was faced with repressing a Jewish uprising in Alexandria in 66, at the time of the outbreak of the First Jewish Revolt in Palestine (66–74). This event entailed great carnage, according to our only source, the Jewish historian Josephus (*Bellum Judaicum* 2.487–498), who blames the uprising and bloodshed mainly on the Jewish community. It is again difficult to know just how to evaluate this highly partisan evidence. And Alexander found himself in 70 on the staff of Vespasian's son Titus, the future emperor, in Jerusalem at the time of the destruction of the temple – an act the responsibility for which Josephus is at pains to deflect from both Titus and Alexander. It is clear, however, that relations between the Jewish and citizen communities in Alexandria were by now fatally poisoned, and the imperial government introduced a tax specifically targeting Jews.

The end of this great Alexandrian community came with the revolt of 115–117 (see **3.2** on its place in the series of disturbances in Egypt in the second and third centuries). Although the revolt apparently did not originate in Egypt, and its origins in Cyrene are hardly clarified by the bald account in Eusebius' *Ecclesiastical History* (4.2), its course and consequences are better known there than elsewhere. We happen to have an archive of family papers concerning Apollonios, who was the governor (*strategos*) of a small Upper Egyptian nome (Apollonopolis Heptakomias) during the revolt, and who corresponded with his family in Hermopolis (*P.Giss.Apoll.*). From these papers it is clear that there was a high level of anxiety among the Greek elite. And it is clear that the slaughter of the Jewish population and the confiscation of their property was widespread and nearly total. It would be more than a century before we can start to see any rebuilding of a Jewish community in Egypt (**4.7**).

Bibliography
Barclay 1996; Blouin 2005; Cowey and Maresch 2001; Gambetti 2009; Harker 2008; Horbury and Noy 1992; Mélèze-Modrzejewski 1997

2.9   Religious change under Roman rule

As we have seen (**2.7**), Egyptian cults and temples faced a number of changes in the early Roman period, some to their disadvantage, and not all yet fully understood. Still, they continued to flourish (cf. **1.8**), with additions made to existing temples and the construction of new ones particularly in the south (in Nubia, for instance, at Kalabsha and Dendur) and the oases (e.g. Deir el-Hagar and Trimithis in Dakhla). Rather than cult scenes of Ptolemaic kings and queens, Roman emperors now appeared on temple walls, accompanied by abbreviated hieroglyphic cartouches. Egyptian gods continued to be worshipped in temples and smaller shrines throughout the land. Besides the major cults, Isis at Philae for instance or Sobek/Souchos in the Fayyum, there were many oracle temples and more popular cults like those of Bes or Shai. Some gods took on new appearances: Isis *lactans* is portrayed giving

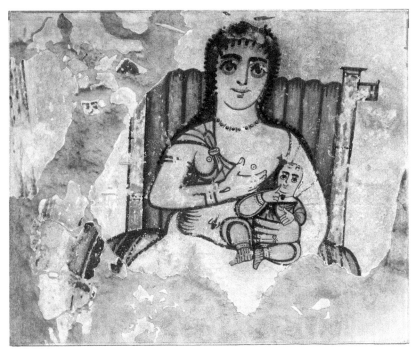

Figure 2.9.1 Isis with Harpokrates in wall painting from Karanis
Isis and Harpokrates, wall painting from southern wall of House B50E, Karanis,
University of Michigan excavation; facsimile painting by Hamzeh Carr over existing
photograph (2003.02.0002). This wall painting, from a house at Karanis in the north
Fayyum, shows the goddess suckling her young son Harpokrates. The cult of Egyptian
Isis spread widely through the Roman world and images of Isis lactans ("providing
milk") served as a prototype for later scenes of the Christian Virgin and Child.

her breast to Harpokrates ("Horus the child") on the wall of a house at
Karanis (Figure 2.9.1); elsewhere an image of Harpokrates-Dionysos – a
deity recognized by both Egyptians and Greeks – is formed in terracotta.
Religion was also affected by the presence of the army. Mithras arrived from
the east. Heron and other military deities were widely portrayed on wooden
panels in Hellenized form. At the entry to the Kom el Shoqafa catacombs in
Alexandria, two figures of Egyptian Anubis stand guard, dressed as Roman
legionaries but wearing Egyptian headdresses (Figure 2.9.2). In funerary cult
a further striking innovation under the influence of Rome was the practice
of providing mummies with realistic portraits, which sometimes
recorded a name.

Other significant changes took place (**2.7**), although their impact and
meaning remain controversial. The state took more control over religion,

Figure 2.9.2 Anubis from Kom el-Shoqafa
Anubis from Kom el-Shoqafa. The jackal god Anubis, who presides over mummification, stands guard in the guise of Roman legionaries on either side of the underground entrance to an Alexandrian tomb. Note the different headdress of the two figures – a composite crown on the left and simple sun-disk to the right. Over their short tunics they wear a cuirass and the lower part of the left-hand jackal takes the form of a serpent.

with, from Hadrian's reign, the appointment of a high priest (*archiereus*) of Alexandria and all Egypt. Regular priests were excluded from holding administrative posts, limiting their local influence. Chief priests (*archiprophetai*) became bureaucrats with limited tenure who regulated their subordinates by granting or refusing them permission to conduct circumcisions. And, whereas under the Ptolemies all priests enjoyed certain tax privileges, the Romans limited the numbers of those so privileged (in Karanis, for instance, fifty-four priests and fifty *pastophoroi*). Sacred land was now managed by the central administration, which took responsibility for the payment of cult and cult personnel. In the reign of Hadrian even the limited financial independence of temples was curtailed, as Rome's control became tighter.

The cult of the Apis bull (see **1.5**, **1.8**, **1.9**) illustrates the effects over time of the Roman takeover. Victorious over Cleopatra, Octavian declined a visit to Apis, opting instead to visit the tomb of Alexander. Despite this snub, the Apis cult continued to flourish, although, as with other animal cults, the state controlled many aspects, as recorded in the official rule book of the "private account" (see **2.1**). The provision of the linen wrappings required for an Apis burial was now imposed on Egyptian temples nation-wide, with fines attached for noncompliance. The cult enjoyed both an international and local following and involved members of the imperial family. Apis' refusal of the sustenance offered by Germanicus was apparently seen as foretelling Germanicus' early death (Pliny, *HN* 8.71). For Hadrian, who visited Egypt, a new Apis was identified after quite an interval. Still later, the appearance of an Apis under Julian (AD 362) was treated as a favorable omen, foretelling good harvests and prosperity (Amm. Marc. 22.14.6). The bull's prophetic and magical powers now came to the fore, as happened elsewhere in other Egyptian cults at this time: Apis had come to be venerated as an oracular god. Finally, however, Theodosius' edict in AD 391 forbidding pagan practices appears to have put an end to this particular cult (see **3.5**).

The imperial cult in Egypt developed from the Ptolemaic dynastic cult in interesting ways. Whereas the Ptolemies had been adopted into Egyptian temples as temple-sharing deities by decree (**1.8**), the imperial cult was based primarily in its own cult centers, especially in the towns and *metropoleis* of Egypt. A prototype of the civic nature of much of imperial cult was the Sebasteion or Caesareum in Alexandria (**2.4**), which became a focus for the imperial cult under Augustus. Lying close to the harbor, the precinct included, in Egyptian fashion, a library and was fronted by two historic stone obelisks, brought from Heliopolis and held in place by large bronze crabs, which record the prefect's dedication in 13/12 BC (Figure 2.4.3). In that year, the same prefect dedicated a temple to Augustus at Philae in Upper Egypt, implying imperial encouragement.

Later Julio-Claudian emperors showed more hesitation on the question of their divinity, as indicated by Claudius in his letter to the Alexandrians (AD 41, Box 2.8.1). While accepting many honors – the celebration of his birthday as a festival, the erection of statues of himself and family, and much else – he deprecated the appointment of a high priest for him or the building of temples; such honors, he wrote, were for the gods alone. Nero responded in similar vein when early in his reign the elite of the Arsinoite nome approached him with similar offers (*SB* 12.11012). The imperial cult thus was endorsed both by the ruling power and by provincial elites seeking preferment.

Throughout the valley the developing rule of Rome was accompanied by the foundation of centers of the imperial cult: Kaisareia, Sebasteia and later Hadrianeia were erected in many locations in both Lower and Upper Egypt. Here, as in Ptolemaic temples, were placed statues of members of the imperial family. The impressive marble busts of Augustus, Tiberius,

Figure 2.9.3 Head of Augustus from Meroe
This over-sized bronze head of the emperor Augustus, broken off at the neck, probably reached Meroe (capital of Nubia) as booty from further north. The eyes are inlaid, with glass pupils set within metal rings and the iris formed of calcite. The head turns slightly to the right and the waves of the hair are typical of portraits of Augustus. H: 46.2 cm (18 in); W: 26.5 cm (10 ½ in); D: 29.4 cm (11 ½ in). British Museum cat. no. 1911,0901.1.

and Livia from Arsinoe may be examples – possibly, too, the fine bronze head of Augustus from Meroe, far up the Nile (Figure 2.9.3), which perhaps came looted from further north. Ritually buried in sand below the entrance to a shrine where it was trodden underfoot, this emperor's head would signify the defeat here of Rome.

In addition to multifarious statues, the imperial cult took other forms, both in homes and within the community. Imperial busts were carried in processions, imperial birthdays were celebrated, and months named after the imperial family. Sebastos (in Latin, Augustus) replaced the month of Thoth, and Hathyr became Neos Sebastos for Tiberius. Other name changes for months show up only some of the time and did not outlast

---

Box 2.9.1 Karanis prayer papyrus: *P.Mich.* 21.827, column 1

Let there be words of good omen! ... pray while performing a sacrifice (?).

(Let this be) a hearth for the Emperor Caesar Trajan Hadrian Augustus, the savior and benefactor of the world. (Let this be) a hearth for the god Augustus Caesar. (Let this be) a hearth for the god Tiberius Caesar. (Let this be) a hearth for the god Claudius Caesar. (Let this be) a hearth for the god Vespasian Caesar. (Let this be) a hearth for the god Titus Caesar. (Let this be) a hearth for the god Nerva Caesar. (Let this be) a hearth for the god Trajan Caesar. (Let this be) a hearth for – - -, prefect (?). (Let this be) a hearth for Haterius Nepos, the prefect (?). (Let this be) a hearth for Zeus the savior. (Let this be) a hearth for Zeus the Olympian. (Let this be) a hearth for Zeus (of Mount) Kasios. (Let this be) a hearth for Zeus the hospitable. (Let this be) a hearth for Zeus of the Capitoline. (Let this be) a hearth for Zeus the – - -. (Let this be) a hearth for Zeus the sender of all ominous voices (?); for Hera the all-powerful; for Hera who presides over marriage; for Athena Nike; for Athena [– - -]; for Ares [– - -] allies; [for Aphrodite (?) – - -]; for the Graces (?) [– - -]; for Poseidon the securer; for Poseidon of the sea; for Poseidon the earth-mover; for the Nile (?) [and Earth (?)] the all-nurturing; for Kronos the great(est?) god (?); for Rhea mother of god (?); for Demeter and Kore, fruit-bearing goddesses; for Hades – - -; for Persephone the beautiful child; for Apollo leader of the Muses; for Artemis the light-bringer; for Hermes – - -; for Herakles gloriously trimphant; for the Dioscuri the manifest [gods?]; for the Olympian Muses; for the Pierian Muses; for the Helikonian Muses; for the Helikonian [– - -] ... ; for Asclepius [– - -].

(Translation Paul Heilporn and Traianos Gagos.)

---

the Julio-Claudians, except for the later introduction of Hadrianos, which survived well into the third century.

Egypt now formed part of the Roman Empire, sharing the festival calendar employed in other provinces. On festive days the *strategos* would lead the procession and all would join in acclamations and prayers. One of the most detailed records comes from the reign of Hadrian, from Arsinoite Karanis. Here, at great length, are listed the recipients of prayers with incense at their altars. First comes the reigning emperor Hadrian, savior and benefactor of the world, then his deified predecessors, from Augustus to Trajan, plus the prefect. The Greek pantheon of Olympian gods follows next – Zeus is both Capitoline Zeus and Zeus Kasios – with the addition of Augustus and Alexander Founder (of Alexandria); more Greek gods follow, including the Nile. Different sectors of the population are named, with prayers for their well-being. A second main section has the local crocodile gods, ending with the Tyche (good fortune) of Karanis and prayers for the local community, its settlers and landowners. The Roman ruler cult was well integrated in its Egyptian context.

Bibliography
Arnold 1999; Clarysse 2009; Claytor and Verhoogt 2018; Frankfurter 1998; Hölbl 2000, 2004, 2005; McKenzie 2007; Monson 2012; Pfeiffer 2010; Rondot 2013

2.10   The people of Roman Egypt

Roman rule in Egypt had different effects on the diverse parts of the population – but what and who were the people of Egypt in this period? As we saw earlier (**1.9**), this question has no simple answer. In the Ptolemaic era Greek immigrants were a relatively small minority of the population compared to the native Egyptians, perhaps a tenth of the total and possibly no more than a twentieth. But neither "Greek" nor "Egyptian" is a tidy or self-explanatory category. As we have observed, the Ptolemies treated a wide range of foreigners as officially Greek, from the tribesmen of the Balkans to the Judaeans and Idumaeans of the nearby Levant. This immigrant body was therefore highly diverse in cultural background, laws, and even native language, for Greek must have been a second language for many.

"Egyptian" might seem simpler, but it is by no means a straightforward description. From the earliest times Egypt drew population from several directions, including Nubia, Palestine, and Libya (see **1.9**). But the power and distinctiveness of Egyptian culture was such that immigrants rapidly became part of Egyptian society and are often distinguishable only by names, if at all. The influx of outsiders never stopped, and the Greeks were only the latest wave of newcomers. But whereas earlier groups were readily absorbed into the majority culture, with their languages barely visible in the mass of Egyptian texts and their images only occasionally visible in Egyptian monuments, the Greeks came to rule and kept a sense of separate identity.

It is easy to exaggerate this separateness, however, because of the continued use of separate written and artistic forms for the two cultures. In reality, many people belonged to both cultures (see **1.10** for an example), and once in a while scholarly detective work can identify those who used Egyptian names in demotic documents and Greek names in Greek texts, sometimes with Egyptian funerary monuments that give no hint of a Greek identity. Because the heavily male immigrant population often married local women, second- and third-generation products of these marriages are particularly likely to have been bicultural. It is often difficult or impossible to tell who belongs to this group and who is a member of an Egyptian family where the father has entered Ptolemaic civil or military service, obtaining a Greek identity through participation in the royal system. And even descendants of Greeks who did not marry Egyptians might well in later generations show a high degree of acculturation to local language and customs. (See **1.12**.)

The Romans thus inherited a situation in which it was not readily apparent who was a Greek or what a natural governing class in the local population was. Their response was clearly unpopular at the time and has been criticized by modern scholars, but it was not irrational. The citizen bodies of the three cities were recognized as Greek, and everyone else was an Egyptian. Within the Egyptian population, the Romans distinguished the descendants of Ptolemaic military settlers from the rest and gave them a lower tax rate. To make this distinction, they had to maintain records; our documents preserve many traces of this record-keeping. To keep this privileged status, one had to marry inside the group. Members of this non-citizen elite guarded their Greek identity jealously, but there must have been many descendants of Greek settlers who were outside this group but culturally as Greek as anyone.

Modern concepts like race and ethnicity, much contested even today, are particularly hard to apply to the population of Roman Egypt. Markers of identity are often ambiguous. As we have seen (**2.3**), the use of demotic mostly retreated within a half-century into the world of the temples, and for all practical purposes people used Greek for writing. Language thus does not distinguish groups of the population. Names are somewhat more useful, but they are full of traps for the unwary. For example, we find families in which alternating generations have Greek and Egyptian names. In many cases, the men of a family tend to have Greek names, but the women bear Egyptian ones. Some people have double names, one Greek and the other Egyptian; even more commonly, members of the elite have double names, both of them Greek. And even the category of "Greek" names is far from simple. Some names are of classical origin, while others reflect old dynastic loyalties (Ptolemaios, Kleopatra, and the like), and even more are expressions of devotion to Egyptian gods wrapped in Greek grammatical form, such as Isidoros ("gift of Isis"). Decoding cultural identity from such evidence is tricky.

Visual evidence is no simpler. Interpretations of the mummy portraits (Figure 2.10.1) found in the Fayyum and other parts of Egypt often reflect the assumptions of modern viewers. Greeks look at them and think they look just like Greeks today. Egyptians think they look like modern Egyptians; and it

Figure 2.10.1 Mummy portrait of Eutyches
Mummy portrait of Eutyches, *c.* AD 100–150. This teenage boy wears a white Roman tunic with a purple stripe; the inscription describes him as a freedman, i.e., a former slave. Uniquely for a mummy portrait, this portrait has a signature, perhaps that of the artist. The provenance is unknown, but probably one of the cemeteries of the Fayyum. Metropolitan Museum of Art, 18.9.2.

should be noted that these portraits were originally attached to sarcophagi of firmly Egyptian character. But this ambiguity points to another key reality: It was possible to be both Greek and Egyptian. It is a mistake to try to separate these people into distinct, exclusive categories. Your sense of culture might embrace the heritage of classical Athens, but Egypt was your country. Perhaps the Romans' classification of the entire population of the countryside as "Egyptians" even gave impetus to this combined identity, a feature much more pronounced in Roman than in Ptolemaic Egypt.

Two additional groups warrant further discussion. One is the Jews (**2.8**), for whom a religion irreconcilable with the cults of Egypt and the rest of the ancient polytheistic world marked out a difference that could not readily be

> **Box 2.10.1 The barbarians attack:** *O.Krok.* 1.87.26–44
>
> To Cassius Victor, centurion of the Second Cohort of Ituraeans, Antonius Celer, cavalryman of the same cohort, (sends) greetings. I wish to inform you that on the 17th of the month of the current month of Phamenoth, 60 barbarians attacked the fort of Patkoua. I fought them with the comrades whom I had with me, from the 10th hour until the second hour of the night, then they besieged the fort until dawn. This day Hermogenes, a soldier of the century of Serenos, was killed, a woman and two children were carried off, and a child was killed. At dawn of the 18th of the same month, we fought them and Damanais, cavalryman of the century of Victor (yours) [was killed ?]; Valerius Firm[– –] was wounded, along with his horse … [So and so] of the Proculeian century […] at the 6th hour of the day.

bridged. The Romans classified Jews as Egyptian, and yet their culture and religion were more Greek than Egyptian, although not entirely Greek, either. Here the legal classification, with its implication of higher taxes and lower status, clashed with the more complex cultural reality, and as we have seen serious conflict resulted. The second group, the Romans, by contrast, benefited from a superior legal status in a province where most of the population was non-citizen. The Roman citizens were not numerous until the Antonine Constitution gave citizenship to the whole population of the empire in 212 (**4.2**), but many were soldiers or their descendants, conferring social prestige and power. Others were freedmen of the emperors or of upper-class Romans engaged in the trade across the Eastern Desert or in tax collection.

The desert also housed nomadic populations, which only occasionally turn up in our documents, called by different terms, including simply "barbarians." Their relationship with the settled population was often complementary and friendly, but they could also turn aggressive and attack Roman military posts (*O.Krok.* 1.87, Box 2.10.1).

The wealthier Greek-speaking Egyptians also came to see themselves as having a third aspect – as Romans. Although this process is not easy to trace, like elites elsewhere in the empire, the upper classes of Egypt came to identify their interests with those of the ruling power, despite signs of hostility to Rome in the most privileged place of all, Alexandria.

Whatever their self-conception and cultural formation, the entire population of Egypt had to contend with the harsh realities of premodern life. Although some people lived to great ages, infant and child mortality was high, and even those who made it to age five would on average live only to their middle forties. Of those who made it to adulthood and married, most would live long enough to produce and raise a family, but many would die leaving young children. Fewer than a third of those who reached adulthood would live to age sixty-five. This stringent demographic regime affected many aspects of life. High infant mortality meant that the average woman who lived through her childbearing years needed to produce six children if the population was to remain stable. That burden weighed heavily on women's health, given the absence of anesthesia and the risks of childbirth in a world without the sanitary conditions we hope to take for granted today. Society could not afford for many people not to marry, and indeed few remained single, though not everyone would remarry after divorce or being widowed.

The quality of life was affected by other factors, as well. The high level of endemic disease, including malaria in some regions, much of it the result of contaminated water and poor sanitation, not only killed many people but left others weakened. Many people lost part or all of their eyesight from diseases, especially bilharzia. And the skeletons and mummies preserved from Roman Egypt also show a high level of trauma, not always causing death but surely leaving people with disabilities. It is not always evident whether these physical traumas resulted from accidents or from violence. Whether one had a shoulder wrecked by a falling beam, suffered a beating from a magistrate, or got into a fight with a neighbor, all contributed to harms that would have made life more painful and less productive.

Short life expectancy had social consequences, too. It was not rare for a child to lose both parents before reaching legal age (fourteen for most purposes). Aunts and uncles would in that case often have to take on their siblings' orphaned children, extra expenses to bear. It is not surprising that they often felt entitled to appropriate whatever assets the orphans had inherited from their parents; litigation resulted when the children grew up and considered themselves to have been cheated. Many petitions to the authorities recount such stories, which were nothing new in the ancient world. And yet people inevitably depended on their families. The ancient world had no pension plans. Those fortunate enough to live to old age would normally rely on their children to take care of them, managing family property and making sure the older generation was properly fed and housed, usually with their offspring. Without children, the elderly might need to adopt someone, or simply keep working until they dropped. In rural communities it was common for brothers to maintain a shared household as they managed the family property. We do not see this pattern in cities, where the nuclear family, in a modern sense, was far more common.

Around a tenth of households – more in the cities, fewer in the villages – owned slaves. Most had only one or a few slaves, but richer families could have more. Those in urban homes were mostly household servants, although some were apprenticed to learn a trade. In the villages, many more worked in agriculture. Their presence had complex effects on the population as a whole. Despite the pressure of reproduction, families sometimes had more children than they wanted, especially girls. Surplus infants could be left out ("exposed"), commonly in a dump. Anyone could pick up such a child and rear it as a slave, to be sold for a profit if it survived childhood. It is clear that male slaveowners often treated their slave women as sexual partners. The children resulting from pregnancies in such cases would be slaves in the household of their own biological father – they had no legal father.

The census declarations show that there were few slaves over age forty. It appears that male slaves were freed in their late twenties or at the latest in their early thirties, while female slaves might be kept enslaved until their reproductive years were over. In the case of men, this pattern may suggest that they were able to work and save enough of their earnings to buy their freedom while they still might hope to have some years ahead of them. But women, mostly working in the house and probably earning no wages, might find themselves on their own with few resources and not attractive as spouses because they were no longer capable of bearing children. We have little information about what happened to them.

Life could be difficult for anyone in Roman Egypt. As in any society, those with little in the way of property, money, and social capital almost inevitably struggled to meet basic needs and to protect themselves from disease, injury, and mistreatment. But even the most privileged found someone above them in the hierarchy, and no one was immune from illness, especially when an epidemic swept the cities (**3.4**).

Bibliography
Bagnall 1993; Bagnall and Frier 1994, 2006[2]; Huebner 2013; Rowlandson 1998

2.11   The origins of Christianity in Egypt

Somewhere in these first centuries of Roman rule in Egypt lie the origins of Egyptian Christianity. The first Christians in Egypt were probably members of the Jewish community. In the first century AD, as we have seen

> **Box 2.11.1 The Ethiopic *History of the Episcopate of Alexandria***
>
> Mark the Evangelist entered Alexandria in the seventh year of Nero; he appointed 12 presbyters and seven deacons, and he gave them the following rule: After the bishop of Alexandria has died, the presbyters will gather and they will lay their hands in the faith of God upon the one, among them, that they all will have selected, and thus they will appoint him as their bishop, at the presence of the corpse of the dead bishop. This doctrine has remained for the bishops whom they elect among the presbyters, from Anianos until the blessed Petros, who is the sixteenth bishop of Alexandria. This happened, not because there was any preference for the juridical principle that the presbyters should <appoint> – this had not been granted – yet because, on the contrary, a bishop had not yet been appointed for every region. (Translation Bausi and Camplani 2016, with normalized spelling.)

(**2.8**), Alexandria and Egypt in general had a large and culturally vibrant Jewish community.

The traditions of the Egyptian church attribute its foundation to the evangelist Mark, said to be the author of the second gospel. This tradition first appears in the fourth-century church historian Eusebius, who dates Mark's arrival in Alexandria to AD 43 (*Ecclesiastical History* 2.16). He does not tell us where he learned about Mark, and most historians suppose that he ultimately relied on oral tradition in the Alexandrian church. A different date (AD 60) is given in an Ethiopian version of the *History of the Episcopate of Alexandria* (Box 2.11.1), although this does not agree with the same text's figure of 255 years from Mark until the bishop Peter at the start of the fourth century. Eusebius also lists ten successors of Mark as bishops of Alexandria, for whom we have only names and years of service (beginning with Annianus, *Eccl.Hist.* 2.24). It is only with Demetrius (189–231; see **3.6**) that a bishop of Alexandria becomes a substantial historical figure. Contemporary scholars often suppose that Alexandria had only presbyters (priests), and not a bishop, until Demetrius. But the deep silence of the sources makes it difficult to say what the situation really was.

It is likely that Egyptian Christianity, with its roots in the Jewish community, suffered a severe blow from the large-scale destruction of the Jewish population when the rebellion under Trajan was suppressed (**2.8**). We know that large numbers of Jews were killed and their property taken

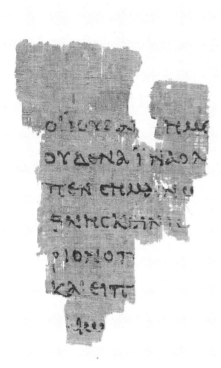

Figure 2.11.1 Christian manuscript, Gospel of John, assigned to the second century
An example of a Christian manuscript commonly dated to the second century and often
claimed to be the earliest known fragment of a Christian text: *P.Ryl.* 457. This is a
fragment from the Gospel of John 18:37–38, the scene of Jesus' appearance before
Pontius Pilate, the Roman governor. It is carefully written and the lines evenly spaced.

by the government, but we cannot say how much the small Christian
population of the time was swept up in this catastrophe.

The silence of our sources for early Christianity has surprised many
people. Christians are not mentioned in any official documents from Egypt
until the third century, but scholars have tried to find earlier traces in
private letters showing a Christian character and in biblical and other
religious texts, all of these being written on papyrus. However, unlike
official documents and contracts, these papyri are not dated by the year
of the emperor's reign and are hard to assign to any particular time. Most
often, the style of handwriting has been the basis of dating them. But dating
the handwriting of book manuscripts and private letters is a difficult art,
about which there is little agreement. Recent scholarship has called into
question the early dates assigned to these manuscripts – most typically, to

the early or middle part of the second century, but in extreme cases even to the first century – and instead proposed much later dates for them, based on more detailed and objective paleographic analysis (Figure 2.11.1). Almost all supposed Christian texts before the time of Demetrius are open to such questions.

We do not know how many Christians there were in Egypt during these early years. Modern mathematical models of the growth of religious groups have led some scholars to think that the numbers were very small to begin with but grew at a small and roughly constant percentage each year. The real process was no doubt more complicated, but it could have led the number of Christians to grow from a few hundreds around the year 100 to 10,000 or so by the time of Demetrius. Even that simplified example helps us to understand why we would not find much evidence of the earliest Christians before the late second century. As Egypt was one of the most populous provinces of the Roman Empire, numbers in other provinces were probably no larger.

Bibliography
Bagnall 2009a; Davis 2004; Huebner 2019; Nongbri 2018; Stark 1996; Wipszycka 2015

3 | Development and crisis in a Roman province

3.1 The continued rise of urbanism and the elite

Egypt was one of the most urbanized provinces of the Roman Empire, with about a fifth to a quarter of the population living in cities. Most of these people lived in the capital cities of the nomes, which the papyri call *metropoleis*. These nome capitals were each at most a sixth or less of the size of Alexandria, which had roughly 400,000–500,000 inhabitants. However, there were a lot of these smaller cities, one for each nome plus the Greek cities Antinoopolis, founded by the emperor Hadrian in 130, and Naukratis, the emporium that already flourished in pre-Ptolemaic times (**1.4**). (Ptolemais, the fourth Greek city, served also as a nome capital.) Although the number of nomes fluctuated and tended to increase, thanks to subdivision, there were around fifty of these *metropoleis*. Nomes varied in size, and so did their capitals, with an average population of around 15,000–18,000, although the largest was bigger than 40,000 and the smallest below 10,000. The smallest, however, had to cover much the same administrative responsibilities as the largest, and it is thus not surprising that they seem to have been larger in proportion to the actual areas of their nomes than larger cities were.

The urban population had certainly grown since the Roman conquest, although there is insufficient evidence to say by how much or how quickly. The foundation of Antinoopolis (Figure 3.1.1) added to the number of Greek cities, but as it drew its citizens from the privileged strata in other parts of Egypt, it probably did not change the size of the urban population very much. The changes in taxation (**2.6**) played a large role in developing the wealthy elite of the cities, as we have seen, and this process continued. But it was only part of what drove urban expansion. The papyrus evidence suggests that no more than about 10–15 percent of urban households – the civic elite – owned agricultural land in the territory surrounding their city. Some of the remainder of the population were employees or slaves of the wealthier landowners, but the cities were not simply living off the nearby countryside. They were, in addition, centers of production and trade.

121

Figure 3.1.1 Antinoopolis, gateway to the theater
This drawing shows the site as it was *c.* 1800, when the scholars attached to Napoleon's
Egyptian army visited it (*Description de l'Égypte* IV 55). The Roman city, founded in
130, was provided with a standard range of public buildings in the architectural style of
the empire.

Wholesale and retail merchants of every variety, with a high level of
specialization, created active marketplaces. Craftsmen produced a vast
range of products from metal, clay, wood, glass, cloth, and leather. The
cities were also centers for services such as law, medicine, and religion.
Petitions were written and books copied. And governmental activities were
largely based in the cities, above all the record-keeping offices with rolls
listing people, land, and tax payments, along with a registry of loans against
property and copies of the innumerable petitions submitted by aggrieved
individuals. Despite the lack of a true professional bureaucracy in our
sense, the imperial and civic officials employed a substantial number of
secretaries and collectors.

Some cities were also active manufacturing hubs. We should not
imagine modern factories, because the mechanization and energy sources
that we associate with modern industrialism were not present. However,
the scale of cloth production in Alexandria and some of the larger nome
capitals, such as Oxyrhynchos and Panopolis, was considerable, and the
production was labor-intensive throughout, from spinning flax, wool, or
cotton into thread to weaving the cloth to fashioning clothing, rugs,
hangings, bedding, and other textile products (Figure 3.1.2). The workers
occupied in textile production may have numbered in the thousands in the

Figure 3.1.2 Funerary shroud of a woman, dated *c*. 170–200
Possibly from Antinoopolis, the shroud is made of linen, Egypt's most characteristic
textile product, which was exported in large quantities. The woman is shown wearing
a fringed linen tunic; the tunic was the most characteristic everyday garment, produced in
great volume, particularly in cities in middle Egypt such as Oxyrhynchos and Panopolis.

largest centers. Egypt occupied a particularly important place in the cloth
economy of the Roman world as the leading producer of linen, with
individual cities each producing tens of thousands of garments a year.
Cotton was a relatively late development, grown mainly in the oases.

Some of the capital invested in such manufacturing enterprises must
have come from the wealthiest part of society. We have little evidence for
that, however, because the surviving documentation is heavily focused on
land, from which the Roman government derived most of its tax revenue.

Land was thought to be a much more stable and thus honorable form of wealth than the more volatile trading and manufacturing activities, even if these might make fortunes more quickly. The wealth and power of the civic elite derived from agriculture, and the city councils of the third century were made up of the larger landowners, those who owned more than 100 arouras (about 27.5 hectares) – with the most powerful owning much more. All of these councillors belonged to the top few percent of society in wealth. Typically, their landholdings were spread around their nomes and even farther afield, managed by agents who leased land out to villagers or managed larger parcels directly. These wealthy urban landowners, with the capital to invest in the necessary irrigation equipment and the time to wait for trees to mature, often acquired or developed the most profitable properties, those planted with olive and other fruit trees or with grapevines. These properties, too, demanded much labor for pruning, irrigation, and processing the harvest, and employed numerous villagers at least part of the time (cf. **3.3**). The landlords' agents could also make loans to villagers from their employers' resources, another way that the rich made their assets generate additional wealth.

The early third century brought a major change in the status of the cities, and as a result significant changes in their administration. Probably in 201, Septimius Severus granted both Alexandria and the nome capitals the privilege of having city councils. This privilege came with duties, as well, and signaled the maturation of the cities into self-governing communities like those in much of the rest of the eastern Roman Empire. Imperial supervision of the cities did not vanish, any more than it did in other provinces, but civic officials now bore responsibility for many local services and tax collection to a degree not present before. It was in large part the development of the propertied elite that made this change possible.

A position as councillor brought abundant duties, costs, and risks. Just entering the council in Oxyrhynchos cost 10,000 drachmas, equivalent to a couple of decades' wages for an ordinary worker (Box 3.1.1). It is not surprising that many new councillors had to pay this entry fee at the time of election by borrowing rather than having ready cash. Even the rich often did not have abundant cash on hand. Council membership brought monthly meetings to attend and, above all, responsibility for public services, the greatest and riskiest of which was taxation. Failure to collect what the government estimated as the tax due meant you were likely to have to fill the gap from your own pocket. This system of compulsory services, or liturgies, imposed burdens that were greatly resented and could bankrupt a councillor. Not only councillors were at risk: the system also drew in both

---

Box 3.1.1 Receipt for entrance fee to the council of
Oxyrhynchos, AD 233: *P.Oxy.* 44.3175

Aurelius Herakleides son of Dorion, (ex-?) agoranomos, councillor, treasurer of the council funds of the city of the Oxyrhynchites, to the heirs of Antonius Priscus, ex-agoranomos, formerly councillor, greetings. You have paid to me on the present day for interest on entrance-fees to the council owed by the aforementioned Antonius Priscus two hundred drachmas, that is, 200 drachmas. Year 12 of Emperor Caesar Marcus Aurelius Severus Alexander Pius Felix Augustus, Tybi 1 ... And on the –th of the month of Phamenoth of the same 12th year you have paid on account of interest on entrance-fees to the council another one hundred drachmas, that is 100 drachmas. Year 12 of Emperor Caesar Marcus Aurelius Severus Alexander Pius Felix Augustus, Phamenoth – -. (Translation A. K. Bowman, alt.)

---

metropolitans and villagers with lesser resources, although still rich enough for the government to consider them good for the money or grain at stake. The city council was ultimately responsible for the villages of the nome as well, increasing councillors' risk, although much of that was pushed down on to the richer villagers. The liturgical system began, as has been mentioned (**2.1**), in the first decades of Roman rule, and it took fuller form in the second century. By the time the councils came into existence in 201, the system was well established. In joining a council, one knew what one was getting into.

We have endless complaints about liturgical service in the papyri, echoed in Late Antique literary sources such as Libanius. It is hardly surprising that this system has been called "responsibility without power" and seen as highly dysfunctional. Because the council was responsible to the *strategos*, an imperial appointee, and through him to the higher levels of the Roman government, it had only limited autonomy. The *strategoi* were generally members of the council in another nome, and they no doubt sympathized with the difficulties of their local colleagues. But they had their own estates at risk if they failed to do the job entrusted to them, so they had every incentive to press the local council hard.

Why did anyone want to be a councillor, faced with such costs, risks, and hard work? Partly it was a matter of status and prestige. Greek and Roman society was extremely competitive, even combative. Councillors were generally treated better by Roman officials and judges than ordinary people, so high status offered some protection against everything from lawsuits to beatings. And two other incentives directly connected to the burdens of service increased the appeal of these positions. First, you might actually make a profit. Targets for tax revenues were set with some allowance for slippage, and if the taxes were collected rigorously enough, you could reap a surplus even after the expenses of collection. And that is to say nothing of the possibilities for extracting more than was really due, through a combination of superior knowledge, extortion, and brute force. Second, if you didn't participate in this system, someone else trying to avoid disaster would make you the victim instead. Better to take risks to ensure one was not in the category of potential victims.

Despite the complaints of the councillors, then, and the sympathy modern scholars have sometimes expressed for these complaints, council membership was apparently on balance a desirable status. The *metropoleis* attracted wealthier families from the villages, and in the third century people with Egyptian names, on becoming councillors, often changed their names to Greek equivalents more suitable to their lofty new position in a Greek civic structure. Only occasionally can we trace this development, but one list of names, probably from a Delta city, that includes councillors and records both old and new names (from the section beginning in the letter iota), gives the game away (Box 3.1.2). From the other end of the social spectrum, we find signs that Alexandrian citizens with extensive landholdings in the nomes sometimes found it attractive to take up residence in the nome capital, where they would be much more important persons than in the megalopolis of Alexandria. They might even hold offices in both places. This trend was probably even stronger in the Delta than up the Nile, because landholdings close to Alexandria had always been attractive to citizens of the capital, who had few opportunities in the immediate vicinity of Alexandria itself and could manage nearby holdings more easily. But we have few papyri from the Delta to show this phenomenon in operation.

The councils were probably not as powerless as modern commentators sometimes think. The Roman government did not have any other good options for ruling the country; they depended critically on these elites to keep order and collect the taxes, as well as to produce supplies for officials and troops as needed. Many documents show that the councils did not always do what the *strategoi* or higher officials demanded, or at least not on time. Polite reminders, then testy notes, and then angry letters, point to just how effective passive resistance on the part of the councillors could be. Whether from unwillingness or plain laziness, they sometimes did not get the job done. One might punish an individual or replace him, but an entire

> **Box 3.1.2 List of persons: *P.Amst.* 1.72.1–20**
> **(cf. van Minnen 1986)**
>
> Ischyrion son of –tion and [– -], councillor, formerly known as
>   Nechtheroous
> Hierax ("hawk") son of Hierax, former exegetes and ... defensor,
>   councillor ... formerly known as Hierax son of Pibichis and [– -]
> Hierax son of Hephaistion and [– -, formerly known as – -] son of
>   Osoroousis and T[– -]
> Isidoros son of Horion and [– -]
> Ischyrion son of Isidoros and [– -]
> Hierax son of Ischyrion and Hephai[– - formerly known as] Pibichis son
>   of Abykis
> Hierax son of Alexandros and T[– - formerly known as] Panibichis son
>   of Pnepheros
> Hierax alias Didiymos son of Isidoros [and – - formerly known as]
>   Piathres son of Petesis and Th[– - through] official notice
>   Didymos son of Isidoros
> Isidoros son of Hierax and Isido[– - formerly known as – -] son of
>   Piathres and Thaesis ...
> Ischyrion son of Eudaimon and [– -] formerly known as Nechtherous
>   Pi[sois ?]

council? It is no wonder that official correspondence often expresses frustration. Of course, our evidence tends to be biased toward failure. *Strategoi* did not need to write letters reminding collectors of their duty if they did it promptly. Trouble always produces more documents than success does.

We should also not underestimate the cultural pull of the *metropoleis* and their upper classes to those who had risen economically under the Romans but who did not belong to the traditional elite families connected with the gymnasium. There is no clear evidence whether membership of this group was required to become a councillor, but it seems unlikely that government put up such a barrier, especially because the gymnasial class was historically a closed group, open only to descendants of those already in it (**2.1**). Financial resources mattered more than birth for the tasks facing the council. However, especially for men from a mixed Graeco-Egyptian background, perhaps with some education but not as extensive a Greek formation as members of the urban upper class, the appeal of political and

Figure 3.1.3 Fragment of Thucydides' *Histories* from Oxyrhynchos
An example of a book in the form of a roll containing a classical author, found in a nome metropolis; written in the late second or early third century AD. The fragment (*P.Oxy.* 34.2703) shows *Histories* 1.110. The handwriting shows detached letters in the so-called "severe" style.

cultural status may have made membership in the council worth taking some risks. And joining it would surely have led many to acquire more education. Councillors were virtually all literate, as they needed to be, and even if only a minority of them were interested in literary culture, it was in their ranks that one would find most of the people who owned books and cared about them (Figure 3.1.3).

This new elite wanted to represent itself before the rest of society as people of high rank. Not only did they think Greek names more suitable than Egyptian for members of this inner circle of Hellenic culture, they also found that they liked double names: not just Apollonios, son of Isidoros, for example, but Heraiskos who is also (known as) Apollonios, son of Isidoros. These names sounded highly important, even distinguished, and perhaps helped suggest the bearers' connection to Roman power. As it happens, their peak popularity coincides with the period of greatest importance for the councils, the third and fourth centuries.

Despite these attractions, keeping councils up to the needed number of members was no doubt a challenge. Even if not bankrupted by their liturgies, councillors might lack adequate resources to support the burdens of membership due to poor management of their property. Moreover, the demographic realities of the ancient world meant that many councillors would die without adult sons to take their places, as membership was in practice highly heritable. Young children might eventually grow up to take on the role, if guardians did not steal their inheritance. But sometimes there would be no son, unless one was adopted – a practice barely documented in the papyri but probably used more than we can see. Or there might be too many sons, and an estate would then be broken up among them, because the population of Roman Egypt practiced, in Egyptian fashion, partible inheritance rather than keeping the estate intact for the oldest son. We are today likely to be sympathetic to an equitable division of an estate, but it was a threat to the Roman model of how a city should work, with a governing class that had large property-holdings. We do not know how families responded to challenges of inheritance or how often such problems cropped up. But it is likely that some renewal of the councils with new members was necessary almost all the time.

The councils presented a Greek and Roman face to the world in another, unmistakable way: building. In the third century, the *metropoleis* began to build extensive public structures to display their status as Greek cities of the Roman Empire, creating avenues lined with porticoes, arches, and government buildings of various sorts (Figure 3.1.4). They mimicked the cities of the Greek East that travelers today know, those of Asia Minor and Syria. The archaeology of these Egyptian cities is unfortunately very poorly known, because in most cases medieval and modern cities have been built over their ruins, and neither politics nor economics allows extensive excavation of such cities and the displacement of people that would be necessary. Alexandria, which had already been outfitted in Greek style under the Ptolemies, is the most striking example of this problem. Only when modern buildings have been torn down has excavation, usually hasty and often incomplete, been possible, with the great exception of the complex at Kom el-Dikka (see **4.3**).

For the nome capitals, even less is known. Only bits of Oxyrhynchos survived to be excavated, rather more of Hermopolis, the best-known *metropolis* of the valley. The oasis city of Trimithis, in the Dakhla oasis, was spared overbuilding (although not quarrying for stone), and it may yet be our best source for a city of the Roman period; how typical it was, however, remains to be seen. Much of what we know about building in the

Figure 3.1.4 Hermopolis, monumental center as reconstructed
Hermopolis, monumental center, reconstruction by D. M. Bailey based on British
Museum excavations. It shows at left the so-called "Bastion," in the center the festival
building called the Komasterion, and the four-columned street intersection
(Tetrapylon) through which the main north-south street passed, and at right a temple in
classical style.

cities of the Nile valley comes from papyri, including a papyrus from
Hermopolis with a detailed accounting of expenditures for repairs to public
buildings in the aftermath of civil disturbances in the third century, the
subject to which we now turn (**3.2**).

Bibliography
Broux 2015; De Ligt 2017; Tacoma 2006; Van Minnen 1986

3.2   Violence from inside, above, and outside

Generally described as a relatively peaceful province, Roman Egypt certainly lacked the more dramatic wars and set battles provoked by Rome's
confrontations with Parthia and Persia or by barbarian invasions in the
western empire in the third century. However, we lack narrative sources for
Egypt for much of the Roman period, and with them any ancient interpretation of the situation. The imperial historian Tacitus thought Egypt
a fractious and unstable land (*Histories* 1.11). Even stitching together the
fragmentary information from a variety of sources, however, forces us to
face the fact that the Roman Peace was far from entirely tranquil in Egypt.
Apart from the first-century disturbances in Alexandria involving the
Jewish population (**2.8**), we cannot underestimate the violence of the
great Jewish Revolt.

This uprising, nowhere fully described in surviving texts by ancient authors, originated as a messianic movement in the region of Cyrene (in modern eastern Libya) in 115, toward the end of Trajan's reign. It quickly spread to Egypt, with its large Jewish population, ending only in 117 at the outset of Hadrian's rule. The small Roman garrison of Egypt was at first unable to cope with the scale of the revolt and suffered defeat in battle. Reinforcements from outside eventually gave the Roman authorities the edge and resulted in a bloody defeat of the Jewish population of Alexandria and the countryside, as well as the confiscation of the property of the defeated. The slaughter was so extensive that for a century and a half Jews are literally invisible in the documentary record, after close to four centuries of frequent appearances (cf. **2.8**).

A half-century of relative peace followed, although with a barely known internal disturbance in the early 150s, until the Antonine plague of the mid-160s (**3.4**). There is still much debate about the severity and consequences of the plague, now generally agreed to have been smallpox, but it certainly had serious effects in at least some areas. It was, however, only one of the ills striking parts of Egypt in the period, for we hear of flight from some villages in the Delta even before the plague, apparently to avoid paying taxes. Such episodes of population movement tended to follow poor harvests, the result of bad years for the Nile flood. These poor flood years may reflect changes in the climate, as the long period of favorable conditions that historians today call (by comparison to less suitable climatic conditions before and after) the Roman Climate Optimum drew to a close. A third element in the disturbance of the period was a revolt attributed in our scanty sources to a group called the Boukoloi ("herdsmen" in Greek) or Nikochites (named after an island in the Delta wetlands).

Although this revolt appears in several literary sources, including fiction, these references are contradictory and problematic. From a rare instance of surviving documentary evidence in carbonized papyri from the Mendesian nome in the Delta, however, the picture can be filled out (Box 3.2.1). We know that attacks on villages in the region began as early as 166/167 and lasted until at least 171/172, when reinforcements sent from Syria under Avidius Cassius, the son of a former prefect of Egypt, helped put down the unrest. (For the Roman army in Egypt, see **2.2**.) In the revolt, villagers were killed and settlements burned down. The official reports describe how these attacks, along with disease and taxpayer flight, had reduced several villages to a handful of residents. The rebels or brigands came from villages in the wetlands of the northern Delta, probably in the vicinity of the modern Lake

---

Box 3.2.1 Excerpts from the reports on trouble in the Delta, from *P.Thmouis* 1

In these conditions, the village secretary, declaring that some cast-net fishermen were dead and that others had been killed by the impious Nikochites, who had attacked the village [Zmounis] – a report on this attack was made to the ex-prefect Blassianus by the *strategos* Horion and the centurion Quadratus – and that the population had been reduced to only 5 men, lifted the sums incumbent upon the 26 missing men (col. 116.2–11).

The village secretary put in a separate account sums for the taxes that had been suspended on men from the village of Psobthon Haryoteos of the Phernouphite toparchy for year 8, declaring that already in year 7 the village had been attacked and burned down, as reported to the former prefect Blassianus; he added that the men of the village had gone down from a great number to only 2, who had fled. Following which, and in accordance with this report, the payments were deferred from that year and until year 10; for which reason, for year 11, also, they are put in a separate account, for, as mentioned above, no decision on them has been communicated to me (col. 114.3–21). (Translation Blouin 2014, alt.)

Menzaleh, where they farmed, fished, and herded, and where it was difficult for the Roman forces to find and defeat them.

This revolt was scarcely past when in 175 Avidius Cassius declared himself emperor, attempting to succeed Marcus Aurelius, whose death had been falsely rumored. Although the revolt of Avidius Cassius, which lasted only a few months in Egypt, did not succeed, it was highly disruptive, coming as it did after the preceding turmoil. All in all, the third quarter of the second century was a difficult stretch for Egypt, even apart from the likely death toll from the plague. Egypt also backed Pescennius Niger's ultimately unsuccessful claim to the throne in 193 and was slow to come over to the side of the ultimate victor, Septimius Severus, an episode that did not predispose that emperor to be favorable to the province.

The Severan period did, however, see major developments: Severus' visit to Egypt in 199/200 led to the restoration of a council to Alexandria and the creation of city councils in the nome *metropoleis*, as we have seen (**3.1**), as well as extensive legislation concerning youths, who were a source of disturbance. But the sources also report measures, including sealing the tomb of Alexander the Great, that suggest that Severus remained worried about the local currents of opinion that had led to Alexandrian support of Niger. In 212, the empire-wide grant of Roman citizenship to the entire population through the so-called Antonine Constitution of Severus' son Caracalla marked a decisive point in the evolution of the Roman Empire into a nation (**4.2**). All of these new citizens took the Roman family name of the emperor, Aurelius, adding it in front of their existing name. A man named Horos thus became Aurelius Horos.

Three years later, at the end of 215 and start of 216, Caracalla visited Alexandria. The visit was not a success. Although many details remain unclear, there was a riot just before or upon his arrival, with deaths as well as fires and destruction of statues, quite possibly those of the emperor or the imperial house. The prefect and some Alexandrian notables were eventually tried and executed for failing to handle this disorder, attributed to craftsmen and the youth, who are said to have mocked the emperor's pretensions as a new Alexander. Caracalla ordered all Egyptians (with a few specified exceptions, including those needed to put on the festival of Sarapis in late April 216) to leave the city and return to their homes in the countryside (Figure 3.2.1). Following continued unrest by the youths of the city, he finally gathered them, perhaps just after the Serapeia, and ordered the army to slaughter them. It is hard to say how we should read the accounts of the ancient sources or how we can estimate either the causes or the damage, both materially and humanly, but the ancients certainly saw his visit as a major occasion of unjustified bloodshed and irrational rage. Caracalla himself, however, may well have thought that he was legally justified in repressing repeated sedition and violence on the part of the youths.

The middle of the third century was a tumultuous time in much of the Roman Empire, but for the most part the decades after Caracalla's visit to Alexandria seem to have been relatively quiet in Egypt. Scattered bits of evidence suggest that Middle Egypt suffered in the mid-third century from attacks by nomadic tribes from the south referred to as the Blemmyes. More damaging, probably, was a revolt by the prefect Mussius Aemilianus, first in 259–261 in the service of the pretenders Macrianus and Quietus, then more briefly on his own account, before he was suppressed by the emperor Gallienus' general Theodoros in early 262. The struggle for control at the end of this rebellion led to serious damage in Hermopolis. In the several years following, Hermopolis had to levy special property taxes to cover the heavy costs of rebuilding much of the city center. We cannot say how many other cities may have suffered in a similar fashion.

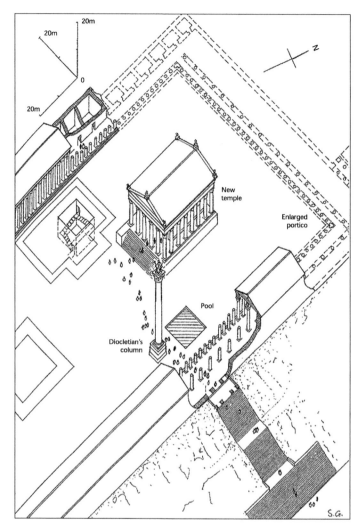

Figure 3.2.1 The Serapeum in Alexandria as rebuilt in the third century AD
Axonometric reconstruction by Judith McKenzie. This vast sanctuary, parts of which
still can be visited, held not only a temple but a library. It was destroyed by Christians
after Theodosius' order of 391 closing the temples (**4.5**).

Despite an attempt at restoration of normal conditions under the
emperor Gallienus, the calm did not last long, as Egypt suffered
invasion at the end of the decade. Taking advantage of the weakness
of the Roman Empire in the 260s after the defeat and capture of the
emperor Valerian by the Persians in 260, the desert trading city of
Palmyra in Syria made a bid for independent regional power, at first
as an agent of Roman power and with Roman consent, but eventually

more on its own. After victories in Arabia and Syria, a Palmyrene army under the general Zabdas invaded Egypt, captured Alexandria, perhaps with some inside help, by November 270, and then defeated the Roman army decisively at Babylon (Old Cairo). The defeated prefect Tenagino Probus, who had committed suicide, was replaced by Statilius Ammianus.

But the Palmyrenes presented themselves publicly as sharers in power with the new Roman emperor Aurelian, not as enemies of the Roman order. Documents from the years 270–272 use formulas referring to both the new emperor Aurelian and the Palmyrene king Vaballathus, the son of the famous queen Zenobia, as colleagues in power. Once free to act, Aurelian thought otherwise, and by June 272 he had defeated Zenobia and retaken control of Egypt with a fleet commanded by the future emperor Probus. Aurelian left the prefect Ammianus in place but added a temporary official, probably above Ammianus, in order to restore order. Some ancient sources suggest that there was civic unrest or even a revolt in Alexandria against Aurelian after reestablishment of Roman rule, but evidence for this is scarce, and some scholars have thought it was fiction. The sketchy sources make it very difficult to understand the background to the Palmyrene invasion and the degree to which it found local support in Alexandria.

It is also far from clear how much damage all the unrest did to Alexandria or other cities in Lower Egypt. Certainly, Alexandria suffered extensive damage at some point during the third century (**2.4**, **4.1**). The entire quarter of Kom el-Dikka, the most extensively excavated part of ancient Alexandria, was rebuilt starting in the fourth century on the ruins of the earlier Roman structures (**4.2**). But archaeological work has not provided a precise enough chronology to say to which events we should attribute the widespread destruction that has been found in the earlier levels. Although the Palmyrene invasion, the recapture by Aurelian, and subsequent unrest are all possible causes, we lack at present any reliable evidence on this point.

A dozen years after Aurelian's recovery of Egypt, and after another series of short imperial reigns, Diocletian came to the throne in 284 and established his control throughout the empire, with the assistance of his co-emperor Maximian, who joined him in the imperial college the next year. In 293, two additional junior emperors brought the number of rulers to four (the Tetrarchy). The changes brought to both Egypt and the whole empire by the two decades of Diocletian's reign have made this reign in retrospect stand out as the beginning of a new era of history. In the standard accounts of Egypt's history, 284 inaugurated a new period. This view, indeed, follows Diocletian's own concept, for he saw himself as representing a new beginning (**4.1**).

But Egypt was not yet settled. A revolt that broke out in Upper Egypt in 293 was put down in person by Galerius, one of the newly appointed junior emperors, who went to Egypt near the end of that year. It may have been limited to the area around Coptos, the great emporium on the Nile that served as the principal gateway to the Eastern Desert and Red Sea ports, but we have only the briefest of references to it in sketchy sources, mostly much later. The statement there that Coptos was razed to the ground is certainly incorrect, as the city was still an active center a few years later, as was nearby Boresis, the other place singled out for mention. The suppression of this rebellion in the Thebaid was, however, sufficiently important for Galerius later to take a victory-title Thebaicus on the basis of it. And it is very possible that he was still in Egypt as late as early 295, which would suggest that the unrest had been more serious than we might guess from the sources. Just a couple of years later came the much more serious revolt of Lucius Domitius Domitianus (**4.1**).

The third century had been eventful – and destructive for Alexandria and some other Egyptian cities. Although the details largely escape us because of a lack of good sources, the Tetarchic government reorganized the garrison of Egypt extensively and built many forts, including in areas such as the western oases that had not had any earlier military presence. It is clear that the government remained very concerned about security. Many of the troubles of the century resulted from external events, but some seem to have been internally generated. It is particularly difficult to tell what was at stake in the rebellion of Domitius Domitianus in 297/298, which clearly had widespread and strong enough support to endure a significant siege of Alexandria. Diocletian's substantial reorganization of many aspects of Egypt's administration and taxation system may have threatened powerful interests that we can barely discern, but too little is known of the background of the revolt to say with any certainty.

Bibliography

Blouin 2014; Bowman 1986; Drew-Bear 1997; Legras 2001; Pollard 2013; Rodriguez 2012; Schwartz 1975; Thomas 1976; Van Minnen 2002

3.3   Intensification of high-value agriculture

Although heritable and alienable private land existed under the Ptolemies, it expanded in the Roman period, and by the fourth century AD even land classified as "public" (paying dues directly to the state; cf. **2.1**) had effectively become private (though still subject to higher rates). The reasons for the growth in private property were complex and have been debated (cf. **2.6**). Likely factors include improved enforcement of property rights, better record-keeping, and the increase in land values due to market integration (**2.5**), as well as population growth. The most crucial factor, however, was probably fiscal, specifically the extension of the low tax rate (generally one artaba per aroura) that had hitherto been accessible only to privileged groups, particularly some Ptolemaic military settlers, to all private land. Since public land yielded more revenue to the state, the Romans made no move to abolish it, but its heavier burdens rendered it more susceptible to abandonment, if it was environmentally or otherwise marginal, as much land in the Fayyum was; if public land was profitable, it was vulnerable to encroachment from individuals seeking to privatize it. Derelict land might be forcibly assigned for cultivation, but it could also be auctioned off, becoming private property in the process. Confiscated land could also exit state possession through the same mechanism, though sometimes (e.g. after the Jewish revolt, **3.2**) it remained public, perhaps because the state was unwilling to depress the land market by flooding it with property.

By virtue of its low tax rate, private land became an attractive investment for groups that under the Ptolemies (and the pharaohs before them) had sought to advance their fortunes through other avenues, principally service to the state and temples. Investment could be either extensive, through the acquisition of more land – it may be noted that the second century apparently witnessed more land under cultivation than any other until the modern period – or intensive, by "upgrading" existing holdings. Improvements could take several forms. The crop grown on a property, for example, might be changed from a cereal such as wheat or barley to something with a higher value, such as grapes. Vines would cost more to acquire and establish, and would require specialist labor and facilities to maintain and exploit, but they also yielded more income per aroura, increasingly so as Egypt's markets became better integrated (**2.5**) and the drinking habits of the population "Hellenized," i.e. shifted from beer to wine. (In pharaonic Egypt, wine was an elite luxury.) Revenue from land might also be increased through the introduction of crop rotation (not

---

Box 3.3.1 A landholder in trouble in the early Roman Fayyum:
***BGU* 2.530 (1st C. AD)**

Hermokrates to Chaeras his son, greetings. First of all I pray that you are well . . . and I beg you . . . to write concerning your health and whatever you wish. Already indeed I wrote you about Tapsoia[?], but you neither answered nor came. And now unless you come I run the risk of having to renounce the property I possess. Our partner has not worked with us, and the cistern has not even been cleaned out, and worst of all, the irrigation channel was filled up with sand, and the holding is uncultivated. None of the tenants was willing to cultivate it; only I continue paying the taxes without getting anything back in return. There is hardly a single plot that the water will irrigate. So you must come since there is a risk of the plants dying.

Your sister Helene greets you and your mother reproaches you because you did not answer her, and particularly [because] she has been pursued by the tax collectors for a long time because you did not send the tax collectors to yourself; but now also send [the taxes(?)] to her. I pray that you are well. Pauni 9. [Address on the back:] Deliver from Hermokrates to Chaeras his son. (Translation Kloppenborg 2006: 490, modified.)

---

typically performed on public land) or other forms of intensification involving greater inputs of labor or capital. Irrigation improvements are a well-attested capital investment. The animal-driven waterwheel (*saqiya*, Figure 3.3.1) enabled the introduction of perennial irrigation to properties and was a far more efficient piece of equipment than its man-powered predecessor (and continuing alternative), the *shaduf*; it also could raise water to a significantly higher elevation. Although already known during the Hellenistic era, the *saqiya* likely did not come into widespread use until sometime in the Roman period. It seems probable that the cost to install the technology became viable only as a result of Roman fiscal reform. Perennial irrigation was indispensable for investment in cash crops such as grapes, and more generally it reduced agricultural risk by making land less subject to the vagaries of the Nile flood. It also offered the possibility of planting two crops a year, though this is poorly attested by our sources.

Investments such as those made in irrigation became more widespread as wealth became more concentrated, and large estates emerged. These were not single large tracts (contrast Apollonios' 10,000 aroura gift-estate, **1.12**) but consisted of fragmented holdings within a single nome or more. Though they are attested earlier in the Roman period, it is not until the

(a)

(b)

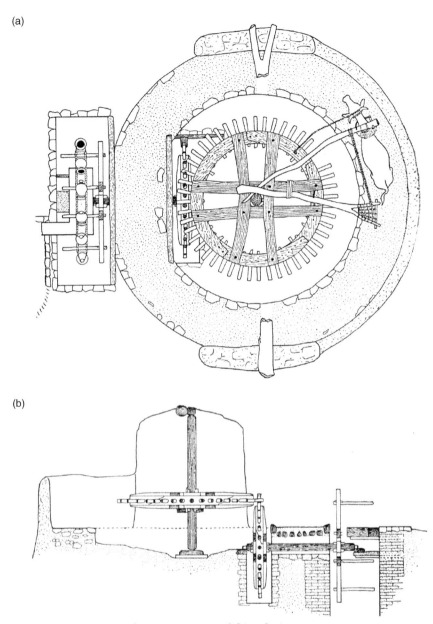

Figure 3.3.1 Drawings of *saqiya*-type water-lifting devices
Referred to as *mechanai* ("machines") or *organa* ("devices") in the papyri, these animal-powered waterwheels enabled the year-round irrigation that vineyards and gardens needed to survive. Requiring a significant capital investment, they were a hallmark of large agricultural estates, and their use expanded as these entities became more common over the Roman period. The top image (a) offers a bird's-eye view of a "pot garland," on which vessels (usually ceramic jars) were used to catch and raise water. The bottom image (b) is a sectional view of a wheel that uses compartments for this purpose.

third century that they become prominent in the extant documentation. The third-century estates undoubtedly did not appear "overnight" – growth in the size of landholdings was gradual during most periods – but it does seem likely that the abandonment of both public and private land resulting from the Antonine plague (**3.4**) and other dislocations that afflicted Egypt in the mid-second century represented an opportunity for rapid growth and consolidation by elite landowners.

Although some archaeological evidence can be cited, this change is most compellingly illustrated by papyrological documentation from the Fayyum village of Theadelpheia (Batn el-Harit). There, in the wake of the Antonine plague, we witness the emergence of a large estate belonging to an Alexandrian notable named Aurelius Appianus, while a register dating to a few decades earlier reveals both a reduction in the total amount of agricultural land and a significant increase in the amount of land paying money taxes (see **4.4** for the continuation of this trend). Money taxes were paid on vineyards and orchards, and it seems plausible that their increase is

Figure 3.3.2 Ancient winery south of Marea
A well-preserved Late Antique winery south of Marea. The vat (*pithos*) is in the foreground. A lion-headed spout (damaged) on the side of the vat farthest from the viewer (in its center) served to deliver the grape juice from the treading floor (*lenos*) behind it. The rectangular hole to right of the spout brought liquid from the mechanical press.

due to investment in such land by elites like Appianus (Figure 3.3.2). Recently, however, it has been suggested that at least some of the taxes in question were due from pastureland, and that the Appianus estate, as a result of decreased local demand for wine, was able to make viticulture profitable only thanks to its deployment of irrigation technology and economies of scale and its access to wider economic networks. That the estate possessed these advantages seems certain; the general difficulty of marketing cash crops in the wake of the Antonine plague is less so. Appianus' enterprise was, in any case, short-lived – its land returned to the state before the end of the century. Theadelpheia itself, owing to its precarious Fayyum environment, would not, however, last much longer, and the broader applicability of the developments apparently attested there is yet to be proven.

Box 3.3.2 Restoring vineyards on the Appianus estate: *P.Flor.* 2.148 (AD 265/266)

The general manager of the Appianus estate (which has been inherited by his daughter Diadora) sends out a letter to his subordinates. Note the close supervision and attention to detail.

From Alypios. Now is the time to take thought for the work. So consider how many of you have irrigated vineyards, now that the land is dried out and ready for hoeing. Before pruning, layer all shoots needing it so that no spot on the "ridges" [reed supports/trellises] is without its vine. Likewise for the [vineyards of] the plain perform the layering before the pruning and do not prune until the spots on the "ridges" lacking new vines are filled. If anyone disregards my instructions, it will not be to his advantage. Gather cuttings of Theban stock and of the white grape, not less than 20 palms in length, but if somewhat bigger or longer provide them like that. Put them into water immediately so that they do not dry out, being aware that for each unit [of the estate] that has been planted I will mark each planting-location with the name of the local manager and vineyard, so that if anybody acts contrary to my orders or puts in any garden stock other than the Theban or white grapes, he will be visited with a penalty that he does not expect. Farewell. I have [already] marked many plantings. [2nd hand] To Heroninos, the manager of [the unit at] Thaso [i.e. Theadelpheia]. Year 13, Tybi. [On the back:] From Alypios to Heroninos the manager of [the unit at] Thraso. (Translation Kloppenborg 2006: 535–536, modified.)

Bibliography
Bowman 2013; Kehoe 1992; Malouta and Wilson 2013; Monson 2012; Rathbone 1991; Rowlandson 1996; Sharp 1999; Van Minnen 2019

3.4   The Antonine plague and its debated consequences

The Roman Empire, along with many other parts of the ancient world, underwent a period of significant stress early in the second half of the second century AD, facing a new set of challenges. A major challenge (**3.2**) was the plague reported by ancient authors to have begun in the reign of the Antonine emperor Marcus Aurelius in 165 and continued until 180, at the start of the reign of his son Commodus; hence the plague is known as "the Antonine plague." It is also known as "the plague of Galen" after the famous Roman medical writer, an eyewitness who gave the earliest preserved medical account of what he called the "great plague." Other contemporary writers (Aelius Aristides and Lucian), as well as later writers, also report the occurrence of the plague. According to these ancient sources, contemporary and later, the plague was severe, with important consequences, and affected many of the key areas of the empire; there are also reports of a plague ravaging other parts of the ancient world, including China and South Arabia, around the same time.

The nature of the epidemic has long been debated. Although smallpox, typhus, and bubonic plague have all been suggested, the generally accepted view among scholars today is that it was some kind of smallpox. This pestilence apparently began in the east in 165 and was introduced to Egypt in 166/167; it is universally believed that it was brought from the east by the armies of Emperor Lucius Verus as they returned from the Parthian War. This was not the first time Egypt had experienced smallpox, as paleopathological evidence shows that an episode of smallpox (perhaps brought from Ethiopia) occurred in the age of Ramesses V, who died in 1150 BC, after reigning for only three years: his mummy, kept at the Cairo Museum, has in fact preserved indelible traces of cutaneous disfigurement attributable to smallpox.

The severity of the plague and its effects in the Roman Empire as a whole and Egypt in particular are not known with certainty. Estimates of deaths range from 1 percent to 30 percent or more of the population, depending on local density and other factors, but the average estimate of loss falls in the 22–24 percent range for the initial outbreak and 16–20 percent for a second wave, corresponding to between 16 and 20 million fatalities in the total population of the empire. However, such overall estimates are drawn from remarks by ancient authors who are not likely to have had reliable information and should be viewed with some skepticism.

The effects of the plague in Egypt, especially with regard to the death toll, can be measured to some extent from the papyrological evidence, especially in the Fayyum. In Karanis in 150–170, the number of inhabitants fell from 3,600 to 2,300. In Soknopaiou Nesos, another (smaller) village at the northern edge of the Fayyum, of the 244 adult males registered in the village in September 178, fifty-nine died in January 179 and another nineteen in February, which means that the village lost almost a third of its population, thus attesting to the long duration, or more likely the recurrence, of the epidemic that had begun in Egypt more than a decade earlier (*SB* 16.12816; Box 3.4.1) (**2.7**). Other evidence has been also connected to the plague: a second-century petition (*BGU* 13.2242) written by a priest from Soknopaiou Nesos, whose house had been robbed while he was out of the village after the death of his two daughters, their husbands, and his wife and many more. A notification of death written in 175/176 (*BGU* 1.79) from the Arsinoite metropolis also reveals multiple deaths in the same family. Funerary inscriptions from Terenouthis, in the Prosopite nome, on the southwestern side of the Delta, record seventeen deaths on the same day, and could be due to a later wave of the epidemic in November 179.

The severest depopulation (between 70 and 93 percent) seems to have been in lower Egypt, in the villages of the Mendesian nome (**3.2**), where, according to a contemporary tax register, more than twenty Mendesian villages were reduced to a handful of inhabitants or abandoned completely in the late 160s. The importance of this tax register

---

Box 3.4.1 Deaths at Soknopaiou Nesos: *SB* 16.12816, col. 4 (AD 179)

Of whom there are 100 men returned as being in abatement, 69 men left enrolled for poll tax at the rate of 40 dr., 2760 dr. With regard to the register of those who died within Hadrianos, 1 (man), 20 dr. Tybi, 59 men at the rate of 22 dr., 1298 dr. Another young man who reached (his 14th year) in the present year 19 and died in the same month Tybi, 1 man, 22 dr. Mecheir, 19 men at the rate of 26 men, 494 dr. Total with regard to the register of dead men, 80; 1834 dr. Total for the village, from the 149 men, 4592 dr. (Translation Hobson 1984.)

is that it makes an explicit connection between epidemic and depopulation or mortality. It seems, however, that the depopulation crisis was present in some of the Mendesian villages even before the outbreak of the plague, as is shown in at least one case in the tax register, and may not have been caused solely by the plague; the plague may only have worsened the situation in places that had faced other problems. Other reasons offered as a cause for the depopulation include *anachoresis* (flight of peasants) to avoid paying taxes. In the Mendesian nome the plague was exacerbated by the development of local brigandage into a major revolt in the 170s (**3.2**); as noted above, the plague, the revolt, and flight are specified as the causes of the depopulation of the Mendesian villages by the official who composed the tax register. It is not clear, however, to what extent this revolt, which ended some years after 172, affected other parts of Egypt. Evidence from other places shows a considerable recovery of the population by the beginning of the third century.

The demographic catastrophe and the shortage of manpower caused by the plague is widely regarded as a leading cause behind the economic changes visible in the late second and third century. Some comparative and statistical studies based on papyrological evidence show that, between the 160s and 190s, prices of wheat and other commodities escalated, accompanied by an increase in real wages. It has also been argued that there was a decrease in the amount of land leased and the length of lease periods, extension of rental terms, decrease of rents in kind, and low tax income. These results, however, remain controversial and have been the subject of revision. Other political, military, or economic causes may have contributed as well. The debasement of currency in 176/177 could well have caused inflation, but this debasement in turn likely resulted from budgetary problems with deeper roots. Climatic disturbance may have favored not only the spread of the plague but also, as noted above, a severely negative impact on agriculture. Egypt had poor inundations during these years, as shown by many declarations of uninundated lands in the Fayyum, the number of which peaked in 164. The crisis therefore seems to have been a complex one, with a network of interacting causes.

Bibliography
Bagnall 2002b; Duncan-Jones 1996; Duncan-Jones 2018; Harper 2016; Rossignol 2012; Scheidel 2002

3.5 Twilight of the temples

As we have seen (**1.8**), the Ptolemies largely preserved the privileges and income of the Egyptian temples and invested substantial amounts in temple-building and decoration. There are signs that some temples were in a weakened condition in the last century of Ptolemaic rule, but in general they remained the centers of their communities, and many were as strong as ever, controlling substantial tracts of land. Income from their estates supported a large priesthood.

With the Romans, much changed, even in the absence of any obviously negative policies on the part of the government (**2.7**). Although the emperors were depicted in temple reliefs making offerings to the Egyptian gods, just as pharaohs had been for millennia, and the imperial cult was introduced into the temples (**2.9**), they did not look to the priests for support or legitimization of their rule. Some of the autonomy enjoyed by the temples in the past was taken away, and even a son's following his father as a priest became subject to a bureaucratic process. Measures of this sort, aligned with broader Roman policies affecting other groups in society, were not specifically aimed at the temples. More importantly still, land that had been directly managed or rented out by the temples was no longer an undisturbed source of income. The temples faced the unpleasant choice of paying rent on the land to the Roman government or of having it taken away entirely in return for a fixed annual cash grant from that government. Neither choice was appealing. The temples had much less control over their revenues than before, while it was private landowners who benefited from the extension of lower rates of tax on their land, even land that had once been controlled by the temples (**2.6**).

The long decline of demotic may also have helped to marginalize the temples. It was mostly in temple schools that the demotic writing system of the Egyptian language had been taught (**2.3**) and the experiments of Old Coptic initiated (**3.7**). The Roman government had no interest in demotic as a language of administration and maintained no court system that could settle legal cases based on contracts in demotic. With the acceleration of the decline of demotic as a language of law and business, already under way in the last centuries of Ptolemaic rule, the temples lost an important social and cultural function. Only priests now had any reason to learn the script. Nonetheless, some temples in which papyri have been preserved, such as Soknopaiou Nesos and Tebtunis, have yielded abundant evidence of the continued literary creativity of these sacred communities, not only

Figure 3.5.1 Mud-brick temple at Umm el-Dabadib, Kharga oasis
The mud-brick north temple at Umm el-Dabadib in Kharga oasis. Most temples in villages and other smaller centers were built of mud brick rather than of the more expensive stone. The temple was subsequently destroyed illegally by treasure-hunters.

preserving and imitating the literature of the past but also producing new compositions that collected priestly knowledge in a systematic way (**2.7**).

Temples had not solely depended on income from landholdings but also benefited from the gifts of individuals living in their communities. Particularly in the villages, where most of the temples stood, they depended on the support of the residents for the construction and maintenance of their buildings, some of stone but many humbler ones of mud brick (Figure 3.5.1). The rural landholdings of Ptolemaic settlers had given these Greek inhabitants of the villages the resources and motive to act as benefactors of their local temples if they wished. Certainly, this kind of giving continued in the Roman period. But as wealth was increasingly concentrated in the *metropoleis* and in the hands of the richer urban residents, and the landed gentry moved away from the villages (**3.1**), there was less wealth controlled by village residents. This process was probably not very noticeable in the first century AD, but as the system of liturgical offices and civic offices expanded in the second century it must have had more of an impact, perhaps already in the first quarter of the century. And the coming of the city councils in the third century, with its mobilization of private wealth in the service of civic life and public responsibilities, can only have intensified the trend.

In addition to temples of the Egyptian gods, many of which had been the core institutions of their communities for thousands of years, the *metropoleis* of the nomes had often built temples dedicated to Greek or Roman gods, imported by Ptolemaic settlers or the Roman government. In general, little is known about these temples, which are mentioned in our documents mainly as structures in the urban landscape or as locations, not as functioning institutions. There is little sign that either they or the urban temples of Egyptian gods attracted an important share of the resources available to the emerging civic elite of the second and third centuries. This newly constituted urban elite concentrated their wealth and effort on competitive civic public life rather than on religious institutions. To the degree that religion figured at all in their priorities, it was in the form of creating a world-class presence in competitive athletic games within the context of festivals, which absorbed resources and energy on a large scale. This shifting focus involved neither any necessary hostility to traditional religion on the part of this elite nor any advocacy by them of an alternative. But it did divert their time and money to other purposes, at a time when all resources were under stress from many sides.

The loss of power and resources for the Egyptian temples, set in motion by changes early in the Roman period, was thus intensified by developments in political, social, and economic life that took time to emerge and take shape. As the Roman Empire faced acute political, military, and economic stresses in the third century, the emperors' priorities did not include support for Egyptian temples. Given all these developments, it would not be surprising if we saw signs of distress already in the second century, and of acute trouble in the third century.

And we do. The indicators are numerous. One important one is the relief inscriptions in temples, recording their construction and decoration, which were always credited to the ruling emperor. This activity was intense under Augustus and fairly widespread throughout the first century, but the entire Theban region and desert oases show nothing after Antoninus Pius (137–161), while other areas show some work continuing until Caracalla (died 217). After that there is almost nothing. With Greek inscriptions dedicating sacred buildings, the situation is hardly different; there is almost nothing after 190. Nor is the papyrus documentation of the priesthoods and their activities much richer; it comes to its gradual end in the middle of the third century. People identified as priests continue to appear in documents, in small numbers, into the fourth century, but their titles serve only to identify them in official or legal contexts, not to reveal any actual priestly activities. Religious imagery disappears from the Alexandrian coinage after the reign of Marcus Aurelius.

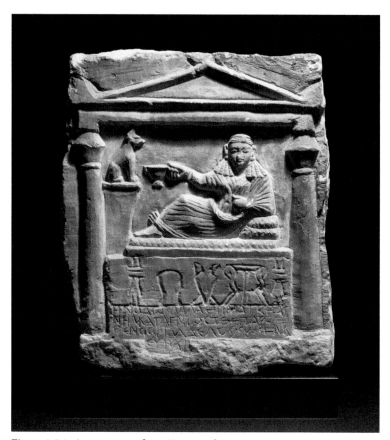

Figure 3.5.2 A gravestone from Terenouthis
This gravestone from Terenouthis (Kom Abu Billou in the west Delta) commemorates
a woman named Heliodora, who is shown reclining and described as unmarried and age
fifty-two, "brother-loving" and a *mathematike*, which seems likely to refer to expertise
in astrology.

Even in subtler, more individual forms of religious expression, by the
middle of the third century we see a sharp decline or disappearance of long-
established practices like the mummy portraits or the carved and inscribed
gravestones of Terenouthis (Figure 3.5.2). Names based on the familiar
Egyptian gods also become notably less popular during the third century,
although those formed from the names of a few popular gods thought to
protect individuals, such as Bes, Tutu, and Shai, remain common.

Despite these signs of stress and decline, it is not easy to chart the fate of
the temples. Hardly any have been excavated with careful attention to
stratigraphy, so that we might find out just when they were abandoned,
demolished, or converted to another use. Even stratigraphic excavation

cannot always tell us what we want to know. A humble example is a mud-brick temple in the agricultural settlement of Ain el-Gedida in the Dakhla oasis, which was turned into a pottery workshop sometime before the middle of the fourth century. Before conversion it was cleaned out so carefully that we cannot give an exact date for either the end of temple use or the conversion into a workshop.

In a few cases, according to evidence from the papyri, temples had been converted to some public purpose during the third century. This is the case with the temple of Triphis on the west bank of the Nile at Atripe, across from Panopolis, which by 298 served as an imperial palace during Diocletian's visit. Both documents and archaeology show that the great temple of Luxor had been turned into a military camp during the third century, although we do not know just when (Figure 3.5.3). Elsewhere we have at least approximate information showing that temples both at major cities such as Herakleopolis and at villages of the size of Karanis were abandoned during the third century, with the temple in Herakleopolis

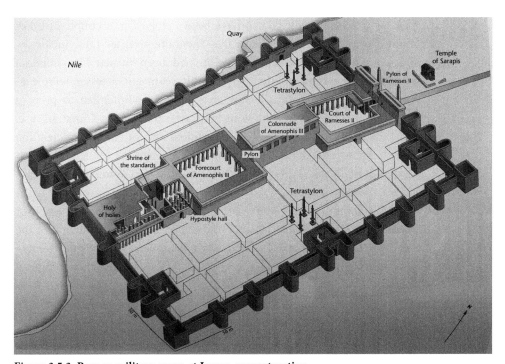

Figure 3.5.3 Roman military camp at Luxor, reconstruction
The Roman military camp built from and inside the Luxor temple, late third century AD. The temple was surrounded by typical Roman fortifications and the area inside laid out in the grid plan normal for the interior of a fort, with tetrastyla marking major intersections.

serving as a quarry for building stone. However, it must be stressed that we have clear information of this kind for only a small number of temples among the large number of known temples, let alone those that must once have existed but have disappeared entirely or lie under modern villages and cities.

Nor can we explain the fate of the temples by reference to Christianity. It has often been supposed that we can fill part of the gap in our knowledge from the accounts of attacks on and destruction of pagan temples that we find in Christian literature, particularly in saints' lives (cf. **2.7**). Far from being trustworthy sources, however, these accounts are partisan, largely fictitious, and prone to magnify the strength of the opposition that saints had to overcome. These exaggerations are a rhetorical means to exaggerate the accomplishments of the hero of a story and not sober history. And most of them were written centuries after the events they claim to describe, many of which happened well after the noted decline.

Matters are different with the writings of Shenoute, the fourth to fifth-century abbot of the so-called White Monastery (outside modern Sohag), who claims to have burned a temple at Atripe, generally supposed to be the great temple of Triphis, and to have been involved in a couple of other temple destructions. It is unlikely that Shenoute invented these incidents, and yet we know that the Triphieion had been turned into imperial quarters in the third century. He may have meant a lesser temple at Atripe, or the purification by fire may have been intended to prepare a former temple, even one long out of service, for Christian use. Shenoute's writings are highly tendentious, and often he is defending himself against attacks that we know only through his replies. Although we cannot easily assess their truthfulness, they do alert us to the possibility – indeed, the near-certainty – that temples fell out of use or were destroyed at widely different times. The common assumption that the emperor Theodosius' edicts against sacrifice and the subsequent destruction of the Serapeum in Alexandria in 391 were part of a universal campaign of temple destruction has no basis, and it is a mistake to date temple abandonments or destructions on the basis of this edict.

These highly visible attacks on temples in a Christian empire of the later fourth and early fifth century, and the rhetorical use of these attacks by Christian authors, should not distract our attention from the fact that, for the most part, the decline of the temples has nothing to do with Christianity, and indeed that there was no systematic campaign of destruction of temples. The impact of Christianity on the temples actually comes later, often much later, in the reuse of building materials from abandoned temples in some churches, and the very rare refitting of temple structures into churches. Even the reuse of materials was not a systematic campaign but a localized phenomenon dependent on needs and opportunities. The decline of building activity and maintenance in most of the temples came at a time when Christians were still a minority disapproved of (and at times persecuted) by the Roman government, not a persecuting majority. As we have seen, much of the decline dates to the third century AD.

However, cultic activities may well have continued in some temples in the fourth century or even later. When the "priests and pastophoroi" of Kellis appear in a receipt for payment of oil in 301/302, we have no reason to think that these titles were meaningless. But a potter is also included in the list under this heading; we should not assume that the priesthood was the main occupation of these men.

Of course, there was nothing new about priests making their living mostly from something other than their priesthoods. That had in fact been the case throughout the Roman period and even earlier. Priests often owned land, for example, or exercised other professions alongside their priestly offices, which they carried out in rotation rather than con-tinuously. And there is good evidence that these ritual experts assembled the major compilations of magical instructions that are preserved on papyri. These texts have a complex history: Egyptian priests composed the Greek spells as early as in the Ptolemaic period in Alexandria or other Hellenized cities, incorporating Hellenistic rather than Egyptian concepts of the priesthood. Only later, perhaps toward the latter part of the first century AD, did priestly circles in southern Egypt adapt these texts into demotic and a shape more faithful to Egyptian conceptions. In any event, it may be that priests in the Theban region in the second and third centuries produced the texts that survive in order to create, as Dieleman 2005 has put it, "an identity that was appropriate for and meaningful within their time, when traditional social structures and religious viewpoints underwent important changes."

It is clear that the transformations we see in Egyptian temples and, more generally, Egyptian religion were not produced by the growth of Christianity, still a marginal and powerless religion during the second and most of the third century. Nor do they necessarily reflect changes in belief about the nature of the world; there may have been such shifts, but they are hard to track. Some of the less formal trends mentioned earlier in this section, such as changes in burial practices and the naming of children, may reflect such developments. Other practices connected with traditional cults had longer lives (**4.5**). But for the most part what we can trace are concrete changes that appear in archaeology and documents, which show above all movements of power and financial resources and the impact of those movements on institutions. These changes are part of larger transformations in the Roman world, as the localism that we traditionally find in religion all around the ancient Mediterranean world begins to give way to an emphasis on universal religion. The Roman emperors bear some of the responsibility for this shift, as the third-century drive for a more unified cult of the emperor and for conformity to imperial orders for sacrifice established an expectation of uniform religious behavior. This drive for centralized control over religion, so foreign to the ancient experience until this time, was to have momentous consequences for the religious history of the later empire.

Bibliography
Bagnall 1993; Dieleman 2005; Frankfurter 1998; Jones and McFadden 2015; Monson 2012; Rondot 2013

3.6 The emergence of the Alexandrian church, then city bishops; the persecutions of Christians

As we have seen (**2.11**), there are only the sketchiest indications of the presence of Christianity in Alexandria before the last years of the second century, and hardly any information at all about the rest of Egypt. In this respect Egypt is similar to most of the Roman world. Starting with the accession of Demetrius as bishop of Alexandria in 189, our evidence gradually becomes much stronger, beginning mainly with literary sources. Once again, this growth in evidence for church institutions can be paralleled elsewhere. Demetrius' long term as bishop, forty-three years, left a strong imprint on the future of the church in Egypt. At the outset, he seems to have been faced with a number of independent house-churches and study groups that did not recognize any central authority. Only over time, and particularly after the Severan persecution (202), was Demetrius able to establish himself in a dominant position and to set the pattern of strong Alexandrian bishops, later called archbishops and patriarchs, that marks Egyptian Christianity from this point onward.

We know much more about Egyptian Christianity in the period from Demetrius until the end of the persecutions in the early fourth century than about the earlier time, but we still have only very fragmentary information. Given the rapidity of change in this period, it is unwise to assume that things we know to have been true in a later century were already the case in the third century. The detailed organization of the church and the clergy that emerges later was nowhere near so formalized and regular as it was to become. We cannot even assume that the classic threefold ordering of the clergy into bishops, *presbyteroi* (priests), and deacons seen in both eastern and western churches later on was widely present at this time. We must therefore balance the knowledge of what was to happen later with the limits of the contemporary evidence.

Most significantly, no archaeological remains from the third century can be identified as distinctively Christian, although by the fourth century we come to have churches in cities and villages, and remains of a few churches have been found and excavated (**4.6**). Similarly, changes in burial practice in the fourth century point to Christian influence on the orientation of bodies and the goods left with them, but none of these changes can be identified with certainty before the fourth century, because most burials lack even approximately exact dates. The lack of archaeological remains of Christianity for this period results in part from the poverty of our archaeological knowledge of Egyptian cities (**3.1**), where most Christians resided in the third century.

The papyri begin to give us useful information only in the second half of the third century. Although this evidence is limited, hard to date, and very scattered, we can at least see that the imperial authorities were aware of the Christians and intermittently sought to repress the practice of the religion, that a network of local churches had developed in the countryside, and that these churches maintained an active correspondence between presbyters and bishops.

It is on the literary side that we first begin to get significant information. Only fragments of the official history of the Alexandrian patriarchate, composed later but drawing on archival sources and generally regarded as largely reliable, survive in late manuscripts and in various languages, including Ethiopic, but those fragmentary sources contribute substantially to the narrative history of the church. Whatever the situation before Demetrius, there was archival material dating back to his term as bishop. Moreover, two of the great figures of Alexandrian theology and philosophy were active during Demetrius' time. The first is Clement ("of Alexandria," *c.* 160–215), who came to Alexandria and taught there in the first part of Demetrius' episcopate but never mentions him in his theological writings – perhaps a sign of the bishop's insecure position in his early years. Clement had an elite education and was evidently wealthy enough to pursue the philosophical life where he wished. He left Alexandria in the early third century.

A still more important figure is Origen. Born into a wealthy Alexandrian Christian family, Origen was impoverished in his late teens by confiscation of the family wealth, when his father Leonides was executed under Septimius Severus, as part of what Christians viewed as a persecution of their faith. The young Origen then worked as a teacher of literature to support his family. His abilities came to the bishop's attention, and he was asked by Demetrius to teach people preparing for Christian baptism, called "catechumens." He began to write extensive treatises and commentaries, with the support of a wealthy patron, and became one of the most prolific Christian authors of the period. His increasing prominence and independence, however, led to conflict with the now-elderly Demetrius, and Origen left Alexandria permanently early in the 230s for Caesarea in Palestine, where he continued to write extensively.

Demetrius also began to build a network of bishops in the nome capitals of Egypt. Although the sources are contradictory, he may have appointed as many as ten bishops while bishop of Alexandria. How many different cities received bishops, however, we do not know. It was Heraclas (*c.* 232–247), Demetrius' successor, who accelerated the rate of network-building in the Egyptian countryside, appointing twenty bishops, according to one source, in a much shorter time. In Heraclas' term we probably begin to see the spread of Christianity in the countryside. Under his successor, Dionysius, we find the first securely dated Christian letter on papyrus, which comes from the 250s or early 260s (Figure 3.6.1). The Christians involved belonged to the highest social level of the Fayyum; the letter discusses the office of gymnasiarch and is written on the back of correspondence from one of the largest estates in the Fayyum. Of course, rich people left more letters behind than poor people, and we cannot leap to the conclusion that most Christians were rich – but they were not all poor, either.

This letter is all the more striking in that it followed by only at most a few years the episode in 250 when Emperor Decius ordered inhabitants of the Roman Empire to affirm that they had sacrificed to the gods in the presence of an official, to taste the sacrificial meat, and to get a certificate showing that they had made such a sacrifice (Figure 3.6.2). Whether this requirement was specifically aimed at Christians and thus can properly be called the "Decian persecution" or thought of as a "persecution" at all is debated, but Christians of the time certainly saw it in that light, and some suffered for failing to comply with an order to do something contrary to their faith. Such individual sacrifice was not a traditional part of ancient cults, and Decius' motives in ordering it are not known. In all likelihood he was seeking empire-wide unity in the worship of the gods, hoping that this

Figure 3.6.1 Early Christian papyrus letter from the Fayyum
An early Christian letter from elite circles in the Fayyum, before the 250s or 260s: *P.Bas.*
2.43v. The letter is on business matters, from Arrianos to Paulos. It belongs to a dossier
connected to a city councillor of Arsinoe who was also involved in the management of
the estate of Aurelius Appianus (**3.3**). It is written by a secretary, but at the end Arrianos
has added his greetings in his own handwriting. The greetings end with the phrase "in
the Lord," with "Lord" abbreviated in a distinctively Christian fashion. It is striking to
find such open witness in a text written not far in time from the Decian "persecution."

would bring him success as a result of the gods' favor. It is clear from the
numerous surviving certificates on papyrus that the administration took it
seriously and followed the emperor's orders diligently, using the well-
established machinery of government. Some Christians took evasive
action, such as getting a substitute to act on their behalf, rather than either

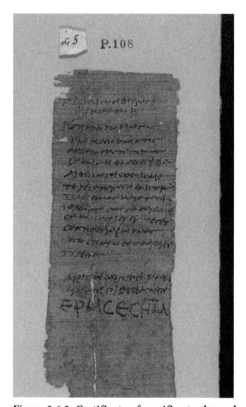

Figure 3.6.2 Certificate of sacrifice to the gods
Certificate of sacrifice to the gods submitted by Aurelius Horion, AD 250; from
Philadelpheia in the Fayyum: *SB* 1.4439 (P.Hamb. gr. 108). Horion declares that he has
sacrificed and poured a libation and tasted the sacrificial offering. Two witnesses to the
act sign below the declaration.

confront the government and risk punishment or betray their beliefs by
complying.

Moreover, a real persecution of Christians took place just a few years
afterward, in 257, under the emperors Valerian and Gallienus. The papyrus
letter mentioned earlier thus was written in an environment in which
repression of Christianity was a current or recent experience, and prominent citizens such as those involved in the letter would hardly have escaped
notice. Their clear use of Christian symbols in the letter suggests confidence that this practice would not put them at risk. Just a year before
Valerian's first edict, a warrant ordered the komarchs (chief village officials,
see **2.1**) of the village of Mermertha, in the Oxyrhynchite nome, to send up
one Petosiris son of Horos, describing him as a "Christian." This is probably not a sign of persecution, although the order is silent on why Petosiris

was to be sent to the city; rather, it likely points to recognition by the authorities of his status as a member of the clergy, a professional Christian. We have no way of knowing the reason for the summons, but given the Roman administration's usual concerns it was probably financial.

In all of these developments, it is important to recognize that the modern habit of classifying people by religion was for the most part foreign to the ancient world. The government did not collect such information; in fact, it is much debated whether the ancients had an abstract concept of religion at all. Even the Jews, probably the first religious group to be recognized as distinct from the rest of society, were originally seen as a people, a nation, rather than a religion. It is quite likely that the Roman administration was, in the middle of the third century, still struggling with the problem of how to conceptualize Christians. Only for publicly identifiable Christians, which meant mainly the clergy, was a Christian identity obvious.

That the church was growing slowly until the last quarter of the third century may be guessed from the numbers of bishops ordained by the next three bishops of Alexandria: twenty-nine for Maximus (264–282); fifty for Theonas (282–300?); and fifty-five for Peter (300?–311). These numbers from the *History of the Episcopate of Alexandria*, if reliable, were enough to build the network of bishops around the country to the point that most of the episcopal seats we find represented at the Council of Nicaea in 325 (**4.6**) were already established by the first decade of the fourth century. Thanks to papyrus finds, we have a number of letters concerning a bishop appointed by Maximus, Sotas of Oxyrhynchos, who probably served for many years, until late in the century. Even before the discovery of an Ethiopic manuscript with part of a history of the Alexandrian patriarchs, Sotas had been identified as a bishop on the basis of five letters to and from him. We see him introducing members or catechumens to other clergymen, and being asked by the priests in Herakleopolis, who address him as "beloved papa," to receive a member of their church. We also see him engaged in fundraising, seeking a donation of land to the church from a prominent Oxyrhychite. He may, in addition, have been involved in the production of books.

The third century has generally been recognized as the time when production of Christian books increased dramatically, particularly the second half of the century, when the network of bishops was growing rapidly. Attempts to quantify this growth, however, have run up against the difficulty of dating handwriting (**2.11**). Christian scriptures are largely written in codex form – that is, in books with pages, and opening from a spine, as we are used to reading today – but the texts cited as parallels for their handwriting come largely from books in roll form. This difference in form has been variously interpreted. It was long claimed that the Christians pioneered the use of the codex, for example, but this idea has largely been abandoned in the face of the evidence. It is also possible that the Christians adopted the codex at much the same time as everyone else, and that the Christian books are not as early as often claimed. Many are undoubtedly dated too early. In any event, it seems clear that many more copies of the scriptures were being produced in the third century than before, and that some of them were being written on parchment, the expensive paper derived from animal skins, rather than on papyrus. In the next section (**3.7**), we shall see that in this period Christians played the key role in developing the use of a new literary form of Egyptian, which we call Coptic, into which the scriptures could be translated. When the authorities went to confiscate Christian books during the persecutions, it is possible that books in Coptic would have been difficult for them to identify (Figure 3.6.3).

Of these persecutions, as the Christians characterized them, three have already been mentioned. The first, which we know mainly from the sixth book of Eusebius' *Ecclesiastical History*, came at the beginning of the third century, not long after Septimius Severus' visit to Egypt, and appears to have been localized and limited. The second is the so-called Decian persecution, launched by the emperor Decius in the first year of his reign, which affected Christians no matter what Decius' actual intentions were. All inhabitants of the empire were required to perform sacrifices to the gods, taste the sacrificial meat, and obtain an official certificate that they had done these things. A number of these certificates survive on papyrus,

Figure 3.6.3 Bilingual papyrus with Coptic and Greek handwritings
An example of a bilingual text with distinct Coptic and Greek handwritings: *P.Brux. Bawit* 22, eighth century AD. The first line is written in a mostly detached Coptic hand, while the second is in a highly cursive Greek hand. The text is a receipt for wine issued by the *oikonomos* Abba Petros to Apa Koum; the part from Abba Petros is in Greek.

Box 3.6.1 Certificate of sacrifice: *SB* 1.4435

To those chosen to supervise the sacrifices, from Aurelius Asesis son of Serenos from the village of Theadelphia. I have both always sacrificed to the gods and now in your presence, according to orders, I have poured a libation and sacrificed, and I have tasted the offerings, and I ask you to subscribe for me. Farewell. Asesis, about 32 years old.

We, Aurelii Serenos and Hermas, saw you sacrificing. I, Hermas, have signed.

Year 1 of the Emperor Caesar Gaius Messius Quintus Traianus Decius Pius Felix Augustus, Pauni 18.

particularly from Theadelpheia in the Fayyum (Box 3.6.1). If Decius was looking to secure the gods' support, however, he failed – he died in battle the next year (251).

After a few years of relief for the church, Valerian began his direct and targeted attack on the church in 257, with a follow-up edict the following year. Although this attack left little trace in the papyri, one very fragmentary papyrus from year 7, probably Valerian's (259/260), twice mentions "Christians" in the plural and seems to be concerned with investigation of the property of the people involved; a prefect's edict is mentioned. This text likely refers to measures taken in the wake of Valerian's edicts. Valerian was captured by the Persians in 260, and according to Eusebius his son Gallienus restored freedom of worship to the Christians.

After that the church had more than four decades without official problems, the so-called "Little Peace" of the church, which coincided with most of Sotas' time as bishop in Oxyrhynchos. It is very likely that a considerable number of undatable papyri containing Christian texts or written by Christians also belong to this time. Only in 303, probably early spring, did Diocletian issue his first edict of persecution, not long after he had been in Egypt for the second time in five years to restore order (**4.1**). A second order, soon after, directed the arrest of bishops. Peter, the bishop of Alexandria, fled. We do not know for certain whether he was newly elected or had been in post for several years. By later in 303, a third edict required the confiscation of church property; we have a reflection of this order in a papyrus from February 304, in which the reader (*anagnostes*) of the "former" church in a village of the Oxyrhynchite nome declares that this church possesses neither gold, nor silver, nor clothing, nor animals, nor slaves, nor building plots, nor any goods received from gifts or wills, except for some bronze material found in the church, which had been delivered to the nome governor (now called *logistes*) for conveyance to Alexandria. He swears an oath by the Fortune of the emperors that his declaration is truthful; and he says that he is illiterate, for which reason someone else writes for him. The whole is drawn up in the detailed and formal prose of a standardized official document, although with some misspellings (Figure 3.6.4).

Figure 3.6.4 The Reader who does not know how to read

P.Oxy. 33.2673. Aurelius Ammonios, the *anagnostes* (Reader) of the "former church of the village of Chysis," declares that the church has no gold, silver, vestments, animals, slaves, or real estate: nothing at all, in fact, except some bronze. He has someone else write on his behalf, claiming to be illiterate. Is this an act of non-cooperation with persecutors? Or did he recite the scriptures from memory rather than actually reading them?

This declaration has given rise to much discussion. Was the Reader Ammonios really illiterate, and if so, how did he read the scriptures? Is his declaration of illiteracy a way to avoid having to write that he swore an oath by the Fortune of the emperors? Was Ammonios the only clergyman for a village church, or had a priest already been arrested or fled? Did the church really have no property except some bronze objects (lamps? liturgical vessels?)? Why are books not mentioned, as they are in many records of persecutions? Although we cannot answer these questions with certainty, we can at least see that the network of churches had spread to villages in the years of the "Little Peace," and that the authorities assumed that such churches might have substantial property, both movable and immovable.

Individual Christians also had property. In another papyrus we can see a similar process of attempted confiscation in the case of a man called simply "Paul from the Oxyrhynchite" mentioned as having been sentenced (to what, it does not say) by the prefect of Egypt. From his name it is likely that he was a Christian. The eminent magistrates charged with finding his property and turning it over to the treasury report that a diligent search of the records has turned up no trace of the man, no indication of a wife, and no sign of any property. If found, Paul could be executed or sent to work in a quarry, but the government was not going to profit from the action. Other Christians avoided trouble by subterfuge; one papyrus mentions having someone else carry out the sacrifice required of litigants in court. Rigorous bishops did not approve of such maneuvers, but they were surely commonplace.

Even this limited papyrus evidence shows us that the persecution was extensive and not limited to the Christian leadership. But the bishops were the most visible representatives of the church, and a number of these were arrested and tried. Their trials gave birth to a literature, recording the proceedings as if in an official court transcript. Of these, the best known is the trial of Phileas, the bishop of Thmouis, an important city in the Delta; there are several known versions of his proceedings, and a letter of his is reproduced in Eusebius' history (Box 3.6.2). Phileas was executed on 4 February 305, after imprisonment and torture. Like other martyrs, he had refused to abandon his faith in the face of pleading from the governor. The persecution created gaps in the ranks of bishops, and Melitios, the bishop of Lykopolis, took it upon himself to appoint new bishops to fill those holes, leading to a major rift with Peter, the bishop of Alexandria, and a long-running controversy in the Egyptian church.

> **Box 3.6.2 From the Letter of Phileas of Thmouis:**
> **Eusebius, *Eccl. Hist.* 8.10**
>
> What account would suffice to reckon up their bravery and courage under such torture? For when all who wished were given a free hand to insult them, some smote them with cudgels, others with rods, others with scourges; others, again, with straps, and others with ropes. And the spectacle of their tortures was a varied one with no lack of wickedness therein. Some with both hands bound behind them were suspended upon the gibbet, and with the aid of certain machines stretched out in every limb; then, as they lay in this plight, the torturers acting on orders began to lay on over their whole body, not only, as in the case of murders, punishing their sides with the instruments of torture, but also their belly, legs, and cheeks. Others were suspended from the porch by one hand and raised aloft; and in the tension of their joints and limbs experienced unequalled agony. Others were bound with their faces toward pillars, their feet not touching the ground, and thus their bonds were drawn tight by the pressure upon them of the weight of the body. And this they would endure, not while the governor conversed or was engaged with them, but almost throughout the entire day. (transl. Loeb)

By Easter 306, Peter was back in Alexandria, supposing that the persecution was finished. It had been spotty and episodic rather than systematic. But he was mistaken; persecution resumed, at first sporadically, then more intensively in late 309 under orders from the emperor Maximinus, who ignored the emperor Galerius' edict of toleration in 311. Only when Licinius defeated Maximinus in 313 did the persecution end definitively.

Bibliography
Bagnall 2009a; Luijendijk 2008; Nongbri 2018; Rives 1999; Schubert 2016; Wipszycka 2015

3.7   The invention of the Coptic writing system

As we saw in the previous chapter (**2.3**), Roman rule led relatively quickly to a decline in the use of the demotic script not only for official documents but also for everyday writing in the private sphere. This decline was not entirely new; the administrative, economic, and social dominance of Greek had already led in Ptolemaic times to a shift in writing practices in favor of the language of power. The depth of the transition can be seen in the fact that not only legal documents but also private letters come to be written in Greek, even between people whose native language was certainly Egyptian. For a quarter of a millennium, there was no written form of Egyptian used in everyday life. It was this gap that Coptic would eventually fill.

But written Egyptian was not dead; it lived in the precincts of the temples, or at least those with the resources to train people competent in hieratic and demotic. The early Roman period is in fact one of creativity and originality in Egyptian literature, especially religious writing. And yet we see signs of stress there, too, as it becomes evident even at the outset of the Roman period that the language had evolved enough that priests had trouble knowing how to pronounce words in hieratic. They responded to this difficulty at first by writing more phonetic versions of words or syllables in demotic above the problem words. As demotic was far closer to the spoken vernacular, the readers could tell from it what the right sound was. Soon, however, some priests took another route and started writing some sounds in Greek characters rather than demotic. Initially, these sounds were mainly the vowels, which were not directly represented in earlier forms of Egyptian. That priests would do this shows unmistakably that Greek was widely used in priestly circles; they wrote their literature in hieratic and demotic not because they were unfamiliar with Greek but because hieratic and demotic were the proper language and scripts for such works and for the temple cults.

The representation of Egyptian words in Greek letters had a long history, dating at least to the sixth century BC. It was not a commonplace or organized practice, and the instances are varied and scattered; most people had no need to do this. But by the second century, the experimental use of Greek signs in Egyptian texts had spread from the hieratic manuscripts into demotic, and we can see the start of an attempt to represent sounds in Egyptian for which Greek had no letter. For example, aspiration, that is, the placing of an /h/ sound at the start of a word, had largely vanished from ordinary spoken Greek by this time, but many Egyptian words required this sound, so a character for /h/, called "hori," was borrowed from demotic. We do not have a large number of surviving texts showing this process, which was far from systematic, but in the course of the second century a full set of the missing consonants was developed. There were multiple lines of development; the consonants were not yet standardized. Other types of experimentation were also going on in the temples, including attempts to create a fully alphabetic demotic script, which we see in some magical texts. But the use of Greek as the alphabetic basis prevailed.

Up to this point, the developments mainly concerned the "glosses" written to help the reader vocalize words that might be hard to pronounce in their traditional writing. It is hardly surprising, however, that people thought to use this new tool, an enhanced Greek alphabet, to write entire texts rather than just glosses. The few early examples emerged gradually after a phase best seen in the ostraca from Narmouthis (Medinet Madi) in the Fayyum, where we start to get longer phrases rather than just short glosses in the late second and early third century. The term "Old Coptic," which has been widely if not consistently applied to this stage, is best reserved for texts that work with a full set of the added consonants in the script, even if not all might appear in a single short piece of writing. Egyptian texts written in Greek characters without these added consonants are indeed known, with the missing sounds either left out or represented by their nearest Greek equivalent. But these are Egyptian written in Greek, not Old Coptic (Figure 3.7.1).

Figure 3.7.1 Egyptian in Greek, with extra signs
O.Narm.Dem. 2.37. In this school exercise from Narmouthis in the Fayyum, of the second half of the second century or the beginning of the third, the writer has first written words in hieratic Egyptian, then tried to transcribe them alphabetically into Greek letters. In some cases, all of the sounds could be represented in Greek characters, but in others a character drawn from the demotic script was needed in order to show a sound for which Greek had no character. This experimentation is part of the long process that led to the development of the Coptic script.

Old Coptic, still unstandardized, represents a phase in which attempts to develop systems of writing Egyptian in modified Greek were under way in a number of places – how many we do not know, but surely more than what we can see from the surviving papyri. The evolution we have been describing is essentially a graphic one, a matter of how the language is written. However, the process was further complicated by questions of language: Egyptian itself was continuing to evolve in this period, from demotic to what is commonly called Coptic. Egyptologists have debated the linguistic character of the independent texts labeled "Old Coptic," but a detailed analysis shows most of them to be essentially demotic. Still, the stages of linguistic development are less clearly marked and sudden than the graphic changes. These texts are mainly religious, astrological, and magical, products of the temple setting in which the earlier experimentation had been taking place. But one private letter on an ostracon, found at Kellis (Ismant el-Kharab) in the Dakhla oasis, linguistically Coptic and using consonantal signs, indicates a use broader than religious or magical. Whether it is properly to be seen as "Old Coptic" or as simply a branch of Coptic that disappeared is not easy to say.

One characteristic of the Kellis ostracon that may mark it as Old Coptic is the absence of any Greek vocabulary. The Old Coptic texts in general almost totally lack loanwords from Greek, unlike classic Coptic, which uses them in abundance. But the ostracon is incomplete. Later Coptic letters from Kellis (to be discussed below), on papyrus, often use Greek words in the opening greeting formula of the letter, which is missing from the ostracon, so we cannot be sure that the ostracon was lacking Greek borrowings. Moreover, the level of Greek loanwords even in later Coptic texts varies substantially, with more vernacular letters less marked by such vocabulary than more literary texts translated from Greek.

It may not be useful to insist too much on categorical distinctions. The process by which Egyptian came to be written in an augmented Greek alphabet was complex, reflected different needs, and took different forms in varied places. It is not surprising that most of the early development can be seen in the temples, where expertise in writing Egyptian was mostly located by the Roman period as demotic faded from the Ptolemaic bureaucracy and was avoided by the Roman administration. It is harder to trace the process by which the earliest forms of "Old Coptic" turn into more ambitious systems for writing entire texts, which must have involved people trained in the temples.

This process probably took place in all parts of Egypt in different ways. In the Alexandrian region there apparently were attempts, eventually unsuccessful, to create a system that minimized the creation of new signs, thus keeping a more purely Greek writing system. What we find in the Kellis ostracon may also have been a dead end, an Upper Egyptian branch without offspring. The standard Coptic of the fourth century and later is ultimately a product, it seems, of Middle Egypt or the Delta, or both, with Upper Egyptian forms deriving from Middle Egyptian ancestors. There was perhaps an original version, with regional variants branching off from one "successful" form. But this remains speculative. We are missing too many of the steps and too much evidence to describe the process with precision. It is particularly difficult to trace the transition from Old Coptic to Coptic, from temple to usage by Christians. Moreover, many of the texts that document the development of Old Coptic cannot be dated with confidence, with proposals ranging over more than a century in some cases. In any case, it must be remembered that Old Coptic is a term used to describe a script, not a language. The Egyptians themselves always called their evolving language "Egyptian," as did everyone else.

The difficulty of dating manuscripts (**2.11**, **3.6**) is also a barrier to understanding just how Old Coptic was succeeded by Coptic proper. As has long been recognized, Coptic has a strongly Christian character. The earliest manuscript evidence for Coptic comes in glosses to biblical manuscripts (Isaiah, minor prophets), generally dated to the third century. The translation of the Bible from Greek into Egyptian made the strongest imprint on the character of the language, and the adoption of Coptic by Christians and its rapid development reflected above all, it is widely believed, the need or desire for Egyptian-language scriptures. That does not mean that the churches of Egypt stopped using Greek in favor of Egyptian; Greek remained the church's main operating language for centuries to come. But it does mean that some Christians who had the means to bring it about very much wanted an Egyptian Bible.

Although finds of Coptic texts are still relatively scarce through the fourth century and even until the sixth century, they include not only biblical manuscripts but several archives of documentary texts. These archives are particularly interesting because they are bilingual, including texts in both Greek and Coptic and, in some cases, texts using both languages. The archives of two abbots of a Melitian monastery in the Kynopolite nome have been published. The private letters are in both Greek and Coptic, but other documents are all in Greek. The earlier of these abbots, Paieous, could sign his name in Greek and received letters in both languages. Later in the century we have the archive of an anchorite named Iohannes (John), probably the John of Lykopolis known from

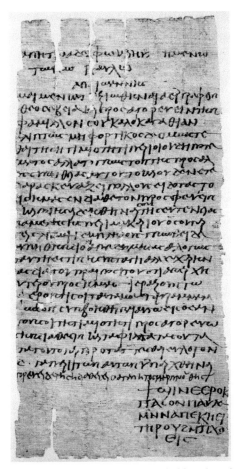

Figure 3.7.2 Letter of John, probably John of Lykopolis
P.Amh. 2.145. The letter has been written in a fluent cursive Greek hand by a secretary; at the bottom, John appends a four-line Coptic subscription at the right side greeting his correspondent Paulos "in the Lord."

literary sources as a powerful monk. Iohannes most likely did not read or write Greek, but he had a secretariat that could do so and received letters in both languages (Figure 3.7.2).

These archives point to an important fact, that Coptic was in this period used especially in monasteries. But the correspondence found at Kellis, which dates to the third quarter of the fourth century, shows that it was by no means limited to monks. Private individuals sent letters back and forth between the oasis and the valley in both languages, and indeed mixed languages within single letters, showing, as with the monks, a substantial degree of fluent bilingualism. This is a critical point: Coptic (as a script) was invented and developed by bilingual individuals as a means of expression; it does not reflect an inability to communicate in Greek. Indeed, the route to learning to write and read Coptic for a long time passed through elementary education in Greek. If anything, written Coptic was a tool of the propertied classes. It is possible that the scarcity of papyri from villages of the Nile valley in this period has obscured a wider use of Coptic in these milieus.

This bilingualism points up a critical fact: Coptic, unlike "Old Coptic," is a term properly used, in this period, only for the script and the stage of the ancient Egyptian language (**6.7**). This language was used by a majority of the population of Egypt, but many members of that majority also spoke Greek, and some of those could write and read Greek, too. The use of Coptic did not separate out a population; it did not distinguish Christians from pagans, for example, or monks from laypeople, or city dwellers from country people. We cannot properly use "Coptic" to refer to anything but the language and script until centuries later.

Bibliography
Bagnall 2005; Choat 2012; Dieleman 2005; Fournet 2009a; Papaconstantinou 2010a; Quack 2017; Richter 2009

4 | The making of Late Antique Egypt

4.1 Diocletian's reforms of administration, coinage, and taxation

The troubles experienced by Egypt in the late second and third century – plagues, political instability, abandonment of land, revolts, invasions, and more (**3.2**, **3.4**) – reflected stresses on the Roman Empire as a whole. A century of adoptive planned succession to the imperial throne had come to an end with the struggle following the death of Commodus in 192, when it was effectively auctioned off to the highest bidder. The Severan emperors could not forget the fact that their power depended on the support of the army. At the same time, inflation following the Antonine plague (**3.4**) and the debasement of the coinage led to not only higher prices but also higher expectations for wages and thus made it harder to keep the army at full strength and content with its pay. The Severans responded with active recruitment and pay increases for troops. Chroniclers of the age disapproved, seeing a deterioration of military discipline and ever-growing greed on the part of the soldiers. What is clear is that imperial resources were not enough to keep up with needs for expenditure, causing repeated rounds of debasement of the coinage by the imperial government.

The decades between the murder of Caracalla in 217 and the succession of Diocletian in 284, in particular, were catastrophic for the empire. They included the assassination of most of the emperors, rebellions by the different armies, conflicts among the usurpers, recurrent outbreaks of plagues, and attacks from barbarian tribes and the Persians. Egypt had suffered from the Palmyrene invasion and Aurelian's recovery of the province; but even before that large amounts of land in Egypt had fallen out of cultivation. Despite the efforts of the emperor Aurelian to patch things back together, when Diocletian ascended the throne in 284 the empire was still in shaky condition. Diocletian tried to resolve the mess left behind by the third century through a series of reforms which he considered a major transformation; historians have agreed.

169

But the fourth century brought much that Diocletian did not foresee or even opposed. His administrative and taxation changes, as continued and modified under his successors, led to a redistribution of power in society (**4.4**), and his attempts to repress Christianity not only failed but were followed by a major, even if piecemeal, transformation of the religious landscape of the empire. Both the institutional church patronized by Constantine (**4.6**) and the more spontaneous and autonomous monastic movement (**4.9**) transformed many aspects of Egyptian life over the century and a half after Diocletian's reign. Constantine also created a new imperial capital, Constantinople, out of the old city of Byzantium. As the empire increasingly became bipolar in the following decades, Egypt found its relationships of power redirected to the new eastern capital, not least because its tax grain began to feed the growing population of Constantinople rather than, as in the previous three centuries, that of Rome.

Administrative reforms

In order to keep his newly acquired grasp over the vast empire, Diocletian divided it into two sections: east and west. In 286, he appointed a colleague as senior emperor for the west, with the title of *Augustus*, and, some years later, junior emperors with the title of *Caesar*, one for each half of the empire, who were intended to become the next senior emperors. He reorganized the provinces by abolishing the distinction between the imperial provinces like Egypt, under the direct supervision of the emperor, and those under senatorial control; separated the civil authority from military; and combined the provinces into larger administrative units, each known as a diocese. The dioceses were twelve large super-provinces, of which seven were in the west. Egypt belonged to the *dioecesis* of the "East" (*Oriens*), together with what is today Iraq, Syria, part of Turkey, and Cyprus. The overseeing governor was known as *comes Orientis* ("count of the East"). Egypt remained under this governmental unit until 382, when it became a separate unit named *Aegyptiaca dioecesis*, ruled by a *praefectus Augustalis*.

Administratively, Roman Egypt had been divided into four sections, the Thebaid in the south, the *Heptanomia* ("seven nomes") in Middle Egypt, the Eastern Delta in the north, and the Western Delta and Alexandria (**2.1**). Diocletian restored the old division of the country into two major parts: the northern part (Lower Egypt) or *Aegyptus*, in which the overall governor, the *praefectus Aegypti*, presided and supervised the governors of smaller units, who were called *praesides*. The southern part of the country was the Thebaïd,

Upper Egypt. This division remained until 314 when *Aegyptus* was divided into two sections: the Eastern Delta and the *Heptanomia* in Middle Egypt were united as *Aegyptus Herculia*, and the other part, with the middle and west of the Delta and Alexandria, became *Aegyptus Iovia*. The Thebaïd remained unchanged. This division lasted only until 324, when Constantine defeated Licinius and took control of Egypt, returning it to its pre-314 division into two sections. In 332, the old *Heptanomia* regained its independence from *Herculia* and became known as *Mercuriana*. (The references in the province names to Hercules, Jove (Jupiter), and Mercury reflect imperial ideology of the period.) However, in 341, after Constantine's death, Egypt was again divided into three parts: *Augustamnica* to include the east part of the Delta and *Heptanomia*, *Aegyptus* in the middle and west of the Delta, and the Thebaïd as the third part beginning from Hermopolis and Antinoopolis. From 381 on, Egypt became again four sections, when *Heptanomia* was separated off to form the state of *Arcadia*.

More significantly, in order to hold a tight grasp over all parts of the country and prevent any one governor from amassing too much power, Diocletian separated civil and military powers; the rulers of the three parts were all civilians, not military men. The army was headed by a military leader known as *dux Aegypti*.

Latin was now considered the main official language in all provinces, including those in which Greek was the traditional language of power and culture, such as Egypt (**2.3**). Despite the increased emphasis on Latin, however, Greek remained the principal language used in courts and governmental departments in Egypt. Judicial reports were partially written in Latin, mainly the heading with address, date, and topic, while the statements of the parties (plaintiff and defendant), witnesses, and judges were still recorded in Greek. In the dating of contracts, the Roman habit of giving the names of the two consuls of the year, the traditional chief magistrates of the Roman state, began to replace dating by the traditional Egyptian years of the emperor's reign. Under Licinius and Constantine the government introduced the indiction, a fifteen-year cycle for the estimation of taxes, which also came to be used to date some types of documents. Only in the reign of Justinian in the sixth century was the use of imperial regnal formulas for the dating of contracts reintroduced.

Under Diocletian, the nome capitals acquired more administrative responsibility, and in the years after his retirement their administrative autonomy was further increased. As a result, the district (or nome) was no longer the main unit of administration, and the old office of *strategos* lost its central role, while that of the royal scribe was abolished. The city council was handed both fiscal and general administrative duties. The *metropoleis* in effect became fully fledged cities, *civitates,* in a Roman sense, with independent administrative systems. The old nomes, now essentially the rural territories of the cities, were divided into regions called *pagi* that replaced the old system of toparchies. Each one had a financial supervisor named the *praepositus*, who was supervised by a nome-level *exactor.*

Monetary reforms

Diocletian's reforms extended to the monetary system. When the Romans took over Egypt in 30 BC, they did not integrate its coinage into the system used in the rest of the empire. Coins minted in Alexandria were not valid outside Egypt, and coins minted elsewhere were not valid in Egypt. Some coins from other provinces are nonetheless found in Egypt, probably because they were brought by soldiers, tradesmen, or tourists, just as Alexandrian coins made their way to other parts of the Roman world. The Alexandrian coinage retained Greek denominations, with the dominant coin the part-silver ("billon") four drachma piece (tetradrachm), with five denominations of bronze smaller coins (Figure 4.1.1–2). Alexandrian coins had Greek inscriptions, unlike imperial coins of other provinces, whose inscriptions were in Latin.

The Alexandrian mint was divided into four workshops, *officinae*, which are distinguishable through the different shapes of their legends. By the

(a)   (b)

Figure 4.1.1–2 Pre-reform tetradrachm of Diocletian, Alexandria, AD 293/294
Obverse: Laureate and cuirassed bust of Diocletian, with his name and title. Reverse: Diocletian mounting a horse. Dated to regnal year 10.

middle of the third century, the number of the workshop was added in the exergue of the reverse (i.e. under the baseline of the standing figure). Following the Ptolemaic tradition, the position of the die in the Alexandrian coins was always in one direction for both obverse and reverse types, so that in turning the coin over, the up direction remained the same. (Roman coins, in contrast, needed to be flipped vertically in order for the coin to be right-side up.) Ptolemaic technique was also applied in the minting of bronze coins, which were struck into convex molds for the obverse, while the reverse was flat in shape. The portrait image was struck on the convex side. Alexandrian coins were executed by local Greek artists, a fact that explains the continuity from Ptolemaic techniques.

The debasements of the coinage throughout the empire during the third century had led by the 260s to a loss of confidence and value in the supposedly silver currency. Diocletian's reform of the monetary system was crucial in that it integrated Egypt into the rest of the empire. From 296, the Alexandrian mint struck coins similar to those minted in the other provinces in their sizes, weights, denominations, minting techniques, and types, as well as in bearing Latin inscriptions (Figure 4.1.3–4). Accordingly, the coins minted in Egypt became valid for use in other provinces, and vice versa. Greek letters (A B Γ Δ) were used only to distinguish the four workshops, not all of which were equally active. Some years witnessed the issuing of a large quantity of coins by one or more workshops while the others remained inactive. Alexandrian minting in any case supplied

(a)   (b)

Figure 4.1.3–4 Post-reform bronze follis of Diocletian, Alexandria, AD 302/303
Obverse: Laureate head of Diocletian with titles. Reverse: *Genius* of the Roman people standing holding a *patera* in his right hand and *cornucopiae* in his left hand.

only a part of the province's needs in the first half of the fourth century, with much of the coin supply coming from external mints.

Imperial coins were in principle minted in gold, silver, and bronze. But the Alexandrian mint did not actually produce all of these at all times, even after Diocletian's reforms, and indeed few gold coins (at 1/60 Roman lb./5 g each) and virtually no purely silver coins (at 1/96 Roman lb./3.3 g) were struck under Diocletian and his successors. A new billon (copper alloy with a small amount of silver) coin of 1/50 Roman lb/6.5 g, usually referred to as the *nummus* in our documents, served for everyday transactions, along with two smaller copper coins, but as its silver content was reduced over the next couple of decades its declining value spurred price inflation.

The coinage reform was followed closely by the revolt of Lucius Domitius Domitianus (297/298; see **3.2**, **4.3**), who declared himself emperor and minted coins in gold and billon in Alexandria in his own name. Domitianus' coins were at first struck in the Alexandrian fashion (Figure 4.1.5–6), but then in line with Diocletian's reformed coinage (Figure 4.1.7–8). The earliest dates in documents by a regnal year of Domitianus are from late August 297, but these come from the Fayyum, and it is likely that the revolt began earlier than that and in Upper Egypt. Domitianus counted 296/297 as his first (partial) regnal year. Most of the evidence dates from the first part of his second year, i.e. the fall of 297. The imperial government soon counterattacked, winning a decisive battle at Pelusium. By January 298, the Fayyum was again under the

(a)   (b)

Figure 4.1.5–6 Pre-reform billon tetradrachm of Domitius Domitianus, Alexandria, AD 296/297
Obverse: laureate head with name and title of Domitianus. Reverse: Nike (Victory) walking right, holding wreath and palm branch. Dated regnal year 2.

(a)   (b)

Figure 4.1.7–8 Post-reform bronze follis of Domitius Domitianus, Alexandria, AD 297/298
Obverse: laureate head with Domitianus' name and titles. Reverse: *Genius* of the Roman people standing left, *modius* on head, holding a *patera* and *cornucopiae*, eagle at foot left.

control of the imperial government, which seems to have also recovered most of the rest of Egypt quickly after some six months of the rebellion.

But the revolt was by no means over. Domitianus still controlled Alexandria, which was besieged for eight months. Diocletian himself, who had been at Pelusium in January, participated in the final stages of the siege in March (Figure 4.1.9). It seems to have ended in vast destruction. Diocletian proceeded on toward the southern frontier, visiting Oxyrhynchos and Panopolis on the way. By summer he was on the frontier, the location of serious trouble with Nubian tribes. He abandoned the attempt to rule directly the area south of the first cataract of the Nile and settled the border at Philae, just south of the cataract, where a legionary garrison was stationed. Everything to the south was left to be stabilized without direct Roman occupation. Diocletian then returned north during the fall and by midwinter was back in Antioch.

The coinage reforms had not ended inflationary pressures in the economy, resulting from the inexorable pressures for higher expenditure for the expanded army and administration, on the one hand, and the shortage of gold and silver on the other. Diocletian clearly felt the need for additional changes. In 301, he issued an edict specifying the maximum prices of goods and wages. The decree prohibited the purchase of goods from areas in which they were sold at low prices in order to resell them elsewhere at higher prices, and threatened the death penalty for violations. We do not

Figure 4.1.9 Diocletian's pillar, 298–299 ("Pompey's pillar"), in the Serapeum.

know how long this decree remained in effect, but within a few years prices had resumed their upward course.

Taxation reforms

Documents from Roman Egypt show that the government collected a large number of both regular and non-recurrent taxes, perhaps more than a hundred in all (**2.1**). Tax collectors were under immense pressure from above to deliver the amounts expected by the government, and they often used violence to collect the taxes. Collective responsibility for payment pushed the demands on to families and indeed sometimes entire communities. In extreme cases, insolvent taxpayers simply fled to other villages, to temples, to larger cities, and even to the marshes of the Delta. Annual lists of runaways were usually prepared to count those who had fled and determine the lands they were obliged to cultivate. Notices went out to other villages to see if the runaways could be located and returned. Owners of the neighboring lands were ordered to farm the abandoned fields (or at least pay the taxes) instead.

Although Diocletian made some changes to the system of obligatory services, liturgies (cf. **2.1**, **3.1**), fundamentally the system was left in place, with some offices disappearing, such as the grain-collecting *dekaprotoi* of the third century, and others introduced, such as the *sitologoi* who replaced them.

By contrast, taxation itself, which had evolved over three centuries of Roman rule, underwent major changes. In 287, Diocletian renewed the practice of conducting a regular census of the population as well as a census of property. The census of the population, which had earlier been carried out every fourteen years, had stopped after the census of 257/258. There is no evidence that Diocletian's renewed census of the population was maintained after his time, perhaps because taxation increasingly fell on property rather than people. The aim of reactivating the census certainly included the counting of taxpayers, but a detailed recording of property was even more essential after a prolonged period of disturbance. In every census, the owners were to declare their property. Landowners had to specify the size and location of their properties as well as their nature, whether private or public property, and the kind of produce, whether grains, olives, or grapes, to mention only the largest categories. A group of officials had to supervise and revise the submitted data and sign for its credibility.

Perhaps most importantly, Diocletian also introduced a new system for calculating land taxes. This system was based upon two fictive units of assessment: *caput* and *iugum*; it is thus known, in modern scholarship, as the *capitatio-iugatio* system. The land tax unit was the *iugum* ("yoke" in Latin, theoretically the amount that could be plowed in a day), while individuals and animals came under the *caput* ("head") unit. Despite the superficial appearance of uniformity, however, the two measuring units did not necessarily refer to the same amount of land or number of individuals, since the meaning of the *caput* varied from province to province and took account of local conditions. In Egypt the assessments based on the *iugum* were translated into the aroura, the local unit of land measurement; the more abstract system is mainly encountered at higher levels of the administration. Exactly how the *caput* side of the reform was implemented in Egypt remains uncertain; evidence is scanty and unclear.

Diocletian's taxation reforms were supposed to be universal and rational, and they were expected to achieve a higher level of fairness in the distribution of the tax burden. But as in any tax reform, there were winners and losers, even if the total burden seems to have changed relatively little; indeed, some land paid much less in tax than before. Those who did not benefit, however, may well have formed part of the support for the revolt of Domitianus, and the new system had the drawback of being more rigid than the old, not taking account of the quality of a year's inundation. Rates thus might seem low in a good year but high in a bad year.

Bibliography
Bell 1948; Boak 2008; Clark 2017; Kent 1920; Milne 1971; Petitt 2012; Robertson 2015; Schwartz 1975; Thomas 1976

4.2   An Egyptian nation in a Roman nation

The turbulent history of the third century in Egypt (**3.2, 4.1**) was succeeded by a very different Late Antiquity, although the three centuries from Diocletian's reforms (**4.1**) to the Persian invasion (**5.8**) were hardly free of trouble. Difficulties with the tribes on the southern frontier continued, and Alexandria remained prone to mob violence. But there were no invasions, no usurpations by prefects, and no major revolts. Explaining an absence is never easy, but part of the reason for the greater stability was probably the increased cohesion of the Roman Empire itself. To some degree, an empire had become a nation.

To readers today, who have known only nation-states, this may seem like a strange statement. But we must recognize that nationalism as we have known it in the past few centuries is largely a modern invention, founded in concepts of national identity. Although in many cases this identity may be largely illusory or imagined, it does not make it less powerful. An inhabitant of one of the provinces of the Roman Empire in the second century is not likely to have had any sense of belonging to a nation. Rome was the ruling power but not a national identity.

As the empire came under more stress in the later second century, and still more in the third century, emperors seem to have recognized that this traditional type of empire was too vulnerable to fracturing. Caracalla's bold move in granting Roman citizenship to the whole population of the empire probably reflects a first big step in trying to reconceive the nature of empire in a more unitary fashion. Diocletian's administrative reforms created a much more uniform structure for the empire, completed the work of unifying the Roman monetary system, and aimed at providing a common taxation system, even with local variations, across an empire that had until then been much more diverse. The repeated but unsuccessful attempts of emperors from Decius to Diocletian to build a common civic religion (see **3.6**) also reflect such concerns. In a sense, they were on the right track in conceiving of the combination of religion and empire as a basis for building identity, indeed of seeing the possibility of religion as a category of identity at all, something largely new in the third century.

But the religion that managed to join with politics to form a durable identity was not the traditional paganism of the Mediterranean world, deeply based in local cults as it was, but Christianity, with its universal claims and network. Christianity's role in forming an identity for the Late Roman world began with Constantine's embrace of this religion and his personal involvement in building the church's institutional capacity and decision-making structures (see **4.6**). The inextricable link between the Roman Empire of the east and the official church was to be a foundational element of the Byzantine world for more than a thousand years.

In a curious irony, however, the same process created the basis for the beginnings of the creation of a national identity in a number of countries. In some, such as Armenia and Georgia, the modern nation is thought to have its origins in just this period. In these cases, the creation of a means of writing the national language was a critical part of the formation of identity, as was Christianization of the population. The same thing was true for Christian Egypt, where the process of identity-building emerges into view most clearly in the period after the reign of Justinian (527–565). That process, central to chapters 5 and 6, created a narrative of the evolution of the Coptic Orthodox Church, with its distinctive character and its distancing from the official Chalcedonian orthodoxy of the future Greek Orthodox Church (see **5.1**). In that narrative, the early centuries of the Egyptian church were retrospectively interpreted as the start of a continuous development of what was to become the Coptic church (see **5.1**). Such divisions, however, were all in the future in the time of Constantine, and we cannot legitimately interpret the developments of the third and fourth century only in that retrospective light. But the later importance that these events took on in community memory must be recognized.

In a curious example of such later reinterpretation, an era based on the accession of Diocletian and used to date events in horoscopes, private inscriptions, and papyrus documents came to be called the era "of the martyrs" in the late eighth century in Nubia (now in Sudan) and from the ninth century in Egypt. The persecution under Diocletian was, of course, the great period of martyrdom in the Egyptian church, and Diocletian was remembered as a persecutor rather than administrative reformer. But the earliest uses of Diocletian's era have nothing to do with Christianity, and even after Christians started to use it, referring to this era in no way distinguished Christians from non-Christians.

All the same, the foundations were laid in the fourth century for the divergences in doctrine and church governance that would ultimately emerge in the fifth and sixth centuries (**5.2**). At first, these divisions were internal and organizational, the product of disagreements over actions taking during the persecutions of the early fourth century, but a major theological divide emerged soon after the end of persecutions with the preaching of the Alexandrian priest Arius, according to which Christ was described as having been created by God the Father rather than having been eternally coexistent with the Father. The dispute between Arius and successive bishops of Alexandria soon spilled outside Egypt and became the object of debate at church councils. Constantine, although not supportive of Arius' theological views, was annoyed by the dispute and eventually sent the bishop of Alexandria, Athanasius, into exile for the last two years of his reign; even after Arius' death and Athanasius' return following Constantine's death, the bishop remained embattled for the rest of his career, clashing repeatedly with other churchmen and with emperors and suffering several periods of exile.

Although Athanasius was in his lifetime a controversial figure inside the Egyptian church, he was by the end of his career, and even more after his death, a revered personage and an embodiment of the church. What could be seen as his persecution thus helped to create a type for the later bishops of Alexandria, who were repeatedly portrayed as defenders of the truth against outsiders. In this vision of Athanasius originated a concept of the church of Egypt as a bastion of orthodoxy.

Bibliography
Bagnall forthcoming; Barnes 1993; Fowden 1993

4.3   Turbulence and renewal in Alexandria

In the third century, as we have seen (**3.2**, **4.1**), the Roman Empire underwent a series of continuous crises. Without experiencing barbarian invasions on the scale of some provinces, Egypt and Alexandria were by no means unaffected by the crises, and indeed responded to the multiple stresses at times by supporting challenges to the established rulers. The reign of Gallienus had been disrupted repeatedly.

But the period of greatest damage in Alexandria begins in 270, when the forces of Vaballathus, king of Palmyra, and his mother Queen Zenobia (Figure 4.3.1–2) marched on Alexandria (**3.2**). The subsequent recovery of Alexandria by Aurelian's army, after a siege, caused severe damage to the city walls and to many buildings, especially in the Royal Quarter, where the Palmyrene army had camped.

Figure 4.3.1 Tetradrachm from the Palmyrene occupation, Alexandria
Obverse: Laureate, draped and cuirassed bust of Aurelian with name and titles. Reverse:
Laureate and draped bust of Vaballathus, with name and titles.

As described by Eusebius (*HE* 7. 21), corpses were scattered all over
the streets among the ruins of buildings. The epidemics of the previous two decades, particularly the so-called plague of Cyprian, had
already cost the city much of its population. Eusebius mentions that
Bishop Dionysius, a former student of Origen, wrote a letter to
another bishop in Upper Egypt complaining about an epidemic that
hit Alexandria in the early 250s, which was so severe that he was not
able to pass through the main road, so numerous were the corpses.

The Soma, the burial complex of Alexander the Great, occupied the
district named after it, located at the intersection of the city's two main
streets, and was the most conspicuous monument of Alexandria. Some
have supposed that the Soma was destroyed in 272 at the time of the
destruction of the Broucheion. However, the last text to mention the
tomb of Alexander is a speech from the late fourth century of Libanius,
who said that the body of Alexander could still be seen in Alexandria
(*Oration* 49.12). If this is correct, it suggests that the Soma survived the
events of 272. The first explicit mention of the disappearance of this tomb
comes from Libanius' student John Chrysostom, Archbishop of
Constantinople (397–404), who said in one of his homilies: "Tell me,
where therefore lies the tomb of Alexander? Show it to me and tell me
the date of his death" (26.12).

More broadly, however, we know that after the additional damage
suffered in Diocletian's subsequent siege of Alexandria, rebuilding was
slow. The royal quarter remained abandoned for almost a century, as
Ammianus Marcellinus (22.16.15) tells us. Interestingly, in spite of his

admiration for the city, which he described as the greatest of all cities, he gives a gloomy account of the royal quarter, mentioning its total destruction along with that of the city walls. Ammianus' account is confirmed by Epiphanius of Salamis, writing in 392, who describes the royal quarter as still in ruins (*Weights and measures, PG* 43, col. 249 C). We should also not overlook the natural disasters that befell Alexandria and caused massive destruction (see **2.4**). The tsunami that hit the coasts of the Eastern Mediterranean in 365, caused by an earthquake off the coast of Crete, is but one example, although perhaps the most dramatic; to use the words of Ammianus Marcellinus (26.10.19), it caused ships to land on the top of the roofs of buildings in Alexandria.

Renewal of Alexandria

The substantial destruction of Alexandria in the second half of the third century left the city in dire need of large-scale reconstruction. Topographical studies show that the reconstruction project began at the beginning of the fourth century, once stability was largely restored. The city walls were rebuilt and strengthened. Sources say that double walls were present, probably in the eastern parts. The seventh-century Bishop John of Nikiu mentions a second eastern gate. We also know that Justinian later built a wall around the lake port named Philae to protect the grain brought from the valley and destined to be shipped to Constantinople (Procopius, *Buildings* 7.2–5).

A new area was chosen to replace the royal quarter as a city center; now called Kom El-Dikka, this area was located to the south of the main Canopic road (Figure 4.3.3). Excavations at Kom El-Dikka, which began in the late 1960s, are still being carried out systematically by a Polish mission from Warsaw University. Kom El-Dikka is the only extensive part of ancient Alexandria now visible that preserves monuments dating to Late Antiquity. It provides us with material evidence of the urban transformations that took place starting at the beginning of the fourth century. A theater-like building has been uncovered along with a garden and a huge imperial bath complex with a large open courtyard surrounded by granite columns, with a black basalt fountain in the middle. Four large cisterns date from the third century, with an aqueduct leading from the cisterns to the bath. Still later, a large number of classrooms was built in this area (**5.3**). As noted above, most of Alexandria remains inaccessible to archaeology because of the modern buildings constructed on the fill that covers the ancient city; our picture of reconstruction is therefore very limited.

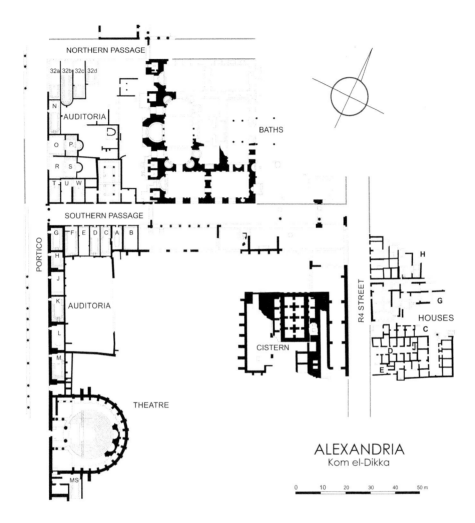

Figure 4.3.2 Plan of Kom el-Dikka
Plan of Kom el-Dikka, showing the imperial baths, theatre, auditoria, and houses.

The area had an older history. Under these massive Late Antique public structures, a residential district in use during the first three centuries was discovered, with peristyle and pseudo-peristyle houses, giving us a sense of Alexandria's elegance before the turmoil of the third century (cf. **2.4**). Among them is House Alpha, the so-called Villa of the Birds, dated to the middle of the first century. The house bears traces of a massive fire that occurred in the third century, causing the house and the neighboring ones to be destroyed and deserted. Stratigraphy shows layers of debris that remained after the area was abandoned for a considerable period before reconstruction began. The destruction of such a residential quarter suggests just how widespread the damage to Alexandria in the third-century conflicts must have been.

To the north of the Canopic street, excavations in the last decade of the twentieth century were carried out in the heart of the royal quarter by the French Center for Alexandrian Studies (CEAlex). These excavations have yielded the remains of some other private and public buildings, including parts of the Caesareum. One of the uncovered houses, the so-called house of Medusa, is dated to the second century. It was destroyed by violence and abandoned at the same time as the fire that destroyed the Villa of the Birds and the other houses in Kom El-Dikka. From this we can again see how extensive the ruin had been, and how partial the recovery.

In Late Antique Alexandria, the Canopic street, or Plataea, was still used, as in earlier periods, for religious processions and important imperial, civic, and other political parades and spectacles. At the intersection of Plataea with the other main north–south street of the city, a Tetrapylon was built. This is a monumental building of four columns carrying four arches and forming four entrances, each of which leads to one direction. The *Lageion*, located to the southwest of the Serapeum, remained functional as the city's chariot racecourse until it was burned during the reign of Zeno (474–491), who financed its reconstruction; it was renovated in the reign of Justinian. As chariot racing became more important in Late Antiquity, racecourses were built elsewhere in Egypt, with various competitors. Hippodromes have also been found in Antinoopolis, Memphis, Herakleopolis, Oxyrhynchos, and Hermopolis.

Early churches of Alexandria

As Alexandria was rebuilt and reshaped in Late Antiquity, churches were constructed. The earliest church we know to have been built in Alexandria was the *Baukalis*. The location of this church is unknown, but John of Nikiu (108.8) states that it was somewhere on the east shore of the city. A martyrium for St. Mark was cut into the rock within the site of this church. The second church to be erected in Alexandria was built by Bishop Peter I (300–311) and named after his predecessor, Theonas. Dedicated to the Virgin Mary, it was located to the west of the Western Harbor at the end of the main east–west street. Expanded by Bishop Alexander (312–328), it remained in use until the beginning of the seventh century. It was later converted into what was called the Western Mosque or the Mosque of 1000 Columns.

Bishop Alexander also built a church inside the courtyard of the Caesareum. It was named after St. Michael but is mentioned in various texts as the church of the Caesareum. It soon became the main cathedral of Alexandria but was destroyed during religious conflicts. The long bishopric of Athanasius (328–373) was the most productive for building churches. The Bendidium (sanctuary of the Thracian goddess Bendis) was converted in 371 into a church and later named after Athanasius. It was located close to the western Agora, near the *Heptastadion*. Rich families funded the building of other churches. By the death of Athanasius, at least fourteen churches existed in Alexandria. But temples had not totally disappeared. At least the temple of Tyche, in addition to that of Osiris at Canopus and the Serapeum, remained standing at that date.

In the last quarter of the fourth century, Bishop Theophilus (385–412) was notably active in constructing churches, either by converting disused temples or building new structures. The temple of Dionysos was replaced by the Martyrium and church of St. John the Baptist, also known as the church of Arcadius, after the son of the emperor Theodosius. Theophilus also dedicated a church in the name of Honorius, the other son of Theodosius. It was a principal church and the episcopal residence of the patriarch. Located probably within the ruins of the Serapeum, this principal church was destroyed in 600, to be rebuilt by Patriarch Isaac (681–684). In 1167, it was deliberately dismantled and its columns thrown into the sea in order to block the harbor against the crusaders. Theophilus also built another church by the name of Raphael on the island of Pharos and yet another church, dedicated to the three young Jews who were thrown into the furnace by the Babylonian king Nebuchadnessar, as well as a third dedicated to the Virgin Mary. The church of Menouthis in east Canopus, also attributed to Theophilus, was the burial place of Bishop Cyril (412–444), St. John, and St. Cyrus, and the district of Canopus was later known by the latter's name, Abu Qir. By the death of Theophilus, at least twenty churches existed in Alexandria and its environs.

Bibliography

Borkowski 1981; Bowman 1986; Carleton Paget 2006; Décobert and Empereur 1998; Derda, Markiewicz, and Wipszycka 2007; El-Falaki 1872; Gascou 1998b; Haas 1997; Lloyd 2010; McKenzie 2007; Pearson 1993; Pearson 2006; Rodziewicz 1984; Roques 1999; Southern 2008; Zibawi 2005

4.4   Elite struggles for wealth and power and the rise of a new aristocracy

There is evidence even during the first century AD for the accumulation of land in the hands of certain rich families, members of the propertied elite that emerged as a result of Roman provincial policy (**2.6**). An emblematic case is that of the Iulii Theones, with holdings in the Oxyrhynchite and other nomes (see *P.Theon.*). But it is in the third century that large estates become a conspicuous feature of the rural landscape, or at least of our rural documentation. The owners of these properties, as was noted above (**3.1**, **3.3**), may have benefited from opportunities for acquisition that arose in the wake of the dislocations of the second century. Many of them were associated with the city of Alexandria and belonged to a social group that drew both from the imperial bureaucracy based in the provincial capital and from its municipal elites, although these are overlapping groups. There was also movement up from the metropolitan class in the *chora* (for which see next paragraph). The best-known representative of the Alexandrians is Aurelius Appianus, whose properties at Theadelpheia and (to a lesser extent) Euhemeria are documented by the Heroninos archive (see **3.3**). This group of texts reveals an enterprise that was overseen by a hierarchy of managers who relied significantly on wage labor to exploit the land and deployed economies of scale in the active pursuit of profit; the estate also spent heavily on irrigation to permit investments in wine production. The extent to which these characteristics were also present in Appianus' other holdings – he is estimated to have possessed 16,000 arouras (4,410 hectares/ 10,900 acres) in just the Fayyum – is not clear, but there is no reason to believe that the Theadelpheian unit was managed differently from others. It is less certain how far we can apply this model of agriculture to the estates of other Alexandrian elites, mostly because our evidence is more scattered. But the use of direct management structures and wage labor, as well as investments in irrigation and cash crops, is documented on the estates of some other owners from this group, such as Calpurnia Herakleia in the Oxyrhynchite. Appianus' estate was confiscated by the treasury before the end of the third century, but an equal danger for other property owners was undoubtedly partible inheritance (**3.1**). During the fifth century, this problem would find a solution in the transformation of large estates into corporation-like entities called "houses."

Alongside the properties of the Alexandrians in the *chora* we find those of the metropolitan elites, the councillor class that arose as part of the municipalization process that culminated in the third century (**3.1**). Their holdings could be substantial in their own right (in the hundreds of arouras), but it is not until the fourth century that this group achieves dominance – presumably at the expense of the Alexandrians, then apparently in eclipse. This shift in the rural power structure need not have brought dramatic changes in the exploitation of the land. Though tenancy may seem to expand under the metropolitan elites, this may reflect the state of our evidence more than anything else; the decision to let out land (or not) was determined by a number of factors, including the owner's resources, the environment, the size and dispersal of properties, crop choice, and available labor. Certain practices – in particular, investments in irrigation and viticulture – continue to be observable in the sources. In the fourth century the landholdings of the metropolitan elite are best documented in the Hermopolis region, thanks to archives from there and two very important land registers (*P.Herm.Landl.*). A certain Hyperechios dominated the region in the early part of the century with well over 6,000 arouras (1,654 hectares/4,087 acres), but within a generation or two partible inheritance had considerably reduced the holdings of his descendants, although they remained among the elite (Box 4.4.1). This elite was a remarkably small group; the majority of landowners based in Hermopolis did not own enough property to live off their rents.

**Box 4.4.1 Landholdings of a son of Hyperechios: *P.Herm.Landl.*
2.241–253**

Herakleon, son of Hyperechios, through Euprepios
6th pagus, 14 arouras … public land 66 $^{13/32}$ arouras
8th (?) pagus, 2 (?) … arouras, public land 48 arouras
3rd (?) pagus, 110 $^{5/32}$ arouras, public land 2 ¼ arouras
10th pagus, 21 ¼ arouras
Through Ailianos, 8th pagus, private land 113 ½ arouras, public land 52
    arouras
6th pagus, 98 ⅛ arouras, public land 5 $^{3/16}$ arouras
12th pagus, private land 12 arouras
14th pagus, 75 ¾ arouras, public land 18 arouras
And in the name of Silvanus, son of Hermapollon
15th pagus, 20 $^{11/32}$, public land 1 $^{13/32}$
15th pagus, 366 ⅛ arouras, public land 1 $^{13/32}$ arouras
(Translation R. S. Bagnall.)

The fifth century brought significant change. This period was once referred to as a "dark age" because the papyrological evidence for it is less plentiful, but to some extent the gap results from editorial choice and the incorrect dates assigned to documents on the basis of handwriting. By the second half of this century the metropolitan class had gone into deep decline, a development traditionally ascribed to increasingly burdensome taxation and service demands. While fiscal and administrative structures are surely part of the explanation, they were not the only factors at work. In fact, by thinking of the problem in these oversimplified terms, we rob the metropolitans of agency, of the possibility that they made choices for their own self-preservation. Surely such choices were made; the question is whether (or why) they were unsuccessful.

That answer lies less in tax burdens and compulsory public services than in competition, specifically competition from a new elite group that had been created by Constantine and owed its loyalty to him. Membership in this new body is clearly demarcated in the papyri: Those on the inside bore the imperial name Flavius as a sort of status designation, marking their membership in the military or the expanding bureaucracy of the empire; those on the outside were Aurelii, a designation going back to the extension of citizenship under Caracalla (**3.2**). While there were plenty of "new men" in Constantine's bloc, the group also drew from the metropolitan elite: Imperial service was the way out of civic responsibility, above all liturgies, and could even culminate in membership in the new senate in Constantinople. "Flight" by metropolitans naturally left an administrative vacuum, one that the empire would have to fill with its own officials (i.e. members of the new "bureaucratic" elite) and through other means, such as co-opting local aristocrats to take responsibility for the councillors' duties (Box 4.4.2; see also **5.5**).

One of the important benefits of membership in Constantine's elite was receipt of a salary in his new gold coin (the *solidus*; see Figure 4.4.1), which from the middle of the fourth century came to be preferred as the medium of payment for private transactions and, especially from the fifth century onward, fiscal ones. The reason for this preference was the coin's stable value throughout Late Antiquity; bronze money and commodities, meanwhile, were volatile. Crucially, the new elites were not limited to receiving gold through their pay. As the imperial bureaucracy expanded into tax collection, the opportunities for profiteering formerly available to the councillors (**3.1**) went to its officials. A culture of extra payments – not yet incorporated into the fiscal system, so still to be seen as bribes and illicit

(a)   (b)

Figure 4.4.1 Gold *solidus* of Constantine I, Constantinople, AD 330
The coin that transformed Late Antiquity: A gold solidus of Constantine I,
Constantinople mint, AD 330. Obverse: bust of Constantine I, rosette-diademed,
draped, cuirassed, facing right; legend: CONSTANTI|NVS MAX(imus) AVG(ustus).
Reverse: Victory advancing left with wreath and palm branch; legend:
CONSTAN|TINVS AVG(ustus), in exergue: CONS (mintmark).

gratuities – offered additional enrichment. Beyond these emoluments
imperial service brought social prestige and occasions for patronage.

The dominance, eventually complete, of this bureaucratic elite enables
us to begin to speak of "the aristocracy" in a narrower sense, of an elite with
a homogeneous career origin and ethos – an "aristocracy of service." Of
course, membership in this elite did not guarantee success, and between the
mid-fifth century and the Arab conquest, it became stratified and then
polarized, as seen in the complex and expanding titulature system
employed by the group (text box 4.4.2 has some examples of the titles in
use). In the mid-fifth century, the Septimii Flaviani, based in the
Herakleopolite nome, appear to have been this aristocracy's most successful members. The first known member of the family, Flavianus I, jumped
from the metropolitan elite into imperial ranks, serving as provincial
governor (*praeses*) at least once. He then became a governor outside
Egypt with higher rank before moving into posts in Constantinople, his
career culminating with service as the palace financial official known as the
count of the sacred largesses – a magnificent trajectory, but one that was
exceptional for the period. In section **5.5** we will see how the evolution of
this aristocracy of service was a critical part of the formation of the great
fortunes of the sixth century.

> **Box 4.4.2 A wealthy landowner, Apion II (5.5), accepts**
> **responsibility for functions of the city council:**
> ***SB* 12.11079 (571)**
>
> In the reign of our most godly and most pious master, greatest benefactor, Flavius Iustinus, the eternal Augustus and Imperator, year 6, in the consulship of his serenity for the 2nd time, Phamenoth 21, indiction 4. To Flavius Apion, the all-praiseworthy and most extraordinary former ordinary consul and patrician, landowner also here in New Iustinopolis [= Oxyrhynchos], who has been allotted responsibility for the office of father of the city, chair of the council [*proedros*], and superintendent of the city [*logistes*] for the fortunate fifth indiction for the house of Timagenes of admirable memory [= a corporate fiscal entity], in the name of Theodos[- – -], through you, Theodoros, [his] venerable representative, from Aurelius Petronios, towhandler, son of Isakios, from the same city, greetings. I acknowledge with willing resolve and of my own free choice that I give surety and pledge to your venerableness for the same fortunate fifth indiction that Aurelius Pekysios … [here the papyrus breaks off] (author's transl.)

Bibliography

Bagnall 1992; Banaji 2007; Bowman 1985; Keenan 1973; Keenan 1974; Laniado 2002; Palme 2008; Rathbone 1991; Van Minnen 2009; Zuckerman 1998

4.5 Paganism, Christianity, and religious pluralism

As we have seen (**3.5**), the decline of the Egyptian temples began at the latest by the middle of the second century, after which we see little sign of building or decorating these structures. In the third century, this decline accelerated. After the middle of the third century, there are no more documents concerning the sources of income of the temples, nor are there references in papyri after 260 to the reports of the priests that were submitted to the Roman officials, registering themselves and their children and the property of their temples. Mentions of temples and officially organized traditional cultic activities in general are rare, with the exception of some inscriptions indicating occasional dedications to some gods toward the end of the century.

With Constantine's recognition of Christianity in the early fourth century and the subsequent issuance of some anti-pagan decisions,

Christianity achieved not only public acceptance but an increasingly dominant position in the public sphere. According to Eusebius, Constantine in 324 prohibited the establishment of cult statues, consulting the pagan oracles, offering sacrifices to the gods, and private activities in homes practiced by fortune-tellers and soothsayers. His successor Constantius II ordered the closure of pagan temples and a prohibition of sacrifices. Although not all of these measures were either as universal as sometimes supposed or as effective as the emperors wished, the cumulative impact on the institutional forms of traditional Egyptian religion certainly increased. Aware of growing imperial patronage of and support for Christianity, the governing classes may have been drawn to the public practice of Christianity.

But the end had not yet quite arrived for the temples. Under Julian, they enjoyed a two-year breathing space and some imperial patronage. But the emperor, who had been brought up a Christian, retained some of its mentality and concepts, including, most strikingly, seeing traditional practice as a coherent religion in opposition to Christianity, a religion that the Christians called paganism. Julian's actions did nothing to reverse the shift from localism to universalism in religion. Imperial moves were relatively muted under Jovian, Valentinian I, and Valens, but anti-pagan legislation resumed under Gratian, Valentinian II, and Theodosius I, who were influenced by activist bishops such as Ambrose, bishop of Milan (374–397). In 391 Theodosius issued edicts ordering governors to close temples and stop public sacrifices, as well as banning domestic sacrifice. His successors followed his policy.

Contemporary chronicles about the end of the fourth century recount many stories of the destruction of temples and images all around the Mediterranean. In the fifth century, some heads of monasteries such as Shenoute of Atripe, Macarius of Tkow, and Moses, the bishop of Abydos, are described in sources, particularly posthumous hagiographic texts, as having led the burning of temples, the killing of priests, and the storming of houses to destroy private shrines. Shenoute, indeed, boasts of such actions in his own writings (**4.10**). This activity resulted not only from imperial decisions but also from the religious zeal of local bishops and monastic leaders. It is not always easy to distinguish rhetoric from fact in these accounts, nor whether the temples that these men attacked were actually still in regular use.

Pockets of public observance of the old religion remained in some remote places, the best known of which is the island of Philae, and within some small communities in rural areas. The temple of Philae was excluded from Theodosius' decision, issued in 391, to close the pagan temples, because it seems to have been governed by a treaty with the southern Blemmyes tribes, who had not Christianized. But in the fourth century, Philae became a pilgrimage destination for Christians as well as pagans because of the presence of the church of St. Stephen in addition to the temple, which was not closed until 553, by Justinian. The evidence for continued activity in shrines in the fifth century is not always reliable. Stories concerning the supposed continuity of worship at the temple of Isis in Menouthis, 20 km (12 miles) from Alexandria, depend on a single witness, Zachariah of Mytilene, whose account has been debunked.

If we have some ability to grasp the public course of Christianization, it is far harder to understand what the process meant in the religious practice of most people. The gradual vanishing of the public forms of Egyptian religion, which had lasted (although not without change) for thousands of years, certainly did not mean that the mentalities and practices associated with it disappeared. People whose lives largely centered on agriculture remained vitally concerned with the Nile and its fertility as well as with everyday preoccupations such as illness, prosperity, love, and reproduction. All of these continued to be the object of practices that we call religious or magical.

These ongoing practices offered both a challenge and an opportunity for Christianity, and later for Islam. Practices that persisted under Christianity included the consultation of oracles for answers about what the future would bring or how to deal with a present problem. Thus the oracular authority shifted in Late Antiquity from temples to the shrines of Christian saints while the process of consultation remained practically unchanged. More broadly, the shrines of saints and holy men, both Christian and subsequently Muslim, inherited much of the devotion previously given to local deities in village sanctuaries. Such practices, right down to the level of spells, represent ways in which people defined their own forms of Christianity.

Indeed, the number of magical amulets and spells that come from the third and later centuries onward is if anything greater than earlier. It is not easy to say why these methods of seeking divine help become more popular. Although it has been suggested that the decline of the more formal structures of traditional religion led to this increase, the Christianization of Egypt did not lead to any reversal in the trend. Rather, people made spells, amulets (Box 4.5.1), and curse tablets against adversaries part of their own form of Christian practice despite the official rejection of these methods by the Church.

Box 4.5.1 A magical amulet: *P.Oxy.* 7.1060

+ The Door, Aphrodite
phrodite rodite odite
dite ite te e Hor Hor
Phor Phor Iao Sabaoth Adone
I bind you, Artemisian Scorpion
Free this house
from every evil reptile
[and] deed – Now! Now!
Saint Phocas is here!
Phamenoth 13, third indiction.
(Translation from Meyer and Smith 1999: 25, alt.)

Some amulets and spells combined the traditional formulas and figures from Egyptian religion with Christian symbols and names, such as the cross or the first letters of the name of Christ (XP) or the symbol of alpha and omega, the first and last letters of the Greek alphabet and symbols of the beginning and the end (AΩ). We cannot classify the people who used these magical methods as Christian or pagan on the basis of their contents, nor do they seem to be the exclusive practice of any social or economic class. Neither Christianity nor Islam succeeded in dispelling the widespread conviction that these practices were effective. It is no exaggeration to say that magic is still practiced, with the substitution of different names for demons. Indeed, the ancient Adonai and Sabaoth invocations are still found in the magical talismans of contemporary Muslims.

Even leaving aside magic, the broad range of these practices was certainly not universally approved. Leaders such as bishops and monastic abbots attacked what they characterized as paganism and what in modern times have sometimes been termed pagan survivals. For these "reformers," such practices were not consistent with a pure Christianity. The surviving literary sources, and even documents, largely come from people in positions of power and show their hostility to activities that reflect the individual choices of ordinary people. But enough evidence survives to show that this official view could not always be imposed, and even some religious leaders took a more benign view of what might instead be seen as the Christianization of social practices.

Similar conflicts emerged later with Islam, where puristic views have also become prominent at times. In recent years, such pressures, amplified by modern media, have led to a decline in visits to the shrines of holy men and to the abandonment of traditional festivals. These celebrations, which were a time-honored tradition of Egypt for thousands of years, are now limited to a few holy men at the shrines of El-Badawy in Tanta, El-Desouki in Desouk, and El-Morsi in Alexandria. Pilgrimage, in contrast, has enjoyed a substantial revival in both Islam and Christianity.

The evolution of burial practices is another area of great complexity. In Egyptian religion, a number of categories of funerary workers held priestly status, and the mummification practices for which the Egyptians were famous in antiquity, and which remain a focus of popular fascination today, were closely tied to religious doctrines about the afterlife and how the preparation of the body was connected to the fate of the individual after death. Despite this general emphasis on mummification, however, actual funerary practices in the Ptolemaic and Roman period varied considerably. Not only did rich people enjoy more elaborate standards of preparation of the body, the presentation of the mummy varied widely from place to place, as did the degree to which visual markers of burial places were provided.

This variety seems only to intensify with Christianization. Mummification became less common, and bodies instead were often wrapped in multiple layers of cloth – or nothing; however, traditional procedures did not altogether disappear for many years. Some cemeteries supposed to house Christian burials have distinctive traits, such as the orientation of bodies to face the east, but the degree to which such characteristics have a religious function remains controversial. Although many cemeteries have been excavated in recent decades, only some of them are fully published so far, and the subject remains a lively area of scholarly debate (Figure 4.5.1, 4.5.2).

The Serapeum

The last reference to a festival in the Serapeum of Alexandria is not later than the first quarter of the fourth century. Some believe that the Serapeum was closed in 325 on the orders of Constantine, but it is clear that it was still in use to some degree until the emperor Theodosius' decree in 391 to close all pagan temples. Seizing on this decision, Bishop Theophilus went to the temple with a large group of Christians hostile to paganism and pagan buildings. Theophilus stood at the entrance and read aloud the emperor's decree in front of the excitable multitudes. He ascended the great stairs with enthusiasm and entered the Holy of Holies, where he struck the cult statue with his ax, separating the head from the body, whereupon the crowd set

Figure 4.5.1 **Eucharist scene in the Tomb of Wescher, Kom El-Shoqafa**
Late third or early fourth century.

Figure 4.5.2 **Tomb VII in Tabiet Saleh, with Christian symbols on the eastern wall of a tomb at Gabbari**
Third century. Christian symbols have been painted on the eastern wall of this originally pagan tomb at Gabbari.

out to loot and destroy the temple's possessions, leaving no stone of it in place (Theodoret, *H.E.* 5, 22; Eunapius, *Vita Aedesii*, 77–78). The head of the cult statue was dragged into the streets of the city and burned, and its ashes were scattered. It is possible that the "daughter library," said to have been located in the rooms of the portico that surrounded the western and southern sides of the temple, was destroyed at the same time, although this is far from certain (Aphthonius, *Progymnasmata* 40; Rufinus, *H.E.* 2. 23.).

For Christians, the destruction of the Serapeum was a great victory worthy of celebration. An illuminated manuscript written in Coptic and dated between the fifth and seventh centuries, kept in the Pushkin Museum in Moscow, is entitled "The Alexandrian World Chronicle." In this manuscript, we can identify a manifestation of this celebration in a painting where Bishop Theophilus is represented standing in ceremonial clothes on the roof of a Greek building with the statue of Sarapis wearing a basket-shaped crown. Theophilus holds a codex book, probably the Bible, with the cross on the cover (Figure 4.5.3).

Hypatia

The most emblematic and celebrated figure of Alexandrian learning in the late fourth and early fifth century was the mathematician Hypatia; however, she also came to be a symbol of Christian intolerance. The daughter of the famous philosopher, mathematician, and astronomer Theon, Hypatia was an eloquent and gifted teacher who drew high-ranking young students from Egypt and abroad. Her students came from various backgrounds, both pagan and Christian, some from prominent families with political influence. These connections offered her an opportunity to play an active role in finding peaceful solutions to some of the conflicts between rival factions in late fourth- and early fifth-century Alexandria.

Hypatia unintentionally became part of a major dispute in 412–415 between the imperial governor Orestes and Cyril, the successor to Theophilus as the bishop of Alexandria. Cyril led a campaign against the Hellenic philosophical school headed by Hypatia. Moreover, he took action against Christians with dissenting views. Cyril also attacked the Jews and is said to have expelled them from the city, an action that provoked Orestes, who saw in Cyril's actions an infringement on his own powers. When Hypatia took the side of the governor, extremist Christians became enraged, regarding her position as a threat because of her character and influence. Cyril's supporters murdered Hypatia. In the account by Damascius (458–538), who visited Alexandria decades later, Hypatia's

Figure 4.5.3 Theophilus standing over the ruins of the Serapeum
Theophilus standing over the ruins of the Serapeum, in a drawing on papyrus in a copy
of the "Alexandrian World Chronicle."

killing was instigated by Cyril out of jealousy. By contrast, John of Nikiu (fl.
680–695), who was a bishop and head of Lower Egypt's monasteries,
portrays her as a famous woman who appeared to work in philosophy
but was in fact a demon working magic to control the minds of the people,
making the Christian governor cease going to church, and attracting
Christian believers to her classes (John of Nikiu, *Chronicle* 88). In John's
account, Hypatia was sitting on her lofty chair when men dragged her into
and through the streets to the church of the Caesareum, where they
stripped off her clothes, tore her body apart limb by limb with tiles and
shells, and then carried the pieces to a place called *Cinaron* and burned

them (cf. Socrates, *Hist. Eccl.* 3.10). The reference to a high seat in John's account indicates that Hypatia was sitting in a lecture hall. Perhaps this was one of those in the complex at Kom el-Dikka (**5.3**).

Religious pluralism

Alexandria in the first three centuries offered a remarkable range of philosophical and religious ideas, around which formed groups of adherents and followers. Modern scholars have tended to see these as a cluster of distinct organized groups. However, with a stronger sense of the fluidity of religious commitments and affiliations, scholars are now more reluctant to take at face value the terms with which ancient polemicists attacked one another.

A good example is "gnosticism," which was not an organized school but rather a set of ideas drawn from Jewish, Christian, and pagan sources. Even that description may be too coherent, and some scholars have rejected the entire concept. The scriptures that embody these ideas indicate their belief in the spiritual knowledge, *gnosis*, which a person can attain only through personal meditation. But the ideas that we associate with "gnosticism" came into conflict early with the strain of Christianity that ultimately established itself at the Council of Nicaea as "orthodox." Eventually the distrust of church leaders for the writings of those described as gnostics reached the point that Bishop Athanasius warned in 367 that their literature was apocryphal and should not be read (Box 4.5.2).

The situation is different with Manichaeism, a religious movement originating with its founding prophet Mani, in Mesopotamia. By the 260s it had found its way to Egypt, where large numbers of its sacred writings have been rediscovered and edited in modern times. Manichaeism embraced a sharply dualistic principle of good and evil. The movement was very wide in its appeal and its missionary activity, which eventually extended deep into Central Asia as well as throughout the Mediterranean. However, Manichaeans in general saw themselves as the true Christians, not as adherents of a separate religion. St. Augustine as a young man was strongly attracted to Manichaeism. In fourth-century Egypt, the Fayyum and Lykopolis were important centers of Manichaeism, as was the oasis of Dakhla, which had an active Manichaean community. Shenoute attacked gnosticism and Manichaeism, perhaps indicating their continuing presence in the fifth century, although it is not always clear that the objects of his attacks are the people he says they are.

> ### Box 4.5.2 Athanasius on prohibited books: *Festal Letter* 39.21–23
>
> Nevertheless, beloved, the former books [the Old and New Testaments] are canonized; the latter [seven other works] are (only) read; and there is no mention of the apocryphal books. Rather, (the category of apocrypha) is an invention of heretics, who write these books whenever they want and then generously add time to them, so that by publishing them as if they were ancient, they might have a pretext for deceiving the simple folk … For truly the apocryphal books are filled with myths, and it is a vain thing to pay attention to them, because they are empty and polluted voices. For they are the beginning of discord, and strife is the goal of people who do not see what is beneficial for the church, but who desire to receive compliments from those whom they lead astray, so that, by publishing new discourses, they will be considered great people. Therefore, it is fitting for us to decline such books. For even if a useful word is found in them, it is still not good to trust them … Therefore, it is even more fitting for us to reject such books, and let us command ourselves not to proclaim anything in them nor to speak anything in them with those who want to be instructed. (Translation Brakke 2010: 61–62.)

As we shall see (**4.7**), the Jewish community of Egypt, despite its destruction in the revolt under Trajan (**2.8**), eventually recovered to some extent in the later third century. Narrative sources say that the Jews joined with the pagans in attacking some churches in the 330s and 370s, but one must be cautious here, again, as Christian preachers were prone to describe as Jews even Christians who disagreed with them. The Jews are said to have tried to destroy St. Michael's Church in the riot that took place in 414/415. Nonetheless, the relationship between Christians and Jews was for the most part one of coexistence, and despite imperial decrees that prevented the marriage of Jews with Christians, this practice also continued.

Religious pluralism, however unwelcome to many, remained a reality in Late Antique Alexandria. A part of the Egyptian church, supporting its bishop Dioscorus, did not accept the decisions of the Council of Chalcedon in 451 (**5.1** and **5.2**), and an anti-Chalcedonian church eventually split from an official church that followed the council's doctrines. But this was a slow process and took full shape only in the later sixth century. The Miaphysite (anti-Chalcedonian) doctrine remained dominant not only in Egypt, but also in Syria, Armenia, Nubia, and Ethiopia (**6.1**).

Bibliography
Bagnall 1993; Bell 1952; Bénazeth and Rutschowscaya 2020; Bowman 1986;
Cameron 2007; Driver 2014; Dzielska 1995; Frankfurter 1998; Frankfurter
2017; Gabra 2002; Geens 2007; Haas 1997; Hobbs 2014; Lewis 1983;
Watts 2006

4.6   The emergence of Christian institutions in public; the church and imperial politics

The persecutions of the Christian church by the Roman government (**3.6**,
4.2) officially ended in 313, perhaps as the result of an agreement in Milan
between the emperors Constantine (who was ruling the west) and Licinius
(who controlled the east). Licinius' edict brought peace to the churches of
Egypt, as far as external threats went, but it was only after Constantine
defeated Licinius in 324 and took control of the east that Christianity
started to have an official status and recovered what the church had lost
during the persecutions. Free from outside threats, the Christians lost little
time in developing internal divisions, which led to conflict within the
church of Alexandria for many years to come.

As we have seen (**3.6**), the imperial government had selected the clergy,
Christian books, and church buildings, as points of attack during the
persecutions. Clergy were arrested, imprisoned, and sometimes executed;
books were burned; and buildings were destroyed or confiscated. It is these
same three visible markers of Christianity that best help us understand the
development of the church after it became legal and the emperors were
Christians (with the exception of the brief reign of Julian). Soon after
Licinius' edict, we start to find men identified in documents as priests
(*presbyteroi*, "elders," in Greek), deacons, and readers. For the first time,
such clergy titles are treated as official designations, as if the men with these
ranks were city magistrates or imperial officials; being a *presbyteros* is also
in a sense an occupation (**3.6**). Where previously the government sometimes called clergy "Christians," in the sense of professional Christians,
now they used the official church titles.

The fourth century also shows a steep increase in the number of
Christian books of which we have surviving fragments. Although these
are difficult to date exactly (**2.11**, **3.6**), because we often have only the
handwriting to guide us, there is no doubt about the rise. The number of
known manuscripts doubles or even triples. Many of these are well preserved, and they show great diversity. Alongside many books of the Bible,

there are works that did not make it into the eventual biblical canon, showing the range of views and practices embraced by Christians during this period. The bishops of Alexandria were not friendly to such diversity and saw many of these books as threats to orthodox belief. The long-serving Bishop Athanasius (in office 328–373) ordered the removal of books viewed as heretical in a circular letter sent to the churches and monasteries at Easter, 367 (cf. **4.5**). Scholars have sometimes explained the physical burial of books as a reaction to official hostility.

Church buildings were the third visible manifestation of the legalization of the church. Most early churches were later destroyed in order to be replaced by larger and grander buildings, and few of these earlier structures have been excavated. The Kharga and Dakhla oases offer an unusual opportunity to see fourth-century churches, because many sites there were abandoned within two or three generations of the building of the first churches and never reoccupied. At sites such as Kellis and Ain el-Gedida in Dakhla, archaeologists have found churches built in the quarter-century after Constantine took control of Egypt. These structures adapted existing buildings to create churches oriented to the east, with benches along the walls and a rectangular or semicircular place for the altar at the east end (Figure 5.4.3). These were soon followed by purpose-built churches of basilica style, found in many cities and villages and probably near-universal by the third quarter of the fourth century. Like most buildings, churches in villages were built of mud brick.

The newly official status of the clergy and the need for more clergymen because of the growth of the Christian population posed significant challenges to the church. The church of Egypt was exceptional in the monarchic role played by the bishop of Alexandria, who ordained and was the direct superior of all the bishops in the province, roughly seventy at the time of the Council of Nicaea in 325, rising to nearly a hundred by the end of the century. Unlike in other regions, there were in this period no intermediate "metropolitan" bishops between the patriarch and the bishops. If the bishops of Alexandria wished to exercise real control over the church – and generally they did – a tremendous effort of management was required. Their absolute power was disliked and contested by many, and the ugliest struggles of the fourth-century Egyptian church reflect this battle for power. Most of the bishops' seats were in cities; bishops had responsibility for their nomes, including supervising the priests and deacons and conducting baptisms in all of the churches of their dioceses.

At least in the fourth century, bishops were drawn mainly from the educated classes, which means that they were in general well off financially, drawn from the same population as the city councils. For the most part, however, it does not appear that the very richest landowners took on the role of bishop. Although being a bishop did not prevent men from managing their estates, bishops did not in general have other occupations or hold civic office. This lack of other occupation was not true of priests and deacons, let alone readers. Except in a few cases, the position of priest did not bring sufficient revenues to substitute for another income, and most priests of necessity exercised professions of one sort or another – managing property, drawing up documents, farming, and crafts. Although there were exceptions, in general the clergy needed to be able to read and write, and they did largely have a good level of literacy, even if most did not have the kind of advanced educations that the social elite could obtain.

Elite culture was more important for bishops, who emerged in the fourth century as key figures in their local communities. From a later standpoint, when bishops were obviously among the most important people in any city, it is easy to lose sight of just how revolutionary the change was. Bishops went from being objects of persecution by governors to sitting in a conference hall with the emperor himself, all within the working lifetime of many individuals. Their closeness to power came in part from the emperors' desire to see both that the church was united and that it did not take a stance hostile to the emperor. The conflict that emerged between Alexander (312–328), the bishop of Alexandria before Athanasius, and one of his priests, Arius (cf. **4.2**), remained a flashpoint of contention for many decades, with different emperors taking different sides. It is perhaps hard today to think of a doctrinal issue of this sort as a potent political battlefield, but the intertwining of theology with politics is closely tied to the quick rise in the political importance of the clergy under Constantine, the first emperor to get directly involved in church politics and engage personally with individual bishops. The relationships were not all friendly; during a confrontation with opposing bishops in 335, Athanasius lost his temper with Constantine, told the emperor "God will judge between you and me" (Epiphanius, *Panarion* 68.9), and was exiled during the last years of this emperor's reign. This was not to be his only exile in a long reign. And the life of a bishop was anything but secure; Georgius, the Arian bishop of Alexandria and one of Athanasius' rivals, was killed by a mob.

Bishops were clearly public figures, none more so than the bishop of Alexandria, with whom the governors of Egypt had to reckon. Like civic and imperial officials, they had staffs to handle their extensive correspondence and records, and they relied on deacons for a lot of daily administrative work. Their offices were organized like those of the imperial administration or the management of large estates. The workload was greatly expanded by two areas of the bishop's work. One was the creation and maintenance of charitable institutions serving vulnerable parts of the community such as widows, orphans, the poor, and the sick. Such institutions were an important novelty in Roman society (**4.8**). The other was the bishop's role as arbitrator and judge. This semi-judicial activity grew partly out of his responsibility for the clergy; only the bishop could settle disputes inside the church's growing ranks of ordained priests, deacons, and readers. But it also came in part from his pastoral role, guiding the lives of baptized Christians. They might bring quarrels to the bishop of their own accord, trusting him rather than the public courts; but increasingly even the imperial government chose to steer disputes to bishops if they concerned private matters seen as relevant to the teachings and discipline of the church.

The efforts to run a much larger clerical hierarchy, to administer increased portfolios of property, and to guide the lives of the swelling number of the faithful all called for rules. How else could one ensure that the church communicated the same message everywhere and treated people fairly? The fourth century therefore saw a great expansion in church rulemaking, with attempts to develop what is called canon law ("canon" being a Greek word meaning "rule"). Although canon law was internal to the church, the imperial administration was quite willing to let bishops run their operations according to these rules and did not generally interfere in ecclesiastical matters – except, of course, when an issue took on political importance.

Bibliography
Schmelz 2002; Wipszycka 2015

4.7   The reappearance of a Jewish community in Egypt

The end of the great "war against the Jews" (as it was later called) in AD 117 involved much slaughter and destruction of property (**2.8**). The property of the Jewish rebels was confiscated by the government, and cities created festivals celebrating the victory over the Jews; these were still being celebrated eighty years later. The memory of the conflict was lasting. But what happened to the Jewish community? Was it utterly wiped out, or only severely damaged? Did it recover, and if so when and to what extent? These questions have been nearly impossible to answer.

The main reason for this difficulty is simply the absence of evidence. For the period from 117 to the fourth century we lack the relatively rich narrative and rhetorical sources on which the story of the preceding centuries has been based, however uncertainly. The documents offered by the papyri and inscriptions, numerous before the revolt, are no more informative. After 117, for example, there is not a single receipt for the "Jewish tax" that had been collected throughout the empire ever since the Jewish War of 66–70. References to people called *Ioudaios* or *Hebraios* virtually vanish; indeed, Hebraios is not to be found in the papyri again until the sixth century. And the most complicated and problematic of the main criteria used to identify Jews of earlier periods, their personal names, also fails us. Identifiably Jewish names are exceptionally scarce after 117. When biblical names do start to appear in the papyri in the third century and increasingly afterward, they are mostly names that had not in fact been used by Jews before 117, and most of the people bearing them in the third century and beyond were probably Christians.

And yet, despite this profound silence in our sources, the catastrophe of 117 was not the end of the story of Jews in ancient Egypt. (The medieval Jewish community that we know from the texts of the Cairo Geniza is a different matter, and continuity is hard to establish.) A fragmentary papyrus from Oxyrhynchos (*P.Oxy.* 9.1205, Box 4.7.1), dated to 291, records the translation into Greek of an agreement in Latin by which a forty-year-old woman named Paramone and her two (or perhaps three) children, ages ten and four, the latter named Jacob, were freed from slavery in return for a considerable sum of money paid by the "synagogue of the

---

Box 4.7.1 Manumission of a slave from the Jewish community of Oxyrhynchos: *P.Oxy.* 9.1205.1–9, AD 291

Translation of manumission. We, Aurelius ... of the illustrious and most illustrious city of the Oxyrhynchites, and his sister by the same mother Aurelia ... daughter of ... the former exegetes and councillor of the same city, with her guardian ... the astounding ..., have manumitted and discharged among friends our house-born slave Paramone, age 40 years, and her children ... with a scar on the neck, age 10 years, and Jacob, age 4 years, ... from all of the rights and powers of the owner; fourteen talents of silver having been paid to us for the manumission and discharge by the synagogue of the Jews through Aurelius Dioskoros ... and Aurelius Justus, councillor of Ono in Syrian Palestine, father of the synagogue ... (Translation in Rowlandson 1998: 193–194.)

Jews." The Jewish community thus appears as a legally constituted organization with significant financial resources, which is represented here by
two men, both Roman citizens (as one would expect after 212), named
Dioskoros and Justus. Neither name in itself would have told us that the
individual was Jewish. Justus was in fact a councillor of the city of Ono in
Syria-Palestine, a striking fact when one considers the difficulty that
Christians had at this period in reconciling the demands of their faith
with the responsibilities of a civic official in an empire where public
sacrifice was routinely expected. It is not clear how Justus reconciled this
requirement with his faith, nor how he came to be connected with
Oxyrhynchos, but possibly the rebuilding of a Jewish community in
Egypt depended on new immigration from Palestine, not simply a
re-emergence of the survivors from the old community.

Jewish communities then become more visible in official contexts in the
fourth century; a recently published papyrus dated to 309 shows the Jews of
Oxyrhynchos addressing the *strategos* of the nome, acting as a legal body
with financial capacity. Although the text is fragmentary, it is confirmed by
other papyri in which this association is headed by an individual (or several
individuals) called the headman (*kephalaiotes*), just as in other associations,
including occupational guilds. Nor is this organizational structure unique
to Oxyrhynchos; it is found also in the Arsinoite nome.

As time goes on, we gradually find more Jews in the papyri, mostly in
completely unremarkable situations. In one papyrus, again from
Oxyrhynchos, dated to 400, two Christian nuns lease a room to a man
specified to be a Jew, Aurelius Ioses son of Judas, an instance of the routine
daily coexistence and cooperation of members of different religious communities, the most typical situation in Egypt in all periods. It remains true,
however, that the number of such documents attesting the presence of Jews
among the Late Antique papyri is extremely small. Those we do have
come from the major cities such as Hermopolis, Oxyrhynchos, and
Apollonopolis Magna; but as these places are the sources for most of our
papyri in this period, that tells us little about where Jews lived.

And it is not easy to interpret even what we do have. For example, an
account from the wealthy Apion family, dated to the third quarter of the
sixth century, records a payment of about a solidus for rent on "the
synagogue" by one Lazar (*P.Oxy.* 55.3805). The natural supposition is
that this synagogue was in or near Oxyrhynchos, but we would have
expected that the congregation that was wealthy enough to pay a high
price to free Paramone and her children would have owned its own
building, rather than paying rent. Was the community now poorer? Or

were there multiple synagogues, some even in the countryside? Without further evidence, we can only speculate.

And the situation is not much clearer in Alexandria. Some Jews may have survived the revolt there, but we know nothing about their fate in the following two centuries. A Jewish community does appear in Christian texts in the fourth and fifth century, with a Jewish mob playing a dramatic role in a violent confrontation in 415/416, for example, and the archbishop Cyril directing much abuse at them in the following years (**4.5**). Although some scholars have taken at face value the claims about the Jewish community that appear in Christian rhetorical and narrative sources, some of which are much later, that may well be misguided. Christian writers of this period (and later periods, too) have a tendency to use terms like "Jew" and "Hellene" (i.e. pagan) to attack their enemies within the Christian church. Since it was taken for granted inside the Christian community of Late Antiquity that "Jew" was a legitimate term of abuse, alleging Judaism was a powerful rhetorical tool. Alexandria was certainly a religiously volatile place, but to think that the Jewish community was one of the "principal players" in the ongoing drama of public violence in the great city is surely naïve.

Still, it is possible that Cyril's conflict with the Jews was not only real but consequential. The only Egyptian document of Late Antiquity written in Hebrew characters to have a date (417) is a marriage contract composed mainly in Aramaic but with a Greek dating formula and list of dowry goods, which was written in Antinoopolis, even though one of the parties was an Alexandrian. The editors speculated that they might have fled from Alexandria in 415 as a result of the conflict there. Although dozens of other Hebrew-character texts from the period survive, their lack of even approximate dates makes it hard to discern their significance for the history of the Jewish community of Egypt.

Bibliography

Balamoshev 2017; Epp 2006; Fikhman 1996; Haas 1997; Harker 2012; Nirenberg 2013; Sirat 1985; Sirat et al. 1986

4.8   The invention of charitable institutions

Philanthropy and charity were not unknown in Egypt, or the Greek east more generally, before the institutional development of the church. But the character of benefaction in Greek cities differed from the charitable institutions of Late Antiquity in a number of critical ways. Most importantly, euergetism (*euergetes* means "benefactor" in Greek) was not specifically directed toward the needy. In fact, the reverse was often true; funds established to pay for the distribution of food were sometimes limited to already privileged parts of the population. Major gifts funded buildings to adorn the civic space but did nothing to help the poor. One might, while allowing for difference in context, compare such gifts to the donation of a new art gallery to a wealthy university today. And ancient governments, whether local or imperial, did not see public welfare in a broad sense as part of their duties. Public distributions of food, even on a large scale as at Rome, had political rather than philanthropic purposes. The grain handed out at Oxyrhynchos went to privileged groups, not the poor. The poor were seen as a permanent part of society, not a group needing help to rise in economic and social status.

Some forms of charitable work, above all the support of the poor, are found already in the early church and mentioned in the letters of Paul and the book of Acts. These undoubtedly reflect the practices, deeply rooted in the Hebrew scriptures, of the Jewish communities to which most of the earliest Christians belonged. But Jewish practices of the early Roman period are not well known in any detail, and there is no consensus about whether the more organized and institutionalized Christian charitable activity of Late Antiquity was strongly influenced by contemporary Jewish practice, in competition with it, or both.

The resources of the church, as it became more institutionalized and systematized in the fourth century, were concentrated in the hands of the bishops. Charitable work was widely recognized in Christian literature as one of the core duties of the bishop and included the distribution of food, and sometimes clothing, to the needy – the giving of alms. Next to maintaining the true faith, the bishop had no higher calling than to organize and lead almsgiving. The money for this activity came from the gifts of the faithful throughout his diocese, transmitted to the bishop by the churches in the city and the villages. Among the poor, bishops had a particular concern for specific groups of vulnerable people, notably the widows and orphans. Often left without property or money at the death of a husband and father, they were sometimes at the mercy of rapacious relatives even if they did have resources.

But the most distinctive characteristic of charitable work by the church, and one with scarcely any precedent in Greek and Roman society, was the foundation of institutions to serve vulnerable populations. These included above all hospitals, but also orphanages, homes for the poor, social service centers, and old age homes. Such institutions involved significant expense, not only for construction but for operating expenses. Their founding therefore generally involved an endowment, typically in landholdings donated to the institution from which the rents would support the cost of staff, food, and other needs.

The bishops did not face these expenses on their own. Although some institutions in major cities were imperial foundations, more typically they were created with gifts from wealthy individuals or families, no doubt in many if not all cases as a result of requests from the bishops. These institutions regularly bore the names of the donors but sometimes of local saints. Whether this philanthropy is to be seen as competitive with that of the bishop or rather an extension of his activity through his recruitment of rich supporters is hard to say; both may have been true.

Similar questions arise with the charitable work of monasteries, which was sometimes considerable. The best known of these, thanks to the surviving works of Shenoute of Atripe, is the White Monastery federation on the west bank opposite Panopolis (**3.5**; Figure 4.8.1). The hagiographic sources credit this monastery with large-scale feeding of the poor; an

Figure 4.8.1 The Monastery of St. Shenoute or "White Monastery"
The Monastery of St. Shenoute, commonly (because of the color of the limestone walls) called the "White Monastery," near Sohag, on the west bank of the Nile across from Panopolis (Akhmim). This is the church of the larger of the two men's monasteries that were part of the federation led and enlarged by Shenoute.

encomium of Shenoute claims as many as five thousand people were fed. It is not clear who donated the money or property that made such programs possible, or whether generating these funds competed with the charitable work of the bishop of Panopolis, who is never mentioned in Shenoute's works. But Shenoute was an unusual figure in monastic history, and it is uncertain how far we can generalize from his activities – or, indeed, take his claims seriously; the archaeological evidence does not suggest a capacity for feeding people on such a scale. One distinctive aspect of the monastery's work was the care of refugees from barbarian raids. An emergency rather than regular part of its charitable activity, this care involved not only food but also clothes, medical treatment, and even ransoming captives.

The institutionalization of charitable activity was neither early nor sudden. It took place over a long period, beginning in the second half of the fourth century and continuing through Late Antiquity. We have a good opportunity to look at at the culmination of all of this institution-building in one part of Egypt as of the early seventh century, thanks to a tax register (*P.Sorb.* 2.69) and other papyrus documents. According to these sources, the neighboring cities of Hermopolis and Antinoopolis had at least a dozen hospitals, called variously by the Greek terms *nosokomeion* (place for care of the sick) and *xenodocheion* (place for receiving strangers), which constitute almost all of the "pious foundations" attested. Two are specifically designated as hospitals for the care of those afflicted with leprosy. Some are named after benefactors, who are of high status; one is named for a woman monastic, who came from a rich family. Another is called the "*xeno-docheion* of the South Church" (of Hermopolis); there is also one called the *nosokomeion* of Saint Abba Leontios. One *xeneon* (another synonym) was founded by a chief doctor of Antinoopolis, who in his will (*P.Cair.Masp.* 2.67151, dated 570) had entrusted its care to his brother. We see here a common pattern, in which the donors who had created charitable foundations kept their management in their families. Of course, families might die out, lose interest, or lack competent leadership. At such points the religious nature of the foundation would be even more important, with the bishop needing to step in to protect and maintain it.

Bibliography
Blanke 2019; Crislip 2005; Gascou 1994; Hamel 2002; López 2013; Wipszycka 2015

4.9 Monasticism

Neither monasticism nor the broader concept of asceticism is easy to define, but they rest on the belief that following certain specific practices can enable a person to form a closer relation to the deity. Such practices did not begin with Christianity nor were they unique to it, in antiquity or today. Monks typically live ascetic lives, forsaking worldly pleasures, controlling their physical needs, and engaging in extensive prayer; but monasticism developed enormous variety over time and remains even now a highly diverse movement. Although Egypt is often described as the cradle of Christian monasticism, the earliest stages of its development are lost to our view. Voluntary acceptance of restrictions on one's way of life certainly can be found in paganism, as in the service of the god Sarapis in the temple of Memphis and other temples. We find the Greek term *katochoi* used to describe people who lived, whether all their lives or only for a certain period, a life of isolation, believing that they were called by the god to this practice. In the second century BC, a sect of Jews called Essenes practiced asceticism. In the first century AD, as described by Philo of Alexandria (*On the Contemplative Life* 21–39, Box 4.9.1), a Jewish sect known as the "healers" (*therapeutai*), are said to have lived communally near Alexandria. Their lifestyle, for both men and women, was based on asceticism and abnegation; they refrained from certain types of food and dedicated themselves to meditation and prayer. But the degree to which either Jewish or pagan groups that followed some form of abnegation influenced the development of Christian monasticism is controversial, given the paucity of evidence on this point.

The two key figures in traditional accounts of the origin of the Egyptian Christian ascetic tradition are Paul of Thebes and Antony. Paul was claimed to be the first; in a life written by Jerome, Paul was said to have become a desert ascetic during the Decian persecution in the middle of the third century. But this account was modeled on Athanasius' *Life of Antony*, which was published first, and it is difficult to know how much factual substance, if any, there is to Paul. The *Life* portrayed Antony as Paul's successor: Antony allegedly visited Paul when the latter was 113 years old, then buried him and inherited his tunic.

The evidence is stronger for Antony (251–356), who came from the region of Herakleopolis in Middle Egypt (Box 4.9.2). Considered to be the father of all monks, Antony was a wealthy Christian who inherited substantial family lands. When he heard the divine instructions (Matthew

> **Box 4.9.1 Philo on the *therapeutai*: *On the***
> ***Contemplative Life*, 22–39**
>
> This place is situated above the Mareotic Lake on a somewhat low-lying hill very happily placed both because of its security and the pleasantly tempered air. The safety is secured by the farm buildings and villages round about and the pleasantness of the air by the continuous breezes which arise both from the lake which debouches into the sea and from the open sea hard by … In each house there is a consecrated room which is called a sanctuary or closet and closeted in this they are initiated into the mysteries of the sanctified life. They take nothing into it, either drink or food or any other of the things necessary for the needs of the body, but laws and oracles delivered through the mouth of prophets, and psalms and anything else which fosters and perfects knowledge and piety … Twice every day they pray, at dawn and at eventide; at sunrise they pray for a fine bright day, fine and bright in the true sense of the heavenly daylight which they pray may fill their minds … The interval between early morning and evening is spent entirely in spiritual exercise. They read the Holy Scriptures and seek wisdom from their ancestral philosophy by taking it as an allegory … They lay self-control to be as it were the foundation of their soul and on it build the other virtues. None of them would put food or drink to his lips before sunset, since they hold that philosophy finds its right place in the light, the needs of the body in the darkness. (Translation Loeb Classical Library.)

> **Box 4.9.2 Childhood of Antony: Athanasius, *Life of Antony*, 1**
>
> Antony was an Egyptian by birth, born to noble parents who were independently wealthy. As they were Christians, he was brought up himself as a Christian. And as a child he was brought up in his parents' house, knowing nothing outside of them and the house. As he grew in age and became a youth and advanced in years, he refused to learn letters, wishing to avoid the company of other boys. All of his desire was, as has been written (in the Scriptures), to live simply in his house. But he went with his parents to the Lord's House.

19:21), "Jesus saith to him: if thou wilt be perfect, go sell what thou hast, and give to the poor, and thou shalt have treasure in heaven: and come, follow me," he gave all his wealth to the poor, withdrew from society, and left for the Eastern Desert, settling near the ruins of an old fort at a place called Pispir. Some of his friends used to visit him, bringing him simple food.

Antony would tell them his experiences with self-denial and resisting demonic temptations and assaults. His reputation in time influenced others toward imitating his way of life. To live away from the Nile, which was the center of Egyptian life, and to seek solitude in the desert, which was a home for wild animals, and believed to be the resort of devils and evil spirits, required patience, endurance, and dedication to prayer; this location led to the common (if misleading) term for Egyptian monks as "desert fathers."

Despite his desire for isolation, Antony became famous, and people came to learn from him about asceticism. Some settled in caves or cells around him. When the number of people became too many, he departed to live in another place. However, he kept visiting and advising his followers. At that time, the idea of an organized monastery had not yet been developed. Antony is said to have left his solitude for a time during the persecutions, visiting prisons and going to Alexandria, an act that put his life in great danger. He again went to meet and support Athanasius against Arius in 338, when the church of Alexandria was at risk of splitting between their followers (**4.6**).

Antony had taught his followers to pursue, like him, a life of purity, austerity, and obedience, which included celibacy as a rule. Monks were to follow the life of asceticism and austerity, but they not only had to pray but also to work, following the footsteps of Jesus, who was a carpenter. Every monk was to build a cell in which to dwell and to live in obedience to such rules.

Monks began to gather in various regions throughout Egypt, such as Latopolis (Esna), Thebes, Antinoopolis, Lykopolis, and Oxyrhynchos. They also settled in northern Egypt, near Alexandria, particularly in Kellia and Wadi El-Natrun, which flourished in the fourth century and later; Wadi El-Natrun remains a group of significant monasteries today. It is said that these communities together included five thousand or more monks. Every monk had the choice of living individually, in company with another monk, or in a group. It seems, not surprisingly, that richer monks chose options with more space and privacy. In Wadi El-Natrun there was a large church, seven bakeries, and a guesthouse for long-term accommodation of visitors.

One of the monasteries of Wadi El-Natrun (Scetis) is attributed to two monks: Amoun, who escaped to the desert in 325, and Macarius, whose name was given to one of the currently present monasteries of Wadi El-Natrun, the Monastery of St. Macarius. Monks of Wadi El-Natrun fell into two groups. The first, living in communities inside the monastery, met on Saturdays and Sundays for prayer in one place, spending the rest of the week in their cells. The second group was of isolated monks, who lived in solitude in caves or cells in the desert. They did not attend the monastery for prayer except on Saturdays and Sundays.

Not all monks were part of such communities. Some lived in more or less complete isolation from any group. These are often called anchorites, a term that derives from the Greek word for "withdraw." Others adopted a kind of halfway practice, living in individual cells rather than a common dwelling, but with some shared facilities for periodic gatherings, especially for the liturgy of worship. But even in such isolation monks remained under the spiritual guidance of an elder, and they often gathered small groups of disciples around them or at least had a servant. The monks were considered to possess spiritual power, and fourth-century papyri indicate that people sent messages asking the monks to pray for blessings for them and pray for them to resist the devil and be cured from diseases.

Over time, however, monasticism became mainly collective rather than solitary. An important approach to such community-based monasticism was developed in Upper Egypt by Pachomius (*c.* 292–348), who was born in Chenoboskion (close to Nag Hammadi in the area of Qena). Pachomius served in the army in the reign of Constantine and Licinius. After his service ended in 314, having connections with ascetics, he became a monk and studied under Palaemon, following the Antonian pattern. It is said that when he was in his cell, he heard a voice calling him to build a house for the monks. Thus the first monastery was built *c.* 318–323 in Tabennesi, near Dendera. He convinced a group of monks to follow him to a newly organized system of collective monasticism rather than the less formalized Antonian approach. The establishment of this new collective monasticism, known as cenobitic, is therefore attributed to Pachomius. The term cenobitic (derived from *koinos bios*, meaning common life) encompasses solitude but also communion and other aspects of a shared communal life, including recognized authority and discipline.

Many monasteries appeared in Upper Egypt following the Pachomian style and adopting his rule of common life. Each monastery was divided into different sections, with every section including between thirty and forty monks under the supervision of one monk as a superior. These monasteries strove to be as self-sufficient as possible. Sections were divided according to trades and different industries, with areas for blacksmiths, carpenters, bakers, and so on. Within these cenobitic monasteries, rules were applied and followed by the monks. Pachomius sometimes punished monks who did not abide by the rules; penalties included reprimands, denial of food, imprisonment, and sometimes expulsion.

Although the majority of the monks were Egyptian speakers, some of them also knew Greek, and monks of other origins were allowed to join the Pachomian monasteries as long as they followed the rules. The Pachomian system required that the applicant must not be a fugitive and should spend three months in training, starting to learn to read and write and beginning to memorize the Bible. Time was split between prayer and work to meet the requirements of the monastery. Monks were to sleep the first half of the night and wake up to pray the next half till sunrise. The new monk attended three lessons per day, and the older monk attended lessons on the inter-pretation of the Bible on Wednesdays and Fridays. Prayers were three times per day: morning, noon, and evening. The two daily meals, one at noon and the other by sunset, consisted of bread, cheese, fruits, vegetables, and soup.

Pachomius set many rules and principles for the monks (brothers) to follow; these rules became known in the West through their translation by Jerome. As for prayer, the Pachomian system was less strict than the Antonian. Monks were free in matters of food, fasting, and praying in their accommodations. Women's monasteries were also built. By the death of Pachomius, there were two monasteries for women and nine for men in the region stretching from Panopolis to Latopolis (Esna). Pachomius had supervised them personally and checked on them from time to time. By 518, more than a century and a half later, Pachomian monasteries had reached eighty-five in number and spread beyond Upper Egypt.

Some monastic movements combined elements of the Pachomian and Antonian systems. Among them was the schismatic Meletian movement, which originated with Meletios, the bishop of Lykopolis, who died after the council of Nicaea (325) (**3.6**), and whose followers built a number of monasteries in Middle Egypt near the Pachomian monasteries.

Another cenobitic monastic movement was attributed to Shenoute of Atripe (348–465), who became a monk and later head of the White Monastery (**3.5**, **4.5**) (Figure 4.8.1). He learned the Pachomian methods but took a different approach; his monasteries had a more strongly Egyptian character, in that the monks were all Egyptian-speaking, lacking the linguistic and cultural diversity that we encounter in Pachomian foun-dations. Meting out punishments freely, Shenoute was stricter in discipline and more uncompromising in his teachings than the Pachomians. Excavations at Shenoute's monasteries have yielded a kitchen, a bakery, dining halls, storehouses, perhaps a library, and a church. Outside the area of the monastery, there were farms and orchards. Much of his writing has survived, although fragmentarily, in much later manuscripts found in the White Monastery in modern times (**4.10**).

In the early period of ascetic practice, some women who adopted an ascetic way of life had separate buildings called Houses of the Virgins in or near the cities. Some of them copied the monks in their attire by wearing black clothes. The church had from an early time valued virginity very highly and discouraged remarriage after being widowed, although it never abandoned its overall positive stance on marriage, which was essential to the survival of society. In a text attributed to Athanasius, bishop of Alexandria, from the fourth century, the author advises the virgins to keep reading the Bible, perform prayers at their times, not to drink wine, and to help the poor.

There were differences between monks and nuns. True solitary monastics were far less likely, if at all, to be women. Nuns did not have the same freedom as monks to connect and socialize with the outside world. For their protection, nuns did not live in solitude in cells like monks in the desert. Women's convents typically followed the rule of one of the male communities, often the Pachomian system, but there was also a women's convent at the White Monastery federation of Shenoute.

By the sixth century, there were hundreds of monastic communities in Upper and Middle Egypt, Sinai, and south and west of Alexandria. The architecture of monasteries differed according to whether the monks were anchorites, semi-anchoritic (the so-called "laura" settlements), or larger or smaller forms of cenobitic communities. Various types of cells developed, ranging from hutlike cells that barely protected from the sun and the cold to more complex mud-brick cells that were surrounded by a wall for solitude and might contain a well. The cell might also, in some types of landscape, be hewn from rock, either completely or partially; the laura of Naqlun in Fayyum provides a good example (Figure 4.9.1). In addition to doors and windows, there were cavities in the walls, typically niches with shelves, to store books and other belongings. Objects of daily life have been found in excavations of monasteries, including axes, double axes, sickles, some furniture such as a dining table and mats for seating and sleeping, in addition to utensils like water jars, grain and bread baskets, dishes, and cooking pots.

Although monks were constantly exhorted to remain rooted in their monasteries and cells, they sometimes intervened outside their monasteries, even in politics and religious conflicts. They considered themselves as protectors of the orthodox faith, even if they did not always agree on what that was. Although most rural monasteries followed the anti-Chalcedonian bishops of Alexandria, there were also pro-Chalcedonian monasteries. As we have seen (**4.5**), monks might occasionally take part in attacks on pagans. Emperors did not approve of such activities, and Theodosius I

Figure 4.9.1 Monastic cell at Deir el-Naqlun
A monastic cell cut into the rock at Deir el-Naqlun, in the Fayyum. This is a characteristic dwelling of a *laura*, a semi-anchoritic monastery, with dispersed cells but common facilities for worship. The cells at Naqlun were extended in front with brick constructions, which have largely disappeared.

ordered monks not to enter the cities because of their supposed religious fanaticism.

Literacy was widespread in monasteries, thanks to the rules laid down by Pachomius and other founders, but we have no way of determining how many monks got past the basics. Most of the literature in monasteries was religious in character, but monks from educated backgrounds sometimes had other books, even from classical literature. Monasteries themselves often had libraries (see **4.10** for the question of whether the Nag Hammadi codices belonged to such a library). And writing was commonly used for record-keeping, receipts, and correspondence. The narrative literature (hagiography), which specialized in the lives of the martyrs and priests who performed miracles, played a major role on annual days of commemoration of the saints.

Bibliography
Bell 1948; Blanke 2019; Brooks-Hedstrom 2017; Drayton 2002; Evelyn White 1936; Geens 2007; Jeppson 2003; Marquis 2012; Wipszycka 2009; Wipszycka 2018

4.10 The development of a Christian literary culture in Coptic

The creation of Coptic as a coherent writing system to express the Egyptian language is, as we have seen (**3.7**), difficult to trace and to place. The earliest manuscripts of texts in Coptic may go back to the third century, but their dating depends on assigning dates to handwriting, based on similarities to Greek papyrus manuscripts, themselves often dated only very approximately. It is clear, however, that in the fourth century the script and language were coming to be well established, and high-quality manuscripts were produced. What did they contain?

The earliest Coptic literature, perhaps not surprisingly for a Greek-based script developed by well-educated and Greek-speaking people, is translated from Greek originals. Above all, this meant the Bible: the Greek Old Testament (the Septuagint) and the New Testament. A few other theological works, notably *On the Passover* by Melito of Sardis, and probably some sermons, also belong to the earliest phase of translation literature. The Bible remains the foundational work of Coptic literature and permeates it; without a knowledge of the Bible, little that was written later is understandable. There is no known Coptic literature, translated or not, from any period, that is not Christian (or by a Christian author), if one allows a broad definition of Christianity that includes Manichaeism and gnosticism. In the case of the Manichaeans, translation also included turning works in Syriac into Coptic. This activity, known to us from the papyri found in the excavation of the village of Kellis in the Dakhla oasis, was going on at least by the third quarter of the fourth century. It is fair to say in general that Coptic was a vehicle for Christian groups; there is no evidence for its use by anyone else in the rapidly Christianizing society of fourth-century Egypt. Of course, the disappearance of institutions not related to the church that might have preserved any non-Christian works in Coptic means that we cannot be sure that such writing never existed; however, nothing has been found in the papyri to suggest that it did.

It is essential to remember, however, that Coptic was not the dominant language of the church as long as Roman rule lasted, even if many monasteries were largely or entirely Egyptian-speaking (**4.9**). And Coptic was certainly not the dominant literary language of the church. The famous Alexandrian theologians of Late Antiquity all wrote in Greek, most notably the great archbishop Athanasius and his successors, just as predecessors such as Clement and Origen had. They wanted to communicate with the educated population not only of Egypt but of the rest of the eastern Roman Empire, and Greek was the proper language for that purpose. The same is true of Didymus the Blind, the biblical commentator and educator (**4.11**). Even as seemingly Egyptian a figure as Antony may have written (or dictated) his letters in Greek, despite Athanasius' description of him as ignorant of Greek; the surviving Coptic fragments would thus be translations. Even in the fifth century, the Alexandrian patriarchate remained Greek-speaking. The history of the church of Egypt commissioned by the patriarch Timothy Ailouros (457–477; **5.1**) was written in Greek, based on the records in the Alexandrian bishop's offices. It was intended to present the history and interpretation of the patriarchate in the era of conflict after the council of Chalcedon. It, too, was soon translated into Coptic, and while the Greek history is lost, parts of the Coptic version survive.

By contrast, the early literature around the figure of Pachomius, the founder of Upper Egyptian cenobitic monasticism, seems to have been composed originally in Coptic and, indeed, to be perhaps the first original corpus written in the language. Not only the Pachomian textual corpus but also a large part (although not all) of the letters written in Coptic in the fourth century come from monasteries. Equally monastic is the first major author of original literature in the language, and the greatest of those known, Shenoute of Atripe (**4.8**). His works survive almost entirely in fragmentary form, and many remain to be properly edited and translated. But his corpus was large; what survives of it comes from copies made five to seven centuries after his death. His earliest writing probably dates to around 380 or soon after, just before he became the abbot of his monastery, and the latest to the middle of the fifth century – for it seems he was exceptionally long-lived and productive until he was a centenarian. Although he is the most important exemplar of original writing in Coptic, he was clearly educated in Greek at a high level.

Shenoute's works consist to a large degree of letters (Box 4.10.1) and sermons. These letters are in many cases addressed to his monastic community or to parts of it, for Shenoute lived a hermit's existence for much of his life and communicated in writing. He probably dictated much of what he composed, mixing formal rhetoric (perhaps a product of his Greek higher education), quotations from the Bible, and more informal speech. His Coptic may as a result be difficult for modern readers to follow, but as his sermons were read aloud in the monasteries of his federation not only in his lifetime but afterward we should not imagine that they were impossible for most people to understand.

Shenoute's exceptional qualities as an author stand out all the more if one observes that he had no real direct successors. There were writers who followed him, including Besa, to whom an encomiastic "life" of Shenoute is

> **Box 4.10.1 Letter of Shenoute: *My heart is crushed, Canon 8*, XO 84: i.3–ii.18**
>
> Also, do not let people among us in these congregations at any time be timid in their endurance because of sons or daughters or a brother or sisters or mothers or any other blood relatives of theirs being thrown out of the holy places of God because of pestilent deeds. Let your love display to God that you love him more than sons or daughters or brothers or sisters or fathers or mothers and more than the world and all those who are in it. Is this not sufficient on the subject of the things we, whether male or female, have done among these congregations until now? (Translation Krawiec 2002: 48.)

(wrongly) attributed, but no one of his stature. The century and a half after Shenoute's literary work is to a large degree one of the continuation of translation of Greek originals. Alongside these are works of which no Greek original is known to have existed; scholars of Coptic have debated whether they are original compositions in Coptic or translations of otherwise unknown works, often ascribed fictitiously to prominent writers. Even apart from these questions, however, the translations are a real part of Coptic literature, and there is no reason to believe that Egyptians reading these works maintained a bright line in their minds between works written in Coptic and works translated into it. They may well not have known which was which, and it probably did not matter to them. Moreover, the ways in which these books were translated, sometimes with changes, and used in the life of the church are important in themselves.

In this respect, it is significant that already in the fourth century the works translated from Greek into Coptic included not only those of Alexandrian theologians, as one might expect, but also those of the patristic writers from or based in Asia Minor, including Melito of Sardis (mentioned above), John Chrysostom, Basil of Caesarea, Gregory of Nyssa, and Gregory of Nazianzus. The use of Coptic texts of these authors does not represent opposition to the traditions of Greek patristic literature in Egypt – the corresponding Greek texts are also found in the papyri. At the same time, many works commonly (although controversially) described as gnostic were also translated from Greek into Coptic; for many of these, only the Coptic version has survived, thanks to various discoveries of papyri, of which by far the most famous is the Nag Hammadi cache. The thirteen codices of this trove, uncovered in Upper Egypt in 1945, contained a variety of "gnostic" treatises and scriptures, including the Gospel of Thomas. Some scholars have supposed the burial of these codices to be the result of obedience by a monastery to Athanasius' orders in 367 (**4.5**) to get rid of apocryphal texts, but the origin of the "library" remains debated.

It is interesting to see what original literature emerged from Egyptians in the period after Shenoute (**5.7**). It is perhaps no accident that in this period, when the Chalcedonian and non-Chalcedonian churches were growing apart (**5.2**), we see the burgeoning of Coptic writing. Also in the sixth century Coptic develops into a language acceptable in more formal contexts, used for example in the first arbitration agreements settling legal disputes written in Coptic in mid-century, and begins to be used by government officials at least for their own internal purposes (**5.7**). As Coptic moved closer to official status, even though it had not yet reached that level, it also became a richer medium for literary composition.

As with Shenoute, this work was composed in the context of the life of the Christian communities, especially its liturgy and preaching (**5.1**). Sermons and hagiographic literature – the praise of saints, or encomia, for use in the liturgy on their feast days – are dominant genres in the work of Pisentius of Koptos, Constantine of Asyut, Rufus of Shotep, and others of the late sixth and early seventh centuries, especially under the bishop Damian (578–605), who though of Syrian origin played a critical role in shaping an anti–Chalcedonian Egyptian church. All this work dates to the last two generations before the Arab conquest. In no case is there a surviving body of work comparable to that of Shenoute; as Stephen Emmel has said, they are "shadows or at best fleeting images" of what once existed. And, of course, much had changed in Egypt since the fourth century. These writers belonged to a much-changed world, in which relations between Alexandria, the *metropoleis* of the nomes, the monasteries, and the country villages had undergone profound changes (**5.6**).

Bibliography
Emmel 2007; Layton 1995; Orlandi 1997

4.11   The development of a Christian educational culture

Roman Egypt, like other ancient societies, had no system of universal public education. As in Ptolemaic Egypt, elementary and secondary education were private matters. To learn how to write and read in Egyptian, one could still get a traditional education in the schools operated by the larger temples (**1.11**). But the decline of the temples (**2.7** and **3.5**) gradually shrank that possibility, and the exclusion of demotic from the public sphere reduced incentives for learning it. As a result, Greek education, provided mainly in small private schools, dominated the world of learning letters.

That education was highly structured and focused on the classical Greek past, above all on the Homeric epics and the literature of fifth- and fourth-century BC Athens. A pupil in Roman Egypt was more likely to know about Pericles than about Hellenistic kings, and little about Rome made it into the curriculum. As they had for centuries, elementary pupils learned how to make their letters and to copy words, then sentences. Handwriting was heavily emphasized in the initial stages. Many students learned little more than the basic skills of literacy, a limitation we see reflected in the poor spelling of many papyrus letters and documents.

At the secondary level, the school of the grammarian, students were more directly immersed in Greek grammar and literature. These students were mostly male, as women only rarely had more than an elementary education, and they came mainly from well-off families, who could afford the cost of private education. At this stage, one learned Greek well enough to use it fluently in public life, with both accurate reading and expressive writing and speaking stressed. The Homeric poems, especially the *Iliad*, were the center of study, accompanied by other poetic authors, such as Hesiod, Euripides, and Menander. Prose was less central, although some of Isocrates' orations were popular. This curriculum was not peculiar to Egypt; Greek education on this model could be found throughout the eastern Roman Empire and was the common foundation of higher education for young men of the higher classes.

This literature was, naturally, permeated by Greek mythology. The Homeric gods were everywhere, and they were widely represented in painting, sculpture, mosaic, and other arts as well. They formed part of a classical culture that was shared by all educated people, and to a lesser extent by the population as a whole, at least at a visual level. Appreciation of Homer did not imply any particular attitude toward Zeus, Hera, Athena, and the rest of the gods who figure in the epics, and by Late Antiquity there was a long tradition of skepticism about the stories about the gods, even among those who practiced traditional religion.

Christians were educated in the same system as everyone else, and indeed Christians taught the classical authors just as pagans did. The emperor Julian saw a contradiction there: How could a Christian teach texts full of what they thought were lies? But he was more clever than realistic, for most upper-class Christians saw classical education for what it was, a social rather than religious formation. They focused on the stories told in the myths as cultural narratives rather than religious doctrines. The major fourth-century theologians were well educated in classical texts, and to a large extent these texts remained the basis of the grammarian's teaching for another two centuries or more. The notary and poet Dioskoros of Aphrodito (**5.4**) had Greek grammatical tables, a copy of the *Iliad*, and a codex of the plays of Menander. Nor did depictions of mythological scenes disappear from the art of Christian households. The Christian poet Nonnus wrote a long poem on the adventures of the god Dionysos alongside his paraphrase of the Gospel of John.

But not all Christians were so comfortable with the inheritance of classical culture. Didymos the Blind, a mid to late fourth-century commentator on biblical texts active in Egypt, was also a teacher, and he applied the methods of the grammarian to Christian texts. In the case of the Psalms and the book of Ecclesiastes, we have, thanks to a find of papyrus manuscripts, copies of what have been argued to be transcripts of his classroom teaching (Figure 4.11.1, Box 4.11.1). He treats these texts just as any other grammarian would the Homeric poems. The methods of analysis and the classroom dialogue between teacher and student are traditional, but the content is explicitly from a different tradition – but not from specifically Christian texts, it is important to notice. Rather, Didymos is teaching from works of the Hebrew Bible translated into Greek in the Septuagint.

The need for a more specifically Christian curriculum was perhaps felt most acutely in monasteries, some of which embraced education as a central part of their life. Although some monks came from proper-tied backgrounds and were well educated, others – particularly in cenobitic monasteries – had more modest origins. Classical culture was by no means entirely absent from the teaching in such monaster-ies, but it survived mostly in extracts, compiled into anthologies of verses extracted from the works of Homer or Menander and thought useful for instruction or practice. It is often difficult to tell if educa-tional texts found in the excavations of monasteries were intended for teaching young children or adult monks. In any case, the role of the Psalms was central, as with Didymos' teaching. They were in any event highly familiar to the monks, who memorized them and recited them on a regular rotation.

It is not surprising that the evidence for education in Coptic follows some of the same lines of complex adaptation of the classical curricu-lum that we see in Greek education in a Christian society. The pedagogical methods are identical, from the practicing of individual

Figure 4.11.1 Didymos the Blind, *Commentary on the Psalms*
Didymos the Blind, *Commentary on the Psalms*, from a manuscript leaf now at Brigham
Young University, gathering 16, folio 1 verso; fifth–sixth century AD. Found in quarries
at Tura, south of Cairo. The Psalms played a major part in Christian education and
devotion, and Didymos taught the Psalms in his class.

Box 4.11.1 Didymos the Blind in the classroom on Psalm 34:9

Question: What is the difference between "over (*epi*) the Lord" and "in (*en*)
the Lord"?

Didymos: Someone who simplistically interprets prepositions will say there
is no difference. But it can be interpreted as follows: for instance someone
rejoices, say, over his child if he is healthy, but he rejoices in the drinking of
wine. He has one reason, then another reason. (Translation Stefaniw
2019: 110.)

letters to the making of word lists and the practicing of grammatical forms. Maxims from Menander can be found in Coptic as well as in Greek. But it seems that the texts copied and practiced by students in Coptic were mostly drawn from the scriptures or other religious writings, such as sermons. However, as many of the surviving educational texts in Coptic are written on ostraca and were found in monastic contexts, it is difficult to trace the evolution of Coptic education outside the monasteries.

Bibliography

Brooks Hedstrom 2017; Cameron 2007; Cribiore 2001; Larsen and Rubenson 2018; Stefaniw 2019

5 | Divergence and division

5.1 Patriarchs and church politics from Chalcedon to Justinian

Despite the many challenges it had faced in the previous two centuries, at the middle of the fifth century Alexandria's wealth and prestige made it still one of the most important cities in the empire. The transformations that Egypt as a whole had undergone in the period from Diocletian to the middle of the fifth century left it more economically and socially unequal, with more power in the hands of a smaller elite. At the same time, it was more closely connected with the rest of the empire, particularly in the east, than ever before. The fifth century is a low point in the papyrological documentation, and it is not easy to track changes at the local level until the rich archives of the sixth century pick up the trail and complicate our view (**5.4**, **5.5**). By way of compensation, however, the fifth and sixth centuries are exceptionally rewarding for the archaeology of Alexandria, as it rebuilt its center after the troubles of the third century (**5.3**). This period also brings a wealth of Christian literary sources, pushing Alexandria and its role in church politics to the center of attention.

The bishop of Alexandria had been able over the years to capitalize on that wealth to gain status and power, and felt his position was sufficiently strong to allow him to disagree repeatedly on religious matters with the emperor. Indeed, since the official establishment of Christianity, the institutional church had been in an almost constant climate of religious tension because of disagreements between groups of theologians regarding the proper way to define the nature of Christ, said to be fully divine and fully human at the same time, which posed an obvious theological puzzle. Tensions arose because of the expectation, set out by Constantine and followed by most of his successors, that there could be only one correct definition, to be determined through theological debate among bishops within the institutional context of an episcopal assembly – a council or synod. All members of the imperial church were then expected to accept those decisions.

Building on the city's long philosophical tradition, the theologians of Alexandria were at the forefront of those debates (**4.2**). This had already strained the relations between the bishops of Alexandria, especially Athanasius and Cyril (**4.5**, **4.6**), and the emperors, but as we shall see, that tension was nothing in comparison with the difficulties created by the decisions of the Council of Chalcedon in 451 (discussed below), which created a lasting division among the Christians of the empire. Because the disagreement between the bishops at that council was very deep and involved important episcopal sees (a "see" is the domain controlled by a bishop), the threat to the religious unity of the empire was greater than it had ever been before. For almost two centuries, until the southeastern provinces were conquered by the Arabs in the mid-seventh century, this religious rift and the political upheavals that ensued dominate the literary sources on all sides.

As a result, we are very well informed about the episcopal see of Alexandria and its occupants for that period – far better informed than we are about secular political matters. Much of our information, however, comes from sources that are rarely objective: writings by historians who were either pro-Chalcedonian or anti-Chalcedonian, and who saw and recounted events from their own perspective. We also have records of Council proceedings and imperial edicts and other decisions relating to the conflict, in which the Alexandrian bishops are often protagonists. Our knowledge of the history of the see is enriched, but also complicated, by the *History of the Patriarchs of Alexandria*, a compilation of biographies of the successive bishops put together in its current form for the first time in the eleventh century and then regularly updated. Although the lives of the early bishops are told in this account from that medieval perspective (see **6.6**, **6.8**), they are based on earlier material and offer precious insights about the inner workings of the patriarchal court in late antiquity (Figure 5.1.1).

The detailed knowledge we have of Alexandria is far greater than our knowledge of the ecclesiastical history of the rest of the province from narrative sources. It is not even possible to compile full lists of bishops for important cities such as Hermopolis or Arsinoe, let alone learn anything about them as individuals. We only have information, often limited, on bishops who wrote works that have been preserved. This gap in our knowledge is filled by papyri to some extent, although they fail to provide a continuous narrative. Instead, they allow us to see some bishops and other clerics in action, in a way that narrative sources seldom do, and give a much better picture of the lower clergy and the more mundane concerns of

Figure 5.1.1 Ivory relief depicting a preaching apostle
Late sixth or seventh century, East Mediterranean origin. This thick ivory relief shows
an apostle or evangelist sitting on a throne before a city gate and surrounded by thirty-
five men shown at a much smaller scale. Scholars have sometimes identified the central
figure as St. Mark, first bishop of Alexandria according to tradition, surrounded by his
successors down to and including Damian (576–605). The thirty-five men, however, are
not dressed in ecclesiastical gear, but in official court clothes, which indicates they were
lay urban elites and not bishops.

churches. These concerns also start to appear in narrative sources from the
late sixth century, when sermons and miracle stories replete with anecdotal
evidence from everyday life become common.

The information from the two sets of sources hardly ever overlaps, not only because narrative sources focus on Alexandria while documentary ones are centered on the valley. One of the most striking differences is that the documentary evidence in no way reflects the theological conflict that dominates the narrative sources. It is as if this conflict had not touched the inhabitants of the country beyond Alexandria and its hinterland, along with a few monasteries that were bastions of anti-Chalcedonian sentiment and produced polemical literature to that effect. This could indicate a degree of consensus in favor of one or the other party that made it unnecessary to raise the issue in documents relating to church management; but it could also reflect the indifference of the average Egyptian toward a conflict couched in obscure theological terms that underpinned a struggle for power among distant elites. It may also reflect the irrelevance of the theological debates to the circumstances and transactions that produced the documents. It is therefore impossible to know whether in the period between Chalcedon and the Arab conquest the population of Egypt was indeed overwhelmingly behind the non-Chalcedonian bishops of Alexandria, as the polemical literature claims, or whether that claim was partly wishful thinking.

The sentiments of ordinary Egyptians aside, the Council of Chalcedon was a turning point in the relations between the churches of Alexandria, Rome, and Constantinople. These were fraught with subtle and not so subtle conflicts over precedence and relative prestige. Where Alexandria and Rome claimed a much earlier origin, Constantinople was the imperial center and ultimately (at least when its bishop and the emperor agreed) had the power to impose its views. The council was called by the emperor Marcian in 451 to settle a dispute that had arisen between the sees of Alexandria on the one hand and Rome and Constantinople on the other after the death of Cyril of Alexandria in 444. Cyril's successor Dioskoros (444–454) defended the Constantinopolitan monk Eutyches, who accused Rome and Constantinople of betraying Cyril's theology on the nature of Christ. Cyril had held that Christ's divine and human nature was one and indivisible, while for the bishop of Rome, Pope Leo I, Christ had two distinct but coexisting natures. Eutyches was eventually condemned by Leo I and exiled by the emperor, but appealed. The emperor Theodosius II eventually called a council at Ephesos in 449 to examine the matter, and asked Dioskoros to chair it. The council reinstated Eutyches, but only after Dioskoros had prevented all his enemies from voting. The hearings also ignored the letter sent by Leo I with his opinion on the issue.

Predictably, the procedures and result of the council of 449 angered Pope Leo I, but Theodosius refused to bow to his pressure and even appointed several bishops who were in agreement with Dioskoros. In 450, however, the emperor died, and his successor Marcian adopted a radically different position on the matter. He called a council at Chalcedon with the intention of restoring the authority of Leo, and even asked the bishop of Rome to chair the council. Leo refused but sent his positions in a long letter that became known in later literature as the "Tome of Leo." Theologically the Council adopted Leo's positions while trying to strike a compromise with those of Cyril, even though the two positions appeared incompatible to many of Cyril's followers (Figure 5.1.2).

The most contentious outcome of the Council, however, was probably the decision to condemn, depose, and exile Dioskoros (Box 5.1.1), and

Figure 5.1.2 Vatican stamp commemorating the 1500th anniversary of the Council of Chalcedon

On October 31, 1951, the Vatican issued a set of five stamps commemorating the Council of Chalcedon. Indeed, the bishop of Rome was instrumental in defining the direction taken by imperial religious policy after 451. This stamp shows Pope Leo's envoy reading his letter to the assembly of bishops and the emperor. In the bottom-left corner is the statement "Peter has uttered this through Leo," referring to one of the acclamations of the bishops on hearing Leo's letter. The phrase highlights the direct descent of the Roman pope from the Apostle Peter, traditionally considered to be the first bishop of Rome, and thus lends legitimacy to the Roman position.

replace him in the see of Alexandria by one of his former confidants, Proterios. The Egyptian delegation to the Council refused to accept its authority to depose Dioskoros, and by implication did not recognize the legitimacy of Proterios. The decision provoked serious riots in Alexandria among the defenders of Dioskoros, who burned alive the first group of soldiers sent to pacify the situation. After more troops were sent by

---

Box 5.1.1 Acts of the Council of Chalcedon, Third Session

99. Notification of deposition sent by the holy and ecumenical council to Dioskoros.

The holy, great and ecumenical council, convoked by the grace of God and according to the decree of our most pious and God-beloved emperors in the city of Chalcedon in Bithynia in the martyrium of the most holy and victorious martyr Euphemia, to Dioskoros.

On account of your contempt for the divine canons and your disobedience to this holy and ecumenical council, because, in addition to the other crimes for which you have been convicted, you did not present yourself even when summoned a third time by this holy and great council according to the divine canons to answer the charges brought against you, know that on the present thirteenth day of the month of October you are deposed from the episcopate by the holy and ecumenical council and deprived of all ecclesiastical rank.

100. To the clergy of Alexandria present at Chalcedon, on the deposition of Dioskoros.

The holy and ecumenical council, convoked by the grace of God and according to the decree of our most pious and Christ-loving emperors in the city of Chalcedon in Bithynia in the martyrium of the holy and victorious martyr Euphemia, to the most devout Charmosynos, presbyter and administrator, and Euthalios, archdeacon, and the other clergy who are there.

May your devoutness be informed that Dioskoros, formerly your bishop, has been found guilty in many ways of infringing the divine canons and ecclesiastical discipline, and furthermore of insulting this holy and ecumenical council after being summoned a third time according to the canons by scorning to present himself, and that in consequence yesterday, which is Saturday, the thirteenth day of the present month of October, by a decision of the holy and ecumenical council and in accordance with the decrees of ecclesiastical law, he was deposed from the episcopate and deprived of all ecclesiastical rank. Therefore guard all church property, since you are going to render account to whoever by the will of God and the decree of our most pious and God-beloved emperors shall be ordained bishop of the church of the great city of Alexandria. (Gaddis and Price [2005] II: 112–113.)

Marcian, things finally settled down, at least superficially. Tensions persisted, however, and throughout Proterios' tenure, his opponents repeatedly threatened to prevent the departure of the fleet that shipped the *annona* grain to Constantinople (**2.5**), to the point that Marcian had to organize the departure of the fleet from Pelusium instead.

Marcian's later attempts to convince the Alexandrians that the Council's decisions were compatible with their theological tradition proved fruitless, and at the emperor's death in 457 the anti-Chalcedonian party moved swiftly to consecrate Timothy Ailouros ("the Cat") as bishop of the city (**4.10**). The imperial reaction was quick: Timothy was arrested and Proterios reinstated, actions that launched more unrest among the partisans of the two sides. In the ensuing riots Proterios was killed, and Timothy took back his position as bishop and consecrated several new bishops among his supporters. The new emperor, Leo I (not to be confused with the pope), eventually exiled Timothy Ailouros, and put in his place a pro-Chalcedonian bishop, also called Timothy and nicknamed Salofakiolos ("Wobbly Turban"), an action that resulted in yet more riots.

Until the emperor Leo's death in 474, imperial policy was consistently pro-Chalcedonian. Basiliskos, who seized power after Leo's death, brought Timothy Ailouros back from exile and received him in Constantinople. The meeting resulted in the *Enkyklios*, a document drawn up by the emperor, which condemned the "innovations" of Chalcedon. This was sent to the eastern churches, where almost 700 bishops signed it. Several new anti-Chalcedonian bishops were consecrated at the same time. But this respite did not last long, because Basiliskos was overthrown a year later. The new emperor, Zeno (effectively ruler 476–491), a supporter of Chalcedon, revoked the *Enkyklios*. Because of his old age, Timothy Ailouros was left in place. When he died in 477, his supporters immediately chose as his successor Peter Mongos ("the hoarse"), a close collaborator of Dioskoros and Timothy. Salofakiolos also claimed the see, however, and was accepted as the legitimate bishop by the emperor. Even though Peter had to leave the see officially, he continued to act as the leader of the anti-Chalcedonians, so much so that Salofakiolos felt threatened and asked the emperor to exile him (Figure 5.1.3).

When Salofakiolos died in 482, Peter Mongos tried to convince the emperor that he was the rightful successor. Zeno and the patriarch of Constantinople, Akakios, seeing an opportunity to find a compromise, agreed to consecrate him in exchange for his support of a statement known as the *Henotikon* ("text of union"), addressed initially by Zeno to the bishops, clergy, and monks of Egypt. The text essentially proclaimed

Figure 5.1.3 Emperor Zeno represented on a gold solidus, Constantinople, 476–491
Zeno reigned fifteen years, and although his policy was overall pro-Chalcedonian, he
was the first to attempt a compromise by appointing Peter Mongos as bishop of
Alexandria and issuing the *Henotikon*. This led to internal dissent among the anti-
Chalcedonian faction, and the memory of his reign remained vivid in early medieval
monastic circles.

that the positions of Chalcedon were consistent with Cyril's theology,
which it reaffirmed as valid. Although this made little real progress compared to the council itself, openly supporting Cyril was an important
symbolic step on the part of the emperor. Peter spent much of his tenure
defending the *Henotikon* before dubious Egyptian assemblies for whom
anything short of an outright condemnation of Chalcedon was insufficient.
This was especially true in some monastic circles, which distanced themselves from Peter and proclaimed themselves independent (*akephaloi* –
"headless," or *aposchistai* – "separatists"). This was the first time a clear
division emerged among the anti-Chalcedonians in Egypt, and it marked
the beginning of almost a century of internal troubles, even while the see of
Alexandria remained securely in anti-Chalcedonian hands until 535.

Despite their internal tensions, the stability of the anti-Chalcedonians in
Egypt was exceptional among the eastern churches. From 518, when Justin
I came to power in Constantinople, the fragile equilibrium achieved by the
Henotikon was broken. Eager to reconcile Constantinople and Rome, Justin
tried to enforce the acceptance of Chalcedon, especially in the provinces of
the Levant and Syria, while Egypt was left undisturbed. The result of this
imperial initiative was that many of the exiled Syrian anti-Chalcedonian
bishops fled to Egypt, reinforcing it as a bastion of resistance to Chalcedon.
Among the exiled bishops was Severus, who had occupied the see of
Antioch since 512 and had the reputation of being one of the most eloquent

interpreters and exponents of Cyril's theology. During his exile in Egypt, from 518 to his death in 538, Severus became one of the most influential theologians in the country and also played an active role in organizing the opposition to Chalcedon from his residence in the Enaton monastery, 15 km (9 miles) west of Alexandria.

Like the Egyptian anti-Chalcedonians, however, the Syrians were also divided. Soon Severus found himself in a long and complex controversy with his fellow exile Julian, bishop of Halicarnassus, over the issue of the corruptibility of the body of Christ. The debate was as obscure as it was intense, and soon both sides had supporters within the ranks of the Egyptian church. This internal division was exacerbated under Justinian, and ultimately led to the formation of the Coptic church as we know it today.

Bibliography
Davis 2004; Maraval 1997; Wipszycka 2015

5.2 Conflicts over doctrine and power from Justinian to Heraclius

The advent of Justinian in 527 changed the terms of the conflict. In part this was due to his own theological interest and his tendency to weigh in on the debate, the terms of which had taken a new turn in the early sixth century around the remarkable personality of Severus of Antioch. Another factor was the empress Theodora's consistent support of the anti-Chaldedonians, who thus found a friendly ear at court – although it also meant they had to contend with a member of the imperial family meddling in their internal affairs. In 535, when the sees of Alexandria and Constantinople both became vacant at the same time, Theodora backed two supporters of Severus, respectively Theodosios and Anthimos. This met with strong opposition in Alexandria, where the partisans of Julian of Halicarnassus had gained traction. The fact that the election of Theodosios had the mark of imperial interference may have reinforced local feeling against him. The supporters of Julian elected Gaianos, who turned out to be just as controversial: He had to be protected by the army from rioters, and his tenure hardly lasted three months (Figure 5.2.1).

With Gaianos deposed, Theodosios, who had taken refuge at court with Theodora, returned to Alexandria and took back his position. The respite did not last very long, however, because in 536 the visit to Constantinople of Agapetus, the strongly pro-Chalcedonian bishop of Rome, turned the

(a1)   (a2)

(b1)   (b2)

Figure 5.2.1 Bronze coins (*nummi*) of Justinian, Alexandria, sixth century
Bronze coins (*nummi*) of Justinian. Struck in Alexandria, sixth century. Justinian
introduced monetary reforms that turned out to be quite successful in Egypt. He
attempted to reinvigorate bronze coinage through new issues of multiples of the
nummus (a low-value copper coin for everyday use). The mint of Alexandria
struck an unusual issue of 33 *nummi* (a) that had little success, as well as issues as
small as 3 and 6 *nummi* (b and c). The *dodekanoummion* (12 *nummi*) was the
most successful one, and was reissued under his successors until the Arab
conquest (d). The value was written in Greek letters on the obverse (12 = IB; 3 =Γ;
6 = ς; 33 = ΛΓ), together with the abbreviated name of the mint: ΑΛΕΞ.

tide at court. Henceforth Justinian adopted a much firmer pro-
Chalcedonian attitude, imposing Chalcedonian bishops throughout the
empire. He replaced Theodora's anti-Chalcedonian patriarch of
Constantinople, Anthimos, with the Chalcedonian Menas, and attempted
to win over Theodosios to the Chalcedonian cause. When this failed,
Justinian replaced him in 537 with Paul of Tabennesi, a Pachomian

(c1)

(c2)

(d1)

(d2)

Figure 5.2.1 (cont.)

monk. The consecration took place in Constantinople, and Paul was sent to Egypt with an exceptional military escort. This was not appreciated locally, affording yet more proof that the Chalcedonians, even when they were of Egyptian origin, were mere pawns of the emperor.

Very unpopular because of his rather violent methods, Paul was replaced in 542 by the much less confrontational Zoilos, himself followed in 551 by Apollinarios, who returned to a regime of terror in trying to impose religious union. The repression resulted in more riots, and many members of the anti-Chalcedonian clergy took refuge in monasteries. This period was marked by reinforced military presence in the city to maintain the power of the Chalcedonian patriarchs, to whom increasing military and civil authority was delegated. It is remembered in later anti-Chalcedonian sources as a time of persecution.

Figure 5.2.2 Portrait of the empress Theodora from Ravenna
This portrait of the empress Theodora is from the church of San Vitale, Ravenna, and dates to the sixth century. Justinian's wife Theodora was one of the most consistent supporters of the anti-Chalcedonian churches, and arguably played a key role in their survival and eventual longer-term establishment in the later sixth century. This famous mosaic from the church of San Vitale in Ravenna is the only extant image of her, despite her very insistent presence in contemporary texts.

At the same time, Theodora continued her patronage of the anti-Chalcedonians, which arguably was crucial to their survival and ultimate revival. She brought the exiled Theodosios to court, from where he was able to continue ordaining Severan clergy, including, in 534, the Syrian Jacob Burd'aya, who eventually set up an entirely new church structure in northern Syria (Figure 5.2.2).

Justinian continued to make attempts at a theological rapprochement with the anti-Chalcedonians until his death in 565, all in vain. His successor Justin II continued his policy with further efforts to conciliate the theological positions of the two sides. Over the years, however, because of what they had construed as persecution by the imperial authorities, most anti-Chalcedonians had hardened their positions and would settle for nothing less than the condemnation of Chalcedon and of the loathed Tome of Leo. After his last attempt at conciliation in 571 failed, Justin changed policy and resorted to repression instead.

Meanwhile, the anti-Chalcedonians had been actively organizing an ecclesiastical hierarchy that was loyal to their cause, creating what was in effect a separate church, even though it still lacked legal validity at that time. In 575, Peter IV, a Severan, was elected patriarch of Alexandria. Following in the footsteps of Jacob Burd'aya in Syria, he proceeded to ordain seventy bishops for Egyptian sees. Justin II's death in 578 helped consolidate that new hierarchy because his two successors, Tiberius II (578–582) and Maurice (582–602), kept a low profile on the religious front, thus making this a key period for the (re)constitution of the Severan church in Egypt.

Peter IV died in 577, and after some conflict, Damian, a Syrian monk from the Enaton monastic complex west of Alexandria, was elected to the patriarchal see in 578, occupying it until his death in 605. Damian was a controversial figure, popular in some Egyptian monastic circles and unpopular in others. He eventually fell out with the patriarch of Antioch, Peter of Kallinikos (Raqqa). Despite his difficulties within the anti-Chalcedonian world, however, Damian turned out to be a key figure in establishing a strong and stable Severan ecclesiastical hierarchy in Egypt. During his entire tenure, this hierarchy functioned in parallel – or in competition – with the pro-Chalcedonian one, but it was left to flourish unimpeded by emperors Tiberius II and Maurice.

Damian did not take over the traditional premises of the patriarchate (namely the principal church of the city), but set up his headquarters in the monasteries of the Enaton, where Severus himself had resided and where Severan support was strongest. This was not surprising given the heavily monastic origin of the Severan party, and it was mirrored at the level of the bishoprics of the valley: from what we know, the anti-Chalcedonian bishops under Damian resided in monasteries in the periphery of the cities of which they were eponymous (**5.6**). This parallel organization, with bishops operating respectively from episcopal cities and from monasteries, continued until the Persian occupation, when the Chalcedonian patriarch of Alexandria, John the Almsgiver, took flight, leaving the ground open for the anti-Chalcedonian Andronikos to take over his church in the city. He was followed by the long-serving Benjamin, whose tenure knew several ups and downs: He was displaced in 633 by Cyrus, whom the emperor Heraclius appointed with exceptional powers with the aim of reestablishing Chalcedonian control, but was able to return after the Arab conquest of the country and remained in place until his death in 665. Benjamin's successors followed him on the patriarchal throne undisturbed, as the Chalcedonians had lost their imperial support.

It is difficult to have a clear idea of the sympathies of the population at the accession of Damian. Our sources on all sides claim that their heroes were popular, as even a cursory reading of such Chalcedonian texts as the *Life of John the Almsgiver* or the *Miracles of Cyrus and John* will demonstrate. The allegiance of the rural population would have depended on two factors: (a) their relations with the monks of rural monasteries, who were far from all being anti-Chalcedonian – a large number of the Pachomian monasteries seem to have been supporters of Chalcedon; and (b) the existence of a clerical structure that could support the needs of the population. In the latter area, the appointments made by Peter IV and Damian in the later part of the sixth century changed the forces at play. Both patriarchs had clearly understood the importance of a tight network of bishops and clergy to win over and maintain the rural areas.

Several of the bishops from that period are known to us today because of their writings, including an important volume of textual production by the Severans in the late sixth century, mostly in Coptic. This is not surprising, as they came from – and resided in – monastic environments that had already been producing Coptic ascetic literature from the fourth century onward. Most probably, the new Severan bishops were wielding their authority essentially in the countryside, in an unwritten division of the ecclesiastical territory with the Chalcedonians, who remained in the urban settings (**5.6**). As well as avoiding direct conflict, this division was ultimately favorable for the Severans: The rural population was larger by far, and Damian certainly knew that winning them over could bring more benefit than holding major cities. It was also a much more Coptic-speaking population, for whose benefit the bishops and clergy spoke – and wrote – in their own language.

Apart from John of Paralos, a city of the Delta, all the other known Severan bishops of this era were appointed south of Hermopolis. This may be partly a coincidence in our sources, but it could also reflect the choice to send the most pastorally active of the new bishops to the south, to areas not in direct contact with Constantinople and less easy to control from outside the country. Distance was a problem, even from Alexandria, as Egypt's topography allows only for a single, linear communication route. This difficulty was addressed through the creation of a new position, that of patriarchal vicar for Upper Egypt, who could relay the bishop's authority and take swift decisions without the necessity to travel up and down the valley. The church thus dealt with administrative issues similar to those faced by civil administrations across the centuries.

The vicar had authority over the bishops, who in turn were appointed to specific cities and were responsible for religious life in those cities and their respective territories. This responsibility involved organizing the cycle of feasts for the year and celebrating them in such a way that the entire community felt included. The bishop thus ensured that over the year he had visited all of the city's churches and celebrated in them at least once. This was especially important in periods when the population was religiously divided, as it encouraged the cohesion of the group around the bishop and asserted control over the church premises. We hear very little of Chalcedonian bishops in the south, but the fact that several Severan bishops operated mainly in the countryside suggests they existed. It seems, however, that Peter IV and Damian created new bishoprics where at first there were no Chalcedonian incumbents.

By the sixth century, bishops were generally chosen among monks and had to display the corresponding ascetic morality to be considered worthy of the episcopate. In practice, their capacity to speak in public played a very important role, as they spearheaded the campaign to win over the population to their cause. This seems to have been the primary criterion, for instance, in the appointment of several Severan bishops to key bishoprics in the valley but also in the Delta. The *History of the Patriarchs* mentions three who were active under Damian, and of the three, we know that Damian consecrated Constantine of Asyut and appointed him vicar for Upper Egypt. Damian also seems to have appointed John of Hermopolis, known by the *History of the Patriarchs* as John the Recluse. We do not know, however, whether the third bishop mentioned, John of Paralos, was appointed by Damian, or if he was part of the first wave of Severan bishops appointed by Peter IV.

The *History of the Patriarchs* insists on the purity and holiness of those bishops. What it does not say is that they were prolific authors, just like some other contemporary bishops that the *History* does not mention, for example Rufus of Shotep/Hypselis, the author of several preserved homilies, and Pisenthios of Coptos, who wrote at least one extant homily. Exceptionally, Pisenthios is also known by a documentary dossier, largely of letters that were addressed to him while he was hiding, apparently from the Persians (**5.8**; Box 5.2.1). These documents throw a vivid light on the concerns of the local population and the reasons why they would have appealed to a bishop. At the same time, it demonstrates the importance, for a church seeking to establish itself in the country, of having a network of bishops to whom the population could turn for their everyday moral grievances.

> **Box 5.2.1 Letter to Bishop Pisenthios:** *SBKopt.* 1.295
>
> First I embrace the sweetness of the holy feet of your truly God-loving fatherliness, which intercedes for us before God; and you are the one who beseeches God for the entire people and whom God has appointed true high priest to make petition for the whole people before God; and you are our patron who intercedes for us before God and men.
>
> I am this wretched one, miserable beyond (all) men on earth, and greatly weighed down with grief and sadness, and heartbroken for my husband who is dead, and for my son whom the Persians beat (?) . . . and my cattle which the Persians carried off.
>
> Now, I beg you of your holy fatherliness to send and bring the headman of Jeme and Amos, and ask them to leave me in my house and not to have me wander abroad. For they said to me, "You are liable for the field."
>
> The son, also, whom I had was heartbroken and took to flight.
>
> And also the pair of cattle which were left from the Persians – the moneylender came forth and carried them off and sold them on account of his loan which I borrowed for the tax.
>
> Be so kind to me as for me to be settled in my house.
>
> *Verso* – Give it to my lord father the holy [bishop] Pesente, from this poor wretched wife of the deceased Pesente. (Translation Bagnall and Cribiore 2006: 242.)

From the same area, another body of episcopal correspondence on ostraca has offered insight on one more bishop from the time of Damian, Abraham of Hermonthis (Figure 5.2.3). It is a varied dossier of documents, some of which pertain to issues of clerical recruitment and discipline, and others to the running of an episcopal tribunal. Abraham is not known from narrative texts, but a portrait of him is extant and he is also mentioned on an ivory diptych found in the area that contains a list of bishops of the see of Hermonthis (Armant) (Figure 5.2.4). His residence was in the Monastery of St. Phoibammon (Figure 5.6.1), from which a substantial archive has been preserved, documenting its existence and activity for more than a century after Abraham's death – although bishops do not seem to have resided there any longer at that time.

Combined with official church rules, Abraham's correspondence gives a vivid image of the everyday management of a bishopric, exemplifying the authority of bishops over the clergy of their territory, but also the responsibilities of the different members of that clergy. They took care of the

Figure 5.2.3 Portrait of Bishop Abraham of Hermonthis
Portrait of Bishop Abraham of Hermonthis, Theban region, early seventh century. This
portrait shows Apa Abraham, bishop of Hermonthis and superior of the monastery of
St. Phoibammon. Combined with his correspondence, it makes Abraham one of the
best-attested provincial bishops in the country. The holes drilled on the four corners
show it was intended to be suspended, and the halo around the bishop's head could
indicate it was made after his death. As he was the monastery's superior, he would have
been commemorated there by the monks.

churches and ran their activities, mainly ensuring religious rites were
carried out in the different localities. Outside the days and times of religious
service, most members of the clergy practiced a trade or worked in agriculture. Others could be scribes or even tax-collectors. Their social origin
varied, and their rank in the clergy did not always correspond to what we
can know of their social status: some deacons, for example, seem to be of
higher social status than some priests. Abraham's correspondence
also shows that injunctions to know the scriptures and church law found
in normative texts were taken seriously, and knowing scriptural texts by
heart was, in Abraham's eyes, an important prerequisite for a priest's
ordination.

Figure 5.2.4 Ivory diptych with list of bishops, Theban region
This is a very rare example of a liturgical diptych from the church of Hermonthis. These
were widely used in church services, containing the names of those who were to be
commemorated by the priest. The list included important figures of the church, and some
who were more locally important. Here the list starts with the bishops of Alexandria
down to Benjamin, and continues with the bishops of Hermonthis, including Abraham
(Figure 5.2.3). One list of names was compiled after 623, and more names were added
after 662 to bring the list up to date, which shows that the object was used continuously in
the liturgy and it contained a "living" text, which was updated as time went by.

Bibliography
Blaudeau 1997; Booth 2017; Booth 2018; Davis 2004; Fournet 2018a;
Godlewski 1986; Maraval 1997

5.3 Alexandria as a university city; the auditoria of Kom el-Dikka

After the damage to Alexandria in the late third century (**3.2**, **4.3**), intellectual life in the city seems to have been centered on the Serapeum, where the "daughter library" still offered a chance for the continuation of academic life, as Ammianus stated in 380 (22.16.17–18). Aphthonius, who is said to have visited the Serapeum around 314, described the rooms surrounding the sanctuary as being used not only to store books but also for classrooms (**4.5**). These rooms had been added as part of the Roman reconstruction and enlargement of the sanctuary *c*. 215/216. Arranged in two stories around the portico that surrounded the entire precinct, the rooms were numerous enough to have served more than one function. We are not sure whether they were used specifically for a library or any other educational purpose, because the *temenos* incorporates a number of other buildings whose original function is also unknown. This center for learning did not last long, as the Serapeum itself was destroyed in 391 (**4.5**).

Diocletian's reforms included the marginalization of both the gymnasium and the training of ephebes by minimizing the authority of their directors, changes that did not improve the educational environment in Alexandria. Even after the great persecution came to an end and Christianity was an officially recognized religion, Alexandria remained a turbulent place (**5.1**, **5.2**), still fraught with religious strife. It is hard to say how much these conflicts affected scientific and scholarly work. Scientists and intellectuals seem to have tried, on the whole, to stay away from direct involvement in such strife and to preserve their city's scholarly distinction, based on its Hellenic heritage. Neoplatonism continued to be taught throughout the fourth and the greater part of the fifth centuries, side by side with more directly Christian education (**4.11**).

In any case, throughout the fifth and sixth centuries Alexandria continued to draw students from other cities in the empire, especially from nearby Gaza. Among those was Zacharias Scholasticus, a Christian who combined his Christian beliefs with classical rhetoric. He moved to Alexandria in 485, studied philosophy for two years, then traveled to study law in Beirut, where he lived until his death in 491.

In the second half of the fifth century, Alexandria faced competition as a center of learning: The Athenian academy witnessed a great revival in the fields of philosophy and medicine, and Constantinople and Beirut became famous for law. But Alexandria kept its reputation for excellence in the fields of philosophy and medicine. After Hypatia's murder in 415 (**4.5**),

Neoplatonism did not wither but continued with great philosophers such as Asklepiodotos, who was said to have been a proximate cause for the destruction of the temple of Isis in Menouthis: Together with his sterile wife, he visited the temple looking for a cure. When a baby was born, it was rumored that the mother was one of the temple priestesses and that the temple was a place for prostitution. In 488–489, a group of Christians attacked the temple, destroyed the cult statue, and burned it in front of the Tycheion; the temple was closed.

The "Life of Isidore" written by his student gives us a glimpse of the relationship between the Athenian and Alexandrian academies. Isidore (*c.* 450–520), himself the student of Asklepiodotos, was the last Neoplatonic philosopher in Alexandria until he left for Athens, where he became the head of its academy. His student and friend Damascius succeeded him in Athens in 515, where he continued until the academy was closed in 529 by Justinian, who accused it of teaching pagan sciences. Justinian's decree prohibited non-Christian teachers and required all syllabuses to be examined to ensure that teaching materials were free of any instruction in divination. Damascius escaped, along with a handful of colleagues, to the Persian king Khosrow. Two years later, a peace treaty between Justinian and the Persians was signed that included the safe return of the philosophers. However, Damascius did not return to Athens but went to Alexandria, where he could find a safe haven to continue lecturing on Neoplatonism.

Along with the known pagan philosophers who lived in fifth- and sixth-century Alexandria, there were other philosophers and orators whose religious affiliations are not known with certainty. Some may have been pagans throughout, some Christians, and some pagans who converted to Christianity. Some philosophers were probably tacit pagans. Among them was Horapollon, a priest in the temple of Menouthis during the reign of Zeno (474–491). He fled after the destruction of the temple and was said to have converted to Christianity. His best-known work was the *Hieroglyphica*, in which he introduced to contemporary readers the historical Egyptian script and language, which had completely disappeared from use during his time. Also living during the reign of Zeno were Heraiskos and his brother Asklepiades. Heraiskos was a Neoplatonist, and when he died in the late 580s, his brother performed pagan rituals as part of his burial (Damascius fr. 174).

The sixth century witnessed a substantial expansion of specifically Christian education, the roots of which date back to the fourth century (**4.11**). Philosophy classes were held by Christian scholars who dealt with and commented on Hellenic works. Scholars came to Alexandria especially after the closure of the Athenian academy, many from Gaza, such as

Agapetus (active at the end of the fifth century), Enius (third quarter of the fifth century), Procopius (465–528), Diodorus (480–485), Thomas (485), Choricios (510–520), Zacharias (480–490), and Silanos (480–485). John the Almsgiver, who became the Chalcedonian bishop of Alexandria (606–610; **5.2**), came from Cyprus, Severus and his brother from Sozopolis in Pisidia (480–490), Proclus from Xanthos in Lycia (320–425), Athanas from Aphrodisias in Caria (470–480), and Agathias the scholiast from Marina in Asia Minor (*c.* 550).

Alexandrian medicine

Since the fourth century medical teachers had flourished in Alexandria. They committed themselves to the compilation and study of the works of great medical authorities of the past and to production of commentaries on their works, in what became known as the Alexandrian canon. This scholarly movement led to great fame for the medical school of Alexandria; Ammianus Marcellinus in the 380s stated that a doctor trained in Alexandria was entitled to special appreciation (22.16.18). Given its excellence in medical studies, Alexandria not surprisingly had well-trained physicians and surgeons who practiced in places that later became hospitals. As we have seen, a family of doctors who lived in Antinoopolis ran that city's hospital for generations (**4.8**).

   Among those famous for their medical contributions was Stephanus of Alexandria (Stephanus Medicus), who also taught and wrote about Plato and Aristotle, geometry, arithmetic, and music. His probable teacher in medicine was Asclepius. John Philoponus (fl. *c.* 510–553), a pupil of an Aristotelian commentator Ammonius, wrote a medical commentary on Hippocrates' book about the fetus. Also a commentator on Aristotle, he was known also as John of Alexandria and in Arab sources as Yehia El Nahwi, John the grammarian, because he was a philologist. Palladius of Alexandria (*c.* sixth century) wrote commentaries on Hippocrates' *On Fractures* and *Epidemics* and on Galen's treatise on the three medical sects. Olympiodorus was the name of more than one intellectual: Olympiodorus of Thebes (fl. *c.* 412–425) was a historian and poet, while Olympiodorus the elder (fifth century) and Olympiodorus the Younger (495–570) were Neoplatonic philosophers and teachers in Alexandria. Some manuscripts attributed to a certain Elias in the second half of the sixth century are believed to have been part of the philosophical and medical school of one of these men named Olympiodorus.

Poetry

Almost all the leading poets who worked in Egypt in this period came from the Theban region, although many were attracted to Alexandria in the course of their careers. Nonnus of Panopolis was a Christian poet who lived in the late fourth and beginning of the fifth centuries. Showing the ease with which a writer could combine classical and Christian culture, Nonnus wrote both the epic *Dionysiaca* and a poetic paraphrase of the Gospel of John. Also from Panopolis was Cyrus (fl. 426–441), a Christian whose poetry included pagan themes and indeed led to his being accused of sympathy with paganism. Panopolis seems to have been an important scientific and religious center in the fourth and fifth centuries.

These poets had important public careers, as did Claudian, who moved west and became a successful panegyrist at the court of the emperor Honorius. But poetry was far from being the exclusive preserve of the mobile upper classes. At a much more modest level, we find the sixth-century village notable, notary, and poet Dioskoros from the village of Aphrodito (**5.4**). His poems are the earliest poetic manuscripts to have reached us in the author's own handwriting. Although the quality of his poetry has been much criticized, it gives a vital sense of the literary culture of a provincial town in the time of Justinian.

Kom el-Dikka and the creation of an academic campus

For the most part, we know little about the spaces in which ancient education took place. Most instruction in Late Antiquity, as in earlier periods, occurred wherever the teacher chose. In many cases this meant the teachers' homes, as with Hypatia and Horapollon, but it might also mean the house of a wealthy man or a philosopher. Some teachers selected rooms in public buildings such as baths or theaters or even porticoes of large streets. Cities might rent rooms to teachers. An individual teacher might teach both at home and in a more public place.

In principle Alexandria was not different from other cities in this respect, at least when it came to elementary education. But the Kom el-Dikka excavations (**4.3**; Figure 5.3.1) provide archaeological evidence about this subject, on which written sources remain almost without exception silent. According to this evidence, the second half of the fifth century saw the establishment in the heart of Alexandria of a fixed place for higher education in a more institutionalized form, a complex of classrooms and lecture halls.

Figure 5.3.1 **Kom el-Dikka, view of auditoria with street and theater**

The first phase of urban reconstruction in Kom el-Dikka, which began at the end of the third century or the start of the fourth, included the transformation of the area into a city center with important public buildings, including the imperial bath complex and the theater-like building (**4.3**).

It seems that after the middle of the fourth century a new program of urban reconstruction took place in Kom el-Dikka. Excavations have uncovered a street running from north to south, not noted in the nineteenth-century map prepared by El-Falaki, that splits the area between El-Falaki's squares L1 and L2 into two unequal parts. It is currently known as the Theater Street, since it passes in front of the theater-like building. Parts of granite columns are found on one side of this street, indicating that it was porticoed. The street is also unique in being wider than the other secondary streets of ancient Alexandria. It could be inferred from the presence of mortar mixed with ashes used in the paving of this street that it might have existed at the same time as or been designed along with the theater-like building.

John of Nikiu speaks about a catastrophic earthquake that hit Alexandria in 535 (*Chronicle*, 90, 81–83). Another earthquake – in 554 – is mentioned by Procopius (*de aedificiis*, 6.1.4; *ancedota*, 26.36). The need for construction thus was not all the result of a single event.

In a later reconstruction phase (second half or end of the sixth century), changes were made to the theater-like building. The upper three rows of seats were removed and used to extend the front of the semicircular cavea (the seating area) to form a horseshoe-like shape (Figure 5.3.2). As a result,

Figure 5.3.2 Kom el-Dikka, theater

the entrance passages were blocked and the stage was removed. Excavations also prove that the building was roofed by a cupola supported by marble columns. Inscriptions dated to the reign of Phocas (602–610) reveal that the renovated building was sometimes used for meetings of certain circus or political factions. The remodeling of the theater-like building was apparently intended to prepare the building to serve its new function: to accommodate a larger audience (600–800 people) for plenary sessions at which famous teachers or orators, either Alexandrians or visiting scholars, might have delivered their public lectures or orations.

To the north of the theater-like building are a number of rectangular halls (so far twenty have been excavated), all highly similar although not identical in their ground plan and architectural features. An east-west passage leading to the bath complex divides the halls into two groups, the earlier southern group and the later constructed northern group. The halls are each characterized by two or three rows of stone benches lining three sides of the walls. In the majority of halls they curve at the short side to form a horseshoe shape, and a lofty chair on a dais is placed at the middle of the head of the horseshoe, with a few steps leading to it. Almost every room also has a low pedestal or a block of stone placed in the middle of the empty space between the lengthwise benches, toward the end opposite the teacher's throne. These halls are all oriented north-south, though they differ in proportions, ranging between 7 m and 14 m (23–46 ft) in length

Figure 5.3.3 Kom el-Dikka, individual auditorium with apse

and around 5 m (16 ft) in width. Each hall in the northern group has an anteroom furnished with one row of stone benches and connected to the main hall by a large opening. However, two of the halls have an different plan: Unlike the others, both are oriented east-west and have projecting apses with semicircular benches (Figure 5.3.3). On two sides of the walls are a number of benches. According to the discoverer, Grzegorz Majcherek, these two rooms could have served as small churches, although he thinks that the absence of any traces of altars would argue against this interpretation. However, the use of movable altars, especially in small shrines, is a possibility – there is evidence of such use in a number of family shrines (*lararia*) at Pompeii – that could support a religious function for these two rooms.

Both iconographic and literary evidence indicates that the hall layout fits the picture of classrooms, or lecture halls. The benches are for the students to sit, the lofty chair for the teacher, and the small pedestal either for a student to stand on while delivering his demonstration or recitation or to support a movable lectern. The anterooms attached to the northern group of auditoria are most probably for those who used to come to listen to certain lecturers or orators for their own interest without becoming involved in systematic learning.

Not all the halls were built at one time; the pottery found in the southern group of auditoria indicates it was built earlier than the others. The later auditoria represent an enlargement of the complex during the sixth century to accommodate the increasing numbers of lectures, most probably for more than one discipline.

Alexandria's academic campus was unique. It is worth mentioning, for the sake of comparison, that in the 1950s a building was discovered on the southern slope of the Athenian Acropolis, dated to the late fourth century and known as House Chi. It is widely thought to have been the house of the Athenian Neoplatonist philosopher Proclus (412–485), head of the Athenian academy. The archaeological evidence indicates that the house was used for education; it had many small rooms surrounding a larger one with mosaics. The house was abandoned around 530, when Justinian's edict closed the Athenian academy. This private building, apparently used for teaching, confirms that Athens, probably like other cultural centers in Late Antiquity, had no fixed public places for education. Justinian's closing of the academy might have been the earliest case of official interference by the imperial government in the educational process. In Alexandria, the municipal authority apparently undertook to build this academic campus in the heart of the city over a period when higher education underwent many changes, with specifically Christian teaching emerging in the course of the fourth century (**4.11**) alongside the traditional disciplines. The final stage of this process roughly coincided with the closure of the Athenian academy, which caused an increasing number of students to flock to Alexandria. However, the closure of the Athenian academy was certainly not the only cause of the flourishing of Alexandrian scholarship in the sixth century; we have many other indications that Alexandria was an intellectual hub long before Justinian. Procopius of Gaza (465–528) called the Alexandria of his time "the mother of world intellects."

Bibliography
Borkowski 1981; Bowersock 1996; Cribiore 2001; Derda, Markiewicz, and Wipszycka 2007; Dzielska 1995; Gascou 1998a; Hendrickson 2016; Karivieri 1994; Majcherek 2010; Pearson 2008; Ruffini 2004

5.4   Egyptian villages in Late Antiquity

Although Egypt was probably the most urbanized province of the Roman Empire, the majority of its people lived in rural villages, as they had for thousands of years. Much of what we know about these villages, however, is based on how they were seen from outside, particularly by the city-based officials who had to keep track of their population and land and collect the taxes from them. In the first few centuries of Roman rule, we are fortunate enough to have many papyri from villages in the Fayyum, particularly Karanis, Theadelpheia, Tebtunis, Philadelpheia, and Soknopaiou Nesos. Whether any of these can be thought of as "typical" is hard to say. Soknopaiou Nesos was small, dependent on caravan trade and pilgrimage to its temple, almost without agricultural land. The others were much larger than average; Karanis and Tebtunis were local administrative centers. Karanis seems to have drawn more Roman veterans as settlers than most places. Still, the texture of life can be seen in some detail.

For later centuries, we are less well served. For the fourth century we have significant documentation from Karanis, Theadelpheia, and Philadelpheia, but little after the 360s. Our perception of villages in the fifth to eighth centuries is dominated by two important and relatively large places: Aphrodito (in the Antaiopolite nome) and Jeme (on the west bank at Thebes, in the Medinet Habu temple enclosure). From Aphrodito we have as many as a thousand papyri, dating to the sixth to eighth centuries, that illuminate both the dynamics of village life and the Arab administration of the Egyptian countryside. From Jeme in the seventh and (particularly) the eighth centuries we have many private documents on papyrus, mostly in Coptic, and a vast number of ostraca, also mainly in Coptic, that give us a lot of information difficult to synthesize.

Villages ranged greatly in size, from a few hundred inhabitants to several thousand, and the land attached to them reflected this range. For the average village, all of its land was probably within an hour's walk of the village center, and even the larger ones, like Aphrodito or Roman Karanis, were still fairly compact, within perhaps an area of 6–7 sq km (2.3–2.7 sq miles) or a corresponding circle. At most one should imagine perhaps 4,000 hectares (around 10,000 acres) for a big village. This area was usually divided up into a large number of small plots, often a small fraction of a hectare, and planted with a range of crops. Perhaps three-quarters or somewhat more of the land, on average, was planted in the typical arable crops: wheat, barley, flax, legumes, and fodder crops. The remainder, apart from land occupied by lanes or dikes, held higher-value crops that required artificial irrigation in addition to the rich floodwaters of the Nile, above all tree and vine crops such as olives, dates, grapes, and an array of less common fruits (**3.3**).

Some of the smaller settlements, called *epoikia* in Greek and usually referred to as "hamlets" in English, might be little more than a large estate belonging to a single family. But most full-scale villages included a substantial group of local landowners, some of whom might own 10–30 hectares (25–75 acres), but most with little more than the 2–3 hectares (5–7.5 acres) that would support a family, or even less. Outside owners, often resident in other villages or the local nome capital, owned most of the rest and leased it out to local farmers. And some villages had a dominant outside owner, a landlord who held a large part of the acreage and was also usually a major lender to farmers needing credit. And, where in Ptolemaic times there had been significant holdings by temples, in the sixth and seventh century we see properties belonging to churches – mostly to the main church in the city – as well as monasteries and other charitable institutions (**4.8**).

Villages were also centers of habitation, of course. Although there were often small outbuildings on agricultural plots, people mainly lived in densely clustered centers, composed mostly of houses. These were built of unfired mud brick, with modest amounts of wood used for doors, windows, and wall reinforcement; some flat roofs also used timbers and palm ribs along with mud, although brick vaults were very common (Figure 5.4.1). Hardly any Late Antique villages have been excavated; Jeme, situated inside the Medinet Habu mortuary temple complex and

Figure 5.4.1 House of Serenos at Trimithis (Amheida), Dakhla oasis, view from above
This 225 sq m (2,420 sq ft) house was built by a wealthy family *c.* 330–340; four of the rooms are decorated with wall paintings. It is preserved up to nearly the top of the walls; there may have been a second story or rooftop living space.

Figure 5.4.2 View of Jeme with Late Antique houses
Jeme was a Late Antique village built inside the mortuary temple of Rameses III at
Medinet Habu. This town was an important center in the seventh and eighth centuries
AD and is the source of many of the documents we have from this period.

unusually well preserved, does not likely offer an example followed in most
places (Figure 5.4.2). The larger Roman villages had not only temples but
also granaries, meeting halls for associations, and some other communal
facilities. These structures are hard to find in later villages; if Aphrodito had
been excavated systematically we might have a better sense of what it had.
What we know of are churches and monasteries. Village churches, mud-
brick buildings like the temples that preceded them, were found almost
everywhere, with a great wave of building beginning in the second quarter
of the fourth century. Only rarely were temples converted into churches,
although some early churches were remodeled houses (Figure 5.4.3). From
the time of Constantius II on, purpose-built churches dominate the landscape. These village centers were not planned settlements with a grid plan;
they had grown organically and might have been difficult for outsiders to
navigate. Depending on environmental conditions, some streets were
roofed to protect from sun and wind, and even gated, adding to the
labyrinthine feeling.

The village churches had their own local priests, deacons, and readers,
although we know relatively little about them compared to the clergy of the
metropolitan churches. There is not much sign that the village churches
had any financial resources beyond the offerings of the members of their
congregations, few of whom were wealthy. Although these churches may
have been able to support a full-time priest in many cases, the lesser clergy

Figure 5.4.3 Church at Ain el-Gedida, Dakhla oasis
The church was created by converting an older building for worship in the fourth
century. At left is the sanctuary with apse, with benches around the walls; at right,
another gathering room of uncertain function. Originally there was an opening between
the two rooms, perhaps for a speaking platform.

certainly were only part-time servants of the church, working at other jobs
or their landholdings to make a living. The clergy were certainly less
numerous than had been the priests of the earlier Roman temples.

Village monasteries are even less well known, but in Aphrodito we have
some information about one founded by Apollos, a village headman turned
monk in his later years and (fortunately) the father of the Dioskoros whose
papers are the main source of our knowledge about the village in the sixth
century. From these documents we can see that the monastery remained a
family-dominated establishment, supported by lands provided by Apollos
and his children. We should not imagine a grand establishment like the
large Pachomian monasteries, the White Monastery, or the foundations of
St. Antony and St. Paul in the Eastern Desert (**4.9**), to name only a few, let
alone the medieval examples like Deir Anba Hadra ("St. Simeon") on the
west bank at Syene. But Apollos' monastery was not the only one at
Aphrodito – Dioskoros rented land from the Monastery of Apa Sorous
(*P.Cair.Masp.* 2.67133).

Even though villages were much smaller than the nome capital cities and
had less money and fewer public institutions, they were not simple communities. As we see particularly from the archive of Dioskoros of

Aphrodito, villages had complex social structures, a range of actors, and a high degree of competition among the leading families. Marginalized groups often invisible elsewhere, such as shepherds, turn out to have been ubiquitous and well connected, even if not always appreciated when their flocks trampled or ate the crops in a field that they were not supposed to be in – or that someone thought they should not be crossing, even if the shepherds claimed a traditional right of passage.

Our documents, mostly created by men, give only a very limited picture of the lives of women in these villages. Women do own somewhat more than one-tenth of the land around the village of Aphrodito, and we find them managing their assets, particularly when the men of the family were away on business or after the death of a husband. But the documents from Aphrodito give us information about ten times as many men as women, even though there must have been roughly equal numbers or perhaps even more women. Women in fact tend not to be documented unless they own land or get involved in some kind of legal business. There are occasional signs of just how difficult life might be for a woman without means. Some wound up in domestic service even though they were not enslaved, and they might well never earn enough to escape their dependent position. However, we do find women like Koloje of Jeme, an active member of a multigenerational family of moneylenders, essentially pawnbrokers. Given the paucity of evidence, we should not generalize too readily about the women of village societies.

Slavery does not play a large role in the papyri from Aphrodito. Although not absent, slave labor was just not as important in rural villages as in the cities, where domestic service and craft production were far more significant (**2.10**). In the relatively small farms of rural Egypt, slave labor was not efficient; slaves had to be fed all year round. It was cheaper to hire people for wages in the seasons when more workers were needed. Because many such laborers owned no property, they – like women – are disproportionately missing from our texts.

The men who appear most in the texts are inevitably those with money and power. We find the village hierarchy and its complex interconnections on display in many papyri, but their relationships are often far from transparent, and patient study of various kinds, including social network analysis, has been necessary to tease out the details. What we find is a world of extensive trust networks, often only barely visible, among the ordinary farmers of the village, and at the same time strong competition between clans for dominance over the machinery of government and for connections with powerful figures outside the village who can affect its fate.

In most villages, the relationship to the imperial government was fairly straightforward, with district and nome-level officials in charge of making sure that the village's records were in order and the taxes collected. Aphrodito happens to present an unusual case, in that it had the right to collect and pay in its own taxes, without the intervention of the pagarch, the nome-level official who controlled the tax collection elsewhere. This degree of independence was unwelcome to the pagarch, and we find intermittent struggles between the governing class of the village and the pagarch, leading even to village embassies sent all the way to the imperial capital in Constantinople. This cannot have been common, but it does show that villages felt capable of approaching the imperial center directly if enough was at stake.

Ordinarily villagers would go with legal complaints to nome-level officials or, if that failed, to the provincial governor, located (in the case of Aphrodito) in Antinoopolis. The effectiveness of the system of justice in Roman Egypt has been a perennial subject of debate among historians. Not only was it cumbersome and subject to long delays, even a judgment in your favor could be difficult to enforce. The system was still in use in the sixth century, although we also find in this period that disputes were increasingly settled outside the court system. These settlements, at least ostensibly amicable, are often extremely long and detailed (e.g. *P.Mich. Aphrod.*), giving us in many cases a full narrative of how the dispute arose. These narratives are of immense interest for the social history of the period, particularly of villages.

Such dispute settlements reflect neither the end of Roman law in the province nor ignorance of the law at the local level. There is good evidence that the latest legislation from Constantinople in fact made its way to rural Egypt and was taken seriously. But there were hazards in getting involved with governors and pagarchs as judges, as they often developed relationships of patronage with village notables. Struggles between village clans over the ability to enlist the support of a higher official on their side in a dispute could turn ugly, and there was a risk of serious loss to one party. Settling might have seemed like a safer strategy. But the formal and less formal approaches to resolving disputes may have both been pursued, even at the same time.

The nastier disputes sometimes turned violent, even to the point of murder. The society of rural Egypt has indeed often been seen as a particularly violent one. This impression may be exaggerated, because such episodes are highly likely to generate documents while more peaceable settlement of disagreements will leave no trace. But violence was in fact widespread, as shown by the extensive trauma on skeletons (**2.10**), even if most daily transactions surely relied on trust and remained undocumented. The struggle of the elites to control local government, and above all local tax collection, was constant. Much money was at stake, both in making a profit from tax collection and in protecting one's own family from being overtaxed – or even being taxed fairly.

Although village economies, and thus revenues, were largely based on agriculture, they also included individuals who made all or part of their livings from other trades. A small hamlet might have very few specialties represented, a larger village a wider array, and a big settlement like Aphrodito a broad spectrum. The Hermopolite village of Temseu Skordon, for example, which we know largely from a tax register, had among its landowning taxpayers wine producers, bakers, oil-workers, butchers or meat-cooks, masons, six carpenters, cobblers, tailors, clothes cleaners, smiths, and a teacher, a doctor, a stonecutter, and a grain-measurer (*P.Lond.Herm.*). The same categories appear at Aphrodito, with substantial groups of construction workers, textile workers, food-related trades, and occupations related to river traffic. Potters must have been numerous at Aphrodito and present almost everywhere, as pottery was used in many activities of daily life and today remains by far the most common artifact on all ancient sites in Egypt. These tradesmen (for they are indeed men) were in many cases, if not all, members of occupational guilds, which often bore a collective responsibility for the taxes of their members but also served to support solidarity among practitioners of a skill. Many of them also owned and farmed land, and we have little way of telling how prosperous they were or what proportion of the local economy they represented.

We may think of rural communities today as isolated, particularly in countries where the amount of land available in the countryside is large compared to the population. This was not the case in Egypt, with each village occupying a modest amount of land and located generally within a few kilometers of another village or at least some smaller settlements. Particularly in Upper Egypt, where few villages were very far from the Nile, it was no great difficulty to travel to a nome capital or even farther. The Egyptian countryside is best understood as a dense network of connected settlements, in many cases competing at their edges over control over land that lay between them; it is Aphrodito's neighbor Phthla that generates the most bitterly resented incursions of shepherds. The large villages, however, could likely not exercise much power over their smaller neighbors. The hierarchy pointed up to the nome capitals, and above them to the provincial capitals. These cities were not remote places but a constant source for services, for credit, and for goods not produced locally. And, as we have seen, even Constantinople might not be out of reach.

Bibliography
Bagnall 1993; Cromwell 2017; Gagos and van Minnen 1994; Ruffini 2008; Ruffini 2018; Wilfong 2002

5.5   The dominance of the wealthy elite

In the fifth to seventh centuries, the most cohesive documentation for the aristocracy comes from the Oxyrhynchite nome, and in that district, the best-documented family by far is the one modern scholars call the Flavii Apiones. The Apiones appear to have begun their ascent in the mid-fifth century; the first known member of the family was one of the new bureaucratic elites discussed in **4.4**, a member of the councillor class who "escaped" that body into senatorial ranks through his service as an administrator of imperial estates. The family's big break came, however, when it was joined by marriage with the extraordinarily successful Septimii Flaviani from the nearby Herakleopolite nome (**4.4**). Service outside Egypt then followed, as did entry into the exclusive ranks of the patricians, the most exclusive subset of the senatorial order. A brief fall (including exile) – perhaps the result of Apion I's association with Severus of Antioch (**5.1**, **5.2**) – occurred during the reign of Emperor Anastasius (491–518), but Apion was rehabilitated by Justin I (518–527), and his heir soared to remarkable heights, serving as count of the sacred largesses and performing special missions for Justin's successor Justinian (527–565), whose confidence he certainly had; the men may have been exceptionally close friends. The family's fortunes reached their peak in the next generation, when Apion II was named ordinary consul, the empire's highest honor and one that only two non-emperors would hold after him (Figure 5.5.1). Later he would receive the title of "first patrician," which was reserved for the eldest and most esteemed senator and conferred the right to speak before his peers.

The Apiones were important enough to appear in literary and ecclesiastical sources, but the focus of the hundreds of papyri connected to them is their undeniably large Oxyrhynchite estate. The first documents concerning this estate appeared in print in 1898, and right away a "proto-feudal" conception of it began to emerge. Scholars supposed that its formation was

Figure 5.5.1 Consular diptych of Apion II

Consular diptych of Apion II (Museo de la Iglesia, Catedral de Oviedo). Apion II was one of the last non-imperial recipients of the ordinary consulship, the Empire's highest honor. This was bestowed (AD 539) when he was still a young man (under twenty-five; note the beardless visage within the medallions) and presumably owed something to his father's close relationship with Justinian (Box 5.5.1). From left to right in the image, the inscription (*CIL* II 2699) reads *v(ir) inl(ustris) com(es) dev(otissimorum) dom(esticorum) et cons(ul) or(dinarius) | Fl(avius) Strategius Apion Strategius Apion*, "*vir illustris* [the highest senatorial rank], count of the most devoted domestics and ordinary consul | Flavius Strategius Apion Strategius Apion" (the long name, an example of the elite polyonomy typical in Late Antiquity, gives Apion's lineage; his individuating name comes last in the sequence).

made possible by the destruction of the metropolitan governing class on the one hand and imperial weakness on the other. It was thought to be populated by a serf-like workforce (the *coloni adscripticii*, as legal sources call them) and to serve as an economic engine through which the owners usurped the power and functions of the state, such as law enforcement and tax collection, in their home district. This "feudal" interpretation of the evidence would come to exert considerable influence on histories of Egypt as a whole during the fifth through seventh centuries (see, for example, Bell 1917).

Despite its impact on modern scholarship, the feudal model has two key weaknesses. First, it may not reflect an accurate reading of the sources. The Apion family seems, for the most part, to have been quite close to imperial power (Box 5.5.1); it is therefore hard to suppose that it needed to usurp authority and responsibility – after all, it was already being given much power by the emperor. Second, the Apiones may have been an exceptional case, both in the Oxyrhynchite – where the papyri concerning their estate

---

Box 5.5.1 The emperor's right-hand man: From the medieval Greek *Narrative on the Construction of Hagia Sophia*

The so-called Holy Well and the entire presbytery, and the site of the ambo and beyond as far as the middle of the nave [of the future Hagia Sophia] was [at that time occupied by] the house of a eunuch and doorkeeper Antiochos, and was worth thirty-eight pounds [of gold]. When he had qualms about selling his house to the emperor [Justinian], the emperor, who loved justice and hated evil, was unwilling to do injustice to anybody, and became dispirited as he did not know what to do. The *magistros* Strategius [II, son of Apion I], the keeper of the imperial treasures [i.e. the count of the sacred largesses], the spiritual brother of the emperor, promised to arrange this by some trick. The aforesaid doorkeeper Antiochos was a great lover of Hippodrome games, and while a race was being held the *magistros* Strategios put the eunuch into prison. On the day of the race, Antiochos began to scream from the prison, "Let me see the Hippodrome games, and I will do the will of the emperor." They brought him to the Stama [facing the finish line] before the imperial loge where the emperor used to sit during the games, and there he made the sale, with the *quaestor* [a palace legal official] and all the senate subscribing before the horses started the race. It was an old custom that, as soon as the emperor went up to the loge, the chariot teams started to race. But because they were delayed by the selling of the eunuch's houses, up to this day the racing chariots of the horses go out slowly. (Translation Berger 2013)

utterly dominate the textual record, even though it is clear that other aristocrats, including some of very high status, were also on the scene – and more importantly, elsewhere in Egypt. In short, we must determine whether the rich and cohesive archive of the Apiones has distorted our historical narratives.

Scrutiny of the sources does not support the feudal model. If the papyri are given a "bottom-up" (inductive) reading instead of a "top-down" (framework-driven) one, they point us to a very different interpretation. Elements of this alternate, source-driven view were already present in the earliest synthesis (Hardy 1931), but it reached maturity in 1985 with the presentation of what is now known as the "Gascou thesis" (after its author, French papyrologist Jean Gascou). According to Gascou and other proponents of this view, aristocrats like the Apiones were not trying to wrest power away from the imperial center; rather, they were more-or-less willing cooperators who had stepped into the administrative vacuum left in the wake of the decline of the councillor class (see Box 4.4.2). Thus fiscal and police (or "military") functions suppposed to have been usurped from the state were in fact undertaken with its blessing if not encouragement, while the supposed proto-serf status simply represented a development or codification of long-standing practices in taxation, a development that may not even have been widespread on the estate. Most (but not all) scholars now accept some variant of the Gascou thesis as their interpretative framework for the relationship between the state and the aristocracy during this period in Egyptian history.

All the same, the Gascou thesis may still be open to question because of its dependency on the Apion papyri. The Apiones may have been fiscally responsible for two-fifths of the Oxyrhynchite and Cynopolite nomes, but substantial space remained for other aristocrats, some of them of quite elevated status, about whom we know almost nothing. Nevertheless, it seems likely, despite the significant gaps in our sources, that any differences between these other elites and the Apiones were matters of degree: The structures through which the region was administered seem to have been applicable to all, and elements considered typical of the Apion estate (e.g. the tied tenantry) are also attested on the holdings of other agents, including the church, which can hardly be ignored when we consider the power dynamics of Byzantine Egypt.

When we look beyond the Oxyrhynchite, the question becomes trickier. The Miaphysite (anti-Chalcedonian) magnate known to scholars as Strategius *paneuphemos* ("all praiseworthy"), who is attested primarily in the Fayyum but also had holdings elsewhere, appears to have managed and

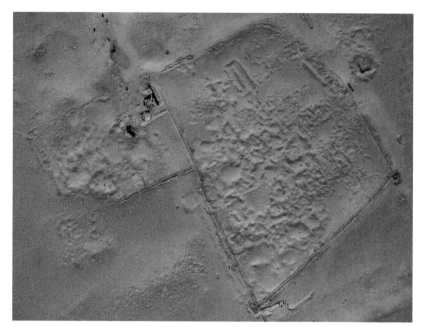

Figure 5.5.2 Aerial image of Oxyrhynchos, possibly showing house of Apion family
Aerial image produced during the Catalan excavations at al-Bahnasa (the ancient
Oxyrhynchos) of a roughly 1-hectare (2.5-acre) complex on the northwest of the site. In
a later phase of its use this complex had a religious function, but it has plausibly been
suggested (Jördens 2016) that it earlier served as the *proastion* (suburban estate house)
of the powerful Apion family. Thus the large zone on the right of the image, for
example, identified as a "funerary basilica" by the excavators, may have earlier
functioned as the estate house's reception hall.

exploited his property in a manner roughly comparable to that of the
Apiones. (The emperor Heraclius is said to have called upon Strategius to
mediate a dispute between the Miaphysite patriarchs of Alexandria and
Antioch – like the Apiones, Strategius seems to have moved in lofty circles.)
Because the evidence from the Fayyum is more diffuse, the public administrative apparatus in Strategius' home district is less clear, but there are
signs that the Oxyrhynchite system was operative. Whether other areas in
Egypt had the aristocratic presence necessary to sustain this system is
another question.

   In very general terms, there seems to have been a north–south progression, rich to poor, in Byzantine Egypt, and the social landscape in places
south of the Oxyrhynchite such as the Hermopolite and Antaiopolite
appears less polarized. This does not mean that elites were absent in
those places, or that they played no role in the local administration, or

that patronage and abuses of power were unknown – the sixth-century papyri from the village of Aphrodito, the other cohesive body of evidence from the period, testify to the contrary – but nonetheless the picture is noticeably different. Despite some recent efforts to argue the contrary, the papyri suggest that the Byzantine Oxyrhynchite was a special case, and extrapolating broader trends from its evidence is risky. In other words, it should be assumed that the "typical" late Roman fiscal and administrative apparatus (**5.4**) was operative unless there is clear evidence that different arrangements applied.

Bibliography
Azzarello 2010; Banaji 2007; Bell 1917; Gascou 1985/2008; Hardy 1931; Hickey 2007; Jördens 1999; Jördens 2016; Keenan 1993; Mazza 2004; Palme 1997

5.6 City and country: dependence and divergence

A persistent theme throughout our study of both Ptolemaic and Roman Egypt has been the growth of its cities in size, importance, and role in governance (**2.1, 3.1**). Particularly after the creation of city councils at the start of the third century, and then with the increased responsibility for administration of the countryside in the fourth century, the cities come to have a dominant position. Much land in the nomes was owned by residents of the cities, and these landowners were in turn an important source of credit for the villagers. For post-elementary education, markets, a range of expertise, and government services, the cities were essential sources of goods and services for their regions. As the two preceding sections (**5.4, 5.5**) have shown, the responsibility of the urban elites for managing the countryside only increased in the fifth and sixth centuries, even as their ranks diminished, and some entire settlements were controlled by metropolitan notables.

And yet, as we have also seen, the villages did not atrophy. They still had their own craftspeople for everyday needs, and they had their own churches and clergy to help provide leadership. They might even, in exceptional cases such as Aphrodito, have tried to contest the dominance of the city in managing their taxation process. A wealthy, cultured villager with literary ambitions might have found it to his advantage to move for part of his life and career to a major city, as Dioskoros of Aphrodito did.

It is just after the period of Dioskoros' career, in the last quarter of the sixth century, that signs appeared of a change in the relationship between city and country, one that was to have important consequences. It has often been remarked that the papers of Dioskoros give us no sense of the growing divide in the Egyptian church between those who adhered to the imperially approved Chalcedonian doctrine, according to which Christ had two natures, human and divine, and those who rejected the Chalcedonian doctrine in favor of a single nature that was both human and divine (**5.2**). The latter was the view represented at Chalcedon by the Egyptian bishops, led by another Dioskoros, the archbishop of Alexandria between 444 and 454. We do not even know for certain which side Dioskoros of Aphrodito himself took (**5.4**), although there are reasons to think he was anti-Chalcedonian.

The divide between the Chalcedonians and anti-Chalcedonians was real, and after some unfulfilled moves toward ordaining separate anti-Chalcedonian bishops, the decisive step was taken by Peter IV, the anti-Chalcedonian bishop of Alexandria in 576–578 (**5.2**). According to John of Ephesos, who did not like Peter, the bishop of Alexandria named seventy bishops during his short reign, thus creating a parallel ecclesiastical hierarchy throughout the land (*Hist.Eccl.* 4.12). The number is suspiciously round and familiar (one thinks of the translators of the Septuagint), but it is likely that anti-Chalcedonian bishops were ordained for most of the main nome-level dioceses in Egypt. From this point on, there were competing church structures throughout the country, and, as we have seen, Peter's successor Damian (578–c. 607) occupies a commanding position in the history of the Egyptian church in this period as the builder of a parallel ecclesiastical hierarchy.

It is not immediately evident how this parallelism could have worked on the ground, or what its consequences would have been for the relationship of city and countryside. The bishops mostly had their seats in the capitals of the nomes, where the representatives of imperial power were also located. These representatives are not likely to have allowed the local cathedral church and the other extensive property of the church to have been taken over by clerics rejecting the doctrinal position ordained by the emperor. The episcopal residence, the revenue-producing lands and urban properties, the charitable institutions (**4.8**): these all must have remained in the control of the Chalcedonian bishops in all but exceptional cases. Where were the anti-Chalcedonian bishops?

From a couple of well-documented cases we have had glimpses of an answer to this question. These are bishops Abraham, the bishop of Hermonthis in the beginning of the seventh century, ordained no later than 601 and probably still in office in 622; and Pisenthios, the bishop of Coptos around the same time, ordained in 599 and still in office after 629. For these bishops, both appointees of Damian (**5.2**), we are fortunate to possess archives, largely of correspondence and other records of their activity as pastors and as supervisors of the lower ranks of the clergy.

Abraham conducted his episcopal duties from the Monastery of Phoibammon, built in the ruins of the Hatshepsut temple at Deir el-Bahri, on the west bank at Thebes (Figure 5.6.1). There is no evidence that he ever resided in Hermonthis, his nominal seat. Pisenthios resided for the most part in the Monastery of Tsenti (Deir el-Gizaz), about 20 km (12 miles) from Coptos, but he spent some part of the Persian occupation in the

Figure 5.6.1 Deir el-Bahri, Monastery of St. Phoibammon
The Monastery of St. Phoibammon as it stood before the removal of the mud-brick structures to make the New Kingdom Temple of Hatshepsut more visible and available for tourism. The Monastery of St. Phoibammon had been built toward the end of the sixth century over the ruins of the temple of Hatshepsut near Thebes. At the end of the nineteenth century, the ruins of the monastery, abandoned around 800, still stood over the temple. The tower on the left, which offered an excellent view toward the valley and the town of Jeme, was a characteristic element of Late Antique Egyptian monasteries in the area. The monastery had a space where guests could spend the night, and housed the relic of the martyr Phoibammon.

Monastery of Epiphanius, again on the west bank of the Theban region. Phoibammon and Tsenti were monasteries in which these men had been monks before election as bishop, and their remaining there while bishop was not unprecedented in the seventh century. Bishops of Antinoopolis, Lykopolis, and perhaps Arsinoe also resided in monasteries, although we know much less about their activity. One earlier instance, before the division of the church, can also be pointed to: a bishop of Oxyrhynchos at the end of the fourth century named Aphou, who despite living at a monastery spent each Saturday and Sunday in Oxyrhynchos. So residence is not in itself decisive for the question of how Abraham and Pisenthios conducted their duties as bishops. What is more striking is that their extensive correspondence deals entirely with matters in rural areas, mainly in villages. Never do they handle a matter relating to the clergy, churches, or faithful of the cities.

It is unlikely that this silence is just an accident of our sources. If it reflects daily reality, however, it has a number of implications. First, these monasteries did not have the wealth or large-scale facilities of the urban episcopates. Being a bishop under such circumstances was likely to be a different experience, and in fact the correspondence of Pisenthios and Abraham has nothing much to say of administration or finance. Second, it remains difficult to see just how the existence of parallel bishops was managed on a day-to-day basis. It is hard to imagine that there was not some sort of agreement, whether tacit or not, between the rival bishops and involving the civil authorities, about just what parts of the rural church the anti-Chalcedonian bishop would be allowed to govern from his monastic base.

However sensible such a tacit agreement may have been in the face of the realities on the ground, it had to have serious outcomes. A division along lines linking cities with Chalcedonian doctrine and rural areas with anti-Chalcedonian principles may well have created, if it did not reflect, a closer tie between the cities and the imperial government than between the villages and that government. And the dominant position of Coptic as a means of communication in these monasteries, which we see reflected in the correspondence of the two bishops, contrasts with the grip that Greek retained on all official correspondence and most legal contracts as the standard language of the cities. We do not have to imagine a separatist nationalism (4.2) to see the potential for an increased divide between the outlooks of the city and the countryside.

We would like to know if a comparable gap opened up in this period, or even earlier, between the Delta and Upper Egypt. It is easy to suppose that the historical divide between the Two Lands or the modern prejudices of the urban populations of the north about the rural south have their counterpart in Late Antiquity. Certainly the Delta nomes were much closer to Alexandria and Pelusium and thus more obviously exposed to the world of the Eastern Mediterranean, and the north was also probably richer than the south (**5.5**).

The evidence of the fourth to sixth centuries, however, gives limited comfort to such regional distinctions. The architectural style of churches in Upper Egypt, despite some possible local traits, does not differ substantially from that of those in the Alexandrian region, and the church of the White Monastery (Figure 4.9.1), and the Basilica of Hermopolis (Figure 5.6.2)

Figure 5.6.2 Basilica of Hermopolis
This grandiose church, with a nave and two aisles, was one of the largest known in Egypt, reusing columns and other materials from Roman public buildings. It was the seat of the bishop of the city.

show that both monasteries and cities in the south could build on a grand scale. Similarly, the lavish decoration of the Red Monastery church does not represent provincial taste but is consistent with international trends of the period. And the great flowering of Late Antique poetry in Egypt is above all the work of natives of Upper Egyptian cities such as Panopolis (**5.3**), and the poems of Dioskoros of Aphrodito show that even at the level of the village elite there was no lack of cultural ambition rooted in the Greek poetic past. The lack of papyri from the Delta, even more acute in this period than earlier, makes it hard to compare many other dimensions of culture, and the archaeology of the Delta remains much more limited than that of the Nile valley. All the same, there is little to suggest that the regions of Egypt were growing apart in the period from Diocletian to Justinian.

Whether this began to change in the last quarter of the sixth century is difficult to say. There continues to be little documentary evidence from the Delta; the chronological imprecision of archaeology hardly allows us to pin any changes down exactly; and the Persian occupation of 619–629 (**6.1**) accounts for more discontinuity throughout Egypt than any domestic developments. It is hard to know how far the economic elite of Upper Egypt was dislodged or destroyed by that decade's turmoil and to what extent that might have had a cultural and political impact on the internal cohesion of the land.

Bibliography
Cameron 2007; McKenzie 2007; Wipszycka 2007; Wipszycka 2015

5.7   Coptic develops a literature and bids for official status

The world of learning in Alexandria functioned exclusively in Greek, the language spoken across the Eastern Mediterranean from where many of the students and even teachers came (**5.3**). For several centuries, higher education and all forms of writing in the public sphere had been in Greek. Literacy in Coptic was acquired only to a level that was sufficient for private communication, except in monastic circles where the language was also used for literary and normative compositions such as biographies and rules.

By the end of the fourth century Greek had been present in Egypt for more than 700 years, and it is clear from the evidence that it was understood as a local language, and that its speakers considered themselves Egyptians. Both Greek- and Coptic-speakers referred to themselves as

Aigyptioi (Egyptians): They did not align themselves ethnically with their language of communication. The term "Egyptian" was also used to describe the local language, with no religious connotation. By the sixth century, it seems clear that the population of Egypt understood itself as bilingual, but did not link that bilingualism to different personal origins.

As in most bilingual societies, including Ptolemaic and Roman Egypt, use of the two languages differed not so much by ethnic or religious group but by areas of life. Because it was the language of the Roman administration, Greek was prevalent in the public domain and was used for documents that were official or institutional. This included not only administrative and legal documents, but also the writings of the bishops of Alexandria and other clerics, and communication of an official nature between ecclesiastical institutions. Greek was also the language of learning, especially in areas such as poetry, philosophy, or theology, which engaged with the broader Mediterranean tradition of learning. Greek was a scholarly *lingua franca*, while writing in Egyptian would have restricted the audience of a work to local consumption. Egyptian, by contrast, was used primarily for private communication, in areas of life not part of the public sphere. It was used very commonly in letters among family members or on local business matters, but also at a larger scale within relatively closed communities, such as monasteries or sectarian groups like the Manichaeans.

During its initial period, Coptic developed a reputation as a less refined language than Greek and therefore as a language that carried lower social prestige. This was partly because Coptic did not develop the formal linguistic features of official texts, which are instrumental in allowing a language to convey power, and partly because it was promoted by monastic circles as the language of those who refused Graeco-Roman learning, believing it increased the distance from God. The first known use of this religious opposition appears in Athanasius' *Life of Antony*, which gives Greek the value of a rational language, while Egyptian, spoken by Antony, was characterized as the innocent, uncultivated language that made possible his unique proximity to God. Used in a rhetorical and symbolic way, this presentation of Coptic as an anti-intellectual language became very popular in monastic circles, and left its mark on the judgments of many later authors, ancient and modern. Ironically, Athanasius launched this spiritualizing view of Coptic in a book that he wrote, like all of his works, in Greek.

In the sixth century, however, this long-standing association of Coptic with circles hostile to learning and with the lower, uneducated strata of society started to break down. Little by little the language appears to have acquired a previously unknown social prestige, something that is visible in a new willingness of the provincial elites to use it in public at a time when the empire's provinces gained a high degree of autonomy and power. This increased autonomy, enabled by Justin II's decision to let episcopal and landowning elites elect the provincial governors, accelerated the tendency toward regional devolution in the Roman provinces, which affected Egypt. The move of Coptic into a much more public role is one of the most striking contemporary developments, and it is probable that the two phenomena are not unrelated.

The rise in the public visibility of Coptic is clear in several areas, but most prominent perhaps in its role as an episcopal language. The bishops appointed by Damian from 575 onward, who reinvigorated the Severan strand of the Egyptian church (**5.2**), used Coptic to write not only their theological commentaries, which could arguably have been addressed mainly to other like-minded clerics, but also their sermons and homilies, delivered before public assemblies. Coptic was thus treated as a rhetorical language at the same level as Greek, and many of those homilies make self-conscious references to the common cultural tradition. These bishops had clearly received a traditional classical education, but they could also admirably handle the Coptic language. The *Panegyric* written by John of Hermopolis in honor of St. Antony closely follows the rules of epideictic rhetoric, and the author places himself in a line of predecessors who wrote similar panegyrics. The other bishops make similar claims, and insist on the necessity to give their own personal perspective on the subject they treat, "according to our ability," as John put it, repeating another rhetorical commonplace, that of the humble, inadequate author.

The bishops appointed by Damian were instrumental in promoting Coptic as a literary and rhetorical language beyond the monastic sphere. Their occasional references to Shenoute as an illustrious (if only newly idealized) predecessor show that they learned much from his rhetorical use of Coptic, even if at the time it had remained within the confines of monastic discourse. This movement was most prominent in the southern part of the country, with figures such as John of Shmun, Constantine of Asyut or Pisenthios of Coptos. The fact that the Severan bishops operated predominantly in the countryside may have also played a role in their choice of language. Yet the titles of several of those homilies claim that they were delivered in the presence of high officials, even if in rural shrines. That alone shows that the language was beginning to be considered in a very different light, and that its practitioners recognized it as a legitimate medium of official public expression.

Even though the return of the Severans as the mainstream Miaphysite (anti-Chalcedonian) faction was instrumental in bringing Coptic more prominently into the public sphere, the use of Coptic was nevertheless building on a tendency that had developed since the end of the fifth century. The Egyptian monastic world, strongly against the Council of Chalcedon (**5.2**), did not refrain from producing texts that promoted their anti-Chalcedonian views. It continued to produce biographies of monks as before, but they were no longer compositions for internal consumption within the monastic world: Their aim was to offer the population examples of holy men who had chosen the right side in the conflict, and thus to persuade them to do the same, with a tone that was unabashedly polemical. Texts such as the *Life of Abraham of Pboou*, the *Life of Manasse*, the *Life of Daniel of Sketis*, or the *Life of Moses of Abydos*, are characteristic examples. Biographies of bishops were produced along the same lines, as were several spurious texts attributed to Severus of Antioch, whose popularity in Egypt reached its peak under Damian and his successors. Along with the invented texts, translations of his works were made at the time.

Apparently also at this time, the work known as the *History of the Church* (**4.10**), an ongoing historical account of the see of Alexandria, started taking the form under which we know it today through the later Arabic *History of the Patriarchs of Alexandria*, which itself is based, for the period before the Arab conquest, on a previous work in Coptic. This account was already organized in the form of biographies of the successive Miaphysite bishops (and their predecessors), which had been collected, and sometimes abbreviated, to form an uninterrupted narrative history. Such biographies of bishops were also produced independently, and some of those separate works are known to us today. Like the polemical biographies of anti-Chalcedonian monks, those texts were intended for circulation among a broader audience, where they could serve as guides and exemplars for those who wanted to find the right doctrinal path.

Using Coptic in public was not the sole prerogative of bishops and monks: It is also visible in epigraphy, perhaps the most unmistakably public form of private expression and self-representation (Figure 5.7.1). The earliest securely dated inscriptions in Coptic go back to the very beginning of the seventh century. Even though most Coptic inscriptions are very difficult to date even approximately, the few securely dated ones indicate that they started being produced in the second half of the sixth century. The choice of language in private inscriptions

Figure 5.7.1 Coptic funerary stela from Esna/Latopolis, sixth–seventh century
This funerary stela commemorates Antonios and is among the early examples of such
monuments with a text in Coptic. The characteristic round top follows the contour of a
circle containing an inscribed cross and a decoration of stylized leaves and flowers.

within a bilingual context is considered to be a good indicator of the
prestige enjoyed by a language, and the rise in the use of Coptic at this
time agrees with the rest of the evidence in reflecting the language's
enhanced status.

Thus religious texts in Coptic started being produced and used outside
the secluded context of monasteries, and individuals used the language to
proclaim private events and acts to the broader community. The language
slowly acquired a more complex and sophisticated repertoire of texts,
fostered initially by an institution, monasticism, which in the sixth century
was no longer the countercultural force it had been in the fourth century
but had become a prestigious and valued part of the establishment. What is
most significant, because more unexpected and less consciously driven by a
specific social group, is the progress made by Coptic in the world of legal
documentary practice.

The first extant legal document written in Coptic that can be dated with some precision is from the middle of the sixth century, and it heralds the appearance of many more to come. Drawn up by the bilingual notary Dioskoros in the Middle Egyptian town of Aphrodito (**5.4**), it records the result of an arbitration of a local dispute. The proliferation of such documents between the mid-sixth century and the Persian conquest of the early seventh century shows the enhanced status of Coptic in this area, too – the urban proprietary elites who usually produced such documents no longer thought it beneath their dignity to use it. Not that they stopped using Greek: these fully bilingual provincial notables produced and ordered documents in both languages depending on the context. In addition to Dioskoros, other members of the Aphrodito landed gentry had documents drawn up in both languages, as did individuals and families elsewhere, such as the dye-seller Aurelius Pachymios from a village near Panopolis, or the family of Patermouthis in Syene. However, Greek remained the normal language of public administration and private contracts.

Although arbitrations were not official documents, since they did not adopt the form of a contract, petition, judicial decision, or any other official deed, they nevertheless needed to be produced in an official context in the event the settlement was not respected and the case had to be reopened. Even in Coptic, arbitration documents had to carry legal validity. At the same time, the gradual decline of the imperial judicial system and of official tribunals, and the concomitant rise of independent notaries with the necessary legal knowledge and authority, made the choice of documentary language less relevant, since either could be used in a procedure that did not go through official channels. This development took place in the bilingual milieu of provincial urban and rural elites, which included the notaries as well as the litigants. Their willingness to use Coptic in their written transactions, even while they aspired, like Dioskoros, to write Greek poetry, is a measure of how far up the ladder of social prestige the language had traveled in the sixth century.

The use of Coptic in legal documents also required specific legal education in that language. In the earlier period, education in Coptic was limited to basic literacy for most, with a more systematic study of the language probably provided in monasteries for those who translated and composed literary texts. This study was not sufficient to prepare people to draw up legal documents; even though the work was done by bilingual notaries who had the legal background and knew the technical language in Greek, it presupposed some specialized training in legal Coptic. The language of the earliest arbitrations was simple, but soon a vocabulary developed that was specific to Coptic and consistent across the country, implying centralized and institutional-ized study of the relevant techniques rather than improvisation on the part of individual notaries.

Returning to the world of the bishops, but this time to their documents, we also see them using Coptic in their relations with their flock. The late sixth- and early seventh-century correspondences of bishops Abraham of Hermonthis and Pisenthios of Coptos (**5.6**) are entirely in Coptic, which may not be surprising for letters dealing with private concerns (Figure 5.7.2). Much of the material in Abraham's archive, however, deals with institutional matters such as ordinations, arbitration decisions, work contracts, guarantees, etc. In the context described above where official tribunals were losing ground, the role of the church in the judicial process (**4.6**) and in arbitrations became more prominent. From the archive of Abraham it is evident that the

Figure 5.7.2 Ostracon with a letter from Bishop Abraham of Hermonthis
O.Crum 71 (late sixth – early seventh century, Hermonthis or Monastery of St. Phoibammon). This letter, like most of his correspondence, was written by bishop Abraham on a piece of limestone. In it he condemns the behavior of a certain Psate, about whose ill treatment the poor have complained to the bishop. Written in the third person, the letter reads as a public condemnation, and is not a direct reprimand to Psate.

> **Box 5.7.1 Arbitration by Bishop Abraham: *BKU* 2.318**
> **(Hermonthis, early seventh century)**
>
> First I greet your sonship. The Lord bless you through God's mercy. God gave us the good *lashane* and those who rule among the people. When therefore he came now to our humbleness with his brothers and the great men and all the people of the town, we asked their sonships for peace, that there would be peace amidst you together with them at once. For it is written: 'Who destroys war, establishes peace'. When we asked them for peace, they said, 'Be so good as to write to them, "We agree on peace". Be so good as to send us the outcome of the matter as it is'. May the Lord bless you and give you peace with those who are amidst you at once. Be so good to us and send me the outcome, how you want to talk to them by God. I pray for the well-being of all of you. Give it to my pious children, Apa Victor and all the great men together, from Abraham, the most humble. (Translation by G. Schmelz in Keenan, Manning, and Yiftach-Firanko [2014]: 529.)

bishop took full advantage of his right to hold audiences of a judicial nature and to make decisions that were binding for members of his flock. In the case of Abraham at least, these were all recorded in Coptic (Box 5.7.1). This did not prevent him from having his will drawn up in Greek on papyrus with all the necessary legal cautions. Outside the episcopal and monastic culture – since Abraham was also the superior of the Monastery of St. Phoibammon at Jeme (Figure 5.6.1) – Greek was still much preferred for writing private acts. Nevertheless, in comparison with the preceding period, Coptic had taken a big step forward: It was now considered a valid language for legal transactions.

Bibliography

Dekker 2018; Fournet 2009a; Fournet 2010; Fournet 2013; Fournet 2018a; Fournet 2020; Papaconstantinou 2008; Papaconstantinou 2010a; Richter 2008

6 | The Persians, the Arab conquest, and another transformation of Egypt

6.1 The Sasanians in Egypt

The Persian invasion and occupation in the early seventh century, coming after a long period of political stability, deeply scarred Egypt and had a lasting effect on its power structure. The origins of the invasion date to the start of the seventh century, when hostilities broke out between Sassanid Persia and the Roman Empire in what would be the last war between these two powers. The conflict was set in motion in 602 with the overthrow of the emperor Maurice by his officer Phocas. The shah Khusraw II, of whom the deposed emperor had been a patron and supporter, invaded the eastern empire in 603, and in relatively quick succession the Sasanians would strip the Romans of Armenia, Mesopotamia, Syria, and Palestine. In 619, Alexandria fell, and in the months afterward Egypt as a whole was lost. The unraveling of these Persian victories, however, would also come rapidly: A series of successful campaigns by the emperor Heraclius, who had overthrown Phocas in 610, would leave the Sasanian Empire on the brink of collapse in 628, and by 630 all of the lost territories in the East would be back in the Roman fold.

The evidence for the roughly decade-long Persian interlude in Egypt includes secular and religious narratives in Greek, Coptic, Arabic, and Syriac; documents on papyri and ostraca in Greek, Coptic, and Middle Persian (Pahlavi); and other archaeological material, including coinage (Figure 6.1.1). The most striking of the narrative accounts appears in the *History of the Patriarchs of Alexandria*, which relates the mass slaughter of monks at the Enaton monastery and elsewhere and the plundering and destruction of monasteries, as well as the execution of all adult males in Alexandria, in the course of the invasion. Though this report is clearly an exaggeration, other evidence confirms that the conquest was violent. Relevant in this regard are the excavations at the pilgrimage center of Abu Mina, not far from Alexandria, which reveal a period of ruin and abandonment that archaeologists have attributed to the Persians. The contemporary Greek and Coptic documents that report atrocities

(a) (b)

Figure 6.1.1 *Dodecanummium* **minted under Sasanian rule, Alexandria**
Dodecanummium (12-*nummus* coin) minted in Alexandria during Sasanian
rule, AD 619-629. Obverse: Facing cuirassed bust wearing crown with *pendilia* and
flanked by a star (left) and crescent (right). Reverse: cross on *globus* with I (=10) to
the left and B (=2) to the right; in exergue: ΑΛΕΞ (mintmark).

committed by the invaders may also be noted. News of the invasion
preceded the Persians' arrival and caused consternation and, in some
instances, flight; again the papyrological record is illustrative, as are the
hoards of coins that anxious Egyptians buried at this time. High-profile
refugees are said to have included the Chalcedonian patriarch John and the
patricius (and cousin of the emperor Heraclius) Nicetas, who together
sailed from Alexandria to Rhodes, as well as Bishop Pisenthios of Coptos
(**5.6**, **5.7**), who initially hid in the Theban necropolis. Another high-
ranking member of the secular elite, the *patricius* Apion III (**5.5**), however,
may have held his ground and perished in battle.

The Persians' aggression, at least as a matter of general policy, was short-
lived, but Egyptians found their freedom of movement curtailed, as would
also be the case later under the Umayyads. There was no systematic persecution of Christians, and the Coptic patriarch Benjamin I seems to have
succeeded Andronicus without incident in 626. Persian officials – most
notably one Saralaneozan (Box 6.1.1), whose authority likely extended to
the entire province – replaced high-ranking governors like Nicetas, but at
lower levels of administration many of the personnel, like Flavius Magistor in
the Hermopolite and the Arsinoite pagarch Menas, remained in place.
Institutions were even more likely to persist. The "house" (**4.4**) of Apion,
for example, survived as a fiscal entity long after its master's death, well into

626 at the least. Egyptians continued to pay their taxes on the same schedule and mostly in the same manner as before, though with the end of the shipment of tax grain to Constantinople, payments in kind were more likely to be converted into cash, and the Sasanians did issue their own version of the copper coinage. The principal Persian presence in the province was undoubtedly military, and this is the aspect of the occupation that the corpus of papyri written in Pahlavi best illustrates (Figure 6.1.2). Communication and contractual relationships with Egypt's inhabitants seem to have occurred in either Greek or Coptic. Though texts in these languages do show borrowings from Persian (e.g. *sellarios* < Persian salar, "official") and vice-versa (ltl' < *litra*, "pound"), such inclusions were hardly typical.

It has recently been suggested that the linguistic resistance of Greek and Coptic to Persian reflects indigenous indifference or even hostility toward the invaders. This view of Egypt's posture toward its occupiers seems more plausible than one popular in the first half of the twentieth century, according to which the predominantly anti-Chalcedonian inhabitants of the province welcomed the Persians as liberators from their Chalcedonian oppressors. In this regard, it should be noted that the *History of the Patriarchs*, probably the source where sympathy for the Sasanians would be most likely to appear, instead views them with hostility.

Box 6.1.1 Feasting the Persian governor: *BGU* 2.377 (619–629)

List of deliveries to the kitchen of the all-praiseworthy Saralaneozan, our master:

As follows:

1st day: vinegar, 5 *sirota*; fish sauce, 1 *knidion*; sheep, 1; lamb, 1; pig [or piglet], 1; chickens, 2; pigeons, 2; eggs, 20.

[second hand] 2nd day: vinegar, 11 *kollatha*; sheep, 1; pig [or piglet], 1; piglets [or pigs], 2; chickens, 2; pigeons, 4.

[third hand] 3rd day: vinegar, 9 *kollatha*; sheep, 1; pig [or piglet], 1; chickens, 3; pigeons, 6; camel, 1; eggs, 27.

On the same day: piglets [or pigs], 3; donkey, 1.

[second hand] To the cithara-player through Narses: sheep, 1.

[third hand] 4th day: sheep, 1; lamb, 1; pig (or piglet), 1; chickens, 2; pigeons, 6.

[fourth hand] Sabur: eggs, 12.

Chorochosro: vinegar, 1 *lagynion*; eggs, 15.

[On the back:] List of expenses . . . (author's translation)

Figure 6.1.2 Fragment of a Pahlavi letter
Hundreds of Pahlavi (Middle Persian) texts dating to the brief Sasanian occupation of
Egypt (AD 619-629) have been preserved. These documents were written on papyrus
(as here), parchment, or sometimes linen. Their script runs from right to left and was
produced using a brush (instead of the reed pen used for other texts written in Egypt
during the same period). Pahlavi documents mainly concern the affairs of the
occupying army, though some private letters are also extant.

Whether Egypt's relationship with the Persians is relevant for assessing
the long-term consequences of the occupation is another question. It has
been argued that Egyptians experienced Sassanid rule as relatively benign,
and that this experience, combined with heightened Miaphysite alien-
ation in the wake of Heraclius' attempts to reestablish "orthodoxy" in
reconquered territories, reduced resistance to the later Islamic invasion.
As we have seen, however, a broadly positive view of the Persians is not
supported by the evidence, and in any case, the argument tries to over-
simplify the answer to the complex question of the rapid growth of the
Islamic state. Nonetheless, the Sasanian occupation did have some long-
term impact: It changed Egypt's power structure (**5.5**). The highest elites
disappear from the scene, and when Egypt is once again Roman, they do
not reemerge. The result was a loss of leadership and resources and, with
the dissolution of the houses, administrative change. This had to have left

Egypt weakened and reduced its capacity to repel the next army that crossed its borders.

Bibliography

Foss 2003; Fournet 2009a; Gariboldi 2009; Gonis 2007; MacCoull 1986; Sanger 2011

6.2   The Arab conquest and lingering uncertainties

The decade that followed the departure of the Persians in 629 is one of the least well known to historians, especially outside Alexandria. We have very few sources, and even papyri that are precisely dated from that period are scarce. The event that dominates Egyptian narrative sources is the replacement in 633 by the emperor Heraclius of the anti-Chalcedonian patriarch Benjamin with the Chalcedonian Cyrus, who was already in Egypt as the deputy of the provincial governor (*topoteretes*). The *History of the Patriarchs*, as well as several texts centered on and partial to Benjamin, understandably cast a very negative light on that event and on the entire period when Cyrus held the patriarchate in the city, leaving Benjamin no choice but to return to the monastic home of earlier Severan patriarchs. Cyrus had been sent to Egypt, however, with a conciliatory mission, namely to unite the two Christian factions under the banner of a new formulation of dogma known as Monoenergism. The new teaching tried to circumvent the thorny issue of Christ's nature, which had divided the churches for so long, by focusing instead on his "energy," which was defined as one, emanating from both natures at once.

In the context of aggressions against the empire by non-Christian forces, the emperor's motivation to reunite different strands of Christianity was strong. Heraclius experienced some success in Egypt, as elsewhere: In 633, the Egyptian Severan church agreed to the formulation promoted by Cyrus and joined the imperial church in a single communion. Although in later Egyptian sources this union is seen as the reluctant outcome of violence and persecution, the context of the time seems to have been one of conciliation, not only in Egypt but also within the Syrian church. A more nuanced position toward Cyrus was also adopted in his *Chronicle* by John of Nikiu, a contemporary of the events and the successor in the see of Nikiu of one of the bishops who had enacted the union of 633.

In the years that followed, however, the Roman state was confronted with a new enemy. After the death of Muhammad in 632, Abu Bakr was

(a)   (b)

Figure 6.2.1 Gold solidus of Heraclius, Constantinople, 610–613
The representation of a cross on steps on the reverse of the coin is characteristic of the
gold coinage of Heraclius. These are the sort of coins that were offered by Cyrus to 'Amr
as tribute, and a large number of them must have circulated among the conquerors even
before they settled in the Levant and Egypt. Some of the earliest coins minted by the
caliphs in the later seventh century reproduced this pattern, but without the transverse
bar of the cross, so that only a vertical pillar appears on the steps.

proclaimed caliph and swiftly moved to continue the initial conquests of
the new Muslim community beyond the Arabian peninsula. The conquests
that followed established the Caliphate as a Muslim polity that posed
a significant threat to its two neighboring empires.

In the face of the rapid advance of Muslim forces in the Levant, starting
with the capture of Bosra in 634, Cyrus was also given civil and military
powers. In 636, after the two important defeats of Heraclius' forces at
Emesa and Yarmūk, Muslim armies seem to have made a first attempt to
march toward Egypt, which Cyrus deflected by negotiating the payment of
a tribute, said by some sources to have been 200,000 solidi (Figure 6.2.1).
According to several accounts (Sijpesteijn 2013: 50, n. 6), this payment was
stopped by Heraclius in 639 and even led to Cyrus' recall to Constantinople
in 640; he was accused of using the money of the treasury and of depleting
the wealth of the province. He was eventually sent back to Alexandria in
641 after the death of Heraclius, only to preside over the tensions that had
developed in the country during his absence between rival anti-
Chalcedonian groups and between civil and military authorities – while
the Muslims were conquering the province. Indeed, upon his return, Cyrus
found that a large part of Egypt, including, crucially, Babylon, which

controlled communication between north and south, had fallen to the Muslim armies.

From the contemporary account of the conquest given by John of Nikiu and corroborated by several Arabic sources, it seems that 'Umar sent two different armies to conquer the country. One, which came from Palestine and moved toward the Delta, its attention centered on the capture of the key positions of Pelusium and Babylon (Figure 6.2.2), was led by 'Amr ibn al-'Āṣ, with whom Cyrus is said to have negotiated the tribute some years earlier. The other army was apparently dispatched to Upper Egypt, crossing the Red Sea directly from the Ḥijāz according to Ibn Ḥawqal, most probably from the port of Medina, al-Jār, to 'Aydhāb on the African shore, and

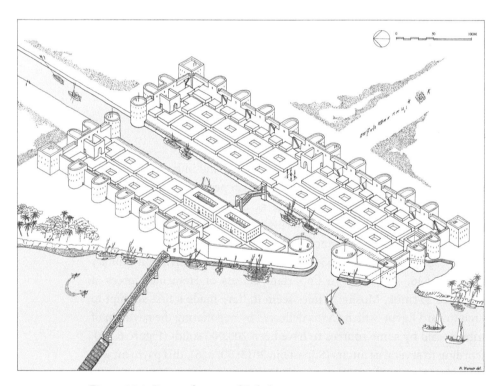

Figure 6.2.2 Roman fortress of Babylon
This is a reconstructed view of the Roman fortress of Babylon, which was a key strategic point in the Arab conquest of Egypt. It controlled the apex of the Delta and therefore also communication between the two parts of the country. The protected harbor inside it marked the end of the so-called Trajan's canal, which connected the Nile with the Red Sea port of Klysma. The point at which the canal reached the Nile is framed by the two round towers. There were several land gates between protruding horseshoe towers: two to the north, and one on each of the other three sides.

moving across the Eastern Desert to Aswān (Syene). This second army was led by 'Abd Allāh b. Sa'd b. Abi Sarḥ, who conquered Aswān and later also subdued the Beja tribes that had been raiding towns in the area for decades. The existence of a second army, coming from the south, is borne out by John of Nikiu, whose *Chronicle* clearly describes an army moving north from Middle Egypt toward the Fayyum and eventually meeting 'Amr's army in Babylon.

The history of the conquest of Egypt has usually focused on 'Amr's advance, as told by the standard Arabic narratives (Ibn 'Abd al-Ḥakam, al-Ṭabarī, al-Balādhurī). These accounts, however, like much of the non-native literary production on Egypt, tend to equate the country with the Delta, to which the Fayyum is sometimes joined. Upper Egypt was usually seen as entirely distinct, perhaps the reason that the traditional narrative neglects it. Indeed, al-Kindī (*Wulāt* 11) states that 'Amr was appointed governor over all of Egypt except Upper Egypt, where 'Umar appointed 'Abd Allāh b. Sa'd, the man who had conquered it according to Ibn Ḥawqal. 'Abd Allāh eventually replaced 'Amr as governor for a short period after the accession of 'Uthmān as caliph (643/644), but 'Amr was able to return after Mu'āwiya's accession (661). The absence from later sources of 'Abd Allāh and the southern army may also reflect the overall favorable treatment Muslim sources reserve for 'Amr, attributing the conquest of the entire country to him alone.

As a consequence, we know next to nothing of the operations in the south until they are picked up in Middle Egypt by John of Nikiu (*Chronicle* 111), who describes a force moving northward on the west bank of the Nile, probably along the Baḥr Yūsuf, which eventually reaches Oxyrhynchos. There they were temporarily stopped by the Roman forces in a first confrontation, but a later attack resulted in Roman defeat; eventually the southern Muslim force reached the Fayyum.

The southern army seems to have moved swiftly northward through Middle Egypt, leaving some of the cities on their way in Roman hands. This may have happened under a cooperation agreement, as John of Nikiu implies in his account, whereby Roman officials from Middle Egypt would provide assistance to the Muslims when the two armies met near Babylon.

Mostly from later sources we have longer and more detailed descriptions of the operations of the army under 'Amr's command, which came overland from Palestine and took Pelusium in 639, possibly because of Heraclius' interruption of the tribute payments. From Pelusium the army headed south to Heliopolis. There 'Amr requested reinforcements from the caliph 'Umar, who sent another 4,000 men (more according to some sources), led by Zubayr b. al-'Awwām. After defeating the Roman army at Heliopolis, 'Amr's army advanced toward Babylon, where they joined up with the southern army. A temporary bridge was constructed to allow the two armies, which were on different banks of the river, to unite. Having taken Babylon, the combined army moved toward Alexandria, which proved impossible to take by force. A treaty was concluded between Cyrus and 'Amr in 641, which stipulated an eleven-month cease-fire between signing the treaty and the transfer of the city to the Muslims, allowing the inhabitants to decide whether to leave and those who had taken refuge there from Valley cities to return home.

There is much confusion in the sources as to the events that followed. In some accounts Heraclius, who was not happy with the treaty, immediately replaced Cyrus with Manuel, who tried to recapture the city, with short-lived success. The story is suspiciously similar to that of Cyrus' recall by Heraclius after the tribute agreement, when the patriarch was purportedly replaced by a certain Manuel. According to other sources, Manuel attempted to recapture Alexandria three years later, in 645, after Heraclius' death. Whatever the case, the second conquest of Alexandria by the Muslim army, said to have been by force, is the subject of a brief account in the *History of the Patriarchs*, which includes a miracle of St. Mark (Box 6.2.1).

Box 6.2.1 On the second conquest of Alexandria: *History of the Patriarchs* **Benjamin I,** *Patrologia Orientalis* **1 (1904) 494–495**

And in the year 360 of Diocletian, in the month of December, three years after Amr had taken possession of Memphis, the Muslims captured the city of Alexandria, and destroyed its walls, and burnt many churches with fire. And they burnt the church of Saint Mark, which was built by the sea, where his body was laid; and this was the place to which the father and patriarch, Peter the Martyr, went before his martyrdom, and blessed Saint Mark, and committed to him his reasonable flock, as he had received it. So they burnt this place and the monasteries around it. And at the burning of the said church a miracle took place which the Lord performed; and that was that one of the captains of the ships, namely the captain of the ship of the duke Sanutius, climbed over the wall and descended into the church, and came to the shrine, where he found that the coverings had been taken, for the plunderers thought that there was money in the chest. But when they found nothing there, they took away the covering from the body of the holy Saint Mark, but his bones were left in their place. So the captain of the ship put his hand into the shrine, and there he found the head of the holy Mark, which he took. Then he returned to his ship secretly, and told no one of it, and hid the head in the hold, among his baggage.

Later Muslim sources were careful to distinguish between cities that surrendered and those taken by force, circumstances that entailed different fiscal obligations. It is unclear, however, whether this distinction was made from the very start, as we do not have the original versions of the treaties signed with conquered cities.

Although papyri do not offer narratives of the conquest, they provide a useful complement, as they show the commanders of Muslim units making requisitions from the local population for the needs of the army: horses, sheep, chickens, grain, oil, milk, grapes and grape juice, wood for burning and other uses, leather, ropes, etc. These were not simply raided but carefully listed in detailed receipts given to the administrators of the districts that provided the goods. This record ensured that the burden on the conquered population was distributed as evenly as possible, but also no doubt served as an inventory of goods for the army itself, allowing the commanders overall control of provisions.

Immediately after the conquest, agents were dispatched to take over the existing system of annual taxation, not letting the change of rule create any disruption in payments. Starting under 'Amr, however, the new rulers began to change the tax system from a territorial organization toward a more centralized structure, based on a general census and, eventually, reoriented to the central requirements of the Caliphate. Also in the immediate aftermath of the conquest, a census was organized of the male population over fourteen years of age, defining the base on which the newly introduced poll tax would be levied. This is known as the census of 'Amr, because it is attributed to him by Ibn 'Abd al-Ḥakam (*Futūḥ*, 152–3) and other later Muslim texts. Although the *History of the Patriarchs* attributes the census to 'Abd Allāh, two Coptic census declarations on papyrus (Box 6.2.2) make it clear that it happened under 'Amr and that it was carried out by village heads who declared to the authorities the adult male population of their village. Such declarations would have been collected and forwarded up the administrative hierarchy.

However, the military situation did not stabilize immediately. The population seems to have been uncertain whether the conquest was a temporary takeover or a permanent state of affairs, and the Muslim consolidation of the borders to the south and west of the valley and Delta took some time and effort. Although the accounts given by different sources vary enormously, the Romans appear to have taken advantage of the instability caused by the civil wars that shook the early Caliphate to attempt to win back some of the lost territories, and these efforts fostered unrest within the respective provinces. Naval raids on both sides continued

---

Box 6.2.2 Census declaration: *P.Lond.Copt.* 1079

+ I, Philotheos the head-man, son of the late Houri, the man from Tjinela,
swear by God Almighty and the well-being of 'Amr not to have left out any
man in our whole village from fourteen years (up), but to have accounted
for him to your lordship.

+ I, Ioustos, the village scribe, swear by God Almighty and the well-being of
'Amr not to have left out any man in our whole village but to have
accounted for him to your lordship +

+ I, Philotheos, together with Esaias, the head-men, and together with
Apater the priest, the men from the village of Tjinela, we write, swearing
by the name of God and the well-being of 'Amr not to have left out any
man in our village from fourteen years on; if you produce any that we have
left behind we will put them in our house.

+ Sign +++ of Philotheos the *protokometes*, he agrees. Sign +++of Esaias, he
agrees.

+ Apater, the humble priest, I agree.

---

well into the eighth century, and the Muslim administration tried energet-
ically to build and maintain a fleet for this purpose. Their main base seems
to have been at Klysma (al-Qulzūm), Egypt's main port on the Red Sea,
a well-protected site surrounded by securely held territories and thus
inaccessible to the Romans. In addition to garrisons stationed in
Alexandria, naval garrisons guarded the mouths of the Delta.

Because of the variety of accounts, it is difficult to build an accurate
chronology of this period. Unsurprisingly, conditions in Egypt seem to
have settled down as the situation stabilized at the level of the Caliphate.
The civil war that shook it from 656 to 661 ended with the advent of
Mu'āwiya, whom 'Amr had helped by occupying Egypt at a crucial
moment. The new caliph confirmed him as governor of the province for
a second mandate, a position he held until his death in 664. This period saw
a first wave of organization and unification of the Caliphate's new acquisi-
tions, and, in Egypt, the beginning of a sustained effort to channel the
wealth of the country toward central Caliphal projects, rather than using it
only for the immediate needs of the soldiers and the war effort.

More was at stake in the control of Egypt than its wealth. Its geographical
position, facing the Ḥijāz, also opened the door to the Maghrib and to the
African continent beyond the Sahara. Its several Mediterranean ports,
which connected easily with the Red Sea, also made it very important
strategically. The campaign for North Africa was launched from Egypt, as

were many naval raids against the Romans. The density of Egypt's population turned out to be a resource both for the raids and for other types of *corvée* (requisitioned) labor, and its expertise in shipbuilding was consistently used for the maintenance of the Arab fleet. Because the province was precious on several fronts, as had been the case with the Roman prefects (**2.1**) its governor had to be someone the caliph could trust. 'Amr's initial governorship was not uncontroversial; the sources preserve anecdotes showing that the caliph 'Umar was ambivalent about letting him take Egypt. 'Umar's successor 'Uthmān recalled him in favor of his own half-brother, 'Abd Allāh b. Sa'd. When Mu'āwiya became caliph after the first Muslim civil war, he returned 'Amr to that position because of his support during the war. When 'Amr died, however, Mu'āwiya immediately replaced him with his own brother, 'Uqba. After the second civil war, the caliph Marwān I appointed as governor his son 'Abd al-'Azīz. When the latter died, his brother 'Abd al-Malik, who had meanwhile become caliph, made sure he appointed his own son 'Abd Allāh to the post. Thus 'Amr was one of just a few early governors who were not members of the reigning Caliph's family and clients, a testament to his high prestige and military expertise as well as his loyalty to Mu'āwiya at a crucial moment. Otherwise, the province was firmly held by the Caliphal family.

In his first period as governor, 'Amr founded the new settlement of Fusṭāṭ, directly to the northeast of Babylon, which provided a special quarter for the soldiers, like a military camp (Figure 6.2.3). The soldiers were not given land, but the taxes paid by the population were to feed and sustain them. Fusṭāṭ also served as the new administrative capital of the province, no doubt chosen for its strategic position at the apex of the Delta, from where both the Valley and the Delta could be easily controlled. From the very beginning of the campaign, 'Amr, who was familiar with Egypt from business he had conducted there before the conquest, saw the importance of that position in mastering and administering the country.

Despite the length of the military campaigns and the ongoing uncertainty, there are hardly any signs of disruption in the countryside. The archaeological record shows no signs of large-scale material destruction, and nothing in the papyri refers to problems faced by the population. There are records of requisitions by the army, but the – admittedly inconsistent – accounts in some narrative sources of violent capture and massacres do not surface in the papyri. In the countryside very little changed, as the new conquerors did not initially settle there, but remained in Fusṭāṭ.

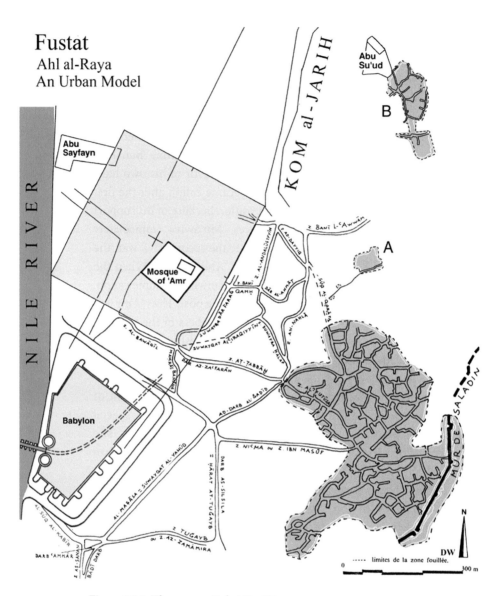

Figure 6.2.3 The new capital at Fusṭāṭ

At first, Fusṭāṭ was built just to the north and slightly east of the fortress of Babylon.
The new settlement was initially conceived as a military camp, much as the fortress itself
had been when it was first built. Both eventually merged into the medieval city, but
maintained something of their previous character in the religious color of their urban
space: Babylon was the center of Christian and Jewish religious buildings, while early
Fusṭāṭ was organized around the mosque of 'Amr, and later, further to the north, that of
Ibn Tulun. Excavations have also revealed urban housing quarters to the east.

During the early years, the economy of the new Caliphate counted on Egypt for money, because of its rich tax base and the wealth of its resources; for labor, because of its large population with expertise in shipbuilding and irrigation; and for produce in kind, as it was a very fertile area that could supply food through easy and secure routes to the Ḥijāz, where the population was growing, and where civil war made other supply routes – notably from Mesopotamia – less viable.

Resource extraction was the first concern of the conquerors. The organization of taxation, as well as more occasional requisitions, is well known from the large number of documents those levies produced. Here, too, it is difficult to offer a precise chronology, but in a process typical of new imperial rulers, the Arabs first took stock of the resources of the province through a census of the population and the land, and initially used the existing human resources and administrative structures in a way that could ensure maximum control and extraction with minimal presence. With time this developed into a more systematically organized and centralized structure, with more direct connections to the Caliphal center. One of the main points of contention seems to have been the destination of the extracted resources: What part would be spent within the province, mainly through the soldiers established there, and what part would go to fund the central treasury. 'Amr's disagreement with 'Umar on this matter mirrors that of Cyrus with Heraclius: Both governors saw the pacifying power of reinjecting money into the economy of a restless province, while the respective central rulers were frustrated at the quantity of resources that escaped them.

Perhaps the more Egypt-centered approach developed by 'Amr made him more popular with the local population, or at least with the local church hierarchy, especially when compared to the various members of the Caliphal family who were sent to the province as governors. Indeed, the *History of the Patriarchs* paints a surprisingly positive image of the conqueror of the country, going so far as to portray him asking Patriarch Benjamin, who had returned to Alexandria after the conquest and Cyrus' departure, for his blessing in the conquest of North Africa (**6.6**).

Bibliography
Booth 2013; Booth 2016; Foss 2009a/2009b; Power 2012; Sijpesteijn 2007a; Sijpesteijn 2013

6.3   Administrative continuity and evolution

The conquerors had an immediate need for resources, and the quickest way to meet it was to rely on existing structures and administrators, with adaptations where necessary (**2.6**). It is unclear how far the last decade of Roman rule had managed to restore effective taxation and other forms of extraction and control after the Persian period, and the Muslims needed in any case to make the system work for them. The existing provincial governors (*duces*) were left in place, but their combined military and civil authority was curtailed: They kept only their administrative role, while the military duties were now carried out by a Muslim commander (*amīr*). Already in the first post-conquest years, 643–644, such a commander appears alongside the governor of the Thebaid, overseeing a vast operation to collect goods from villages, through regional hubs situated in the local administrative units (still called by the Roman term "pagarchies"). He had with him a garrison, whose members are described in papyri as *moagaritai* (from the Arabic *muhajirūn*, "emigrants," the name given to the first followers of Muhammad), or *sarakenoi* (Saracens, a common term used for Arabs before the conquest). The commander was also allocated messengers to facilitate communication.

This army-assisted approach seems to have been an immediate post-conquest arrangement, which only served as an initial investment intended to set up a system of control and supervision. Although Arab commanders continued to be appointed alongside the governors, garrisons are no longer mentioned in later documents – and there is indeed no sign of stable Arab settlement in the countryside, especially in Upper Egypt, before a much later date. Soldiers were much more necessary in other parts of the new empire, as military operations against the Romans, as well as the Muslim civil wars, continued until at least the end of the century. Most of the soldiers in Egypt seem to have lived within the specially allocated sectors of Fusṭāṭ.

In running the country, the Muslims resorted to the same basic principles as the Romans: direct taxation of land and people, extraordinary levies (especially for the supply of the army), conscription, and requisitioned labor, but otherwise a high degree of autonomy left to local communities. They redrew the boundaries of the tax-collection units, reintroduced a poll tax/capitation levy, a quick and efficient fundraiser that had long been used by the Romans, and maintained the surviving landed elites on their land with the same tax obligations. The takeover of the existing system of state taxation is well illustrated by a receipt for

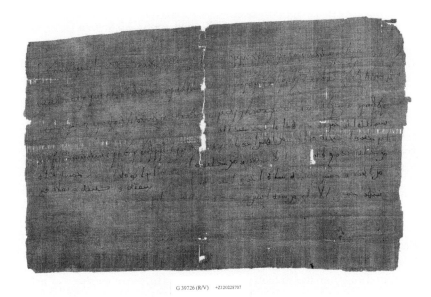

G 39726 (R/V)   +Z120228707

Figure 6.3.1 Receipt for requisitioned sheep: *SB* **6.9676**
On this receipt, issued by an army commander (Box 6.3.1), the Greek text occupies the first
four lines, which are rather widely spaced, from left to right. The Arabic text is written in
five lines from right to left, and starts just under the third line of the Greek, using the space
left free by the shorter fourth line. Its content is more precise than that of the Greek text, as
it details the destinations of the requisitioned sheep, and gives the patronymics of the
individuals involved – revealing that the two pagarchs of Herakleopolis were brothers.

requisitions issued in 643 by a commander of the army, which mentions
moagaritai and others traveling upstream "for the collection of the public
taxes of the first indiction," thus inscribing their new dominance in absolute continuity with what they found in place (Figure 6.3.1). This continuity
of centralized state taxation helped the new empire expand and consolidate
its conquests and eventually create a stable political entity. There is a clear
sense from the start that the assets and resources of the different provinces
were managed centrally with skill and knowledge, and Egypt was unsurprisingly used to supply the same services it had always supplied.

After the years of the conquest the most important concern of the new
administration would have been to restore order and control over the
province. In the preceding century, the region had seen regular outbreaks
of plague, religious conflict, a short-lived but brutal conquest by the
Persians, another short-lived and conflict-ridden reconquest by the
Romans, and finally long years of armed conflict and civil wars associated
with the Muslims. For most of Egypt's inhabitants in the 640s, instability

**Box 6.3.1 Receipt for requisitioned goods: *SB* 6.9676
(643, Herakleopolis)**

Greek

+ In the name of God! I, 'Abdallāh the *amīr* to you, Christophoros and
Theodorakios, pagarchs of Herakleopolis. I received from you for the
expenses of the Saracens who are with me in Herakleopolis 65 sheep, that
is sixty-five and no more, and as an acknowledgement I made out the present
receipt, written by me Ioannes the notarios and deacon, in the month of
Pharmouthi the 30th of the first indiction.

Arabic

In the name of God, the merciful, the compassionate! Here is what 'Abd
Allāh b. Jabir, and his companions, took as of animals for slaughter from
Ihnas. We took from the representative of Theodorakios, the younger son of
Abu Qir, and from the representative of Christophoros, the elder son of Abu
Qir, fifty sheep from the animals for slaughter and fifteen other sheep, which
were butchered for the men on his ships, his cavalry and his infantry in the
month of Jumādā the first in the year twenty-two. Written by Ibn Hadīd.

and conflict were all they had ever known. The structures put into place by
the new rulers were to a large extent successful in achieving the desired
stability.

The province was run by a governor who was appointed by the caliph,
with special care, as we have seen, because Egypt was a very sensitive and
important province. Later narrative sources present us with a coherently
organized governing group assisting the governor and made up of a head of
finances (*ṣāḥib al-kharāj*), a head of police (*ṣāḥib al-shurṭa*), and a judge
(*qāḍī*), but it is difficult to know whether this tradition reflects reality or is
a projection of later order onto what was still a developing system. The
papyri do not mention a *qāḍī* before the 'Abbāsid period (beginning 750).
Several documents from the Umayyad period are responses on judicial
matters coming from the governor, but it is impossible to know whether he
was making the decisions himself or relaying those of a *qāḍī*, whose title
and role are simply not mentioned. Be that as it may, from the 'Abbāsid
period onward the *qāḍī* took on increasing importance, and he was
appointed directly by the governor or even the caliph. As noted above,
under the Umayyads the army remained mostly in Fusṭāṭ, with garrisons at
sensitive points like Alexandria and probably the other Mediterranean
ports, as well as on the southern frontier (probably Aswān and the southern

parts of the Eastern Desert). Its commander (*amīr*) was also part of the main governing group.

These top positions were held from the start by Arab Muslims, while administrative positions further down the hierarchy were mostly held by locals. The four big subdivisions of the country – two in the Delta, two in the Valley – were headed each by a *dux*, whose authority was controlled by an *amīr*. Each of these big regions was made up of pagarchies, as was already the case under Roman rule (**5.4**), each headed by a pagarch who was answerable to the *dux*. The pagarchy was the main administrative unit, ensuring the control of the territory and the collection of the taxes. The pagarch had the relevant staff at his disposal: secretaries, police and guards, messengers, money changers – and also a network of informers and collaborators. The pagarch's office seems to have been the lowest echelon with which the central administration would transact business directly. Below it were the village headmen, two in each village, with whom the pagarch kept in constant contact and to whom he relayed any demands or instructions. They were responsible for their village's compliance with those demands, and at the same time they were essential actors in the administration of rural society, as most internal village conflicts were referred to them and rarely went further up the hierarchy.

The village was the basic tax unit, and the tax sum assigned to each one depended on the number of adult males. The internal distribution of that burden was left to local officials, an arrangement that seems to have prompted unfair assessments, and we sometimes see the assessment made directly by higher-ups – the *dux* or even the governor's office. This seems to have been done ad hoc, either as a corrective measure or as an extraordinary one, because contemporary documents show that pagarchs were still responsible for individual assessments.

During the first seventy to eighty years of Muslim rule, a large part of the tax revenue, as well as other requisitions and *corvée* labor, were used primarily for the continuing war effort and for the establishment of the new structures and trappings of power, including the military and administrative center of Fusṭāṭ (Figure 6.3.2). While in the seventh century the levies still retained their traditional names, in the early eighth century the governor Qurra b. Sharīk calls them "the taxes of the Commander of the faithful" – a marked departure from the idea prevalent under Rome that levies constituted an abstract entity called "the public taxes" (*demosia*). This did not mean that they went directly to the Caliph: Most of the taxes were used for similar purposes as before, but such purposes were now described as part of the Caliph's project.

Figure 6.3.2 Old Cairo – Fusṭāṭ
This aerial photograph shows the contemporary state of the area in Figure 6.2.3: In the foreground is what remains of the Roman fortress, with the church of St. George occupying the northern tower of the entrance to the port, and just south of the south tower the entrance to the church of al-Muʾallaqa, which is built along the southern wall of the fortress. At the top left of the picture is the mosque of ʿAmr.

The most obvious beneficiary of the taxes in the early decades was the army. The soldiers stationed in Fusṭāṭ were paid in gold and given rations of wheat and possibly other produce. The poll tax was therefore levied directly in gold. From the correspondence of Qurra it is clear that contingents from Fusṭāṭ took part in the maritime raids against Roman ports, and they had to be paid in advance. Other sums, as well as *corvée* labor, contributed to the building, maintenance, and manning of the fleet. Animals for the army also had to be provided and maintained.

The government also invested in infrastructure, including a postal system for swift communication, the maintenance of canals and irrigation systems, and, crucially, the reopening and constant maintenance of the Nile–Red Sea canal. Blocked by the Romans, the canal was reopened by ʿAmr during the military campaigns; its ongoing maintenance became very important because it was the route by which the fleet reached the Mediterranean from its base in Klysma for the raids. The timing of the entire canal enterprise was very tight, as taxes – and labor – could not

Figure 6.3.3 Mosque of ʿAmr
In its current state, the mosque of ʿAmr is the result of several rebuildings, a process that
started very early. A first intervention attributes to Muʿawiya the building of four minarets.
The governor ʿAbd al-Aziz b. Marwan expanded the structure at the end of the seventh
century, and in the early eighth century, as the Muslim population of the city grew, the
further extensions were added, enlarging the mosque quite considerably. Later in the
century, ʿAmr's house and the tomb of his son ʿAbd Allah were incorporated in the
mosque. Several additions were made to it in subsequent centuries, and it took its current
form in the twentieth century.

be levied before the harvest in May–June, the raids were impossible to carry
out too late into the autumn because of the weather, and the canal could
only be used during the flood, which in Lower Egypt lasted until October.
The whole administrative machine had to function like clockwork for the
system to work.

The revenue was also invested in imperial building works – in the early
years, the material set-up of the new ruling power. From the 640s, an
extractive operation was organized whereby building materials such as
bricks and wood, as well as pack animals and *corvée* workers, were requisitioned from villages and sent down the river to Fusṭāṭ to build the new
capital. Even though we have documentation only from the 640s and the
710s for this sort of operation, it is plausible that it was ongoing throughout
the first 70 or so years. Construction projects in Fusṭāṭ included the palace
of the governor, the revenue building, a mosque (the first version of today's
"Mosque of ʿAmr," Figure 6.3.3), storage buildings, and of course, in the
earliest years, the army's living quarters. By the early eighth century,

material and human resources were also being requisitioned for projects beyond Egypt, namely the vast building programs initiated by 'Abd al-Malik and continued by al-Walīd in Damascus and Jerusalem, including the palace of the Commander of the Faithful, the Great Mosque of Damascus, and the mosque in Jerusalem.

Finally, as it had done for the seven Roman centuries, Egypt contributed to the new empire's food supply. As noted above, grain was levied for the soldiers' rations in Fusṭāṭ, and we have evidence of ad hoc levies for emergencies, such as a period of drought in Medina. However, there was apparently no regular levy like the Roman *annona* – the population of the Ḥijāz as compared to that of Rome or Constantinople would hardly have warranted one. It seems that Egypt's contribution to the food supply of the Ḥijāz and later Damascus was rather through commercial channels, to the benefit of great landowners, both Christian and, with time, Muslim. The state's share would have come through the land tax on their estates.

The use of the revenue – for the support of the occupying empire – was not different from the preceding period. What changed was the system of collection and the toll on human resources, particularly heavy during the initial period. Yet this was not a radical or sudden change, but well within the range of reforms that the country had known under successive Roman emperors. In that sense, the new order would not necessarily have been perceived as any more alienating than previous impositions from a distant imperial center; nor was the change of capital in Egypt (**6.6**) likely to have affected perceptions.

Bibliography
Legendre 2016; Morelli 2010; Papaconstantinou 2015b; Sheehan 2010; Sijpesteijn 2013; Tillier 2017

6.4   Old and new elites

The result of the administrative approach taken by the new rulers was that for several decades very little changed in the overall structure and composition of the local elites. As we have seen, the conquerors held mainly military positions at the highest levels and key nodes of the administrative pyramid. This foreign governing and military elite at the very top controlled as best it could the existing local potentates, on whom it relied to manage matters at the local echelons.

The newcomers were mostly Muslims with military roles, or roles of high civil and judicial responsibility, who at least at the very beginning seem to have been Arabs with enough proximity to the caliph to be considered trustworthy. With time, Christians with high administrative duties were brought in from other provinces – especially Syria – to serve alongside the governor, such as the Edessan Athanasius Bar Gūmōyē, chosen by ʿAbd al-Malik as the secretary and mentor of his brother ʿAbd al-Aziz when he appointed him governor of Egypt. Within twenty years of the conquest, there was in Fusṭāṭ a substantial chancery whose members were able to bridge the linguistic divide, producing requests for information and resources in both Arabic and Greek and processing the paperwork that came from below. The Arabic documents produced there show that their authors were trained in a different tradition than the local notaries and had probably come to Fusṭāṭ along with the other members of the central administration. The chancery also included local documentary specialists, who had to work closely with the newcomers to produce the necessary paperwork in forms familiar to the lower echelons of the administration. When the governor traveled through the province, his suite included a secretary for Arabic and one for Greek.

The largest group of newcomers were the soldiers stationed in Fusṭāṭ. As noted above, they received rations of wheat and probably other foodstuffs, and were paid directly from the taxes. Later sources are consistent in describing them as listed on a register (*dīwān*), which entitled them to that stipend and the free distributions. Their main duty seems to have been to participate in the annual naval raids, which for the soldiers stationed in Egypt seem to have targeted the Roman province of Africa before it was also conquered. In the interest of the ongoing military effort, initially the soldiers were prohibited from settling on the land and stayed mostly in Fusṭāṭ except when on missions. Very little is known from contemporary sources about their internal social differentiation, but from fragments of early registers it appears that their levels of pay could range from 10 to 200 dinars a year. With time, the *dīwān* expanded as new emigrants came from the Ḥijāz, but also through conversion and procreation, so that by the ʿAbbāsid period the soldiers no longer formed a military group entirely foreign to the country. The naturalization of the Arab population was accelerated when soldiers started to settle on Egyptian land and participate in agriculture as a result of the gradual phasing out of the military pension payments. There is evidence of Muslim landowners in the Delta by the first half of the eighth century, but we do not know if they were newcomers who had settled or locals who had converted.

From at least the 660s, there seems to have been a limited but permanent Arab presence outside the centers of power that ensured the smooth running of the postal system, essential for a vast empire in which power was delegated to local elites. As swift and trustworthy communication was a very sensitive matter, both the staff of the postal stations and the messengers sent from the center were Arabs with no ties to the local population.

Most positions nearer the base of the pyramid were occupied by locals, generally from the social groups who had occupied them before the conquest. The office of *dux* was thus filled by a Christian Egyptian, but under the control of a Muslim military *amīr*. The two were obliged to collaborate, but when their interests did not coincide, the *dux* could count on his local network, while the *amīr* had the backing of the caliphal structures. At the level below were the pagarchs, who saw their autonomy partly curtailed by more direct control from the center, and under them the village headmen, who were answerable to the pagarch. Between all those levels there was a subtle interplay, depending on the context and the levels of pressure from the center.

Until well into the first half of the eighth century we see Christian Egyptians in all of those positions, communicating among themselves and with the central authorities in Greek. In the earliest decades, they maintained the cultural habits they had acquired as members of the Hellenized Roman urban and semi-urban elites (Figure 6.4.1): They were Greek-educated landowners with well-developed networks of patronage among the villagers under their control and a strong sense of the balance between protecting their clients and pleasing the imperial authorities. With time, that organization lost some of its appeal for the central authorities, who found it more expedient to appoint Muslims to many of those positions. Here again, it is usually impossible to know whether those Muslims were converted locals who had changed their names or Arabs from outside. Christians from well-to-do families with a good education did however continue to serve in the administration, even in high positions, until the Fatimid period and beyond.

Papyri offer the unparalleled opportunity to observe in more detail how this system worked at the level of pagarchies and local administrative nodes as well as within villages. Several groups of documents preserved from the first century of Arab rule give us priceless glimpses into the new system and the ways in which it evolved and settled in otherwise unremarkable parts of the Valley.

Texts from the first decade after the conquest show several individuals who retained their positions, and in some cases were even promoted to

Figure 6.4.1 Gold necklace and armbands, Asyut, *c.* 600
The jewelry found in provincial Egyptian towns testifies to the wealth and refined taste
of their elite inhabitants. It is often mentioned in documents, especially in women's
wills or monetary transactions. Here a well-preserved set of earrings and necklace of
excellent execution, which are part of an early twentieth-century find known as the
Asyut hoard.

a higher rank. Although they had to come to terms with the demands of
the new authorities, they were not unused to pressure from above; they
had developed ways of cushioning such demands to prevent or minimize
unrest or flight – the two most common reactions of the population to
rising burdens – and at the same time were prepared to deal with these
reactions when they occurred. In Hermopolis, for example, one local
official, concerned that a new tax might provoke some inhabitants to
flee, instructed his subordinates to anticipate such a response. Other
officials had to organize the collection of various requisitions in kind,
for which they used the administrative structures already in place or
reorganized them in order to follow up on requests. Thus, immediately
after the conquest, we see a notary – usually a member of landowning
elites – taking on the role of "manager" of the northern part of the
Hermopolite pagarchy and coordinating the dispatch of building

materials from his district to the pagarchy so it could be forwarded to the capital (Morelli 2010).

From the period of Muʿāwiya, we have the papers of Flavius Papas, pagarch of Apollonos Ano (Edfu), many of which concern requisitions imposed from the center (*P.Apoll.*). Among other things, they show that the governor was especially keen for labor specialized in shipbuilding, a direct consequence of Muʿāwiya's decision to build a war fleet for the Caliphate. The papers also make clear that the positions of pagarch were still held by the Christian Hellenized landowning elites of the valley, who formed a network among cities, exchanging favors and mutual assistance.

By the early eighth century the administrative system had settled into place. An excellent snapshot of it is offered by the archive of another local administrator, Basileios, whose sector of responsibility was centered on the town of Aphrodito and its territory (Papaconstantinou 2015c), part of the pagarchy of Antaiopolis. Basileios was its financial manager and administrator (*dioiketes*), a role that appears to have been directly subordinate to the pagarch, who was from the same social circle. That archive brings to the surface the tension between those local elites and the two levels with which they interacted: the authorities in Fusṭāṭ above and the village headmen below. The letters sent by the governor reveal that the *dioiketes* could be partial and given to corruption (Box 6.4.1), an impression reinforced by cases of local inhabitants trying to circumvent him with direct appeals to the governor for justice.

Basileios' correspondence with the lower echelons shows that the landed elites (Figure 6.4.2) of the intermediate levels were indeed abusing their power, enriching themselves and favoring their own clients. For those seeking justice in the villages, the linguistic and cultural barrier was even stronger than before, and until a proper centralized judicial system was put into place in the ninth century, judicial decisions were taken by the local officials.

Pagarchs and other local worthies could, with some success, play their local knowledge against the central authorities, who had to rely on their cooperation but could never be sure that it was forthcoming. The authorities therefore increased their control and surveillance, which in turn necessitated more and more non-local personnel to be brought into the country. Between the first quarter and the middle of the eighth century, a number of decisive changes seem to have taken place that were intended to break the local trust networks and create an administration more loyal to the caliph than to its clientele. Coupled with measures to protect the

---

Box 6.4.1 Letter from the governor to a local official showing concern about equality of treatment: *P.Lond.* 4.1345

[...] fearing God and preserving justice and equity in the assessment of the quota apportioned by them in accordance with [the work that ?] each undertook and to the best of his ability; and cause the overseer with four other notable persons in your district to [assist?] them in the said assessment. And when they have finished this, send to us a register containing particulars as to the amount assigned to each person among them, showing us in it the name and patronymic and place of residence of those who assessed the said fine. And let it not come to our knowledge that you have in any respect at all cheated the people of your district in the matter of the fine distributed by you, or that you have shown any preference or antipathy at all to any one in the assessment of the said fine. For we know that the persons who are to assess it will certainly not disobey you in any instructions given them by you, and if we find that they have assessed any one too lightly through partiality or too heavily through antipathy, we shall requite them both in their persons and in their estates by God's command. Therefore exhort them and warn them about this and also (tell them) not to assess any of the officials beyond his means, even if he is at a distance from them and does not join them in the assessment of the said fine, but to treat each with justice as aforesaid and assess him according to his means; and cause the assessors of the said fine first of all to make a written agreement in which they declare that if they are proved after the assessment to have assigned to anyone an apportionment beyond his means and to have assessed another too lightly, that they (themselves) in equal shares will make up the deficiency caused through the person too heavily burdened in their assignment, and will be liable besides to severe punishment for their disobedience and disregard of our command; and the said agreement send to us with the register of the quota assessed for the fine upon each person. Written the 6th Tybi, 8th ind.

    By Basil . . . . 200.

    By the officials. . . . . 200.

    Total . . . . 400. (Transl. H. I. Bell)

---

population from unfairness despite the heavy burden, these adjustments no doubt aimed to secure the adherence of the overall population to the new regime.

The changes brought about significant shifts in the upper echelons of local society, either through new officials coming from outside or through the conversion of at least some of the locals. It is in this period that Arab

Figure 6.4.2 Fragment of a woolen hanging, seventh–ninth century
This woven tapestry shows two hunters in action in two different sections, with two
decorated frames, one floral and the other aquatic. A fine and certainly expensive object,
it must have decorated the wall of an elite house. Hunting had long been a very popular
theme among Roman elites, and that popularity continued in the Islamic period.
Associated with masculinity and high status, it was also sometimes practiced as a rite of
passage to adulthood – which could be represented here, as both human figures are
rather small and seem to be wearing boys' tunics.

names start appearing in the valley outside the army and the postal service.
Pagarchs are the first local officials to be more and more commonly Arabs,
but we also see individuals with Arab names take part in everyday activities,
such as guaranteeing debts – even for Christians – or owning estates
employing Christian supervisors and laborers. Still, Arab presence

remained relatively limited, especially in the south, until soldiers started to leave Fusṭāṭ and settle on agricultural land.

A similar social structure, with a group of well-to-do families monopolizing all positions of power, seems to have been reproduced at a smaller scale within villages. Decisions on cases of conflict, especially regarding property rights, were made by the two village headmen (**6.3**), whose mandate was annual. They were also responsible before the higher authorities for the members of their village and had to guarantee their behavior and financial compliance. Papyri from villages reveal a group known as the "Great Men" – a sort of council of elders from which the headmen were chosen, and which they consulted regarding the resolution of more complex disputes (e.g. *P.KRU* 42.11–12; *P.KRU* 46.47–49). Although sometimes priests can be found among the "Great Men," they had no specifically reserved place and at times might not be represented.

Apart from the most central figures like the patriarch, clerical elites seem to have played a small part in the very early Muslim period. This is not to say that clerics lacked influence, but without any official power their social weight came predominantly from their symbolic standing. Priests or monks could be notaries, witnesses, or signatories of petitions, indicating that at least a contingent of them had a rather high social status within the village. Many were well educated and certainly helped drive the proliferation of Coptic literary texts in the late seventh and eighth century, not only in the capital and the bigger cities but also in rural monasteries.

By the ninth century the situation had changed; as will be discussed below, church careers were becoming more appealing for the Christian elites – especially because they could, as clerics, also take on civil authority in towns and villages. By the tenth century, a learned Arabic-speaking bishop such as Severus b. al-Muqaffaʿ could spend more time debating theology in the capital than at his see of Hermopolis.

Bibliography
Berkes 2016; Debié 2016; Kennedy 1998; Legendre 2016; Papaconstantinou 2012b; Papaconstantinou 2015c; al-Qadi 2015; Tillier 2015; Sijpesteijn 2009; Sijpesteijn 2013; Wickham 2005

6.5 Impact on the rural population

The autonomy granted local communities to manage their affairs had mixed results on the ground. Along with the welcome continuity of familiar interlocutors and practices, the structural changes ultimately left local elites with absolute power – and the rest of the population entirely dependent on them. Narrative sources, produced by those who benefited from the system, give the new rulers credit for leaving them that local control. By contrast, documentary sources, which are a mine of information on village life, make it clear that, for much of the ordinary rural population, this communal autonomy meant even more dependence than before.

Taxation had always been the means through which local elites exploited the rural population, and in that respect things did not change (**3.1**). The changes in taxation, however, had cumulative effects. It is difficult to estimate the weight of taxation on the population as a whole. The changes introduced presumably had a differential impact on different social groups. Some of the pressure of taxation would have been offset by the cessation of the levy of the *annona*, but there has been no attempt as yet to quantify this commutation, or to identify the social groups most concerned by it.

The introduction of a poll tax very soon after the conquest – during ʿAmr's second mandate at the latest – hit new sectors of the population. As noted above, the new tax was demanded in gold, so that the soldiers taking part in the naval raids could be paid in advance. As a result, even individuals who owned no land and therefore had not previously paid tax needed to find enough gold for their payments. Although the Egyptian economy was already thoroughly monetized under Roman rule, the shift of more of the tax burden to a poll tax left many rural inhabitants unable to meet their obligations, with no choice but to borrow from the richer members of the community. They could either borrow the tax money directly or let the lender pay their tax for them, signing an acknowledgement of debt. Repayment of that debt could be in cash, in kind, or in labor. The non-landed population who normally made a living from wage labor, both in agriculture and in crafts (Figure 6.5.1), were thus often compelled to work for free for part of their time to repay contracted debts, resulting in a spiral downward, as their wage income then decreased, making them even less able to pay the following year's installment of the poll tax. Documents show that debt was rampant among the rural population, with interest rates higher than those set by Roman imperial legislation.

The second component of the caliphal extractive enterprise, forced labor and conscription, also weighed heavily on villages. Every village had to provide a given number of individuals, assigned on the basis of the tax registers provided annually by the district. The village headmen were

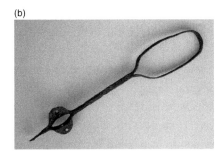

Figure 6.5.1 Spindles from textile production, Thebes
Spindles from Thebes, sixth–seventh century (a) and third–twelfth century (b). Contrary to other provinces, Egypt has preserved many textiles because of its favorable climate. Even without the end products, however, archaeology has preserved other material remains of textile production, which was clearly a very lively sector of the Egyptian economy. Weaving was strongly gendered, usually done by women within their homes, or in adjacent workshops, and it also involved the preparation of the wool or flax using combs and spindles. Hundreds of such spindles have been found; here (a) is one of several found at the site of the monastery of Apa Elias, where presumably the monks worked raw wool or flax into yarn.

required to guarantee the good behavior of those individuals, and the village collectively was also liable for their salary and expenses. This burden may have hit Egypt especially heavily, because its population had always been higher than that of other provinces. However, it was important to leave enough men in each village for the agricultural operations to run smoothly as well, and this would have been much more difficult in more thinly populated provinces.

The most common destinations of the requisitioned individuals were the ships of the war fleet and the imperial building projects in Fusṭāṭ, Damascus, and Jerusalem. The fleet seems to have been the most dreaded of all, as it was far from certain that those conscripted would ever return to their village. Many attempted to avoid conscription and forced labor, often with the explicit or tacit help of the village headmen. In some cases it was possible to buy out the requisitioned workers with a sum of money. These payments were made by the headmen to the district administrator and sent up to the capital. Most probably those sums represented a collective financial effort by the village's landed elite in order to maintain a local workforce, ensuring a certain quantity of free labor in exchange for the favor – although such a transaction could also have been made between individuals and passed through the headmen. If the individual conscripted was himself wealthy, he could have provided the sum himself. In some cases, however, the service could not be bought out, and the authorities in Fusṭāṭ demanded that the workmen be sent in person.

Another way to avoid forced labor was to take flight. Papyri have preserved several registers with lists of fugitives by name, whom the administrators were ordered to track down (Box 6.5.1). The phenomenon seems to have become difficult to control by the early eighth century, when we see a system of fines for those harboring fugitives and rewards for those turning them in, as well as restrictions on free movement outside one's home district (**6.1**). The fines were sometimes paid by villages to allow their own fugitives to return. Mostly, people fleeing were hidden by villagers in neighboring districts, where they would have been more difficult to identify. Those hiding them were risking high fines, as were the fugitives themselves, but the price of being conscripted could sometimes be much higher. Our documentation thus shows that solidarity networks functioned not only within, but also between villages.

Overall, extractive pressure created tension within village communities and made exploitation of the weak much easier for the more fortunate members. The image we get of village society is of one riddled with networks of patronage and protection functioning as safety nets for a population that was under pressure and highly dependent on the locally powerful. The increased difficulty of moving without a pass or guarantee from a figure of authority reinforced that dependence and favored the heads of protection networks, who were thus able to control the rural population of their district.

> **Box 6.5.1 List of fugitives: *P.Lond.* 4.1460, 38–48 (Aphrodito, 709)**
>
> From 15 years and under,
>   as follows:
> Senouthios, son of Atres, from Pakerkout, in the pagarchy of Panopolis
> Phoibammon, son of Kyriakos, from St. Kyriakos in the same pagarchy
> John, son of George, from Akom in the same pagarchy
> George, son of Isaac, from the city of Apollo
> Horsiesios, son of Jacob, from the same village
> Mousaios, son of Abraham, from Tse in the pagarchy of Panopolis
> Senouthios, son of Phoibammon, from Pem in the pagarchy of Thinis
> Phoibammon, son of Menas, from the same in the same
> Elias the shepherd from the village of Psoipoi in the same
> Apollo, son of Kollouthos, from Akort . . . in the pagarchy of Panopolis.

The burden of dependence was especially important in the first seventy years or so of Muslim rule, when, as noted above, it was all but impossible for villagers to appeal to any system of justice beyond the village. Complaints were meant to be heard by the *dioiketes*, but abuse and favoritism seem to have been rife in that office so that villagers lacked equal access to justice. As for the richer members of rural society, they were able to send appeals directly to Fusṭāṭ, something that was beyond the means of most ordinary villagers.

Thus the caliphal extractive operations were at the root of many difficulties for the rural population, not only through their direct weight but also through their side effects. The situation was not entirely new, however, as many of the issues faced by the rural population in this period were present under Ptolemaic and Roman rule, and even before, under different names and in different forms.

In difficult circumstances the population in the countryside turned most readily to members of the church. Already before the conquest, letters requesting help with the authorities against the exactions of the local wealthy were addressed to bishops, priests, or monks with great regularity, and this continued in the first century after the conquest (see Box 5.2.1). The requests made of these clerics show that they were seen by the rural population as figures of authority, even though they had no direct administrative functions or power of decision. Most of the churchmen solicited were linked to monastic institutions, even if they were not monks themselves. Clerics seem to have been especially approached by women with no male protectors such as widows, who were among the most vulnerable members of rural communities, even when they owned some property.

With time, monasteries came to occupy what seems like a disproportionate place in village life. In the eighth century there are fewer, but arguably bigger, monastic establishments, possibly through the abandonment of smaller sites to merge into the larger ones. In the eighth century a huge, semi-urban settlement like Bawit (in the region of Hermopolis, Figure 6.5.2) may not have been the exception. The social make-up of those monasteries is not easy to determine, but their very close relations – both economic and religious – with surrounding villages are obvious from the documents they produced or archived.

Villages were linked to rural monasteries by production and consumption, and they facilitated monastic trade (Figure 6.5.3). There were also other types of transactions, involving various forms of transfer of property (sales, donations, bequests), generally from villagers to monasteries. Bequests to monasteries were made for religious reasons, in exchange for prayers for the deceased. Although ostensibly motivated purely by piety, donations were a more complex phenomenon, involving land and productive assets as well as children transferred by their parents to monasteries as slaves (Box 6.5.2). The status of monastic property during the early Caliphate is not entirely clear, but if it remained inalienable as it had been under Justinian, such operations could well be understood as a way to protect family land and assets from seizure. The transfer of children with the explicit status of slaves could also have been protective, as slaves were not liable for poll tax or requisitions.

While a large number of the monks seem to have been active in agriculture, many monasteries also continued as centers of learned activities, housing libraries with religious books and archives where they kept their documents and titles of ownership; their members could act as arbiters or notaries. It was in such rural monasteries that many texts of Coptic literature were produced and copied. This literary activity indicates the presence of at least a proportion of monastics from the upper echelons of rural society, and probably also members of urban educated circles within some of those establishments, making them into a privileged point of contact between city and village.

Figure 6.5.2 Monastery of Apa Jeremias at Saqqara, ground plan
Ground plan of the monastic complex named after Apa Jeremias at Saqqara to the west
of the Nile. Only the excavated buildings are shown, and the same density probably
prevailed in the unexcavated areas. Recent work indicates that the late seventh and the
eighth century were a time of intense building activity.

Despite the internal tensions, villages had a strong sense of community. In the late sixth century, a village community in Western Thebes
collectively donated a piece of communal land to a group of monks who
wanted to settle there. They describe themselves in the donation deed as
"We, the whole village" (*P.KRU* 105). Another collective donation is
known from the eighth century involving "the entire community" of
Jeme (*P.KRU* 108). That term likely refers to the male propertied inhabitants of the village, whose voices were preponderant, especially where

(a)

(b)

(c)

(d1)

(d2)

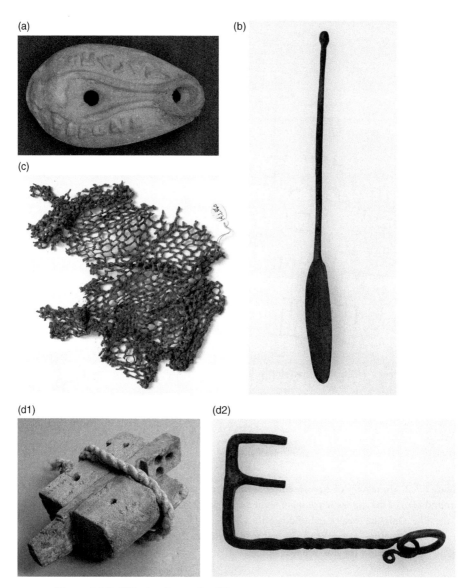

Figure 6.5.3 Objects of everyday life

Excavations of late antique and early Islamic sites in Egypt have uncovered a host of everyday objects that illustrate the rural population's activities and material culture. Here is a choice of such objects, among the most commonly used: oil lamps were the main form of indoor lighting (a); spoons were used as the main eating utensil, even though the earliest known forks appeared in Late Antiquity in elite circles (b); fishing in the Nile provided for one of the staples of the Egyptian diet, and nets were a simple fishing method (c); and doors – especially external doors – were routinely locked, as the proximity of the desert raised the danger of intrusions (d).

Box 6.5.2 Child donation of Tachel: *P.KRU* 86 (29 August 766)

In the name of the Holy, life-giving, and consubstantial Trinity, the Father, the Son, and the Holy Spirit. Written in the month of Thoth, on the first, of the fifth indiction year.

I, Tachel, the daughter of Sophia, from Ape in the district of the city of Hermonthis, and also my sister Elizabeth partaking in this together with me, we are providing, hereafter, a scribal assistant who will sign for us and we are asking trustworthy witnesses to let them bear witness to this inviolable and, through the existing laws, unchangeable donation document.

I write to the holy monastery of Apa Phoibammon on the mountain of Jeme, this one which is yielding to the superiority of the most glorious fatherly ruling lord, master Psmo, the administrator of the holy monastery and the entire *kastron*, greetings.

Since the laws of God, the compassionate, encourage the entire human race toward an accomplishment of the good, so that the forgiveness of their sins is obtained, since there is no sinless one, except for God, this sinless one. Moreover, there is no authority, who will rule at any time, hindering anyone from doing what he wants with that which is his own.

At this time in which we are now, a small male child was born to me, Tachel, the wife and married woman. In his seventh month, I pledge him as a servant to the holy monastery of Apa Phoibammon on the mountain of Jeme, in the following manner: "If God saves him from death, I shall donate him to the holy place (*topos*)." Afterward, when God let the small boy grow up and he developed, this one whom I have named Athanasios at the holy baptism, my confused reasoning led me into great sin, deciding with respect to the young boy, that I shall not donate him to the holy place. When God looked onto the lawlessness I had committed, he cast the young boy into a severe illness, which lasted a long time, so that I, and anyone who saw him, assumed that he died. When I remembered the sin and audacity I had committed, I turned around again and I entreated the saint in his place in the following manner: "If you entreat God and he grants healing to this small child, I shall place him in the *topos* eternally in accordance with my first agreement." Now, the merciful God, the compassionate, took pity on the young boy and granted him healing. I had carried him in my arms and had placed him in the holy place, because he had fallen into a demonic illness. Everyone saw him and marvelled at him.

With respect then to the security for the holy place, this donation document was asked from me concerning my beloved son Athanasios, this document with which I have proceeded, while being alive, my mind

Box 6.5.2 (cont.)

with me, my reasoning strong, without any physical impairment on me, but through my inner desire and my very own decision, without any guile, fear, force, deceit, or deception, I acknowledge and assign my son Athanasios to the aforementioned holy monastery, from now on until eternity and for any time coming after me until eternity. The person who shall dare to come forth regarding this particular young child will submit to the condemnation of my sacrifice at God's tribunal and I will litigate with him.

As security then for the holy place, I have produced this donation document, it being firm and valid at any place at which it will be shown.

I, the deacon Papas, and Georgios, son of Philotheos, and Chael, son of John, these men, residents of Ape, we bear witness.

I, Senaga, have written for them.

(Translation Schenke 2016.)

landed property was concerned. The representatives of several villages could also coordinate actions in their mutual interest. Thus in the early eighth century we know of a complaint lodged by the inhabitants of a number of villages and monasteries of the districts of Panopolis and Ṭaḥṭā regarding the behavior of a tax collector. The sixty-eight representatives of the villages and institutions acted collectively not only to submit the claim, but also to retract it after a settlement had been reached. They present themselves as the "heads of the people" of the district, a revealing self-designation that shows how village elites perceived their own importance, but also how the villages of a district were seen as an organic whole. Significantly, they put the bishop of Panopolis at the top of the list of signatories (*P.Cair.Arab.* 3.167).

From the first half of the eighth century, the central authorities reinforced their efforts to control local favoritism and ensure a more equal distribution of burdens, partly through the appointment of non-locals to key positions. This move disrupted the existing patronage networks, introducing individuals whose ties were to the capital rather than the district's other "heads of the people," and who, crucially, did not belong to the same families who had controlled village life generation after generation. Accompanying the increasing settlement of Muslims in the countryside, it constituted the first step

Figure 6.5.4 Hanging decorated with crosses and floral motifs, from Bawit
Fifth-seventh century. Cotton with indigo and red pigment. High-quality hangings with
figural scenes were common in elite houses. This one, from the large Middle-Egyptian
monastery of Bawit, shows only crosses and floral motifs, possibly because it was woven
specifically for a monastic or ecclesiastical setting. It gives a clear indication that some
inmates with considerable financial means also lived in those monasteries, bringing
their aesthetics and habits of comfort with them.

toward a more organized Muslim justice system, which ultimately
offered the population once again a venue of appeal external to the
village.

Bibliography

Berkes 2016; Boud'hors and Garel 2016; Legendre 2016; Morelli 2010; Papaconstantinou 2015c; Papaconstantinou 2016a; Papaconstantinou 2020a; Sijpesteijn 2009; Sijpesteijn 2013; Tillier 2015; Tillier 2017

6.6   The evolution of the church and the dominance of the Miaphysites

For the institutional church, the consequences of the conquest were profound. The rendition of Alexandria was negotiated between 'Amr and the Chalcedonian patriarch Cyrus, as had been the earlier peace treaty in return for tribute. Despite the initial success of his conciliatory mission, and his circumscribed acceptance by the local population, later Egyptian sources have painted Cyrus in a very negative way. They describe the union he achieved as the result of coercion, and mainly remember him as the imperially sponsored holder of the Alexandrian see whose presence had forced the anti-Chalcedonian patriarch Benjamin into exile.

No clear picture has emerged of the situation in the years immediately following the conquest. Byzantine sources all but stop discussing Egypt after the final capitulation of Alexandria, and as mentioned above (**6.2**), the very circumstances and chronology of that event are blurred. By contrast, Egyptian sources offer a host of details but are partial and philologically problematic: Some, like the *History of the Patriarchs of Alexandria*, have been heavily and probably repeatedly redacted; others, such as the *Chronicle* of John of Nikiu, are only extant in abbreviated translations; still others are hagiographical in nature; and many were simply composed at a later date and relate a received truth that does not always reflect the circumstances of the time.

To understand the development of the church in Egypt after the conquest we are largely dependent on the *History of the Patriarchs of Alexandria*, which offers the only continuous narrative on the subject. It must be kept in mind, however, that this monumental historical work is neither a religious history of Egypt, nor a history of Christian Egypt, but an internal institutional history of the non-Chalcedonian patriarchate of Alexandria – and later Cairo – written in the form of a collection of biographies of the holders of the office. From this vantage point, the story of Christianity in Egypt is narrated in a way that aims to establish the continuity of that church from the first incumbent of the see of

Alexandria (St. Mark) to the time after the Muslim conquest and the departure of the Romans.

The earliest post-conquest years are covered in the section written in the early eighth century by George the Archdeacon, a member of the patriarch's court. George wrote the biographies of Benjamin (623–662) and four of his successors until Simon (692–700), but also those of the sixth-century holders of the office. His account is arguably one of the most influential and defining narratives in the historiography of the anti-Chalcedonian church of Egypt. It demonstrates the continuity of the post-conquest church headed by Benjamin with the "Severan" (i.e. influenced by Severus of Antioch) church so masterfully established by Peter IV and Damian (**5.2**), dismissing Cyrus as an imperial imposition and the attempts at union as ultimately insignificant. From other sources, it is clear that the situation was not quite so clear-cut in the early years, and that the struggle for power against other Christian groups – both Chalcedonians and rival non-Chalcedonian factions – was still a reality in the immediate post-conquest decades. The Muslim rulers had no special interest in Christian theological niceties and were not going to show preference on that account, so the leaders of the different groups had to convince them of their legitimacy on non-theological grounds. The Severan church was eventually the most successful in that endeavor, by arguing for its essentially native nature as opposed to that of the other groups, described as foreign and intrusive.

From the very start, the Severans positioned themselves as the most willing and useful collaborators of the new rulers. By the second half of the seventh century, their network of bishops probably offered the best territorial coverage of the country, and they commanded the loyalty of most of the rural monasteries. This network connected them to the rural population in a way no other group could hope to achieve, and it proved an invaluable asset in their relations with the governors. The *History of the Patriarchs* romanticizes the very foundation of that relationship through its description of the meeting between 'Amr and Benjamin (Box 6.6.1). Avoiding the question of 'Amr's earlier negotiations with Cyrus, George focuses on the conqueror's immediate recognition of Benjamin's sanctity when he set eyes on him. In the spontaneous spirit of cooperation that ensued, 'Amr is said to have asked Benjamin for prayers during his upcoming campaign against the Libyan Pentapolis. An early version of the story even claims that 'Amr was sent to Egypt by the caliph specifically to liberate Benjamin from the yoke of Cyrus and restore him to his rightful place.

> **Box 6.6.1 The meeting of Benjamin and 'Amr: *HPA* Benjamin I,**
> ***PO* 1 (1904) 495–497**
>
> Then Amr, son of Al-Asi, wrote to the provinces of Egypt a letter, in which
> he said: "There is protection and security for the place where Benjamin, the
> patriarch of the Coptic Christians is, and peace from God; therefore let him
> come forth secure and tranquil, and administer the affairs of his Church,
> and the government of his nation." Therefore when the holy Benjamin
> heard this, he returned to Alexandria with great joy, wearing the crown of
> patience and sore conflict which had befallen the orthodox people through
> their persecution by the heretics, after having been absent during thirteen
> years, ten of which were years of Heraclius, the misbelieving Roman, with
> the three years before the Muslims conquered Alexandria. When Benjamin
> appeared, the people and the whole city rejoiced, and made his arrival
> known to Sanutius, the duke who believed in Christ, who had settled with
> the commander Amr that the patriarch should return, and had received
> a safe-conduct from Amr for him. Thereupon Sanutius went to the com-
> mander and announced that the patriarch had arrived, and Amr gave orders
> that Benjamin should be brought before him with honour and veneration
> and love. And Amr, when he saw the patriarch, received him with respect,
> and said to his companions and private friends: "Verily in all the lands of
> which we have taken possession hitherto I have never seen a man of God like
> this man." For the Father Benjamin was beautiful of countenance, excellent
> in speech, discoursing with calmness and dignity. Then Amr turned to him,
> and said to him: "Resume the government of all thy churches and of thy
> people, and administer their affairs. And if thou wilt pray for me, that I may
> go to the West and to Pentapolis, and take possession of them, as I have of
> Egypt, and return to thee in safety and speedily, I will do for thee all that
> thou shalt ask of me." Then the holy Benjamin prayed for Amr, and
> pronounced an eloquent discourse, which made Amr and those present
> with him marvel, and which contained words of exhortation and much
> profit for those that heard him; and he revealed certain matters to Amr, and
> departed from his presence honoured and revered. And all that the blessed
> father said to the commander Amr, son of Al-Asi, he found true, and not
> a letter of it was unfulfilled.

A key figure in the narrative of the *History of the Patriarchs*, Benjamin is
presented not only as close to the governor but also as the one who
reconciled the rival Christian factions through his gentle and consensual
approach. Even though this is not entirely borne out by the few other
sources we have – including other biographies in the *History of the*

Patriarchs itself – it does correspond to what we can discern of the Severan church's strategy in the first decades after the conquest. However fictionalized the initial encounter may be, it reflects a pattern that was probably established very early on, whereby the patriarch was part of the entourage of the governor and on good terms with him.

The new political geography of the country, however, complicated this relationship. The patriarchate was in Alexandria, which had been the capital of the Roman and Byzantine province. With the move of the political center to Fusṭāṭ, the governor and the patriarch were no longer in the same city. For the first century or so, this potential gap was manageable because Alexandria retained its political importance and governors spent part of their time there. As the center of attention of the Caliphate moved away from the Mediterranean toward Baghdad and the Red Sea, however, the political importance of Alexandria diminished. At the same time, Fusṭāṭ was growing and becoming an increasingly attractive capital, one that the patriarch was induced to visit more often. Yet Alexandria remained important for the patriarchate, not only symbolically but also because of its monastic hinterland, which was the intellectual and theological powerhouse of the Severan church and its main center of support. Thus for several centuries the patriarchate found itself torn between the two cities, neither of which could be ignored. The situation was resolved only under the Fatimids, when the decision was taken by Patriarch Cyril II (1078–1092) to move the patriarchate permanently to the newly founded capital, Cairo.

Although it is clear that they were quickly overtaken by the Severans in the race for official status, we know very little about the politics of the other Christian groups during that early period. The same can be said about the institutional church in the valley: Narrative sources all but ignore it, and the only information we have comes from papyri, which shed little light on the different denominations and the balance of power between them. This lack is compensated for by a wealth of detail on the place of ecclesiastical institutions in everyday life.

Perhaps the most striking feature of the early post-conquest years is the continuity in the way religious life functioned in local communities. The relations of trust and moral guidance that the population had built with monks and members of the clergy from the fourth century onward persisted, and translated, as they always had, into a sacred economy that tied religious institutions very closely to the villages and cities to which they were attached. Despite their symbolic and moral importance, however, clerics were not the official leaders of their communities, which were defined territorially and entrusted administratively to the lay elites. Only heads of monastic establishments had administrative status, as monasteries were generally counted as villages for tax and other administrative purposes. With time, monastic establishments became more and more important, and being a monk became a prerequisite for any career in the church. This was as true in the villages and cities of the valley as it was near the centers of power. Rural bishops were drawn from the ranks of monks, as were patriarchs (Figure 6.6.1).

The role and purpose of the Egyptian church was continually redefined and elaborated inside the most prestigious of those monasteries, which came to hold a central role in the existence of the church. As the relative numbers of Christians and Muslims changed over time and the Christians became a minority, church institutions became more important within Christian communities. By the tenth century, church careers had come to

Figure 6.6.1 Fresco from the Monastery of Apa Jeremias, Saqqara, showing a group of monks

This fresco (sixth–seventh century) from the monastery of Apa Jeremias at Saqqara shows a group of monks who are also known by their biographies. On the left is Onophrios the anchorite, with a long beard that hides his nudity, followed by Apa Makarios, Apa Apollo "the great," and Apa Pamoun. The depiction of these founding figures of monasticism in the monastery shows the prestige they enjoyed and allowed the monks to feel part of that great tradition. The small figure kneeling at the feet of Apa Apollo may have been the individual who paid for the execution of the fresco.

be the main choice of the Christian elites who wanted to participate fully in the life of the Caliphate. Under the Fatimids (969–1171), this evolution had come to its high point: Provincial bishops like Severus b. al-Muqaffaʿ, who mastered Arabic well enough to work for the government and participate in court debates, were, alongside the patriarch and the most prominent members of monastic establishments, the new face of the Christian elites.

Bibliography
den Heijer 2000; Papaconstantinou 2006; Papaconstantinou 2007a; Swanson 2010

6.7 The formation of a Coptic identity

The success of the Severans as the preponderant Christian denomination after the conquest decisively and lastingly reshaped Egyptian Christianity. Indeed, despite the lack of narrative sources describing the situation in the valley, it is clear that from the late eighth century at the latest the Severan church had no competition in the countryside – even though there remained a rival patriarch in Alexandria, appointed by the emperor. The *History of the Patriarchs* claims to chronicle this victory, but in effect it participated in it. The *History*'s narrative of cooperation, and even friendship, between patriarch and governor was part of the negotiating position adopted by the Severan church after the conquest, presenting itself as the privileged interlocutor of the new regime. Central to this negotiation was a redefinition of the Severan church as the only native – and therefore the only legitimate – Christian institution. This redefinition was done in a number of ways and formed the basis of a new discourse on the identity of that church and the community it claimed to represent.

Continuity was a key theme of that new discourse. First, as we saw in the previous section, came the institutional continuity of that church. From its earliest establishment in the country to Benjamin and the patriarchs who followed him, the see of Alexandria and its holders were seen to form a long, direct line, interrupted only by usurpers who had obtained their positions through external support, not internal consensus. Imperial support was construed as theologically misguided foreign meddling, which used the prerogative of the imperial office to impose on the Egyptian church a version of Christian dogma that was wrong.

The implication of this institutional argument was that the Severan church was in direct doctrinal continuity with such Egyptian patristic giants as Athanasius and Cyril, whose theology was the foundation of orthodox belief. Indeed, according to this narrative, the first time that an empire-wide theological controversy broke out, Athanasius had not hesitated to oppose the emperors because he realized they were wrong, and he was forced into exile. He was only able to return because later emperors recognized he was right. The emperors who came after Chalcedon, however, mostly insisted on supporting a doctrine understood as being at odds with the teachings of Cyril, remaining unconvinced even by great theologians. Thus while the Egyptian patriarchs remained loyal to their predecessor and professed the proper faith, the emperors remained in error. For John of Nikiu, this refusal to accept the right belief eventually cost the Roman Empire its eastern provinces: The Muslims were sent by God to punish its rulers for their erroneous doctrine. From the years following the Council of Chalcedon until the last attempts at reconciliation under Cyrus, the acceptability and rightness of that doctrine were measured against Cyril's uncontested and non-negotiable definition of the nature of Christ. Once again, an Alexandrian patriarch and his theology became the yardstick of proper belief, and naturally the Egyptian church could legitimately claim to be his best and most authorized interpreter.

The few narrative texts we have from the period espouse and promote this view, underpinning the formation of a distinct Egyptian Christian identity, separate from that of the rest of the Christian world and predicated on the indigenous character of the institution and the community it represented. Indeed, the *History of the Patriarchs* assumes a "community" of like-minded Christians throughout the country, who stood as one behind the patriarch from the very days of the conquest onward. It thus shows Benjamin speaking for the entire population when he meets 'Amr, and it does the same with his successors. In one case, under Michael I (744–768), a Muslim judge who received the two competing patriarchs (5.2) during a hearing allegedly referred to them as "the father of the Jacobites" and "the father of the Melkites," thus considering them de facto the heads of those communities (*HPA*, Michael I, referring respectively to non-Chalcedonians and Chalcedonians). If we look at the papyri, however, there is nothing to show that there was a strong sense of a "Jacobite community" across the country: in the first century after the conquest, the only form of communal self-ascription that is obvious in documentary texts is that of the village (6.5). With time, the forms of worship and the textual production of the newly redefined church spread through the country and gradually became the norm, defining the population's Egyptian Christian identity. And as the Muslims slowly started settling in the countryside, they provided a religious other against whom this identity became better defined. It was then, with the spread of Arabic beyond the big cities, that this Egyptian church came to be called "Coptic."

An important aspect of this Coptic community's self-perception was its continuity – ethnic and religious – with the community that produced the many local martyrs. A host of stories about martyrs were written – or rewritten – at this time, insisting on the Egyptian origin of their main characters. For the most part, these were victims of Diocletian's persecution, whose capacity to withstand torture with the help of an angel was a sign of the favor they found with God. Many of these stories, which today constitute an important part of Coptic literature, form thematic groups, almost like series, because they concern martyrs who are said to have met each other, or even to have been related – but for each one a separate, individual story was told. Interestingly for a church that followed Severus of Antioch, many of the stories concern martyrs who came from Antioch to suffer martyrdom in Egypt, and who were all somehow related.

Read together, those martyrdom accounts tell a coherent story. They demonstrate the continuity of the line of patriarchs not only with the theologians Athanasius and Cyril but also with the martyrs Mark (**2.11**) and Peter I (**3.6**) and claim the legacy of the persecutions for what came to be the Coptic church (Figure 6.7.1). Egypt's many martyrs provided the foundational sacrifice for that church, and their indigenous identity provided its legitimacy. The Chalcedonian church, initially called "Roman," and later "Melkite," had no claim to that sacrifice or to the community it created. Popular non-Egyptian saints like Victor were naturalized and given Egyptian connections, while eventually even the emperor Diocletian was said in one narrative to have come from Egypt and to have reneged on his Christian upbringing to turn against the Christians. By co-opting the head persecutor himself, the entire story of the persecutions became an Egyptian affair, and no external intervention was needed for the great founding sacrifice to take place. This history of suffering and resistance, already in gestation during the later stages of the Chalcedonian conflict from Justinian to Heraclius, became so central for the Coptic church that it adopted the "Era of the Martyrs" as its own, peculiarly Egyptian, reckoning of time, with its starting point in 284, the date of

Figure 6.7.1 Icon with Patriarchs of Alexandria, from the church of St. Merkourios in Old Cairo
This thirteenth-century icon depicts three patriarchs of Alexandria: from right to left, Peter I, Athanasios, and Cyril. All three played a key role in the self-definition of the Coptic church: Peter as the last of the martyrs, whose sacrifice is understood as foundational, and Athanasios and Cyril for their theology and uprightness against doctrinal deviations, even from the emperors.

Diocletian's accession. In this way, the "great" persecution came to mark the starting point of the institution's history – even though the foundation by Mark in the first century also remained an essential aspect of that history.

Besides telling the story of the suffering and sacrifices that went into the establishment of the Egyptian church, martyrdom accounts complement several other texts to offer a narrative of the sanctification of the Egyptian landscape. The bodies of the martyrs were buried in shrines that formed a dense network, giving the country an especially holy character. It was also at this time that the story known as the "flight into Egypt," recounting how Mary and Joseph took the baby Jesus to Egypt to escape King Herod's massacre of all babies in Judaea, became popular and was told in much more detail than the initial short mention in the gospel of Matthew allows (Mt 2:13–23). For any Christian, this was the ultimate form of sanctification, as it made Egypt a part of the holy lands that were trod by Jesus. As in Palestine, specific places were associated with specific moments in the gospel narratives, creating more holy focal points of high symbolic value. What's more, during that short visit, a young Egyptian man called Eudaimon is said to have recognized Jesus as the Messiah, and to have been killed for saying so (Synaxarion, 18 Mesore; *PO* 17, 732–734). Thus the first Christian martyr was also an Egyptian, further justifying the identity of the Coptic church as the "church of the martyrs" and linking it to the very time of Jesus.

Unlike the *History of the Patriarchs*, which served as the official history of the see of Alexandria and was probably read only by learned clerics and urban elites, those martyr stories circulated very widely. Copies were kept even in rural monasteries, and they were read out during the feasts of the respective martyrs. As the calendar year was full of these feasts, congregations heard many such stories every year, and reheard them year after year. They were therefore much more decisive in disseminating a given worldview than the more structured and continuous historical works. As texts, they were lively and entertaining, capturing the attention of the audience and easy to remember. They reinforced the social cohesion of the relevant congregation by repeatedly restating a number of cultural and religious beliefs, thereby enhancing their validity and creating an expectation of recurring events along the same lines. The congregation hearing those stories day after day, year after year, gradually acquired a common social memory and a set of shared textual references, which formed the basis of a communal identity as part of that "church of the martyrs," the Coptic church.

Although initially martyr shrines were independent of monasteries, by the seventh century the two had become intricately intertwined. Many monasteries not only preserved texts on martyrs but also housed their shrines, either because the bodies of martyrs had been moved there, as in the case of the Monastery of St. Phoibammon near Jeme, or because monasteries had developed around earlier shrines, as in Abu Mina. Over time, monasteries had become central to Christianity everywhere, but perhaps nowhere as much as among Christians in Muslim-held lands, where they took on increasing importance in the life of the surrounding Christian communities. Along with the martyrs, they were central to the definition of Coptic identity, not least because as an institution, monasticism also claimed Egyptian origin. Indeed, as in other areas, the continuity of that institution with its pre-Chalcedonian origins was greatly stressed, as was its intellectual and spiritual filiation with the early Egyptian monastic pioneers. The stories of the early monks were copied and circulated, as well as kept in monastic libraries to read out during assemblies, generally in the refectory. Even though most of the monastic biographies in Coptic that have come down to us were composed between the fourth and the seventh century, they are invariably preserved in manuscripts copied well after the Arab conquest, sometimes even close to the end of the Middle Ages. The combination of biographies in some of those manuscripts shows the tendency to connect the early monks with later figures in a sort of spiritual genealogy – a connection that was also made visually in representations of great monks in monasteries (Figure 6.7.2).

More generally, the production of manuscripts with stories that told the history of Christianity in Egypt, often through the deeds of important,

Figure 6.7.2 Painting showing monks, from the Monastery of St. Antony
The paintings in the church of the monastery of St. Antony in the Eastern Desert represent many early monks, from the founding times of the monastic movement. Here Abba Arsenios on the right is described as "teacher of emperors" and is holding a scroll with thoughts on salvation. To the left of Arsenios are Abba Sisoes, Abba John the Little, and Abba Bishoi the Great.

exemplary figures, was essential to both preserving and developing the common textual heritage. Indeed, monasteries not only collected and copied older works, probably continuing to translate some from Greek, they also produced new literature in Coptic, thus creating a living and ever-evolving communal memory rooted in the country's Christian past.

In the new texts, a strong anti-Chalcedonian position was expressed until at least the end of the eighth century, during which the debate still felt relevant. The last really polemical text to have come down to us in Coptic is the *Life of Samuel of Qalamūn* (Figure 6.7.3), probably dating from the end of that period. In the framing story, the narrator

Figure 6.7.3 **Monastery of Samuel of Qalamun**
Situated south of the Fayyum where it turns into desert, the monastery founded in the seventh century by Samuel is still in operation today. It was a big and wealthy monastery, which suffered from regular Berber raids, and was twice pillaged in the ninth century. We know that in Fatimid times it paid a guard to protect its property and its trade activity.

offers a sort of genealogy of transmitters (like an *isnād* in Muslim sources), as he describes how his account was based on that of "our holy fathers," who "heard from their fathers who were before them, and they heard from their fathers, who were the disciples of the great one (. . .) those who have seen with their eyes and heard with their ears, their hands have touched him . . ." Among other anecdotes, the text recounts how Samuel tore to pieces a missive from the patriarch Cyrus – most probably an allusion to the latter's attempt to reconcile the two sides in 633 (**6.2**) – and threw it outside, calling it "the Tome of Leo" (**5.1**; Box 6.7.1). The *Life of Samuel* shows how, three centuries after Chalcedon and a century after the country had been separated from the Roman Empire, the subject could still arouse very strong feelings among Egyptian Christians. This virulence receded in later texts, whose authors seem to take the dominance of the Coptic church for granted within Egypt and do not feel compelled to refer to the times of conflict with Rome and Constantinople.

The prestige of monasteries grew with time, as did their power within Christian communities (**6.6**). The importance of a monastic

---

Box 6.7.1 Samuel tears up a letter from Cyrus: Passage from the *Life of Samuel of Qalamun*

And at that moment the holy Apa Samuel leaped up, ready to give his life to death and to show fortitude. He said to the magistrianus, "What do you want us to do for you? We do not accept this Tome or that which is written in it, nor yet do we accept the Council of Chalcedon nor do we have any archbishop but our father Apa Benjamin." After this the magistrianus became angry and ground his teeth at Samuel. He said to him, "By the power of kings, I shall make you subscribe to this Tome first and you will confess all the things in it, because you have acted shamelessly and spoken evilly." The holy Apa Samuel prepared himself to give his life to death. He said to the magistrianus, "This is a mere trifle which you have adjured me to perform. Bring the Tome here to me, and I shall convince you." The magistrianus, overjoyed, caused it to be given to him. When it was placed in his hand, Samuel held it out toward the people, saying, "My fathers, do you accept this Tome? Anathema to this Tome. Anathema to the Council of Chalcedon. Anathema to the impious Leo. Anathema to everyone who believes according to it." He hastily tore up the Tome and threw it outside the door of the church. (Translation in Alcock, A., ed. and trans. [1983] *The Life of Samuel of Kalamun by Isaac the Presbyter*. Warminster.)

background proved especially relevant under the Fatimids, as ecclesiastical elites were much closer to circles of power. At the same time, these monastic elites played a significant role in enhancing the status of the monasteries by providing institutional, financial, and intellectual support.

All these developments were gradual, and most had already been under way from the late sixth century with the patriarch Damian's consolidation of the Severan church (**5.2**, **5.6**) and his foresight in creating a dense and reliable network of rural bishops. That was the legacy on which the definition of Coptic identity as not only anti-Chalcedonian but also fundamentally Egyptian could be built in the eighth and ninth centuries. It was in that period that "Copt" – initially merely an Arabic word for "Egyptian" – came to mean what it does today. This redefinition was a direct consequence of the Egyptian church's successful negotiation of its position in the new empire of the Arabs.

Bibliography
Booth 2017; Booth 2018; Orlandi and Suciu 2016; Papaconstantinou 2006; Swanson 2010

6.8   The evolution of language use and gradual extinction of Coptic as spoken and business/legal language

With the conquest began a slow evolution, over centuries, of the linguistic situation in Egypt, as a new language, Arabic, joined the two already present. At the beginning texts were produced in all three languages, but by the end of the Fatimid period (1171) Arabic was the only language in common use. The pace, order, and geography of that transformation are not easy to trace, however, despite the priceless information that papyri offer on everyday linguistic practice. As we saw (**5.7**), at the time of the conquest Greek was dominant in official situations, and Coptic in private ones, although Coptic was by that time much more likely to be used in private legal transactions than it had been in its early centuries.

It is through the official domain that Arabic made its entry into the country – beyond, that is, Fusṭāṭ and internal communication between Arab newcomers. Unsurprisingly, the first known Arabic documents come from the administration. From the immediate post-conquest years until the mid-eighth century, documents were produced by the rulers and their offices in both Arabic and Greek (Figure 6.8.1), reflecting the bilingualism

Figure 6.8.1 Bilingual tax demand, Aphrodito, 709
Like the document in Figure 6.3.1, this is bilingual and concerns taxation. In the intervening six decades, however, with the establishment of a stable polity in Egypt, much has changed. The sum demanded here is part of regular taxation, not an extraordinary levy, and the document was produced in the governor's chancery in Fusṭāṭ, not on the spot. Even though it is still bilingual, the Arabic text now comes before the Greek one. *P.Heid.* inv. Arab 13r.

of the administrative structure itself, since most of the lower positions were held by locals, whose working language in administrative matters was Greek. Little by little, Arabic gained ground in this area, as Muslims began to be appointed to the lower positions from the early eighth century. Scholars have generally seen this linguistic shift as the direct result of decisions under ʿAbd al-Malik and al-Walīd intended to Arabicize and unify the administration of the Caliphate. The existing evidence, however, shows that there was little change in language use under both those Caliphs, and even under their immediate successors. We do encounter individuals with Muslim names in positions such as pagarch, but it is not clear whether they were converted locals or Arabs appointed centrally – and therefore, whether their first language was Arabic. Thus, even though Arabic documents become more numerous, the use of Greek alongside Arabic in administrative contexts was common until the mid-eighth century.

Under the ʿAbbāsids, the Arabicization of administrative documents accelerated considerably, and by the end of the eighth century there are hardly any Greek documents produced at all. This change indicates that Arabic was increasingly employed among the local population, as the representatives of village communities had to use it in their dealings with the district administrators. In the early eighth century the village representatives drew up documents in Coptic addressed to their administrators, who understood it because of their local origin. Although the then governor Qurra b. Sharīk (709–715) accepted the practice it did not work with non-native local administrators, thus creating a need for Arabic speakers in each community to serve as mediators and interpreters.

The exclusive use of Arabic by the chancery also meant that members of the local elites with ambitions of rising in the administrative structure needed to learn Arabic. Much as was true of Greek from the early Ptolemaic period onward, Arabic became a means of upward social mobility for ambitious locals. By the tenth century, an Egyptian Christian with good Arabic could have a career in government service. The most famous example in Egypt is the tenth-century theologian and bishop of Hermopolis Severus b. al-Muqaffaʿ, who started out as *kātib* (secretary) in the administration under the name Abū al-Bishr. The Christian ʿĪsā ibn Nasṭūrus (994–996) was also among the early viziers of the Fāṭimids in Egypt. From his writings, we know that Severus mastered Arabic, an important competence that must have been refined during his years in the administration. This was probably true of other Copts in government service, and indicates that al-Muqaddasī's statement regarding tenth-century Syria was also true for Egypt: Christians were employed in great numbers in the administration because their Arabic was very good.

The increase of Arabic in the administration quickly gave it the status of *lingua franca* for all economic activity, reinforced by the gradual settlement of Arabs in the countryside and their participation in the agricultural economy. The earliest evidence we have comes from the Fayyum: a letter in Arabic from a Muslim landowner to his estate manager while he was away on business, having taken his merchandise to the market in Alexandria (Sijpesteijn 2004). From the letter, we learn that he had a sizeable estate with a diversified production including wine, that he employed Christian workers, and that he did business with neighboring landowners, who were still predominantly Christian although he gives the Arabic version of their names. There is a strong likelihood that these neighbors interacted with him in Arabic, if only with the help of interpreters or with a mere smattering of the language. As for the waged agricultural workers, who made up a large portion of the Egyptian population, the increased presence of Arab landowners alongside the native ones would have encouraged them to be at least functionally bilingual in Arabic and Coptic to increase their prospects of finding work.

Another factor contributing to the growth of Arabic among the working population in the very early period was the levy of *corvée* workers who were sent to building sites either in Fusṭāṭ, where Arabic was the majority language, or to projects in Syria and Palestine, in which Arabic would have been the main language of communication. Work at shipyards would have taken place under the orders of Arab commanders, and so would conscription in the fleet. Apart from building work in Fusṭāṭ, such forced labor involved moving to a different province and meeting speakers of different languages, making Arabic, as Greek had been before it, essential for communication. Those workers thus returned to their villages having been exposed to Arabic on a daily basis and most likely able to communicate in the language.

After the conquest, and throughout the eighth century, private transaction documents such as deeds of sale, transfers, and guarantees, but also marriage contracts and wills, were invariably in Coptic if they were between Christians. By the ninth century, Christians were having such documents drawn up in Arabic, and even though Coptic continued to be used in transaction documents, it lost its earlier prominence. The latest known documentary texts in Coptic date from the eleventh century. Most come from the archive of Raphael, son of Mina, which contains documents related to his private business transactions, dated between 1022 and 1063, from Teshlot (Dashlūt), near al-Ashmunein (Hermopolis) (Green 1983). These documents include some texts in Arabic, a fact that shows that although Coptic was the local vernacular, some members of Raphael's network were more comfortable writing in Arabic.

In recent years, more texts in Coptic have been published from the ninth century and after, suggesting that the language persisted as a vernacular, especially in the valley. Even though most documents produced in private transactions between Christians were in Arabic, several indicate that the final reading of the document to the parties before they proceeded to sign them was done both in Arabic and "in the foreign language" (*bi-l-ʿajamiyya*), namely Coptic. This replicates a practice common under the Romans, when documents drawn up in Greek would be read to the parties in Egyptian before they accepted the terms and signed. This practice did not necessarily mean that the parties were not competent in Greek or, later, Arabic, but rather that their competence did not extend to legal terminology. Under Rome, the choice of Greek gave the document legal validity before an official court, and that was presumably also the reason for using Arabic from the ninth and especially the tenth century onward. We know that Christians – like Jews – referred their cases to Islamic courts with increasing frequency as time went by.

The tenth century was important economically for Egypt particularly because the Fāṭimids revived the Nile route for the trade with India. As in the Roman period, the trade route left the bend of the Nile at Qūṣ, or sometimes further south at Aswān, and crossed the Eastern Desert to the Red Sea port of ʿAydhab, which replaced the Roman-period port of Berenike. As a result, the south of Egypt developed from a backwater of imperial trade during the late Roman period and the first three Muslim centuries into a center of trade and exchange, and cities such as Qūṣ developed wealth and prestige. Indeed, the trade with India was complemented by a lucrative slave trade to the Ḥijāz and the renewed exploitation of the gold mines of the Eastern Desert, and the bend of the Nile became one of the meeting points of *ḥajj* caravans crossing the Red Sea to Jedda. This economic boom, and in particular the trade with India, is evident in the documents of the Cairo Geniza, which show the important involvement of the Jewish community in that trade (Figure 6.8.2). Hundreds of business letters and contracts from that period found discarded in a synagogue of the Fatimid capital document the relations of local Jews with agents and partners in Aden and in ports on the western Indian coast. Despite less abundant evidence, it is clear that Christians, still the majority in the south of the country, also participated in the economic expansion. Participation in this integrated trade would have depended on Arabic as a common language, as it involved organizing transport up and down the Nile as well as through the desert, setting up control points at key Nile ports, and

Figure 6.8.2 Indian textile found in Egypt
Found in Fustat, probably eleventh century, this fragment of block-printed textile –
a characteristically Indian technique – is one of hundreds of such pieces testifying to
the intense commercial relations with India during the Middle Ages. The journey along
the Red Sea route and down the Nile was one of the main pathways for that trade. It
not only served Egypt but also catered to the entire Mediterranean, which explains the
large flow of goods that went through the country.

communicating with contacts in Aden, an important port of call on the
voyage to India. The new class of merchants that emerged was religiously
diverse but had to be linguistically unified if they were to understand each
other.

An important turning point for the Arabicization of Egypt was the
adoption of Arabic by the church as its official language. To a large extent,
the patriarchate had to live up to its own narrative of cooperation with the
governors, and therefore have at least the means to communicate with
them. With the establishment of the Fatimids in Egypt and the foundation
of Cairo at the apex of the Delta, the capital attracted both educated
theologians and those in search of political and social influence. In addition
to proximity to the ruling family, the court in Cairo offered a lively
intellectual environment, with theological debates staged that involved
members of all faiths. Severus b. al-Muqaffaʿ, for example, was among the
most prominent debaters. Despite the traditional prestige that accompanied the patriarchate, its location in Alexandria was an impediment to the
patriarch's full participation in the life of the Caliphate's upper social
stratum. As a result, patriarchs spent more and more time in Cairo, away
from their official headquarters in Alexandria, until in the late eleventh
century Cyril II (1078–1092) took the definitive step of moving the patriarchate to Cairo officially.

This move had far-reaching consequences on the linguistic front. Even though Arabic had been used by members of the patriarchal court as well as by other clerics, the official language of the Egyptian (Severan) church had been Coptic since the early decades after the conquest. The prevailing narrative within the church at that time maintained that Coptic had been the official language ever since Chalcedon, however inaccurate that statement may have been. Several histories of the Egyptian church had been written in Coptic, and so had the narratives relating the struggles of its heroic martyrs. It was a language with a powerful symbolic value for many Egyptian Christians. The move of the patriarchate to Cairo and the close involvement with court life of learned clerics, generally members of the wealthy Christian elites, made the continued use of Coptic as an official church language almost impossible. Although the liturgy itself remained in Coptic, historical, hagiographical, and theological works were henceforth composed in Arabic, and many older texts were translated.

It is at this time that the *History of the Patriarchs of Alexandria* was compiled into a single work based on the translation into Arabic of existing Coptic histories, and then continued directly in Arabic. The scholar at the center of this enterprise was Mawhūb b. Manṣūr b. Mufarrij, who also wrote the first two biographies originally composed in Arabic, those of patriarchs Christodoulos (1047–1077) and his successor Cyril II. The systematic translation of Coptic religious texts into Arabic was carried out between the mid-eleventh and the late thirteenth century, transferring into the new language almost the entire textual tradition of the Egyptian church.

Many of the texts translated in this period – and intermittently from the mid-tenth century on – were collected from the monastic libraries where they had been copied and kept for centuries. Monks did not see this translation movement in a positive light, and they complained bitterly about it. In a famous text composed at the Monastery of Qalamun in the Fayyum, purporting to relate the words of its founder, Samuel, the adoption of Arabic is criticized as a form of assimilation to the Muslims; it is further castigated because it entails the loss of communal memory and of the specifically Christian understanding of God (Box 6.8.1). For the author, who echoes many other critics, Arabic allowed Muslim vocabulary to penetrate the Christian faith, an argument used previously against Greek, presented as the language of pagans.

> ### Box 6.8.1 Arabic replaces Coptic: Apollo of Qalamun, *Discourse* ["Apocalypse"] *of Samuel, head of the Monastery of Qalamun,* Ziadeh 379–381
>
> Woe upon woe!! What shall I say, my children, about those times and about the great idleness that will overtake the Christians? At that time they will move away from uprightness and start to assimilate themselves to the Hagarenes in their actions: they will give their names to their children, discarding the names of the angels, the prophets, the apostles, and the martyrs. They will also do something else, which if I were to tell you of it, would greatly pain your hearts: they will abandon the beautiful Coptic language, in which the Holy Spirit has often spoken through the mouths of our spiritual fathers; they will teach their children from an early age to speak the language of the Bedouin, and will take pride in it. Even the priests and the monks – they too! – will dare to speak in Arabic and to take pride in it, and that within the sanctuary.
>
> Woe upon woe!! Oh, my dear children! What shall I say? At that time the readers in the church will no longer understand what they read nor what they say because they will have forgotten their language, and they will truly be miserable and deserving to be wept over because they will have forgotten their language and will speak the language of the Hagarenes. But woe to every Christian who teaches his son the language of the Hagarenes from an early age, causing him to forget the language of his fathers! (. . .) Many books of the Church shall fall into disuse, because there shall be nobody among them to take care of the books, their hearts being attracted by the Arabic books. They will forget many martyrs at that time because their biographies will fall into disuse and there will be none left. If the few biographies that will be found are read, many people will not understand what is read because they will not know the language. And many churches, at that time, will fall into ruin, and they shall be deserted on the eves of the feasts and on the eve of Sunday, too. (Translation Papaconstantinou 2020c.)

Despite the resistance, the patriarchate's approach was ultimately successful, and Arabic eventually became the language of all ecclesiastical institutions, including the monasteries. Even though this linguistic change was in part a political decision, it was also – and perhaps primarily – intended to develop intellectual and theological exchange and to integrate Egyptian Christianity and the Egyptian church within the community of non-Chalcedonian Christians across Islamic lands. Only Arabic could allow those connections to develop, and its adoption signaled the onset of a period of intellectual flourishing, featuring important Egyptian theologians who became widely known outside the country.

What remains much more difficult to assess is the effect of those high-level changes on the linguistic practice of the population of the valley. We do not know whether the church was acting partly in response to the Arabicization of the population, or whether it led the way, influencing the language choices of local communities. In other words, it is difficult to know whether Arabicization happened primarily from the top down or from the bottom up – or whether the two processes were simultaneous. Private correspondence remained in Coptic throughout the eighth century; there are relatively few Coptic letters after that, which could simply reflect how few Christian documents from later periods have been published rather than a real decline in the number of Coptic documents. Although we cannot capture oral communication, even through papyri, in the tenth century, the geographer al-Muqaddasī states that the non-Muslims in Egypt spoke Coptic (Box 6.9.2), and the Teshlot archive shows that in the eleventh century, in the area of al-Ashmūnayn (Hermopolis), the locals were still bilingual and used Coptic alongside Arabic. In the late tenth century, a bishop of al-Ashmūnayn wrote a letter in Arabic to his congregation addressing a matter internal to the Christian community, the excommunication of "Father" Abraham because of his involvement in sorcery (Reinhardt 1897). Although the letter has no precise date, it is tempting to identify this bishop as Severus b. al-Muqaffaʻ, who held the see of al-Ashmūnayn until at least 987, possibly until the end of the century. If that is the case, his choice of language may have been intended to promote the use of Arabic locally rather than reflecting a lack of competence in Coptic among his flock. Be that as it may, most of the Christian population of the valley was manifestly bilingual by that time, using Arabic not only in transactions with Muslims but also for internal communication.

Bibliography

den Heijer 1989; den Heijer 1991; Griffith 1996; Papaconstantinou 2007a; Papaconstantinou 2012b; Papaconstantinou 2021; Reinhardt 1897; Richter 2009; Richter 2010; Rubenson 1996; Sijpesteijn 2004; Zaborowski 2008

6.9 Linguistic change and religious conversion

Linguistic change in and of itself did not imply conversion, although the two are often confused. Indeed, the tendency to consider Arabic as a quintessentially Muslim language is very strong and has a long history;

as we shall see, the conflation of the language and the religion dates back to the Middle Ages. Yet Arabic was a language spoken by Christians before even the birth of Muhammad, and after the establishment of the Caliphate it was adopted by both Christians and Jews in different parts of the new empire as a language of learning as well as everyday communication without the adoption of Arabic resulting in a change in religion. Ultimately, Arabic became a medium in which much subtle Christian and Jewish theology came to be expressed. It offered the means to explain, debate, and defend one's creed before the Muslim authorities, thus reinforcing rather than weakening the various groups' theological sophistication. The culmination of this religious use was the culture of religious debates held at the court of the caliph, which had important symbolic value, even if such meetings were not very common.

As noted above (**6.8**), the use of Arabic to express Christian theology was not uncontroversial. Critics accused Christian texts in Arabic of using tropes also found in the Qur'ān, which sparked fears of assimilation to the ways and ideas of the Muslims. Those fears are reflected in several texts that present themselves as prophecies predating the conquest, although none were written before the tenth century. The most famous of these texts, the only one to address at length the question of language, is the one commonly known as the *Apocalypse of Samuel of Qalamūn*. It was produced in the Monastery of al-Qalamūn in the Fayyūm and, although claiming to be the transcript by the monk Apollo of the words of its founder Samuel (Box 6.8.1), was evidently written at a much later date and presented the situation of its time as Samuel's prophecy. The text criticizes the church's adoption of Arabic (Figure 6.9.1) at length, not only for the surreptitious introduction of Muslim theological terms into Christian theology, but also for enabling other forms of assimilation. One of these was the more and more common choice of Arabic names by Christians, leading to the abandonment of saints' names and the protection they were thought to offer. By facilitating interaction with Muslims, the adoption of Arabic was also seen as encouraging Christians to imitate Muslim ways and deeds while abandoning their own traditional practices. The examples include Christians taking several wives or concubines and adopting the eating and drinking patterns of the Muslims, thus neglecting the Christian periods of fast.

Assimilation resulting from interaction between the religions was a constant fear on the Muslim side as well; literature opposing assimilation and regulations to prevent it were produced throughout the Caliphate. The proximity was real, and various forms of mutual acculturation and

Figure 6.9.1 Bilingual manuscript with sections of the New Testament
From the thirteenth century onward manuscripts of the Scriptures and liturgical books start becoming bilingual in Coptic and Arabic. This illuminated mid-thirteenth century manuscript follows the early practice of presenting the two languages asymmetrically, with Coptic occupying the main part of the page, and Arabic in the margin, giving the impression it is an auxiliary linguistic aid. The page shown here is the beginning of the epistle of James. From the Church of St. Merkourios (Abu Sayfayn), Old Cairo. Coptic Museum, inv. 146.

influence in religious practice were inevitable. The eleventh-century canons of the patriarch Christodoulos, for example, prohibit entering the church with shoes and prescribe leaving them outside (Burmester 1932: 74–79). The canons also reveal that, by this time, Christians were wearing turbans as a matter of course, and that church authorities had some difficulty preventing them from doing so (although, as we have seen, Timothy Salofakiolos in the fifth century already wore a "wobbly" turban: **5.1**). Even though such external behavior (Figure 6.9.2) was not considered religiously wrong by those who adopted it, it enormously worried religious leaders on all sides, who saw it as the first step toward conversion to the religion of the other group. Leaders were therefore vigilant, resorting to rhetoric to reinforce their group's sense of identity. As a result, many of the narrative sources for the period tend to be polemical and exclusionary, even

Figure 6.9.2 Shawl with bilingual inscription
The image shows part of a late ninth-/early tenth-century shawl woven in wool and linen, which carries two protective inscriptions, one in Coptic and one in Arabic. They invoke Christ, asking him to protect a certain Raphael and to help him prosper. Despite its unequivocally Christian character, the item seems to have been produced in a wool-weaving factory in Tutun/Tebtunis that was under the control of the caliph.

though the conditions on the ground were more fluid. The role of Arabic as a *lingua franca* facilitated that fluidity.

If Arabic was not sufficient for conversion, it was mostly necessary. Individual converts, especially in the early period, had to merge into the Muslim community, as they would no longer have been religiously synchronized with their own, at a time when religious observance shaped the rhythms of social life. This meant, in most cases, moving to a city, which in the early period was almost exclusively Fusṭāṭ. We know from funerary inscriptions and papyri that converts changed their names to Muslim ones, or simply used the Arabized versions of their Christian names while giving Muslim names to their children. Early converts had to attach themselves to Arab Muslim patrons as *mawlā* (pl. *mawālī*, clients), thus creating a bond of patronage within the broader Muslim community of the city. In such conditions, they also had to adopt Arabic as their main language. Naturally they also remained competent in Coptic, thus slowly creating a growing bilingual group among the Muslims of the country. When converts did business with each other, they still used Coptic, even in writing.

At the same time, there are indications that, under the Umayyads at least, it was possible to be a *mawlā* without converting. At the Monastery of Apollo at Bawit, an eighth-century graffito with a short prayer was left by

> **Box 6.9.1 Graffito from Bawit with a short prayer: text from Fournet 2009b**
>
> Lord God, Jesus Christ, be our *boethos*. Georgios, son of Sergios, *mawla* of 'Abd Allah, son of 'Amr.
>   Moager, son of Eeglan, coming from Saleen.

two companions who visited the site: one was a Christian who was the *mawlā* of a Muslim, and the other was a Muslim himself (Box 6.9.1). This shows the degree of social fluidity that prevailed in this area and the forms of proximity that could emerge in a society with a long tradition of cultural exchange and interaction. Elite sources tend to obscure this aspect of social life because of their strong normative purpose.

The rhythm and geography of the conversions remain unclear, as do their motivations and the form they took. Some were clearly individual decisions; we do not know whether there were collective conversions and what weight they carried in the overall movement. Various attempts have been made to study and understand the phenomenon, but the lack of crucial information hampers these efforts.

Following the assertions of the narrative sources, scholars have generally argued that what lured non-Muslims to Islam was the prospect of paying lower taxes, as they would no longer have to pay the poll tax. This neat story of fiscal oppression driving conversion is, for example, the one told by the *History of the Patriarchs*, where it serves in part to explain the phenomenon as indirectly imposed by the regime, thus somewhat exonerating the converts, and in part to galvanize its remaining flock so as to retain its loyalty. When compared with other sources, it is clear that the narrative of the *History of the Patriarchs* is based on a lived reality, but the way in which it interprets that reality is filtered by its point of view.

Becoming a Muslim could indeed involve lower taxation, especially at the beginning when Muslim presence was restricted to the cities. In that period, only non-Muslims (whether city or village residents) owned land and therefore were the only ones paying the land tax in addition to the poll tax. It seems, however, that at least until 'Umar II (717–720), converts continued to pay the poll tax, to which upon conversion would be added the alms payment (*sadaqa*). The only category of Christians who would have benefited financially from conversion in that period were landowners who abandoned their land to move to Fusṭāṭ. Toward the mid-eighth century, as Muslims started to settle in the countryside, they started paying land tax, too – and presumably so did converts who retained their land. Thus it seems that taxation was not a straightforward affair: its early phases are still not well understood and probably varied regionally, and considering the differences in status, landowning patterns, and forms of wealth, we cannot assert that conversion always represented a tax benefit.

Other advantages came with entering the Muslim community (*umma*), of course, such as greater possibilities for networking with influential people and opportunities for upward social mobility. On the whole, these options were more accessible to individuals who were already members of local elites, with some education and perhaps mastery of Arabic. But as we have seen, excellent careers could be had by Christians and Jews without conversion – in government service, but also in commerce (Box 6.9.2). Indeed, merchants came to play a very important role in medieval Egyptian society. They gradually formed a group controlling lucrative forms of trade

---

Box 6.9.2 On languages of trade: al-Muqaddasi, *The Best Divisions for Knowledge of the Regions* (Collins 2001)

On Syria, 153:

> I must say that the scribes here, as in Egypt, are Christians, the Muslims simply depending on their knowledge of their language, they themselves not undertaking the literary discipline even as foreigners do.

On Egypt, 171–172:

> Their language is Arabic, but incorrect and lax; the non-Muslims converse in Coptic.
>
> Egypt is a country of commerce; it is an important source of very fine leather, resistant to water, sturdy, and pliant; leather of sheep and asses' skins, leggings, and cloth of three-ply yarn of camelshair and goats wool – all these are from the metropolis. From Upper Egypt come rice, wool, dates, vinegar, raisins. From Tinnis, (but not from Dimyat), cloth variegated in colour; from Dimyat, sugar cane. From al-Fayyum, rice, and a linen of inferior quality; from Busir, shrimp, and cotton of superior quality; from al-Farama, fish, and, from the towns around it, large baskets, and ropes made of fiber of the finest quality. Here are produced white cloth of the greatest fineness, wraps, canvas, the mats of 'Abbadani style of very fine quality, grains, grass peas, oils of rape, and of jasmine, and of other plants besides these.

Figure 6.9.3 Gold dinar of Fatimid caliph al-Mu'izz
As in the Late Antique period, under the successive caliphates the gold coin (the dinar) set the standard for the currency system. Human figures disappeared from the coinage from the late seventh century onward, after the reforms of 'Abd al-Malik, and were replaced by inscriptions. These are always religious, and generally include the name of the caliph and information on the date and the place they were struck. Here we are told that "In the name of God this dinar was struck in Misr [Egypt] the year eight and fifty and three hundred" (AH 358/AD 969).

that included not only agricultural produce but also, with time, the revived India trade (**6.8**) and the caravans for the pilgrimage to Mecca (*hajj*), and they held some important passage points of the Nile traffic in cities of the valley. Under the Fatimids, trade was not religiously exclusive, and great fortunes were made by Christians and Jews who took part in it (Figure 6.9.3).

Scholars have attempted to understand and explain the transformation of Egypt from a majority Christian to a majority Muslim country by invoking mundane and broadly economic and political reasons more relevant to better-off Christians, such as opportunities for advancement. Very little attention has been paid to specifically religious – and by implication social – factors. A recent study of the overall distribution of religious groups over the long term shows that, from the Middle Ages to the twentieth century, conversions to Islam have been much more common among the least prosperous. The situation in Fusṭāṭ, and later Cairo, is more complex, and certainly very different from Valley cities and villages. In the latter, communities were divided internally between the elite stratum and the others. The local elites filtered the tax burden in such a way that everyone was covered, but not without obtaining favors – or simply debt acknowledgements – in return (**6.4**). The weight of obligations on the average villager must have been very heavy, and much of it was justified through assertions of social status and religious rhetoric invoking biblical precedents of debt to God. That a religion advocating a less oppressive system based on equality within the *umma* should have appealed to those villagers is hardly surprising. This appeal is also indicated by the strong tendency within the Christian and Jewish communities to bring cases for litigation before the *qāḍī* rather than their communal courts, because they perceived his judgment as more objective and just.

This is not to deny that there were also worldly advantages – but the two need not be strictly separated. Those of high status hardly needed conversion for their advancement, and by remaining within their own community they kept control over it, which gave them more negotiating power with the rulers. It was for the weaker portion of the Christian population that conversion represented a real progression, not only financially but also in terms of independence.

As already noted, it is difficult to capture the overall chronology of conversion, largely because we lack any means of measuring the population as a whole, let alone by religion. The Christian sources repeat that "many" converted or "left their religion." It is, however, impossible to quantify that "many," and al-Muqaddasī tells us that in the tenth century Christians were still an overwhelming majority in the valley. He gives no numbers or proportions, but says that Egypt has "very few cities," because according to Muslim classification, a settlement only counts as a city if it has a mosque. This comment implies that many Valley cities still had no Muslim community at all at that time. Papyri from the period are scarce and inconclusive on this issue.

It seems clear, however that there was no big moment of conversion, at least not until the Fatimids; conversion was an ongoing process rather than an event. There were converts from the early years, often active in the administration, like Abū Sahl "the son of the blessed Shenute," who was *amīr* of al-Ashmūnayn in the eighth century (*P.Ryl.Copt.* 199). Among the local elites to whom the regional administration was entrusted, several seem to have converted over time, assimilating even further into the ruling class, much as they had earlier adopted Greek *paideia* and Roman cultural norms. Our evidence shows that converted *mawālī* in Fusṭāṭ often served as essential mediators with the Christians of the capital. According to the sources, among the most important *mawālī* in Fusṭāṭ was the Armenian 'Amīr, a *mawlā* of 'Abd Allah b. Yazīd b. Bardha' al-Jamalī, who after converting to Islam in Syria accompanied the general 'Amr b. al-Āṣ in the conquest of Egypt, and was so successful that he became the general's personal adviser. Even if the story is not true, it reveals the importance put on inclusivity by the conquerors, a discourse that was bound eventually to attract large sectors of the conquered populations.

Bibliography

Boud'hors 2016; Bouderbala 2014; Brett 1973; Bulliet 1978; Décobert 1983; Dennett 1950; Fournet 2009b; Frantz-Murphy 1991; Gellens 1992; Lapidus 1972; Papaconstantinou 2007a; Papaconstantinou 2012b; Papaconstantinou 2015d; Saleh 2018

Epilogue

That the millennium and a half from the time of the Persian Empire to Fatimid rule in Egypt witnessed much change in the land of the Nile will not surprise anyone. Empires and their dynasties came and went, and Egypt experienced two major religious transformations. With the Ptolemies and Fatimids, Egypt was in a sense independent, although the dynasties were not indigenous. With the Persians, Romans, and the early Arab regime, Egypt was part of a larger empire.

But these changes and many more coexisted with a number of continuities that helped to shape early medieval Egypt. These continuities do not point to an unchanging or "eternal" Egypt, as it has sometimes been depicted to the wider public. But they do suggest some important traits that helped to shape change. Perhaps the most obvious is Egypt's wealth, above all in agricultural production. Even this was not quite constant, for as we have seen the growing inequality of wealth fostered by Roman taxation and governance policies led to productive investment, the fruits of which went disproportionately to the elite. Still, Egypt was always rich; only the extent of its wealth varied over time. Its riches made it attractive to outside powers and help to account for the effort by larger empires to absorb it.

Egypt was also wealthy in documentation, and thanks to the environmental peculiarities of the country its texts were disproportionately preserved. It is likely that writing was used more and more widely and pervasively in Egypt over the centuries we have described here, but it is always hard to say just how much varying patterns of disposal and discovery of documents have distorted the picture that we have of the production of texts in different periods. As Marina Rustow (2020) has shown from chancery documents preserved in the Cairo Geniza, the idea that Fatimid Egypt was somehow an exception to Egypt's long traditions of creating and archiving official documents is a mirage created by scholarly myopia. Every new ruling power brought its changes to the ongoing documentation of public business and revenues, but none was about to do without the information that the archives offered. How unusual Egypt was in this respect is much harder to say; perhaps not very much (Bagnall 2011). But at least in the documentary heritage that survives, it is undeniably the most productive part of the ancient world.

One clear change over this millennium and a half was in the direction of Egypt's integration into the wider world. Not that Egypt was somehow isolated before the Persians: Even the brief sketch we have offered of the Third Intermediate Period and the Saites shows the country's connectedness. But with the Persians began a long period of deeper integration, both with the Near East, with which Egypt had deep cultural ties going back millennia, and with the Eastern Mediterranean. The gradual assimilation of Egypt into the Roman Empire, particularly in Late Antiquity, made it much less insular and distinctive than it had been even under the Ptolemies. And we should not ignore the degree to which the doctrinal disputes of the fourth to seventh century integrated Egypt into the larger anti-Chalcedonian community of the region, a connection that survived the coming of the Arabs and Islam. By the time of Justinian, Egypt was an essential part of the Late Roman world, economically, culturally, and religiously. And by the arrival of the Fatimids, Egypt was in turn a central hub of the Islamicate world.

What did not alter was Egypt's openness, a characteristic sometimes obscured to modern eyes by its distinctive and often conservative culture. In all periods it had the capacity to absorb immigrants and influences from their cultures without losing its Egyptianness. Nowhere is this more visible than in the Christianization of Egypt, which took place in multiple dimensions. There is a narrative – fairly well represented in the sources – of the workings of power, in which Egypt becomes part of an imperially sponsored and supposedly unified Christian empire, although that had far more fissures than the emperors wanted. And there is another, and much more complicated, narrative involving the agency of the Egyptian population across a wide span of attitudes, beliefs, and rituals, ranging from doctrinal zealotry to the ways in which Christian life adapted to traditional practices and vice versa. The Egyptians made Christianity their own, sometimes in ways paralleled elsewhere in the Late Antique world and sometimes in much more distinctive fashion. And, of course, this same population in large part eventually adopted Islam in a similar way.

Not surprisingly, openness and adaptability resulted in diversity. Roman Egypt, in its broad sense, was far from a uniform society. Its variety did not necessarily lead to tranquillity; there is much evidence that it was often a contentious and violent place, both in the capital and in the countryside. But this combativeness also may be amplified by the sources, as trouble tends to be. It is not news when a population diverse in wealth, culture, and religion gets along from day to day, and the near-total lack of reflection of the theological controversies of Late Antiquity in the documentary sources suggests that they were not a major factor in daily life, whereas family matters, making a living, and managing property were much more central concerns.

Glossary

amīr: (Arabic = prince) term used to describe a leader or commander.

annona/annona civica: food supply, city food supply, often referring to the free or low-cost distribution of grain to citizens.

apse: commonly semicircular extension in the center of one end of a hall or church.

aroura: unit of measurement of land area used in Egypt, about two-thirds of an acre or 0.27 hectare.

artaba: Persian grain measure used in Egypt, usually about 39 liters.

billon: mixture of (mostly) bronze and silver used in some coin issues.

catechumens: individuals learning the main tenets of Christianity in view of becoming Christians through baptism.

cavea: seating area of a theater.

Chalcedon/Chalcedonian: city in Asia Minor, across from Constantinople, where a church council was held in 451, or referring to the decisions of that council.

chora: the "country" of Egypt, as opposed to Alexandria.

chrematistai: panel of Greek judges in Ptolemaic Egypt.

corvée: (French) term used for compulsory labor required by the state.

cupola: a dome-shaped structure on the roof of a building.

curia (adj. curial): the body or meeting-place of a senate; the adjective is used to refer to the councils of cities.

Bendidium or –eion: sanctuary of the goddess Bendis.

daric: a Persian gold coin.

demosion/demosia: "public," with reference to the treasury; in the plural often means "taxes."

demotic: "popular," term used to refer to an Egyptian cursive script.

dioecesis: super-province in the post-Diocletianic organization of the Roman Empire.

dioiketes: "manager," term used to refer to the Ptolemaic chief royal minister, in charge particularly of finances; but in the Roman period used to refer to other officials.

drachma: Greek unit of weight and basic unit of coinage; it had different weights in various local standards.

dux: general, military governor of an Egyptian province.

ephebe: a young man undergoing a period of training in a Greek gymnasium.

epigraphy: the study of inscriptions.

episcopate: office of the bishop.

epistrategos: official like but of higher rank than a *strategos*, in charge of an area larger than a nome.

epistrategia: the office or jurisdiction of an *epistrategos*.

equestrian/equites: Roman order of "knights," the level of society just below senators.

euergetism: the practice of benefaction by wealthy citizens, particularly in Greek cities.

exactor: a tax official in Late Antique Egypt.

exegetes: a civic official connected with the gymnasium.

exergue: the space under the main design on a coin.

gnostics: members of different Christian groups for whom personal knowledge of the divine was more important than the institutional forms of Christianity.

gymnasium/gymnasial: the athletic and military training institution of a Greek city, sometimes also with broader cultural programs.

hajj: the Muslim pilgrimage to Mecca.

Heptastadion: seven-stadia long causeway connecting Alexandria to the island with the lighthouse (Pharos).

hieratic: an Egyptian script.

hieroglyphic: the classic formal Egyptian script using stylized pictures.

indiction: tax-year, generally in fifteen-year cycles beginning in AD 312.

kosmetes: a civic official connected with the gymnasium.

laokritai: Egyptian judges in Ptolemaic Egypt.

lararia: shrines for the family cult.

liturgies: compulsory services in public offices (as opposed to physical labor, see *corvée*) in Roman Egypt.

Manichaeism/Manichaeans: a dualistic religion founded by Mani, viewed by some Christians as a heresy.

mawlā: client, a newly converted Muslim; plural *mawālī*.

metropolis: "mother city," used to refer to the main city of each Egyptian nome.

Miaphysite: adherent of a theological position about the nature of Christ, asserting union of human and divine in a single nature.

Monoenergism: Christian theological doctrine that the Father and Son shared a single energy.

Neoplatonism: a philosophical current ultimately deriving from Plato, popular in the later Roman period.

nome: geographical and administrative subdivision of Egypt.

obol: a coin, one sixth of a drachma.

ostracon/ostraca: potsherd used for writing (also used for inscribed stone fragment).

Pachomian: connected with the monastic federation or way of life created by Pachomius.

pagarch/pagarchy: official in charge of (usually) a nome in Byzantine Egypt.

pagus: a subdivision of a nome in the fourth century.

papyrology: the study of ancient texts written on papyrus and other everyday materials.

patriarch: an archbishop with regional responsibility (as of Constantinople, Alexandria, Antioch, or Jerusalem).

patricius/patriciate: "patrician," archaic Roman aristocratic social group used as a mark of distinction in the Later Roman Empire.

polis: the Greek term for a city.

politeuma/-ta: a civic-style organization in Ptolemaic Egypt, usually on an ethnic basis.

portico: covered passageway with columns.

praepositus: official in charge of a pagus or a military unit.

praeses: regional governor in Late Antique Egypt.

praetorium: headquarters in a Roman military camp.

prefect/*praefectus*: the governor of Egypt or commander of a military unit.

presbyteroi/**presbyters**: "elders," term used both for village elders and (later) for Christian priests.

qāḍī: a Muslim judge.

qanat: a water channel cut in the rock underground that uses natural gradient to feed an irrigation system.

royal scribe: chief official for record-keeping in a nome.

saqiya: a water-lifting wheel.

see (ecclesiastical): a bishop's seat or area of control.

senatorial (Roman): belonging to the Roman Senate or its members.

senti: Egyptian term for finance minister, equated to Ptolemaic *dioiketes*.

shaduf: a water-lifting device.

stele: stone slab, usually with carved decoration or text.

strategos: "general," the governor of a nome in the Ptolemaic and Roman periods.

talent: Greek unit of weight or money, equal to 6, 000 drachmas.

temenos: the sacred area attached to a temple.

tetradrachm: a coin worth four drachmas.

titulary: the series of titles used for a ruler.

toparchy: a subdivision of a nome.

topoteretes: deputy governor of Egypt in the sixth–seventh centuries.

Tripheion: sanctuary of the goddess Repit.

Tycheion: sanctuary of the goddess Tyche (fortune).

umma: the Muslim community.

vizier: (Arabic) term for chief minister.

Bibliography

Papyri are cited according to the *Checklist of Editions of Greek, Latin, Demotic, and Coptic Papyri, Ostraca, and Tablets*: www.papyri.info/docs/checklist.

Classical authors, both Greek and Latin, can be found listed in the *Oxford Classical Dictionary*, 3rd edition. For Greek authors both classical and later, the *TLG Canon* (stephanus.tlg.uci.edu/canon.php) provides a more complete list of authors and works, including Christian authors.

The fullest reference list for Coptic authors, although not easy to use, is the *Clavis Coptica*: www.cmcl.it/~cmcl/chiam_clavis.html.

Adams, C. (2007) *Land Transport in Roman Egypt: A Study of Economics and Administration in a Roman Province*. Oxford.

Agut-Labordère, D. (2013) "The Saite period: the emergence of a Mediterranean power." In *Ancient Egyptian Administration*, ed. J. C. Moreno García: 965–1027. Leiden.

Agut-Labordère, D. (2014) "L'orge et l'argent. Les usages monétaires à ꜥAin Manâwir à l'époque perse." *Annales HSS* 69: 75–90.

al-Qāḍī, W. (2015) "Death dates in Umayyad stipends registers (*dīwān al-ꜥaṭāʾ*): the testimony of the papyri and the literary sources." In *From Bāwīṭ to Marw: Documents from the Medieval Muslim World*, ed. A. Kaplony, D. Potthast and C. Römer: 59–82. Leiden.

Alston, R. (1995) *Soldier and Society in Roman Egypt: A Social History*. London.

Arnold, D. (1999) *Temples of the Last Pharaohs*. Oxford.

Azzarello, G. (2010) "Vecchi e nuovi personaggi della famiglia degli Apioni nei documenti papiracei." In *PapCongr.* 25: 33–46.

Bagnall, R. S. (1984) "The origin of Ptolemaic cleruchs." *Bulletin of the American Society of Papyrologists* 21: 7–20. Reprinted in Bagnall 2006: chapter VIII.

(1992) "Landholding in late Roman Egypt: the distribution of wealth." *Journal of Roman Studies* 82: 128–149.

(1993) *Egypt in Late Antiquity*. Princeton.

(2002a) "Alexandria: library of dreams." *Proceedings of the American Philosophical Society* 146: 348–362. Reprinted in Bagnall 2006: chapter IX.

(2002b) "The effects of plague: model and evidence." *Journal of Roman Archaeology* 15: 97–114.

(2005) "Linguistic change and religious change: thinking about the temples of the Fayyum in the Roman period." In *Christianity and Monasticism in the Fayoum Oasis*, ed. G. Gabra: 11–19. Cairo.

(2006) *Hellenistic and Roman Egypt: Sources and Approaches*. Aldershot.

ed. (2007) *Egypt in the Byzantine World, 300–700*. Cambridge.

(2009a) *Early Christian Books in Egypt*. Princeton.

ed. (2009b) *The Oxford Handbook of Papyrology*. Oxford.

(2011) *Everyday Writing in the Graeco-Roman East*. Berkeley.

(forthcoming) "Egyptian religious identities under Roman imperial rule: critical reflections." In *Egypt and Empire: Religious Identities from Ancient to Modern Times*, ed. E. O'Connell. Leuven.

Bagnall, R. S. and Cribiore, R. (2006) *Women's Letters from Ancient Egypt, 300 BC–AD 800*. Ann Arbor.

Bagnall, R. S. and Derow, P. (2004) *The Hellenistic Period: Historical Sources in Translation*. Oxford.

Bagnall, R. S. and Frier, B. W. (1994, 2006^2) *The Demography of Roman Egypt*. Cambridge.

Bagnall, R. S. and Rathbone, D. W. (2017) *Egypt from Alexander to the Copts: An Archaeological and Historical Guide*. 2nd edition. Cairo and New York.

Balamoshev, C. (2017) "The Jews of Oxyrhynchos address the Strategos of the nome: an early fourth-century document." *Journal of Juristic Papyrology* 47: 27–43.

Banaji, J. (2007) *Agrarian Change in Late Antiquity: Gold, Labour, and Aristocratic Dominance*. 2nd edition. Oxford (1st edition 2001).

Barclay, J. M. G. (1996) *Jews in the Mediterranean Diaspora from Alexander to Trajan (323 BCE–117 CE)*. Edinburgh.

Barnes, T. D. (1993) *Athanasius and Constantine: Theology and Politics in the Constantinian Empire*. Cambridge, MA.

Bausi, A. and Camplani, A. (2016) "The history of the episcopate of Alexandria (HEpA): Editio minor of the fragments preserved in the Aksumite Collection and in the Codex Veronensis LX (58)." *Adamantius* 22: 249–302.

Bell, H. I. (1917) "The Byzantine servile state in Egypt." *Journal of Egyptian Archaeology* 4: 86–106.

(1948) *Egypt from Alexander the Great to the Arab Conquest*. Oxford.

(1952) *Cults and Creeds in Graeco-Roman Egypt*. Liverpool.

Benaissa, A. (2012) "Greek language, education, and literary culture." In Riggs 2012: 526–542.

Bénazeth, D. and Rutschowscaya, M.-H., eds. (2000) *L'art copte en Egypte: 2000 ans de christianisme*. Paris.

Berger, A. (2013) *Accounts of Medieval Constantinople: The Patria, 4.4, With Explanatory Additions*. Cambridge, MA.

Berkes, L. (2016) *Dorfverwaltung und Dorfgemeinschaft in Ägypten von Diokletian zu den Abbasiden*. Wiesbaden.

Bingen, J. (2007) *Hellenistic Egypt: Monarchy, Society, Economy, Culture.* Edinburgh.

Blanke, L. (2019) *An Archaeology of Egyptian Monasticism: Settlement, Economy and Daily Life at the White Monastery Federation.* New Haven.

Blaudeau, P. (1997) "Le voyage de Damien d'Alexandrie vers Antioche puis Constantinople (579–580): motivations et objectifs." *Orientalia Christiana Periodica* 63: 333–361.

Blouin, K. (2005) *Le conflit judéo-alexandrin de 38–41. L'identité juive à l'épreuve.* Paris.

(2014) *Triangular Landscapes: Environment, Society, and the State in the Nile Delta under Roman Rule.* Oxford.

Boek, J. A. (2008) *Taxation in the Later Roman Empire: a study on the character of the late antique economy.* MPhil thesis, Leiden University. Online: openaccess.leidenuniv.nl/handle/1887/18524.

Bogaert, R. (1994) *Trapezitica Aegyptiaca. Recueil de recherches sur la banque en Égypte gréco-romaine.* Florence.

Booth, P. (2013) "The Muslim conquest of Egypt reconsidered." In *Constructing the Seventh Century*, ed. C. Zuckerman: 639–670. Paris.

(2016) "The last years of Cyrus, patriarch of Alexandria (†642)." In Fournet and Papaconstantinou 2016: 509–558. Paris.

(2017) "Towards the Coptic church: the making of the Severan episcopate." *Millennium* 14: 151–190.

(2018) "A circle of Egyptian bishops at the end of Roman rule (c. 600)." *Le Muséon* 131: 21–72.

Borkowski, Z. (1981) *Inscriptions des factions d'Alexandrie.* Warsaw.

Bosch-Puche, F. (2008) "L' 'autel' du temple d'Alexandre le Grand à Bahariya retrouvé." *Bulletin de l'Institut français d'archéologie orientale* 108: 29–44.

Boud'hors, A. (2016) "Degrès d'arabisation dans l'Égypte du VIIIe siècle: *CPR* II 228 revisité." In Fournet and Papaconstantinou 2016: 71–89.

Boud'hors, A. and Garel, E. (2016) "Que reste-t-il de la bibliothèque du monastère de Saint-Phoibammon à Deir el-Bahari?" In *Aegyptus et Nubia Christiana: The Włodzimierz Godlewski Jubilee Volume on the Occasion of his 70th Birthday*, ed. A. Łajtar, A. Obłuski, I. Zych: 47–60. Warsaw.

Bouderbala, S. (2014) "Les *mawālī* à Fusṭāṭ aux deux premiers siècles de l'islam et leur intégration sociale." In *Les dynamiques de l'islamisation en Méditerranée centrale et en Sicile: nouvelles propositions et découvertes récentes = Le dinamiche dell'islamizzazione nel Mediterraneo centrale e in Sicilia: nuove proposte e scoperte recenti*, ed. A. Nef and F. Ardizzone: 141–151. Bari-Rome.

Bowersock, G. W. (1996) "Late Antique Alexandria." In Hamma 1996: 263–270.

Bowman, A. K. (1985), "Landholding in the Hermopolite nome in the fourth century A.D." *Journal of Roman Studies* 75: 137–163.

(1986) *Egypt after the Pharaohs, 332 BC–AD 642: From Alexander to the Arab Conquest.* London and Berkeley.

(2013) "Agricultural production in Egypt." In *The Roman Agricultural Economy: Organization, Investment, and Production,* ed. A. K. Bowman and A. I. Wilson: 219–253. Oxford.

Bowman, A. K. and Rathbone, D. W. (1992) "Cities and administration in Roman Egypt." *Journal of Roman Studies* 82: 107–127.

Bowman, A. K. and Wilson, A. I. (2009) "Quantifying the Roman economy: integration, growth, decline?" In *Quantifying the Roman Economy: Methods and Problems,* ed. A. K. Bowman and A. I. Wilson: 1–84. Oxford.

Bowman, A. K., Coles, R., Gonis, N., Obbink, D., and Parsons, P. J. (2007) *Oxyrhynchus: A City and Its Texts.* London.

Brakke, D. (2010) "A new fragment of Athanasius's thirty-ninth *Festal Letter*: Heresy, apocrypha, and the canon." *Harvard Theological Review* 103: 47–66.

Breccia, E. (1909) "Un ipogeo cristiano ad Hadra." *Bulletin de la Société archéologique d'Alexandrie* 10: 278–288.

Brett, M. (1973) "The spread of Islam in Egypt and North Africa." In *Northern Africa: Islam and Modernisation,* ed. M. Brett: 1–12. London.

Brooks Hedstrom, D. (2017) *The Monastic Landscape of Late Antique Egypt: An Archaeological Reconstruction.* Cambridge.

Broux, Y. (2015) *Double Names and Elite Strategy in Roman Egypt.* Leuven.

Brun, J.-P, Faucher, T., Redon, B., and Sidebotham, S. (2018) *Le désert oriental d'Égypte durant la période gréco-romaine: bilans archéologiques.* Paris.

Bulliet, R. W. (1978) *Conversion to Islam in the Medieval Period: An Essay in Quantitative History.* Cambridge, MA.

Burmester, O. H. E. (1932) "The canons of Christodoulos, Patriarch of Alexandria (A.D. 1047–1077)." *Le Muséon* 45: 71–84.

Cameron, A. (2007) "Poets and pagans in Byzantine Egypt." In Bagnall 2007: 21–46.

Caneva, S. G. (2016) *From Alexander to the Theoi Adelphoi: Foundation and Legitimation of a Dynasty.* Leuven.

Capponi, L. (2005) *Augustan Egypt: The Creation of a Roman Province.* New York.

(2018) *Il mistero del tempio: la rivolta ebraica sotto Traiano.* Rome.

Carleton Paget, J. (2006) "Jews and Christians in ancient Alexandria from the Ptolemies to Caracalla." In *Alexandria: Real and Imagined,* ed. A. Hirst and M. Silk: 143–166. Cairo.

Choat, M. (2012) "Coptic." In Riggs 2012: 581–593.

Christensen, T., Thompson, D. J., and Vandorpe, K. (2017) *Land and Taxes in Ptolemaic Egypt: An Edition, Translation and Commentary for the Edfu Land Survey* (P. Haun. *IV 70*). Cambridge.

Clark, P. (2017) *Taxation and the Formation of the Late Roman Social Contract.* Berkeley.

Clarysse, W. (1984) "Bilingual texts and collaboration between demoticists and papyrologists." *PapCongr.* 17.3: 1345–1353.

(1985) "Greeks and Egyptians in the Ptolemaic army and administration." *Aegyptus* 65: 57–66.

(1993) "Egyptian scribes writing Greek." *Chronique d'Égypte* 68: 186–201.

(2000) "The Ptolemies visiting the Egyptian chora." in *Politics, Administration and Society in the Hellenistic and Roman World*, ed. L. Mooren: 29–53. Leuven.

(2009) "Egyptian religion and magic in the papyri." In Bagnall 2009b: 561–589.

(2010) "Egyptian temples and priests: Graeco-Roman." In Lloyd 2010: 1.274–290.

(2019) "Ethnic identity: Egyptians, Greeks, and Romans." In Vandorpe 2019: 299–313.

Clarysse, W., and Thompson, D. J. (2006) *Counting the People in Hellenistic Egypt, 2: Historical Studies*. Cambridge.

Clarysse, W., and Vandorpe, K. (1998) 'The Ptolemaic apomoira." In Melaerts 1998: 5–42. Leuven.

Claytor, W. G. and Verhoogt, A. (2018) *Papyri from Karanis: The Granary C123 (P. Mich XXI)*. Ann Arbor.

Colburn, H. P. (2019) *Archaeology of Empire in Achaemenid Egypt*. Edinburgh.

Collins, B. A. (2001) *Al-Muqaddasī, The Best Divisions for Knowledge of the Regions/Aḥsan al-taqāsīm fī maʿrifat al-aqālīm*. 2nd edition. Reading.

Collombert, P. (2000) "Religion égyptienne et culture grecque: l'exemple de Διοσκουρίδης." *Chronique d'Égypte* 75: 47–63.

Connor, A. J. (2014) *Temples as economic agents in early Roman Egypt: the case of Tebtunis and Soknopaiou Nesos*. Ph.D. dissertation. Cincinnati. Online: rave.ohiolink.edu/etdc/view?acc_num=ucin1430749580.

Cowey, J. M. S. and Maresch, K. (2001) *Urkunden des Politeuma der Juden von Herakleopolis (144/3–133/2 v. Chr.)*. Wiesbaden.

Cribiore, R. (2001) *Gymnastics of the Mind: Greek Education in Hellenistic and Roman Egypt*. Princeton and Oxford.

(2009) "Education in the papyri." In Bagnall 2009b: 320–337.

Crislip, A. (2005) *From Monastery to Hospital: Christian Monasticism and the Transformation of Health Care in Late Antiquity*. Ann Arbor.

Cromwell, J. (2017) *Recording Village Life: A Coptic Scribe in Early Islamic Egypt*. Ann Arbor.

Davis, S. J. (2004) *The Early Coptic Papacy: The Egyptian Church and Its Leadership in Late Antiquity*. Cairo.

De Ligt, L. (2017) "The urban system of Roman Egypt in the early third century AD: an economic-geographical approach to city-size distribution in a Roman province." *Ancient Society* 47: 255–321.

Debié, M. (2016) "Christians in the service of the caliph: Through the looking-glass of communal identities." In *Christians and Others in the Umayyad State*, ed. A. Borrut and F. Donner: 53–71. Chicago.

Décobert, C. (1983) "Review of Bulliet 1978." *Studia Islamica* 58: 182–187.

(1992) "Sur l'arabisation et l'islamisation de l'Égypte médiévale." In *Itinéraires d'Égypte. Mélanges offerts au père Maurice Martin, s.j.*, ed. C. Décobert: 273–300. Cairo.

Décobert, C. and Empereur, J.-Y., eds. (1998) *Alexandrie médievale 1.* Alexandria.

Defernez, C. (2012) "Sur les traces de conteneurs égyptiens d'époque perse dans le Delta." In Zivie-Coche and Guermeur 2012: 1.387–405.

Dekker, R. (2018) *Episcopal Networks and Authority in Late Antique Egypt.* Leuven.

Delia, D. (1988) "The population of Roman Alexandria." *Transactions of the American Philological Association* 118: 275–292.

(1992) "From romance to rhetoric: The Alexandrian library in Classical and Islamic traditions." *American Historical Review* 97: 1449–1467.

den Heijer, J. (2002) "Le patriarcat copte d'Alexandrie à l'époque fatimide." In *Alexandrie médiévale 2*, ed. C. Décobert: 83–97. Cairo.

(1989) *Mawhūb ibn Mansūr ibn Mufarriğ et l'historiographie copto-arabe. Étude sur la composition de l'Histoire des patriarches d'Alexandrie.* Leuven.

(1991) "History of the Patriarchs of Alexandria." In *The Coptic Encyclopedia*, vol. 4, ed. A. Atiya: 1238–1242. New York.

(2000) "La conquête arabe vue par les historiens coptes." In *Valeur et distance: identités et sociétés en Égypte*, ed. C. Décobert: 229–231. Paris.

Dennett, D. C. (1950) *Conversion and the Poll Tax in Early Islam.* Cambridge, MA.

Depauw, M. (2003) "Autograph confirmation in demotic private contracts." *Chronique d'Égypte* 78: 66–111.

Derda, T. (2006) *Arsinoites Nomos: Administration of the Fayum under Roman Rule.* Warsaw.

(2019) "A Roman province in the eastern Mediterranean." In Vandorpe 2019: 51–69.

Derda, T., Markiewicz, T., and Wipszycka, E., eds. (2007) *Alexandria: Auditoria of Kom el-Dikka and Late Antique Education.* Warsaw.

De Romanis, F. (2020) *The Indo-Roman Pepper Trade and the Muziris Papyrus.* Oxford.

Dieleman, J. (2005) *Priests, Tongues, and Rites. The London-Leiden Magical Manuscripts and Translation in Egyptian Ritual (100–300 CE).* Leiden.

Drayton, J. M. (2002) *Pachomius as Discovered in the Worlds of Fourth Century Christian Egypt, Pachomian Literature and Pachomian Monasticism: A Figure of History or Hagiography?* Sydney.

Drew-Bear, M. (1997) "Guerre civile et grands travaux à Hermoupolis Magna sous Gallien." *PapCongr* 21: 237–243. Stuttgart.

Driver, R. E. (2014) *Temple conversion and cultural, ritual and topographic memory in Alexandria, Cyrene, and Carthage.* M.Phil. thesis, University of Birmingham. Online: etheses.bham.ac.uk/id/eprint/5528/.

Dunand, F. and Zivie-Coche, C. (2004) *Gods and Men in Egypt.* Ithaca, NY.

Duncan-Jones, R. P. (1996) "The impact of the Antonine plague." *Journal of Roman Archaeology* 9: 118–136.

(2018) "The Antonine plague revisited." *Arctos* 52: 41–72.

Dzielska, M. 1995: *Hypatia of Alexandria*, trans. F. Lyra. Cambridge, MA.

el-Abbadi, M. A. H. (1992). *The Life and Fate of the Ancient Library of Alexandria*. 2nd edition. Paris.

el-Falaki, M. H. (1872) *Mémoire sur l'antique Alexandrie*. Copenhagen.

el-Masri, Y., Altenmüller, H., and Thissen H.-J. (2012). *Das Synodaldekret von Alexandria aus dem Jahre 243 v. Chr.* Hamburg.

Emmel, S. (2007) "Coptic Literature in the Byzantine and Early Islamic World." In Bagnall 2007: 83–102.

Empereur, J.-Y. (1998) *Alexandria Rediscovered*, trans. M. Maehler. London.

Epp, E. J. (2006) "The Jews and the Jewish Community in Oxyrhynchus: Socio-Religious Context for the New Testament Papyri." In *New Testament Manuscripts: Their Texts and Their World*, ed. T. J. Kraus and T. Nicklas: 13–52. Leiden.

Evelyn White, H. G. (1936) *The History of the Monasteries of Nitria and of Scetis*. New York.

Fikhman, I. F. (1996) "Les Juifs d'Égypte d'après les papyrus publiés depuis la parution du 'Corpus Papyrorum Judaicarum' III." In *Studies in Memory of Abraham Wasserstein I (= Scripta Classica Israelica 15)*, ed. H. M. Cotton, J. J. Price, and D. J. Wasserstein: 223–229.

Fischer-Bovet, C. (2011) "Counting the Greeks in Egypt: Immigration in the first century of Ptolemaic rule." In *Demography and the Graeco-Roman World: New Insights and Approaches*, ed. C. Holleran and A. Pudsey: 135–154. Cambridge.

(2014) *Army and Society in Ptolemaic Egypt*. Cambridge.

Foss, C. (2003) "The Persians in the Roman Near East (602–630)." *Journal of the Royal Asiatic Society* 13: 149–170.

(2009a) "Egypt under Muʿāwiya, I: Flavius Papas and Upper Egypt." *Bulletin of the School of Oriental and African Studies* 72: 1–24.

(2009b) "Egypt under Muʿāwiya, II: Middle Egypt, Fusṭāṭ, and Alexandria." *Bulletin of the School of Oriental and African Studies* 72: 259–278.

Fournet, J.-L. (2009a) "The multilingual environment of late antique Egypt: Greek, Latin, Coptic, and Persian documentation." In Bagnall 2009b: 418–451.

(2009b) "Conversion religieuse dans un graffito de Baouît? Révision de *SB* III 6042." In *Monastic Estates in Late Antique and Early Islamic Egypt: Ostraca, Papyri, and Essays in Memory of Sarah Clackson*, ed. A. Boud'hors, J. Clackson, C. Louis, and P. Sijpesteijn: 141–147. Oxford.

(2010) "Sur les premiers documents juridiques coptes." In *Études coptes XI. Troisième journée d'études (Marseille, 7–9 juin 2007)*, ed. A. Boud'hors and C. Louis: 125–137. Paris.

(2013) "Culture grecque et document dans l'Égypte de l'Antiquité tardive." *Journal of Juristic Papyrology* 43: 135–162.

(2016) "Sur les premiers documents juridiques coptes (2): les archives de Phoibammôn et de Kollouthos." In *Études coptes XIV. Seizième journée d'études (Genève, 19–21 juin 2013)*, ed. A. Boud'hors and C. Louis: 115–141. Paris.

(2018a) "Sur les premiers documents juridiques coptes (3): les 'archives' d'Apa Abraham." In *Études Coptes XV. Dix-septième journée d'études (Lisbonne, 18–20 juin 2015)*, ed. A. Boud'hors and C. Louis: 199–226. Paris.

(2018b) "Les documents bilingues gréco-coptes dans l'Égypte byzantine: essai de typologie." In *Written Sources About Africa and Their Study. Le fonti scritte sull'Africa e i loro studi*, ed. M. Lafkioui and V. Brugnatelli: 59–83. Milan.

(2020) *The Rise of Coptic: Egyptian versus Greek in Late Antiquity*. Princeton.

Fournet, J.-L. and Papaconstantinou, A., eds. (2016) *Mélanges Jean Gascou: textes et études papyrologiques (P.Gascou)*. Paris.

Fowden, G. (1993) *Empire to Commonwealth: Consequences of Monotheism in Late Antiquity*. Princeton.

Frankfurter, D. (1998) *Religion in Roman Egypt: Assimilation and Resistance*. Princeton.

(2017) *Christianizing Egypt: Syncretism and Local Worlds in Late Antiquity*. Princeton.

Frantz-Murphy, G. (1991) "Conversion in early Islamic Egypt: the economic factor." In *Documents de l'islam médiéval: nouvelles perspectives de recherche*, ed. Y. Rāġib: 11–17. Cairo.

Fraser, P. M. (1972) *Ptolemaic Alexandria*. 3 vols. Oxford.

Fuhrmann, C. J. (2012) *Policing the Roman Empire: Soldiers, Administration, and Public Order*. Oxford.

Gabra, G. (2002) *Christian Egypt: Coptic Art and Monuments through Two Millennia*. Cairo.

Gaddis, M. and Price, R. , eds. (2005) *The Acts of the Council of Chalcedon*. 3 vols. Liverpool.

Gagos, T. and van Minnen, P. (1994) *Settling a Dispute: Toward a Legal Anthropology of Late Antique Egypt*. Ann Arbor.

Gambetti, S. (2009) *The Alexandrian Riots of 38 C.E. and the Persecution of the Jews: A Historical Reconstruction*. Leiden.

Garcin, J.-C. (1976) *Un centre musulman de la Haute-Egypte médiévale: Qūṣ*. Cairo.

(1987) "L'arabisation de l'Égypte." *Revue de l'Occident musulman et de la Méditerranée* 43: 130–137.

Gariboldi, A. (2009) "Social conditions in Egypt under the Sasanian occupation." *Parola del Passato* 64: 335–350.

Gascou, J. (1985/2008) "Les grands domaines, la cité et l'état en Égypte byzantine." *Travaux et Mémoires* 9: 1–90; revised edition in Gascou 2008: 125–213.

(1994) *Un codex fiscal hermopolite (P.Sorb. II 69)*. Atlanta.

(1998a) "La vie intellectuelle alexandrine à l'époque byzantine, IVe – VIIe siècle." In *Actes du XXXe congrès international de l'Association des professeurs de langues anciennes de l'enseignement supérieur*, ed. M. L. Freyburger: 41–48. Mulhouse.

(1998b) "Les églises d'Alexandrie: questions de méthode." *Alexandrie médiévale* 1: 23–44.

(2008) *Fiscalité et société en Égypte byzantine.* Paris.

(2013) "Arabic taxation in the mid-seventh-century Greek papyri." In *Constructing the Seventh Century*, ed. C. Zuckerman: 671–677. Paris.

Geens, K. (2007) *Panopolis, A Nome Capital in Egypt and the Roman and Byzantine Period (ca. AD 200–600).* Leuven.

Gellens, S. I. (1992) "Egypt, Islamization of." In *The Coptic Encyclopedia*, vol. 4, ed. A. Atiya: 937–942. New York.

Godlewski, W. (1986) *Le monastère de St Phoibammon.* Warsaw.

Gonis, N. (2007) "Recent news from Flavius Magistor & sons." *Journal of Juristic Papyrology* 27: 125–133.

Gorre, G. (2009) *Les relations du clergé égyptien et des Lagides d'après les sources privées.* Leuven.

Green, M. (1983) "A private archive of Coptic letters and documents from Teshlot." *Oudheidkundige Mededelingen uit het Rijksmuseum van Oudheden* 64: 61–121.

Griffith, S. (1996) "The *Kitāb Misbāh al-'Aql* of Severus Ibn al-Muqaffa': a profile of the Christian creed in Arabic in tenth-century Egypt." *Medieval Encounters* 2: 15–42.

Gruen, E. S. (1984) *The Hellenistic World and the Coming of Rome.* vol. 2. Berkeley.

Haas, C. (1993) "Alexandria's Via Canopica: political expression and urban topography from Alexander to 'Amr ibn al-'As." *Bulletin de la Société archéologique d'Alexandrie* 45: 123–138.

Haas, C. (1997) *Alexandria in Late Antiquity: Topography and Social Conflict.* Baltimore.

Haensch, R. (2008) "Die Provinz Aegyptus: Kontinuitäten und Brüche zum ptolemäischen Ägypten. Das Beispiel des administrativen Personals." In *Die römischen Provinzen: Begriff und Gründung*, ed. I. Piso: 81–105. Cluj-Napoca.

(2010) "Der exercitus Aegyptiacus – ein provinzialer Heeresverband wie andere auch?" In *Tradition and Transformation: Egypt under Roman Rule. Proceedings of the International Conference, Hildesheim, Roemer- and Pelizaeus-Museum, 3–6 July 2008*, ed. K. Lembke, M. Minas-Nerpel, and S. Pfeiffer: 111–132. Leiden.

(2012) "The Roman army in Egypt." In Riggs 2012: 68–82.

Hagedorn, D. (2007) "The emergence of municipal offices in the nome-capitals of Egypt." In Bowman et al. 2007: 194–204. London.

Hamel, G. (2002) "Poverty and charity." In *The Oxford Handbook of Jewish Daily Life in Roman Palestine*, ed. C. Hezser: 308–324. Oxford.

Hamma, K., ed. (1996) *Alexandria and Alexandrianism: papers delivered at a symposium organized by the J. Paul Getty Museum and the Getty Center*

for the History of Art and the Humanities and held at the Museum, April 22 –
25, 1993. Malibu.

Handler, S. (1971) "Architecture on the Roman coins of Alexandria." *American*
Journal of Archaeology 75: 57–74.

Hardy, E. R. (1931) *The Large Estates of Byzantine Egypt.* New York.

Harker, A. (2008) *Loyalty and Dissidence in Roman Egypt.* Cambridge.

(2012) "The Jews in Roman Egypt: trials and rebellions." In Riggs 2012:
277–287.

Harper, K. (2016) "People, plagues, and prices in the Roman world: the evidence
from Egypt." *Journal of Economic History* 76: 803–839.

(2017) *The Fate of Rome: Climate, Disease, and the End of an Empire.* Princeton.

Hendrickson, T. (2016) "The Serapeum: dreams of the daughter library." *Classical*
Philology 111: 453–464.

Hickey, T. M. (2007) "Aristocratic landholding and the economy of Byzantine
Egypt." In Bagnall 2007: 288–308.

(2009) "Tebtunis on the Arno and beyond: two 'archives.'" In *100 anni di*
istituzioni fiorentine per la papirologia: 67–81. Florence.

Hobbs, L. M. (2014) *The Religion of Constantine: An Analysis of the Modern*
Scholarly Hypotheses and Interpretations of the Contemporary Evidence.
Ottawa.

Hobson, D. W. (1984) "P.Vindob. Gr. 24951 + 24556: new evidence for tax-exempt
status in Roman Egypt." In *PapCongr* 17: 3.847–864. Naples.

Hoffmann, F., Minas-Nerpel, M., and Pfeiffer, S. (2009) *Die dreisprachige Stele des*
C. Cornelius Gallus. Berlin.

Hölbl, G. (2000) *Altägypten im römischen Reich. Der römische Pharao und seine*
Tempel, I: Römische Politik und altägyptische Ideologie von Augustus bis
Diokletian, Tempelbau in Oberägypten. Mainz.

(2001) *A History of the Ptolemaic Empire*, trans. T. Saavedra. London and
New York.

(2004) *Altägypten im römischen Reich. Der römische Pharao und seine Tempel,*
II: Die Tempel des römischen Nubien. Mainz.

(2005) *Altägypten im römischen Reich. Der römische Pharao und seine Tempel,*
III: Heiligtümer und religiöses Leben in den ägyptischen Wüsten und Oasen.
Mainz.

Horbury, W. and Noy, D. (1992). *Jewish Inscriptions of Graeco-Roman Egypt. With*
an Index of the Jewish Inscriptions of Egypt and Cyrenaica. Cambridge.

Huebner, S. R. (2013) *The Family in Roman Egypt: A Comparative Approach to*
Intergenerational Solidarity and Conflict. Cambridge.

(2019) *The Papyri and the Social World of the New Testament.* Cambridge.

Huss, W. (2001) *Ägypten in hellenistischer Zeit.* Munich.

Iskander, J. (1998) "Islamization in medieval Egypt: the Copto-Arabic 'Apocalypse
of Samuel' as a source for the social and religious history of medieval Copts',
Medieval Encounters 4: 219–227.

Jansen-Winkeln, K. (2012) "Libyer und Ägypter in der Libyerzeit." In Zivie-Coche and Guermeur 2012: 2.609–624.

Jeppson, K. (2003) *Gender, Religion and Society: A Study of Women and Convent Life in Coptic Orthodox Egypt*. Uppsala.

Johnson, A. C. (1936) *Roman Egypt to the Reign of Diocletian*. Baltimore.

Jones, M. and McFadden, S., eds. (2015) *Art of Empire: The Roman Frescoes and Imperial Cult Chamber in Luxor Temple*. New Haven.

Jones, P. (2011) "Cleopatra VII (69–30 BCE)." In *Dictionary of African Biography*, ed. E. Akyeampong and H. L Gates, Jr.: 101–104. Oxford.

Jones, R. N., Hammond, P. C., Johnson, D. J., and Fiema, Z. T. (1988) "A second Nabataean inscription from Tell Esh-Shuqafiya, Egypt." *Bulletin of the American Schools of Oriental Research* 269: 47–57.

Jördens, A. (1999) "Die Agrarverhältnisse im spätantiken Ägypten." *Laverna* 10: 114–152.

(2012) "Government, taxation and law." In Riggs (2012): 56–67.

(2016) "Ein oxyrhynchitisches *proastion.*" *Zeitschrift für Papyrologie und Epigraphik* 200: 470–480.

Karivieri, A. (1994) "The 'House of Proclus' on the southern slope of the Acropolis: a contribution." In *Post-Herulian Athens: Aspects of Life and Culture in Athens A.D. 267–529*, ed. P. Castrén: 115–139. Helsinki.

Keenan, J. G. (1973) "The names Flavius and Aurelius as status designations in later Roman Egypt." *Zeitschrift für Papyrologie und Epigraphik* 11: 33–63.

(1974) "The Names Flavius and Aurelius as status designations in later Roman Egypt." *Zeitschrift für Papyrologie und Epigraphik* 13: 283–304.

(1993) "Papyrology and Byzantine historiography." *Bulletin of the American Society of Papyrologists* 30: 137–144.

Keenan, J. G., Manning, J. G., and Yiftach-Firanko, U. (2014) *Law and Legal Practice in Egypt from Alexander to the Arab Conquest: A Selection of Papyrological Sources in Translation*. Cambridge.

Kehoe, D. (1992) *Management and Investment on Estates in Roman Egypt during the Early Empire*. Bonn.

Kennedy, H. (1998) "Egypt as a province in the Islamic caliphate, 641–868." In *The Cambridge History of Egypt, I: Islamic Egypt, 640–1517*, ed. C. F. Petry: 62–85. Cambridge.

(2015) 'The Middle East in Islamic late antiquity." In *Fiscal Regimes and the Political Economy of Premodern States*, ed. A. Monson and W. Scheidel: 390–403. Cambridge.

Kent, R. G. (1920) "The edict of Diocletian fixing maximum prices." *University of Pennsylvania Law Review and American Law Register* 69: 35–47.

Kitchen, K. A. (1986) *The Third Intermediate Period in Egypt (1100–650 B.C.)*. 2nd edition. Warminster.

Kloppenborg, J. S. (2006). *The Tenants in the Vineyard: Ideology, Economics, and Agrarian Conflict in Jewish Palestine*. Tübingen.

Klotz, D. (2009) "The statue of the *dioikêtês* Harchebi/Archibios." *Bulletin de l'Institut français d'archéologie orientale* 109: 281–310.

Klotz, D. and LeBlanc, M. (2012) "An Egyptian priest in the Ptolemaic court: Yale Peabody Museum 264191." In Zivie-Coche and Guermeur 2012: 2.645–698.

Kolataj, W. (1983) "Recherches architectoniques dans les thermes et le théâtre de Kôm el-Dikka à Alexandrie." In *Das römisch-byzantinische Ägypten: Akten des internationalen Symposions, 26–30 September 1978 in Trier,* ed. G. Grimm, H. Heinen, and E. Winter: 187–194. Mainz.

(1998) "Theoretical reconstruction of the late Roman theatre at Kom el-Dikka in Alexandria." In *Proceedings of the Seventh International Congress of Egyptologists, Cambridge 3–9 September 1995,* ed. C. J. Eyre: 631–638. Leuven.

Kramer, B. (1997) "Der κτίστης Boethos und die Einrichtung einer neuen Stadt, Teil I." *Archiv für Papyrusforschung* 43: 315–339.

Krawiec, R. (2002) *Shenoute & the Women of the White Monastery: Egyptian Monasticism in Late Antiquity.* Oxford.

Kruse, T. (2019) "The branches of Roman and Byzantine government and the role of cities, the church, and elite groups." In Vandorpe 2019: 119–138.

Kuhrt, A. (2007) *The Persian Empire: A Corpus of Sources from the Achaemenid Period.* 2 vols. London.

La'da, C. A. (2003) "Encounters with ancient Egypt: the Hellenistic Greek experience." In *Ancient Perspectives on Egypt,* ed. R. Matthews and C. Roemer: 157–169. London.

Lampela, A. (1998) *Rome and the Ptolemies of Egypt: The Development of their Political Relations, 273–80 B.C.* Helsinki.

Laniado, A. (2002) *Recherches sur les notables municipaux dans l'empire protobyzantin.* Paris.

Lapidus, I. M. (1972) "The conversion of Egypt to Islam." *Israel Oriental Studies* 2: 248–262.

Larsen, L. I. and Rubenson, S. (2018) *Monastic Education in Late Antiquity: The Transformation of Classical Paideia.* Cambridge.

Layton, B. (1995) *The Gnostic Scriptures: A New Translation with Annotations and Introductions.* New Haven.

Legendre, M. (2015) "Islamic conquest, territorial reorganization and empire formation: a study of 7th-century movements of population in the light of Egyptian papyri." In *The Long Seventh Century: Continuity and Discontinuity in an Age of Transition,* ed. A. Gnasso, E. Intagliata, T. MacMaster, and B. Morris: 235–250. Oxford.

(2016) "Neither Byzantine nor Islamic? The duke of the Thebaid and the formation of the Umayyad state." *Historical Research* 89/243: 3–18.

Legras, B. (2001) "Droit et violence: la jeunesse d'Alexandrie sous les Sévères (à propos du P.Oxy. LXIV 4435." In *PapCongr* 22: 777–786. Florence.

Lerouxel, F. (2016) *Le marché du crédit dans le monde romain (Égypte et Campanie)*. Rome.

Lesquier, J. (1918) *L'armée romaine d'Égypte d'Auguste à Dioclétien*. Cairo.

Lewis, N. (1970) "'Greco-Roman' Egypt: fact or fiction?" In *PapCongr* 12: 3–14. Toronto; repr. in Lewis 1995: 138–149.

  (1983) *Life in Egypt under Roman Rule*. Oxford.

  (1984), "The Romanity of Roman Egypt: a growing consensus." In *Atti del XVII Congresso Internazionale di Papirologia (Napoli, 19–26 maggio 1983)*: 1077–1084. Naples; repr. in Lewis 1995: 298–305.

  (1995) *On Government and Law in Roman Egypt*. Atlanta.

Lichtheim, M. (1980) *Ancient Egyptian Literature, III: The Late Period*. Berkeley.

Lloyd, A. B. (2000) "The Late Period (664–332 BC)." In *The Oxford History of Ancient Egypt*, ed. I. Shaw: 369–394. Oxford.

  (2010) *A Companion to Ancient Egypt*. 2 vols. Chichester.

  (2011) "From satrapy to Hellenistic kingdom: the case of Egypt." In *Creating a Hellenistic World*, ed. A. Erskine and L. Llewellyn-Jones: 83–105. Swansea.

López, A. G. (2013) *Shenoute of Atripe and the Uses of Poverty: Rural Patronage, Religious Conflict and Monasticism in Late Antique Egypt*. Berkeley.

Ludlow, F. and Manning, J. G. (2016) "Revolts under the Ptolemies: A paleoclima-tological perspective." In *Revolt and Resistance in the Ancient Classical World and the Near East: In the Crucible of Empire*, ed. J. J. Collins and J. G. Manning: 154–171. Leiden.

Luijendijk, A. (2008) *Greetings in the Lord: Early Christians and the Oxyrhynchus Papyri*. Cambridge, MA.

MacCoull, L. S. B. (1986) "Coptic Egypt during the Persian occupation: the papyrological evidence." *Studi Classici e Orientali* 36: 307–313.

Mairs, R. (2018) "Language, identity and migrant communities: Cyrenaeans in Hellenistic Egypt." In *Migration and Migrant Identities in the Near East from Antiquity to the Middle Ages*, ed. J. Yoo, A. Zerbini, and C. Barron: 26–40. London.

Majcherek, G. (2010) "The auditoria of Kom el-Dikka: a glimpse of late antique education in Alexandria." In *PapCongr* 25: 471–484. Ann Arbor.

Malouta, M. and Wilson, A. I. (2013) "Mechanical irrigation: Water-lifting devices in the archaeological evidence and in the Egyptian papyri." In *The Roman Agricultural Economy*, ed. A. K. Bowman and A. I. Wilson: 273–305. Oxford.

Manning, J. G. (2003) *Land and Power in Ptolemaic Egypt: The Structure of Land Tenure*. Cambridge.

  (2010) *The Last Pharaohs. Egypt under the Ptolemies, 305–30 BC*. Princeton.

  (2019) "The Ptolemaic governmental branches and the role of temples and elite groups." In Vandorpe 2019: 101–117.

Manning, J. G., Ludlow, F., Stine, A. R., Boos, W. R., Sigl, M., and Marlon, J. R. (2017) "Volcanic suppression of Nile summer flooding triggers revolts and constrains interstate conflict in ancient Egypt." *Nature Communications* 18: 900.

Maraval, P. (1997) *Le Christianisme de Constantin à la conquête arabe.* Paris.

Marquis, C. L. (2012) *Haunted Paradise: Remembering and Forgetting Among Ascetics of the Egyptian Desert.* Durham, NC.

Masson-Berghoff, A. and Villing, A. (2016) "Egypt and Greece: early encounters." In *Sunken Cities: Egypt's Lost Worlds*: 33–70. London.

Mattha, G. and Hughes, G. R. (1975) *The Demotic Legal Code of Hermopolis West.* Cairo.

Mazza, R. (2004) "Noterelle prosopografiche in margine ad alcune pubblicazioni recenti riguardanti gli Apioni." *Simblos* 4: 263–280.

McGing, B. (1997) "Revolt Egyptian style: internal opposition to Ptolemaic rule." *Archiv für Papyrusforschung* 43: 273–314.

McKenzie, J. (2007) *The Architecture of Alexandria and Egypt c. 300 BC to AD 700.* New Haven and London.

Melaerts, H. (1998) *Le culte du souverain dans l'Égypte ptolémaïque au IIIe siècle avant notre ère.* Leuven.

Mélèze-Modrzejewski, J. (1983) "Le statut des Hellènes dans l'Égypte lagide: bilan et perspectives de recherches." *Revue des études grecques* 96: 241–268.

   (1997) *The Jews of Egypt. From Rameses II to Emperor Hadrian*, trans. R. Cornman. Princeton.

Messerer, C. (2012) "La situation des prêtres entre le Ier et le IIIe siècle en Égypte romaine." *PapCongr.* 26: 529–536.

   (2017–) *Corpus des papyrus grecs sur les relations administratives entre le clergé égyptien et les autorités romaines.* 2 vols. (to date). Paderborn.

Meyer, M. W. and Smith, R. (1999) *Ancient Christian Magic: Coptic Texts of Ritual Power.* Princeton.

Mikhail, M. (2014) *From Byzantine to Islamic Egypt: Religion, Identity, and Politics after the Arab Conquest.* London.

Milne. J. G. (1971) *Catalogue of Alexandrian Coins [in the Ashmolean Museum].* Oxford.

Miquel, A. (1972) "L'Égypte vue par un géographe arabe du IVe / Xe siècle: al-Muqaddasī." *Annales islamologiques* 11: 109–139.

Monson, A. (2012) *From the Ptolemies to the Romans: Political and Economic Change in Egypt.* Cambridge.

   (2014) "Late Ptolemaic capitation taxes and the poll tax in Roman Egypt." *Bulletin of the American Society of Papyrologists* 51: 127–160.

Morelli, F. (2010) *L'archivio di Senouthios anystes e testi connessi: lettere e documenti per la costruzione di una capitale.* Berlin.

Morgan, T. (1998) *Literate Education in the Hellenistic and Roman Worlds.* Cambridge.

Morkot, R. G. (2000) *The Black Pharaohs: Egypt's Nubian Rulers.* London.

Muhs, B. (2018) "The institutional models for Ptolemaic royal banks and granaries." *Ancient Society* 48: 83–101.

Myśliwiec, K. (2000) *The Twilight of Ancient Egypt: First Millennium B.C.E.* Ithaca, NY.

Naunton, C. (2010) "Libyans and Nubians." In Lloyd 2010: 1.120–139.

Nirenberg, D. (2013) *Anti-Judaism: The Western Tradition.* New York.

Nongbri, B. (2018) *God's Library: The Archaeology of the Earliest Christian Manuscripts.* New Haven.

Orlandi, T. (1997) "Letteratura copta." In *L'Egitto cristiano: Aspetti e problemi in età tardo-antica*, ed. A. Camplani: 39–120. Rome.

Orlandi, T. and Suciu A. (2016) "The end of the library of the monastery of Atripe." In *Coptic Society, Literature, and Religion from Antiquity to Modern Times. Proceedings of the Tenth International Congress of Coptic Studies, Rome, 17–22 September 2012, and Plenary Reports of the Ninth International Congress of Coptic Studies, Cairo, 19 September 2008*, ed. P. Buzi, A. Camplani, and F. Contardi: 2.891–918. Leuven.

Palme, B. (1997) "Die *domus gloriosa* des Flavius Strategius Paneuphemos." *Chiron* 27: 95–125.

(2008) "Flavius Flavianus – von Herakleopolis nach Konstantinopel?" *Bulletin of the American Society of Papyrologists* 45: 143–169.

Papaconstantinou, A. (2006) "Historiography, hagiography, and the making of the Coptic 'Church of the Martyrs' in early Islamic Egypt." *Dumbarton Oaks Papers* 60: 65–86.

(2007a) "'They shall speak the Arabic language and take pride in it': Reconsidering the fate of Coptic after the Arab conquest." *Le Muséon* 120: 273–299.

(2007b) "The cult of saints: a haven of continuity in a changing world?" In Bagnall 2007: 350–367.

(2008) "Dioscore et le bilinguisme dans l'Égypte du VIᵉ siècle." In *Les archives de Dioscore d'Aphrodité cent ans après leur découverte. Histoire et culture dans l'Égypte byzantine*, ed. J.-L. Fournet: 77–88. Paris.

(2009) "'What remains behind': Hellenism and *romanitas* in Christian Egypt after the Arab conquest." In *From Hellenism to Islam: Cultural and Linguistic Change in the Roman Near East*, ed. H. Cotton, R. Hoyland, J. Price, and D. Wasserstein: 447–466. Cambridge.

(ed.) (2010a) *The Multilingual Experience in Egypt from the Ptolemies to the 'Abbāsids.* Farnham.

(2010b) "Administering the early Islamic empire: insights from the papyri." In *Money, Power and Politics in Early Islamic Syria*, ed. J. Haldon: 57–74. Farnham.

(2011) "Hagiography in Coptic." In *The Ashgate Research Companion to Byzantine Hagiography: Periods and Places*, ed. S. Efthymiadis: 323–343. Farnham.

(2012a) "Egypt." In *The Oxford Handbook of Late Antiquity*, ed. S. F. Johnson: 195–223. Oxford.

(2012b) "Why did Coptic fail where Aramaic succeeded? Linguistic developments in Egypt and the Near East after the Arab conquest." In *Multilingualism in the Graeco-Roman worlds*, ed. A. Mullen and P. James: 58–76. Cambridge.

(2015a) "Language and writing." In *Egypt: Faith after the Pharaohs*, British Museum exhibition catalogue, ed. C. Fluck, G. Helmecke, and E. O'Connell: 198–205. London.

(2015b) "Fusṭāṭ and its governor: administering the province." In *A Cosmopolitan Community: Muslims, Christians and Jews in Old Cairo*. Catalogue of the exhibition at the Oriental Institute Museum, Chicago, February 2015– September 2015, ed. T. Treptow and T. Vorderstrasse: 43–47. Chicago.

(2015c) "The rhetoric of power and the voice of reason: Tensions between central and local in the correspondence of Qurra ibn Sharīk." In *Official Epistolography and the Language(s) of Power. Proceedings of the 1st International Conference of the Research Network Imperium and Officium: Comparative studies in Ancient Bureaucracy and Officialdom, University of Vienna, 10–12 November 2010*, ed. S. Procházka, L. Reinfandt, and S. Tost: 267–281. Vienna.

(2015d) "Introduction." In *Conversion in Late Antiquity: Christianity, Islam, and Beyond. Papers from the Mellon Foundation Sawyer Seminar, Oxford, 2009/10*, ed. A. Papaconstantinou, N. McLynn, and D. Schwartz: xv–xxxvii. Farnham.

(2016a) "Credit, debt, and dependence in early Islamic Egypt and Southern Palestine." In Fournet and Papaconstantinou 2016: 613–642. Paris.

(2016b) "'Choses de femme' et accès au crédit dans l'Égypte rurale sous les Omeyyades." In *Le saint, le moine et le paysan. Mélanges d'histoire byzantine offerts à Michel Kaplan*, ed. O. Delouis, S. Métivier, and P. Pagès: 551–561. Paris.

(2020a) "Hagiography in the archives: Real-life miracles and the sacred economy in eighth-century Egypt." *In Culte des saints et littérature hagiographique*, ed. V. Déroche, B. Ward-Perkins, and R. Wisniewski: 55–75. Leuven.

(2020b) "'Great men', churchmen, and the others: Forms of authority in the villages of the Umayyad period." In *Village Institutions in Egypt from Roman to Early Arab Rule*, ed. M. Langelotti and D. Rathbone: 178–189. Oxford.

(2020c) "A monk deploring the imitation of the Hagarenes by the Christians." In *Conversion to Islam in the Pre-modern Age: A Sourcebook*, ed. N. Hurwitz, C. Sahner, U. Simonsohn, and L. Yarbrough: 167–171. Berkeley.

(in press, 2021) "Arabic: language of empire, language of Egypt." In *Egypt and Empire: Religious Identities from Ancient to Modern Times*, ed. E. O'Connell. Leuven.

Pearson, B. A. (1993) "The *Acts of Mark* and the topography of ancient Alexandria." *Bulletin de la Société archéologique d'Alexandrie* 45: 239–246.

(2006) "Egypt." In *The Cambridge History of Christianity, 1: Origins to Constantine*, ed. M. M. Mitchell and F. M. Young: 331–350. Cambridge.

(2008) "The Nag Hammadi 'library' of Coptic papyrus codices." In *What Happened to the Ancient Library of Alexandria?*, ed. M. El-Abbadi and O. M. Fathallah: 109–128. Leiden.

Pestman, P. W. (1995) "Haronnophris and Chaonnophris." In *Hundred-Gated Thebes: Acts of a Colloquium on Thebes and the Theban Area in the Graeco-Roman Period (P. L. Bat. 27)*, ed. S. P. Vleeming: 101–137. Leiden.

Petitt, J. E. (2012) *The Extension of Imperial Authority under Diocletian and the Tetrarchy, 285–305 CE*. Orlando.

Pfeiffer, S. (2010) *Der römische Kaiser und das Land am Nil. Kaiserverehrung und Kaiserkult in Alexandria und Ägypten von Augustus bis Caracalla (30 v. Chr. - 217 n. Chr.)*. Stuttgart.

Pollard, N. (2013) "Imperatores castra dedicaverunt: security, army bases, and military dispositions in Later Roman Egypt (third-fourth century)." *Journal of Late Antiquity* 6: 3–36.

Porten, B. and Yardeni, A. (1999) *Textbook of Aramaic Documents from Ancient Egypt, 4: Ostraca*. Winona Lake, IN.

Power, T. (2012) *The Red Sea from Byzantium to the Caliphate, 500–1000*. Cairo.

Prada, L. (2018) "Multiculturalism in Ptolemaic and Roman Egypt: language contact through the evidence of papyri and inscriptions." In *Beyond the Nile: Egypt and the Classical World*, J. Paul Getty Museum exhibition catalogue, ed. T. Potts, J. Spier, and S. E. Cole: 148–154. Los Angeles.

Quack, J. F. (2017) "How the Coptic script came about." In *Greek Influence on Egyptian-Coptic: Contact-Induced Change in an Ancient African Language*, ed. E. Grossmann, P. Dils, T. S. Richter, and W. Schenkel: 27–96. Hamburg.

Quaegebeur, J. (1983) "Cultes égyptiens et grecs en Égypte hellénistique: l'exploitation des sources." In *Egypt and the Hellenistic world. Proceedings of the International Colloquium Leuven 24–26 May 1982*, ed. E. Van 't Dack, P. Van Dessel, and W. Van Gucht: 303–324. Leuven.

  (1998) "Documents égyptiens anciens et nouveaux relatifs à Arsinoé Philadelphe." In Melaerts 1998: 73–108.

Rahyab, S. (2019) "The rise and development of the office of *agoranomos* in Greco-Roman Egypt." *New England Classical Journal* 46.1:37–61.

Rathbone, D. W. (1991) *Economic Rationalism and Rural Society in Third-Century A.D. Egypt: The Heroninos Archive and the Appianus Estate*. Cambridge.

  (1993). "Egypt, Augustus and Roman taxation." *Cahiers du Centre Gustave Glotz* 4: 81–112.

  (2007) "Roman Egypt." In *The Cambridge Economic History of the Greco-Roman World*, ed. W. Scheidel, I. Morris, and R. Saller: 698–719. Cambridge.

  (2013) "The Romanity of Roman Egypt: a faltering consensus?" In *Papyrology AD 2013: 27th International Congress of Papyrology. Keynote Papers = Journal of Juristic Papyrology* 43: 73–91.

Ray, J. D. (1988) "Egypt 525–404 B.C." In *The Cambridge Ancient History, IV²: Persia, Greece and the Western Mediterranean c. 525–479 B.C.*, ed. J. Boardman and D. M. Lewis: 254–286. Cambridge.

Reinhardt, K. (1897) "Eine arabisch-koptische Kirchenbann-Urkunde." In *Aegyptiaca: Festschrift für Georg Ebers zum 1. März 1897.* Leipzig: 89–91.

Richter, T. S. (2000) "Spätkoptische Rechtsurkunden neu bearbeitet (II): Die Rechtsurkunden des Teschlot-Archivs." *Journal of Juristic Papyrology* 30: 95–148.

   (2008) *Rechtssemantik und forensische Rhetorik. Untersuchungen zu Wortschatz, Stil und Grammatik der Sprache koptischer Rechtsurkunden.* 2nd edition. Wiesbaden.

   (2009) "Greek, Coptic, and the language of the *hijra*: The rise and decline of the Coptic language in late antique and medieval Egypt." In *From Hellenism to Islam: Cultural and Linguistic Change in the Roman Near East*, ed. H. Cotton, R. Hoyland, J. Price, and D. Wasserstein: 403–414. Cambridge.

   (2010) "Language choice in the Qurra dossier." In Papaconstantinou 2010a: 189–219. Farnham.

Riggs, C., ed. (2012) *The Oxford Handbook of Roman Egypt.* Oxford.

Ripat, P. (2006) "The language of oracular inquiry in Roman Egypt." *Phoenix* 60: 304–328.

Rives, J. B. (1999) "The decree of Decius and the religion of empire." *Journal of Roman Studies* 89: 135–154.

Robertson, S. (2015) *The crisis of the 3rd century A.D.: Wage increases and inflation in Roman Egypt*, PhD thesis, Durham University. Online: etheses.dur.ac.uk/11323/.

Rodriguez, C. (2012) "Caracalla et les Alexandrins: coup de folie ou sanction légale?" *Journal of Juristic Papyrology* 42: 229–272.

Rodziewicz, M. (1984) *Les habitations romaines tardives d'Alexandrie à la lumière des fouilles polonaises à Kom el-Dikka.* Warsaw.

Rondot, V. (2013) *Derniers visages des dieux d'Égypte: iconographies, panthéons et cultes dans le Fayoum hellénisé des IIe–IIIe siècles de notre ère.* Paris.

Roques, D. (1999) "Alexandrie tardive et protobyzantine, IVe–VIIe siècle. Témoignages d'auteurs." In *Alexandrie: une mégalopole cosmopolite. Actes du 9ème colloque de la Villa Kérylos à Beaulieu-sur-Mer les 2 & 3 octobre 1998*, ed. J. Leclant: 203–236. Paris.

Rossignol, B. (2012) "Le climat, les famines et la guerre: éléments du contexte de la peste antonine." In *L'impatto della peste Antonina*, ed. E. Lo Cascio: 87–122. Bari.

Rowlandson, J. (1996) *Landlords and Tenants in Roman Egypt: The Social Relations of Agriculture in the Oxyrhynchite Nome.* Oxford.

   ed. (1998) *Women and Society in Greek and Roman Egypt.* Cambridge.

   (2010) "Administration and law: Graeco-Roman." In Lloyd 2010: 1.237–255.

Rowlandson, J. and Harker, A. (2004) "Roman Alexandria from the perspective of the papyri." In *Alexandria, Real and Imagined*, ed. A. Hirst and M. Silk: 79–113. Aldershot.

Rubenson, S. (1996) 'Translating the tradition: some remarks on the Arabization of the patristic heritage in Egypt." *Medieval Encounters* 2: 4–14.

Ruffini, G. R. (2004) "Late Antique pagan networks from Athens to the Thebaid." In *Ancient Alexandria between Egypt and Greece*, ed. W. V. Harris and G. R. Ruffini: 240–257. Leiden.

(2008) *Social Networks in Byzantine Egypt.* Cambridge.

(2018) *Life in an Egyptian Village in Late Antiquity: Aphrodito Before and After the Islamic Conquest.* Cambridge.

Rustow, M. (2020) *The Lost Archive: Traces of a Caliphate in a Cairo Synagogue.* Princeton.

Rutherford, I., ed. (2016) *Greco-Egyptian Interactions: Literature, Translation, and Culture, 500 BCE–300 CE.* Oxford.

Ryholt, K. (2005) "On the contents and nature of the Tebtunis temple library: a status report." In *Tebtynis und Soknopaiu Nesos: Leben im römerzeitlichen Fajum*, ed. S. Lippert and M. Schentuleit: 141–170. Wiesbaden.

Saleh, M. (2018) "On the road to heaven: taxation, conversions, and the Coptic-Muslim socioeconomic gap in medieval Egypt." *Journal of Economic History* 78: 394–434.

Sanger, P. (2011) "The administration of Sasanian Egypt: new masters and Byzantine continuity." *Greek, Roman, and Byzantine Studies* 51: 653–665.

Schäfer, D. (2011) *Makedonische Pharaonen und hieroglyphische Stelen: historische Untersuchungen zur Satrapenstele und verwandten Denkmälern.* Leuven.

Scheidel, W. (2002) "A model of demographic and economic change in Roman Egypt after the Antonine plague." *Journal of Roman Archaeology* 15: 114–120.

(2012) "Roman wellbeing and the economic consequences of the Antonine plague." In *L'impatto della peste antonina*, ed. E. Lo Cascio: 265–295. Bari.

Schenke, G. (2016) "The healing shrines of St. Phoibammon: evidence of cult activity in Coptic legal documents." *Zeitschrift für antikes Christentum* 20: 496–523.

Schmelz, G. (2002) *Kirchliche Amtsträger im spätantiken Ägypten.* Munich.

Schubert, P. (2016) "On the form and content of the certificates of pagan sacrifice." *Journal of Roman Studies* 106: 172–198.

Schwartz, J. (1975) *L. Domitius Domitianus (étude numismatique et papyrologique).* Brussels.

Sharp, M. (1999) "The village of Theadelphia in the Fayyum: land and population in the second century." In *Agriculture in Egypt from Pharaonic to Modern Times*, ed. A. K. Bowman and E. Rogan: 159–192. Oxford.

Sheehan, P. (2010) *Babylon of Egypt: The Archaeology of Old Cairo and the Origins of the City.* Cairo.

Sidebotham, S. (2011) *Berenike and the Ancient Spice Route.* Berkeley–Los Angeles.

Sijpesteijn, P. M. (2004) "Travel and trade on the river." In *Papyrology and the History of Early Islamic Egypt*, ed. P. M. Sijpesteijn and L. Sundelin: 115–152. Leiden.

(2007a) "The Arab conquest of Egypt and the beginning of Muslim rule." In Bagnall 2007: 437–459.

(2007b) "New rule over old structures: Egypt after the Muslim conquest." In *Regime Change in the Ancient Near East and Egypt from Sargon of Agade to Saddam Hussein*, ed. H. Crawford = *Proceedings of the British Academy* 136: 183–200.

(2009) "Landholding patterns in early Islamic Egypt." *Journal of Agrarian Change* 9: 120–133.

(2013) *Shaping a Muslim State: The World of a Mid-Eighth-Century Egyptian Official*. Oxford.

(2020) "Establishing local elite authority in Egypt through arbitration and mediation." In *Transregional and Regional Elites: Connecting the Early Islamic Empire*, ed. H.-L. Hagemann and S. Heidemann: 387–406. Berlin.

Sirat, C. (1985) *Les papyrus en caractères hébraïques trouvés en Égypte*. Paris.

Sirat, C., Cauderlier, P., Dukan, M., and Friedman, M. A. (1986) *La Ketouba de Cologne. Un contrat de mariage juif à Antinoupolis*. Opladen.

Southern, P. (2008) *Empress Zenobia: Palmyra's Rebel Queen*. London.

Speidel, M. A. (2019) "Egypt's specificity and impact on Roman history." In Vandorpe 2019: 573–580.

Stadler, M. A. (2008) "On the demise of Egyptian writing: working with a problematic source basis." In *The Disappearance of Writing Systems: Perspectives on Literacy and Communication*, ed. J. Baines, J. Bennet, and S. D. Houston: 157–181. London.

Stark, R. (1996) *The Rise of Christianity: A Sociologist Reconsiders History*. Princeton.

Stefaniw, B. (2019) *Christian Reading: Language, Ethics, and the Order of Things*. Berkeley.

Stefanou, M. (2013) "Waterborne recruits: the military settlers of Ptolemaic Egypt." In *The Ptolemies, the Sea and the Nile: Studies in Waterborne Power*, ed. K. Buraselis, M. Stefanou, and D. J. Thompson: 108–131. Cambridge.

Stoneman, R. (1991) *The Greek Alexander Romance*. Harmondsworth.

Swanson, M. (2010) *The Coptic Papacy in Islamic Egypt, 641–1517*. Cairo.

Tacoma, L. E. (2006) *Fragile Hierarchies: The Urban Elites of Third-Century Roman Egypt*. Leiden.

Thomas, J. D. (1976) "The date of the revolt of L. Domitius Domitianus." *Zeitschrift für Papyrologie und Epigraphik* 22: 253–279.

(1983) "Compulsory public service in Roman Egypt." In *Das römisch-byzantinische Ägypten: Akten des internationalen Symposions, 26–30 September 1978 in Trier*, ed. G. Grimm, H. Heinen, and E. Winter: 35–39. Mainz.

Thompson, D. J. (1999) "Irrigation and drainage in the early Ptolemaic Fayum." In *Agriculture in Egypt from Pharaonic to Modern Times*, ed. A. K. Bowman and E. Rogan: 107–122. Oxford

(2001) "Hellenistic Hellenes: the case of Ptolemaic Egypt." In *Ancient Perceptions of Greek Ethnicity*, ed. I. Malkin: 301–322. Cambridge, MA.

(2009) "The multilingual environment of Persian and Ptolemaic Egypt: Egyptian, Aramaic, and Greek documentation." In Bagnall 2009b: 395–417.

(2012) *Memphis under the Ptolemies*. 2nd edition. Princeton.

(2018) "Ptolemy I in Egypt: continuity and change." In *Ptolemy I and the Transformation of Egypt, 404–282 BC*, ed. P. McKechnie and J. A. Cromwell: 6–26. Leiden.

Tillier, M. (2013) "Du pagarque au cadi: ruptures et continuités dans l'administration judiciaire de la Haute-Égypte (Ier–IIIe/VIIe–IXe siècle)." *Médiévales* 64: 19–36.

(2015) 'Dispensing justice in a minority context: the judicial administration of Upper Egypt under Muslim rule in the early eighth century." In *The Late Antique World of Early Islam: Muslims Among Christians and Jews in the East Mediterranean*, ed. R. Hoyland: 133–156. Princeton.

(2017) *L'invention du cadi: la justice des musulmans, des juifs et des chrétiens aux premiers siècles de l'Islam*. Paris.

Torallas Tovar, S., and Vierros, M. (2019) "Languages, scripts, literature, and bridges between cultures." In Vandorpe 2019: 485–499.

Trapp, M., ed. (2003) *Greek and Latin Letters. An Anthology, with Translation*. Cambridge.

Treptow, T. (2015) "A history of excavations at Fustat." In *A Cosmopolitan Community: Muslims, Christians and Jews in Old Cairo. Catalogue of the exhibition at the Oriental Institute Museum, Chicago, February 2015–September 2015*, ed. T. Treptow and T. Vorderstrasse: 99–107. Chicago.

Tuplin, C. J. and Ma, J., eds. (2020) *Aršāma and his World: The Bodleian Letters in Context*. 3 vols. Oxford.

Van den Hoek, A. (1997) "The cathechetical school of early Christian Alexandria and its Philonic heritage." *Harvard Theological Review* 90: 59–87.

van Minnen, P. (1986) "A change of names in Roman Egypt after AD 202? A note on *P.Amst*. I 72." *Zeitschrift für Papyrologie und Epigraphik* 62: 87–92.

(1998) "Boorish or bookish? Literature in Egyptian villages in the Fayum in the Graeco-Roman period." *Journal of Juristic Papyrology* 28: 99–184.

(2000) "Agriculture and the 'taxes-and-trade' model in Roman Egypt." *Zeitschrift für Papyrologie und Epigraphik* 133: 205–220.

(2002). "Αἱ ἀπὸ γυμνασίου: 'Greek' Women and the Greek 'Elite' in the Metropoleis of Roman Egypt." In *Le rôle et le statut de la femme en Égypte ptolémaïque, romaine et byzantine*, ed. H. Melaerts and L. Mooren: 337–353. Leuven.

(2009) "Hermopolis and its papyri." In *100 anni di istituzioni fiorentine per la papirologia*: 1–15. Florence.

(2019) "Economic growth and the exploitation of land." In Vandorpe 2019: 251–268. Hoboken.

Van 't Dack, E. (1983) "Les relations entre l'Égypte ptolémaïque et l'Italie. Un aperçu des personnages revenant ou venant d'Alexandrie ou d'Égypte en Italie." In *Egypt and the Hellenistic world. Proceedings of the International Colloquium, Leuven, 24–26 May 1982*, ed. E. Van 't Dack, P. Van Dessel, and W. Van Gucht: 383–406. Leuven.

Vandorpe, K. (2002) *The Bilingual Family Archive of Dryton, His Wife Apollonia and Their Daughter Senmouthis (P. Dryton)*. Brussels.

(2010) "The Ptolemaic period," in Lloyd 2010: 159–179.

(2011) "A successful, but fragile biculturalism: the Hellenization process in the Upper Egyptian town of Pathyris under Ptolemy VI and VIII." In *Ägypten zwischen innerem Zwist und äusserem Druck. Die Zeit Ptolemaios' VI. bis VIII.*, ed. A. Jördens and J. F. Quack: 292–308. Wiesbaden.

(ed.) (2019) *A Companion to Greco-Roman and Late Antique Egypt*. Chichester.

Vandorpe, K., and Clarysse, W. (2019) "Cults, creeds and clergy in a multicultural context." In Vandorpe 2019: 407–427.

Veïsse, A.-E. (2004) *Les "révoltes Égyptiennes". Recherches sur les troubles intérieurs en Égypte du règne de Ptolémée III à la conquête romaine*. Leuven.

Vierros, M. (2012) *Bilingual Notaries in Hellenistic Egypt: A Study of Greek as a Second Language*. Brussels.

Villing, A. (2018) "Wahibreemakhet at Saqqara. The tomb of a Greek in Egypt." *Zeitschrift für ägyptische Sprache and Altertumskunde* 145: 174–186.

Vittmann, G. (2003) *Ägypten und die Fremden im ersten vorchristlichen Jahrtausend*. Mainz.

Vleeming, S. P. (1994) "Some notes of Demotic scribal training." In *Proceedings of the 20th International Congress of Papyrologists, Copenhagen 23–29 August 1992*, ed. A. Bülow-Jacobsen: 185–187. Copenhagen.

von Reden, S. (2019) "Monetization of the countryside." In Vandorpe 2019: 217–232.

Walker, S. and Ashton, S.-A., eds. (2003) *Cleopatra Reassessed*. London.

Watts, E. J. (2006) *City and School in Late Antique Athens and Alexandria*. Berkeley.

Whitcomb, D. (2015) "Fustat to Cairo: an essay on 'Old Cairo'." In *A Cosmopolitan Community: Muslims, Christians and Jews in Old Cairo. Catalogue of the Exhibition at the Oriental Institute Museum, Chicago, February 2015– September 2015*, ed. T. Treptow and T. Vorderstrasse: 93-98. Chicago.

Wickham, C. (2005) *Framing the Early Middle Ages: Europe and the Mediterranean, 400–800*. Oxford.

Wilfong, T. G. (2002). *Women of Jeme: Lives in a Coptic Town in Late Antique Egypt*. Ann Arbor.

Wipszycka, E. (1992) "Le nationalisme a–t–il existé dans l'Égypte byzantine?" *Journal of Juristic Papyrology* 22: 82–128; repr. in Wipszycka 1996: 9–61.

(1996) *Études sur le christianisme dans l'Égypte de l'antiquité tardive.* Rome.

(2007) "The institutional Church." In Bagnall 2007: 331–349.

(2009) *Moines et communautés monastiques en Égypte (IVe–VIIIe siècles).* Warsaw.

(2015) *The Alexandrian Church: People and Institutions.* Warsaw.

(2018) *The Second Gift of the Nile: Monks and Monasteries in Late Antique Egypt.* Warsaw.

Worrell, W.H. (1923) *The Coptic Manuscripts in the Freer Collection.* New York.

Yiftach-Firanko, U. (2009) "Law in Greco-Roman Egypt: Hellenization, fusion, Romanization." In Bagnall 2009b: 541–560. Oxford.

(2014) "Law in the Roman period." In *Law and Legal Practice in Egypt from Alexander to the Arab Conquest: A Selection of Papyrological Sources in Translation, with Introductions and Commentary,* ed. J. G. Keenan, J. G. Manning, and U. Yiftach-Firanko: 20–23. Cambridge.

Yoyotte, J. (1969) "Bakhthis: religion égyptienne et culture grecque à Edfou." In *Religions en Egypte hellénistique et romaine. Colloque de Strasbourg 16–18 mai 1967,* ed. P. Derchain: 127–141. Paris.

(1989) "Le nom égyptien du 'ministre de l'économie' – de Saïs à Méroè." *Comptes rendus de l'Académie des inscriptions et belles-lettres* 133: 73–90.

Zaborowski, J. R. (2003) "Egyptian Christians implicating Chalcedonians in the Arab takeover of Egypt: The Arabic *Apocalypse of Samuel of Qalamūn.*" *Oriens Christianus* 87: 100–115.

(2008) "From Coptic to Arabic in medieval Egypt." *Medieval Encounters* 14: 15–40.

Zibawi, M. (2005) *Bagawat. Peintures paleochrétiennes d'Égypte.* Paris.

Zivie-Coche, C. and Guermeur, I. (2012) *"Parcourir l'éternité". Hommages à Jean Yoyotte.* 2 vols. Turnhout.

Zuckerman, C. (1998) "Two reforms of the 370s: recruiting soldiers and senators in the divided empire." *Revue des études byzantines* 56: 79–139.

Index

'Abd al-Aziz, 297
'Abd Allāh b. Sa'd b. Abi Sarḥ, 283
'Abd al-Malik, 296, 297, 329
Abraham of Hermonthis, 240, 264, 274
absentee ruler, 5, 9, 48
Abu Mina, 276, 323
Achilles Tatius, 71, 85
Actium, 44, 46
Aegean, 3, 9, 15
agriculture, 15, 39, 94, 137–141, 186–188, 251
Ain el-Gedida, 149, 201
Akoris, 60
ala, 60
alchemy, 81, 86
Alexander III "the Great", xxiii, xxv, 9, 11–14,
    22, 29, 71, 111
  tomb, 108, 181
Alexander, bishop, 184, 202
Alexander, Tiberius Julius, 51, 105
Alexandria (Iskanderiya), 47–49, 52, 71–87,
    180–185, *See also* university, Alexandria,
    Jews in Alexandria, houses, Alexandrian,
    Kom el-Dikka, Serapeum of Alexandria,
    lighthouse (*Pharos*), Library of
    Alexandria, Mouseion, science,
    Alexandrian
  archives, 59
  bishop of, 201, 202, 215, 225, 226, 269, 314
  Christianity in, 117–118, 152–162
  churches, 184–185, 197, 284
  coinage, 172
  conquest of by Arabs, 284
  council, 57, 124, 132
  culture, 23–24, 82–87
  foundation, 71
  garrison, 60, 63
  harbors, 21, 22, 23, 73, 80, 185
  language use, 34
  population, 77
  port, 21, 22, 40, 182
  property holdings in countryside, 186
  quarters, 21
  trade, 80–82, 89

alms, 207, 339
Amasis, 4, 9, 10, 30
amīr, 290, 292, 293, 342
Ammianus Marcellinus, 71, 74, 85, 181,
    243, 245
'Amr ibn al-'Āṣ, 282–289, 295, 304, 314, 315,
    320, 342
Amun, God's Wife of, 2, 3
Amun-Ra, 2, 12
Amyrtaios, 8
Anastasius, 258
anchoritic monasticism, 215
animal cults, 8, 108
annona, 92, 231, 296, 304
anti-Chalcedonian church, 199, 228–241,
    270–271, 278, 280–282
Antinoopolis, 54, 92, 121, 171, 184, 206, 209,
    212, 245, 256, 266
Antinoos, 48
Antioch, 175, 232, 321
Antiochus IV Epiphanes, 18, 43
Antonine Constitution, 115, 133
Antoninus Pius, 74, 147
Antony, Mark, 44, 46, 79
Antony, monk, 210, 211, 218, 254, 269, 270
Aphrodito, 222, 246, 251, 253, 254, 255, 257,
    263, 268, 273, 300, 307
Apiones, Flavii, family of, 258–262, 277
Apis bull, 10, 12, 25, 27, 31, 36, 100, 108
Apollonios, *dioiketes* under Ptolemy II, 30, 36,
    37, 138
Apollonios, *strategos*, 106
Apollonius of Rhodes, 24
apomoira, 26, *See also* taxes, tax collection
Appianus, Aurelius, 141, 186
Apries, 4
Arab conquest, 280–289
Arabic, 297, 303, 319, 321, 327–343
Aramaic, xxiv, 5, 8, 33, 103, 206
arbitration, 220, 273, 275
archaeology of cities, 129
Archimedes, 23
archives, church, 166, 265, 308

aristocracy of service, 188–189
Arius, 180, 202, 212
army, Muslim, 282–284, 290–295
army, Ptolemaic, 14, 25, 103
army, Roman, 60–67, 107, 135, 169, 171,
    175
Arshama, 7
Arsinoe. *See* Fayyum (Arsinoite nome)
Arsinoe II Philadelphos, 22, 26, 28
Arsinoite nome. *See* Fayyum (Arsinoite nome)
Artaxerxes I, 8
Artaxerxes III, 8, 12
asceticism, 210–216
assimilation, 333, 336
Assyria, 1, 3
Aswan dam, 39
Athanasius, bishop, 180, 185, 198, 201, 202,
    210, 215, 217, 220, 226, 269, 320, 321
Athens, 6, 8, 22, 23, 84, 114, 221, 244, 250
Atripe (Triphieion), 149, 150
auction, 38
Augustine, 198
Augustus (Octavian), 44, 46–47, 49, 58, 65, 80,
    81, 83, 84, 93, 109–112, 147
Aurelian, 86, 135, 169, 180
Aurelius as status designation, 133, 188
auxiliary units, 60
Avidius Cassius, 49, 64, 131, 132

Babylon (Old Cairo), 135, 281, 283, 287
banks, 38
Bar Kokhba revolt, 62
Basil of Caesarea, 219
Basileios, *dioiketes*, 300
Basiliskos, 231
Bawit, 308, 338, 339
Beirut, 243
Benjamin, bishop, 237, 277, 280, 284, 289, 314,
    315–316, 319, 320
Berenike II, 24
Berenike, port, 81
Bes, 106, 148
Besa, 218
Bible manuscripts, 119, 166, 196
Bible, Coptic, 166, 217
Bible, Hebrew, 24, 222
bilingualism, 33, 167, 269, 327
bishops, 118, 152–161, 180, 191, 201–203,
    207–208, 215, 225–228, 231–233,
    238–241, 264–266, 270–275, 307, 315,
    318, 327
Blemmyes, 63, 133, 192
Boethos, 24

book production, 69, 86, 122, 157, 200
Boubastis, 2
Boukoloi, 64, 131
bureaucracy. *See* administration
burial practices, 151, 153, 194

Caesar, Julius, 43, 71
Cairo, xxiv, 314, 317, 332, 341
Cairo Geniza, 204, 344
Caligula, 103
Caliphs, Caliphate, 285, 286–289, 292, 293, 300,
    317, 329, 336
Callimachus, 23
Calpurnia Herakleia, 186
Cambyses, 4, 6, 12
canon law, 203
Canopus, 18, 28, 34, 71, 185
Caracalla, 49, 78, 83, 133, 147, 169, 178, 188
Carians, 9, 29
Caromemphites, 9, 30
cemeteries, 73, 194
cenobitic monasticism, 213–214
census, 37, 58, 93, 117, 177, 285, 289
Chalcedon, Council of, 199, 218, 228–233,
    320, 326
charity, 206–209, 252
Chios, 29
chora, 49, 54, 59, 60, 65, 78, 186
Christ, nature of, 225, 228, 280
church, Alexandrian, 118, 152, 200, 228, 267
church, outside Alexandria, 201
churches, outside Alexandria, 151, 153, 159,
    192, 214, 241, 253, 263, 267
cities, foundation of. *See* foundation of cities
citizenship, 52, 54, 60, 67, 79, 93, 105, 115,
    133, 178
Claudian, 246
Claudius, 49, 56, 79, 83, 104, 109, 111
Claudius Ptolemy, 86
Clement of Alexandria, 153, 217
Cleopatra II, 18, 70
Cleopatra III, 20
Cleopatra VII, 43, 58, 84, 86, 108
clergy, Christian, 153, 157, 161, 200–203, 226,
    230, 235, 240, 253, 263, 317
cleruchic system, 15, 29
climate change, 131
codex, 157
cohort, 60, 63
coinage, 10, 41, 147, 169, 172–176, 276
commerce, 10, 90, 340
Commodus, 142, 169
conquest, Arab, 280–289

Constantine, 171, 179, 180, 188, 190, 194, 200, 201, 202, 213
Constantine of Asyut, 220, 239, 270
Constantinople, xxiv, xxv, 182, 188, 189, 228, 231, 232, 233, 238, 243, 256, 258, 278, 281, 296, 326
Constantius II, 191, 253
contracts, 6, 17, 30, 36, 38, 56, 59, 70, 82, 89, 104, 119, 145, 171, 206, 266, 273, 274
Contrapollonopolis Magna (Redesiyah), 63
conventus, 50
conversion to Islam, 297, 301, 335–343
Coptic, 69, 162–168, 217, 238, 266, 268–275, 278, 327–335, 340
Coptic identity, 319–327
Coptic literature, 217–220, 224, 238, 268–275, 303, 321, 324, 333
Coptos (Qift), 60, 63, 65, 81, 91, 136, 239, 265
Cornelius Gallus, C., 63, 67
corruption, 300
corvée labor, 287, 293, 294, 295, 330
Council. *See* Chalcedon, Ephesos, Nicaea
councils, city, 54, 124–125, 126–129, 132, 146, 202, 263
culture, Greek, 36
Cynopolite nome, 261
Cyprian, plague of, 181
Cyprus, 8, 15, 43, 170, 245
Cyrene, 4, 12, 15, 29, 43, 106, 131
Cyril, bishop, 185, 196, 206, 226, 228, 232, 320, 321
Cyrus, bishop and governor, 237
Cyrus, poet, 246

Dakhla oasis *See* Great Oasis
Damascius, 196, 244
Damascus, 296
Damian, bishop, 220, 237–241, 264, 270, 315, 327
Darius I, 6, 8
Darius II, 8
dating of documents, 171, 206
debt, 20, 40, 302, 304, 341
Decius, 154, 158, 178
Delta, xxiv, 1, 3, 4, 8, 9, 18, 53, 126, 131, 166, 170, 176, 239, 266, 268, 282, 283, 285, 287, 293, 297, 332
Demetrius, bishop, 118, 120, 152, 153
demography, 102, 115–116, 121, 142–144
demotic Egyptian, 6, 8, 18, 26, 30, 33, 36, 47, 67–70, 112, 145, 162–165, 221
Dendera, xxiv, 16, 213
Dendur, 106

Didymus the Blind, 218
Dio Chrysostom, 80, 85
diocese, 170
Diocletian, 53, 135, 149, 159, 169–177, 178, 179, 181, 243, 321
Diocletian, era of, 179
Diodorus of Sicily, 29, 35, 36, 71
dioiketes, 15, 37, 43, 52, 300, 307
Dionysius, bishop, 154, 181
Dioscorides, Pedanius, 85
Dioskoros of Aphrodito, 222, 246, 254, 268, 273
Dioskoros, bishop, 228, 231
disease, 116, 117, 131, 213, *See also* plague
dispute settlement, 256
Domitius Domitianus, 136, 174

earthquake, 73, 182, 247
Eastern Desert, 63, 81, 91, 115, 136, 211, 254, 283
economy, 39–41, 87–92, 121–124, 257–258
Edfu (Apollonopolis Magna), xxiv, 16, 24, 25, 26, 27, 38, 63, 95, 300
Edomite, 34
education, 35–37, 220–224, 243, 244, 246–250, 263, 268
Egyptian population, 29–33, 58, 78, 112, 121
Elephantine, 4, 6, 29, 63, 102
elites, 92–95, 113, 138, 146, 154, 186–189, 270, 279, 296–303, 304, 307
Elkab, 8
embalming of sacred animals, 25
Enaton monastery, 233, 237, 276
endowment, 6, 208
Enkyklios, 231
Ephesos, Council of in 449, 228
Epiphanius of Salamis, 182
epistrategos, 54
equestrians, 49
Era of Diocletian/Martyrs, 179, 321
Eratosthenes of Cyrene, 24, 86
estates, 6, 59, 94, 125, 138, 154, 186, 202, 203, 296, 302
estates, imperial, 52, 258
Ethiopia, 60, 65, 142, 199
ethnicity, 29, 30, 32, 59, 78, 80, 113, 269, 321
Euclid, 23
Eusebius, 106, 118, 158, 159, 161, 181, 191
Eutyches, 228
exports, 23, 40, 79, 81, 86

families, 116–117, 129
famine, 40

Fayyum (Arsinoite nome), 28, 29, 36, 39, 80, 93, 98, 106, 109, 113, 137, 141, 143, 154, 164, 174, 186, 198, 215, 251, 261, 283, 330, 333, 340
festivals, 22, 25, 78, 109, 111, 133, 147, 194, 203
feudalism, 260
finances, 12, 25, 26, 37, 39–41, 52–53, 57, 176–177, 266
Flavius as status designation, 188
fleet, Alexandrian, 60
fleet, Arab, 286, 287, 294, 300, 306
flight (*anachoresis*), 131, 144, 277, 299, 306
flight into Egypt (by Holy Family), 322
fortifications, 8
foundations, city, 24, 72, 92
Fourth Syrian War, 20
funerary monuments, 38, 143
Fusṭāṭ, 287, 290, 293–296, 306, 307, 317, 330, 338, 339, 342

Galen, 85, 142, 245
Galerius, 136, 162
Gallienus, 133, 156, 159, 180
garrisons, 4, 5, 12, 29, 34, 60, 65, 81, 92, 131, 136, 175, 286, 290
Gascou thesis, 261
Gaza, 29, 243, 244
gender in naming, 34
George the Archdeacon, 315
Germanicus, 109
gnosticism, 198, 217, 219
governance, civic, 24, 56–57, 124–129
grammarian, 84, 221, 222, 245
Great Oasis, 6, 54, 129, 149, 165, 198, 217
Greek language, xxiv, 14, 16, 18, 30, 32, 33–34, 67–70, 162–168, 217, 221, 266, 268–270, 297, 298, 325, 327–331, 333
Gregory of Nazianzus, 219
Gregory of Nyssa, 219
gymnasium, 21, 24, 25, 31, 74, 75, 79, 93, 127, 243

Hadrian, 48, 54, 74, 76, 81, 108, 109, 111, 121, 131
hagiography, 216, *See also* saints
Hakoris, 8
Halicarnassus, 6
hamlets, 251
Harpokrates, 107
Hebrew, 103, 206
Heliopolis, xxiv, 11, 25, 74, 102, 109, 283
Hellenomemphites, 9
Henotikon, 231

Heraclas, bishop, 154
Heraclius, 237, 262, 276, 279, 280–284
Herakleopolis (Ihnasiya), 2, 103, 149, 157, 184, 210, 292
Hermonthis, 240
Hermopolis (Ashmunein), 205, 209, 238, 239, 267, 299, 303, 308, 329, 330, 335
Herodas, 29
Herodotus of Halicarnassus, 6, 9, 10, 30
Heroninos archive, 186
Herophilus, 23
hieratic, 36, 69, 163
hieroglyphs, 6, 18, 33, 34, 36, 38, 67
Ḥijāz, 282, 286, 289, 296, 297
history of the church of Egypt, 218, 271
History of the Patriarchs of Alexandria, 226, 239, 271, 276, 278, 284, 289, 314, 316, 320, 323, 333, 339
Holy Family, 322
Homer, 37, 72, 221, 222
Horapollon, 244
Horus, 14, 16, 25, 34, 107
hospitals, 207
House of Life, 6, 36
houses, Alexandrian, 21, 76, 183
Hypatia, 196–198, 243, 246
Hyperechios, 187

idios logos, 52, 100
Idumaeans, 31, 112
immigrants, Greek, 4, 30, 31
immigration, 29, 31, 205
imperial service, 188–189
imports, 10, 58, 92
Inaros, 8
independence, 5
India, 81, 88, 90
inflation, 144, 169, 174, 175
inheritance, 59, 129, 187
inscriptions, 6, 34, 67, 147, 179, 190, 271, 338
institutions, charitable, 203, 206
integration, economic, 87–92
intermarriage, 31, 112, 199
irrigation, 39, 44
Isis, 12, 28, 36, 106, 244
Isis-Astarte, 34
Iulii Theones, 186

Jacob Burd'aya, 236
Jeme, 251, 252, 255, 275, 309, 323
Jerusalem, 102, 106, 296, 306
Jewish revolt, 62, 106, 118, 130
Jewish settlers, 31

Jewish soldiers, 6, 102
Jews in Alexandria, 21, 79, 102–106, 114, 117, 196, 199, 206
Jews in Islamic Egypt, 336
Jews in the *chora*, 203–206
Jews, in Herakleopolis, 31
John Chrysostom, 181, 219
John of Ephesos, 264
John of Lykopolis, 166
John of Nikiu, 182, 184, 197, 247, 280–283, 314, 320
John the Almsgiver, 237, 245
Josephus, 105
Judaea, 29, 63, 102
judges, 16, 59, 125, 171, 256
Julian of Halicarnassus, 233
Julian, emperor, 109, 191, 200, 221
Justin I, 232
Justin II, 236, 237, 270
Justinian, 171, 179, 182, 184, 192, 233–236, 244, 246, 250, 258, 260, 308, 345

Kaine (Qena), 63
Kalabsha, 106
Karanis (Kom Aushim), 57, 107, 108, 111, 143, 149, 251
Kaunos, 31
Kellia, 212
Kellis (Ismant el-Kharab), 151, 165, 167, 201, 217
Kerkeosiris, 38
Khusraw II, 276
Kleomenes of Naukratis, 12
Klysma (al-Qulzūm), 286, 294
Kom el-Dikka, 76, 129, 135, 182–184, 243–250
Kush (Nubia), xxiii, 1

Lake Mareotis (Mariut), 21, 80
Lake Moeris, 6
land grants to soldiers, 14
land reclamation, xxiv, 30, 39, 44
language learning, 33–34, 273
language use, 33–34, 67–70, 97, 100, 113, 171, 214, 217–218, 238, 268–270, 278, 298, 327–335
Latopolis (Esna), 212, 214
laura monasticism, 215
law, church, 203, 241
law, Egyptian, 8, 16, 30
law, Greek, 16, 30
law, Jewish, 31
law, Roman, 52, 59, 92, 103
legions, 48, 60, 62, 79

Leo I, emperor, 231
Leo I, pope, 228
Libanius, 125, 181
Library of Alexandria, 24, 83, 86, 196, 243
Libya, 1, 29, 112, 315
Licinius, 162, 171, 200, 213
lighthouse (*Pharos*), 21
literacy, 161, 202, 216, 221, 268, 273
literature, Coptic. *See* Coptic literature
liturgical system, 57, 94, 124, 129, 146, 176, 188
Lucius Verus, 84, 142
Luxor. *See* Thebes
Lykopolis (Asyut), 161, 212, 266

Macedon, xxiii, 9, 29
Manetho, xxv, 16
Manichaeism, 198, 217
manufacturing, 122
manuscripts, dating, 119, 166, 200, 217
Marcian, 228
Marcus Aurelius, 49, 65, 70, 132, 147
Mark, evangelist, 118, 284, 321, 322
marriage, brother-sister, 20
martyrs, era of, 179, 321
martyrs, martyrdom, 161, 179, 216, 321, 323, 333, 334
Maurice, 237, 276
Maximian, 135
Maximinus, 162
Maximus, bishop, 157
Mazakes, 11
medicine, 82, 85, 122, 243, 245
Medina, 282, 296
Melitians, 166
Melitios, bishop of Lykopolis, 161
Melito of Sardis, 217
Memphis (Mit Rahineh), 3, 4, 5, 8, 9, 10, 11, 12, 18, 20, 22, 25, 27, 30, 34, 36, 80, 102, 184, 210
Menander, 221, 222
Menches son of Petesouchos, 38
Mendesian nome, 131, 143
Menouthis, 185, 192, 244
mercenaries, 78
metropolis of nome, 24, 31, 53, 56, 59, 93, 121, 124, 129, 154, 171, 257, 264
Miaphysite. *See* anti-Chalcedonian, Severan
Misenum, 60
Mithras, 107
monasteries, monasticism, 166, 208, 210–216, 217, 218–220, 222, 237, 238, 254, 265, 268, 271, 307–312, 315, 318, 323–324, 326, 333, 338

monetization, 41, 304
Monoenergism, 280
Mons Claudianus, 63
Mouseion, 21, 24, 82, 86
Muʿāwiya, 283, 286, 300
mummification, 8, 25, 28, 40, 41, 194
mummy portraits, 113, 148
Muslim army. *See* army, Muslim
Mussius Aemilianus, 133
Myos Hormos, 81

Nabataean, 34
Nag Hammadi, 213, 216, 219
names, as indicator of ethnicity, status, or
    religion, 30, 126, 128, 148, 204, 302, 338
Narmouthis (Medinet Madi), 164
nation, nationalism, 20, 178–180, 266
Naukratis (Kom Giʿeif, el-Nibeira, el-Niqrash),
    10, 22, 54, 92, 121
navy, 4, 9
Necho II, 4
necropolis, Memphite, 31
Neith, 6, 10, 30
Nektanebo I, 8, 9, 10
Nektanebo II, 9
Neoplatonism, 243, 244
Nero, 76, 83, 84, 109
Nicaea, Council of in 325, 157, 198, 201,
    214
Nicetas, 277
Nikopolis, 62, 73
Nile, 18
Nile flood, 18, 20, 39, 43, 44, 131, 138
Nile-Red Sea canal, 4, 8, 294
nomes, 16, 24, 27, 53–57, 93, 121, 171, 201,
    256, 263
Nonnus, 222, 246
Nubia, xxiv, 2, 9, 63, 106, 112, 179, 199, *See also*
    Kush
Nubians, 31, 175

oases, western, 7, 30, 94, 106, 123, 136, 147, 201,
    See also Great Oasis
obelisks, 47, 74, 109
Octavian. *See* Augustus
Orestes, 196
Origen, 154, 181, 217
orphanages, 207
orthodoxy, 179, 180, 279
ostraca, 33, 37, 70, 164, 224, 240,
    251, 276
Oxyrhynchos, 53, 60, 86, 122, 124, 129, 157,
    175, 184, 204, 205, 207, 212, 266

Pachomius, 213, 216, 218
pagarch, 256, 277, 293, 298, 300, 302, 329
pagi, 172
Palestine, 29, 31, 62, 105, 112, 154, 205, 276,
    282, 283, 323, 330
Palmyra, 63, 134, 180
Palmyrene occupation, 48, 135, 169, 180
Panopolis (Akhmim), 122, 149, 175, 208, 214,
    246, 268, 273, 312
Papas, Flavius, pagarch, 300
papyrus documentation, gaps in, 188, 251, 266
Paraetonium (Mersa Matruh), 12
Parthian War, 63, 142
patristic authors, 219, 320
patronage, 97, 189, 256, 263, 298, 306, 312, 338
Paul of Thebes, 210, 254
Pelusium (Tell el-Farama), 11, 12, 80, 174, 175,
    231, 267, 282, 283
persecutions, 152, 154, 158, 159, 161, 179, 200,
    210, 212, 235, 243, 280, 321
Persians, Persian occupation, 5–9, 33, 134, 159,
    239, 276–280, 291, 345
Pescennius Niger, 132
Petaus son of Petaus, 57
Peter I, bishop, 184, 321
Peter IV, bishop, 237, 238, 239, 264, 315
Peter Mongos, bishop, 231
petitions, 49, 50, 59, 65, 116, 122, 303
Pharos, 37, *See also* lighthouse (*Pharos*)
Philadelpheia (Gharabat el-Gerza), 28, 251
Philae, 42, 63, 65, 67, 106, 109, 175, 191
philanthropy, 146, 206–209
Phileas, bishop of Thmouis, 161
Philo, 210
philosophy, 84, 153, 243–245, 269
Phocas, 248, 276
Phoenicia, 3, 8, 23
pilgrimage, 71, 192, 251, 276, 341
Pisenthios, bishop of Coptos, 265, 270, 274, 277
plague of Cyprian, 181
plague, Antonine, 131–132, 140, 142–144, 169
pluralism, religious, 198–199
Plutarch, 71, 84, 85
poetry, 23, 29, 85, 246, 268, 273
polis (city), as used in Egypt, 24, 54
politeuma, 24, 31, 79, 103
poll-tax, 58, 79, 98, 103, 143, 290, 294, 304,
    308, 339
Polybius, 20, 78
Pompeii, 249
population, sources of, 29–33, 77–79, 112–113
Porphyrites, 63
Poseidippos, 37

postal system, 6, 294, 298

praepositus pagi, 172

prefect of Egypt, 49–52, 103, 104, 109, 111, 133, 159

priests, 36, 38, 40, 52, 58, 69, 94, 95–102, 108, 147, 151, 163, 190

Proclus, 245, 250

procurators, 52

Proterios, bishop, 230, 231

Psammetichos (Psamtek) I, 3, 4, 9

Psammetichos (Psamtek) II, 3, 47

Ptah, 16, 27, 30

Ptolemaic empire, 28, 41, 80

Ptolemaios son of Pasas, 27

Ptolemais, 22, 28, 54, 92

Ptolemais Hormou (El-Lahun), 57

Ptolemy I Soter, son of Lagos, 13, 17, 24, 25, 29, 41

Ptolemy II Philadelphos, xxv, 22, 26, 41

Ptolemy III Euergetes, 18, 21, 25, 28, 40

Ptolemy IV Philopator, 18, 20, 22

Ptolemy VI Philometor, 18, 24, 43, 79

Ptolemy VIII Euergetes II, 18, 24, 40, 43, 84

Ptolemy X Alexander, 43

Ptolemy XII Auletes, 25, 43, 58, 84

Puteoli, 81

qanats, 7

Qurra b. Sharīk, 293, 329

Ramesses V, 142

Raphia, 3, 20

Red Sea, xxiv, 4, 34, 81, 90, 104, 136, 282, 286, 317

regionalism, 166, 266–268, 340

registry office, 36, 70, 122

requisitions, 66, 285, 287, 289, 291, 293, 299, 308

resident king, 16

revolts, 18, 64, 97, 131, 133, 135, 136, 144, 169, 174, *See also* Jewish revolt

rhetoric, religious, 191, 206, 269, 337, 342

Rome, xxiii, 23, 42, 46, 47, 54, 57, 71, 75, 80, 81, 84, 85, 86, 88, 178, 221, 228, 233, 296

Rosetta stone, 18, 26, 34, 67

Royal Quarter, 73, 83, 86, 180

royal scribe, 54, 171

Rufus of Shotep, 220, 239

ruler cult, 18, 22, 24, 28, 109–111, 145

sacrifice, 11, 55, 78, 111, 150, 152, 154, 161, 191, 205

saints, 150, 192, 208, 216, 220, 321, 336

Sais (Sa el-Hagar), 2, 3, 4, 6, 10, 30

salt-tax, 33, 36, 41

Samaria, 29

Samuel of Qalamūn, 325, 333, 336

Saqqara, 4, 31

Sarapis, 27, 74, 133, 210

Sasanians, 276–280

satrap, 7, 8, 9, 11

schools. *See* education

science, Alexandrian, 23, 85–86

scribes, 33, 36, 69, 241, 340

senti, 3, 16

Septimii Flaviani family, 189, 258

Septimius Severus, 49, 57, 124, 132, 154, 158

Septuagint, 24, 103, 217, 222, 264

Serapeum of Alexandria, 21, 28, 74, 83, 86, 150, 184, 185, 194, 243

Serapeum of Memphis, 36, 37

Serapis *see* Sarapis

settlements, legal, 256

Severan party/church, 236–239, 270–271, 280, 315–317, 319–320

Severus b. al-Muqaffaʻ, 303, 319, 329, 332, 335

Severus of Antioch, 233, 237, 245, 258, 271, 321

Shai, 106, 148

Shenoute of Atripe, 150, 191, 198, 208, 214, 218–219, 270

shipbuilding, 287, 289, 300

Shoshenq I, 2

Siwa oasis, 12

slavery, slave trade, 29, 117, 121, 160, 204, 255, 308

Small Oasis (Bahariya), 14, 54

Soknopaiou Nesos (Dime), 101, 102, 143, 145, 251

Sotas, bishop of Oxyrhynchos, 157, 159

Strabo, 60, 75, 80, 83

Strategios *paneuphemos*, 261

strategos of nome, 54, 55, 111, 171, 205

Syene (Aswan), 6, 60, 63, 254, 273, 283

synagogue, 74, 102, 204, 205

Syria, 15, 18, 29, 32, 60, 62, 81, 131, 170, 199, 276, 297, 329, 340

Tabennesi, 213

Tachos, 9, 41

Taharqa, 3

taxes, tax collection, 18, 26, 31, 33, 36, 38, 39–41, 54, 57–58, 93–95, 106, 124, 137, 176–177, 256, 257, 285, 289, 290, 293–295, 304–305, 339–340, *See also apomoira*

Tebtunis (Umm el-Brigat), 98, 102, 145, 251

temple library, 6

temples, 6, 8, 16, 25–28, 36, 95–102, 106–112, 145–152, 163, 190–192, 253
Temseu Skordon, 257
Terenouthis, 143, 148
Teshlot archive, 330, 335
Theadelpheia (Batn el-Harit), 140, 141, 159, 186, 251
Thebes (Luxor), 2, 3, 12, 18, 22, 33, 34, 40, 62, 149, 212, 251, 265
Theocritus of Syracuse, 23, 29
Theodosius I, 109, 150, 185, 191, 192, 194, 215
Theodosius II, 228
theology, 153, 179, 201, 202, 225–241, 264, 303, 320, 336
Theonas, bishop, 157, 184
Theophilus, bishop, 185, 194
Thmouis, 132, 161
Thoeris, 30
Thonis-Herakleion, 8, 10
Tiberius, 49, 70, 94, 103, 109, 111
Tiberius II, 237
Timothy Ailouros, bishop, 218, 231
Timothy Salofakiolos, bishop, 231, 337
titulary, pharaonic, 6, 12
Titus, 105, 111
Tome of Leo, 229, 236, 326
toparchies, 53, 172
tourism, xxiii, 9, 10, 42, 172
traders, 4, 9, 10, 29, 79, 81
translation, 24, 103, 166, 204, 214, 217, 271, 314, 333
transportation, 40, 88, 331
tribute, 3, 6, 281, 282, 283, 284, 314

Trimithis, 106, 129
Tutu, 148

Udjahorresnet, 6
'Umar, 282, 283, 287, 289
university, Alexandria, 243–250
'Uthmān, 283, 287

Vaballathus, 135, 180
Valerian, 134, 156, 159
Vespasian, 48, 63, 74, 81, 105, 111
vicar, patriarchal, 238
village scribe, 38, 57, 286
villages, 36, 57, 93, 102, 117, 125, 131, 143, 146, 153, 161, 168, 201, 250–258, 263, 290, 295, 300, 303–313, 317, 330, 341
violence, 20, 116, 130–136, 176, 184, 206, 256, 280

Wadi El-Natrun, 212
Wahibre-em-akhet, 4
walls of Alexandria, 77
wheat, 23, 40, 46, 79, 89, 137, 144, 251, 294
White Monastery, 150, 208, 214, 254, 267
wine, 22, 32, 40, 79, 90, 137, 141, 186, 215, 223, 257, 330
women, in villages, 255, 308

Zachariah of Mytilene, 192
Zeno, emperor, 184, 231, 244
Zenobia, 48, 86, 135, 180
Zenon of Kaunos, 23, 30, 31, 32, 37, 41
Zeus, 111